Social Work Models, Methods and Theories

A Framework for Practice

2nd Edition

Edited by

Paul Stepney and Deirdre Ford

RHP

Russell House Publishing

First published in 2000
Second Edition published in 2012 by:
Russell House Publishing Ltd.
58 Broad Street
Lyme Regis
Dorset DT7 3QF

Tel: 01297-443948
Fax: 01297-442722
e-mail: help@russellhouse.co.uk
www.russellhouse.co.uk

British Library Cataloguing-in-publication Data:
A catalogue record for this book is available from the British Library.

ISBN: 978-1-905541-83-6

Typeset by TW Typesetting, Plymouth, Devon
Printed by IQ Laserpress, Aldershot

About Russell House Publishing

Russell House Publishing aims to publish innovative and valuable materials to
help managers, practitioners, trainers, educators and students.

Our full catalogue covers: families, children and young people; engagement and
inclusion; drink, drugs and mental health; textbooks in youth work and social
work; workforce development.

Full details can be found at www.russellhouse.co.uk
and we are pleased to send out information to you by post. Our contact details
are on this page.

**We are always keen to receive feedback on publications and new ideas
for future projects.**

Contents

Preface

Professor Nigel Parton, University of Huddersfield, England

I am delighted to be invited to write the Preface for the second edition of this excellent book edited by Paul Stepney and Deirdre Ford. Not only has it been thoroughly brought up to date but it has been extended and its contents thoroughly reviewed. The book's major strength is its focus on providing students with a clear grounding in a wide range of theories, models and methods and a very clear and accessible framework for practice while demonstrating the important influences arising from the changing political, economic and social contexts in which practice takes place. In this respect, the period since the publication of the first edition in 2000 has seen considerable changes and these are helpfully discussed throughout and in chapter one in particular. Here the changing contexts to UK social work are discussed in some depth as well as developments in Europe.

The first edition was written in the very early years of the New Labour Government in the UK while this second edition has been written in the early years of the Conservative-Led Coalition government following the election in May 2010. It has also been written in the context of – what the editors call – 'the post Baby Peter era' following the very high profile scandal that erupted into media, public and political arenas in November 2008 following the tragic and terrible death of a young child. While it can be seen as one of over a hundred such tragedies which had received similar high profile responses since the early 1970s many have commented that the intensity, rancour and anger generated by the case was greater than anything experienced before (see for example Parton, 2011). However, what the reaction to the case did was to raise the profile of social work in interesting and important ways.

One of the developments which was evident with the *Modernisation* pro-gramme of New Labour from the late 1990s onwards was that it was very ambivalent about social work and even using the words 'social work'. It was almost as if social work was too associated with Old Labour and, in particular, with the failings of local authority Social Service Departments. For a government which was wanting a positive image with the media social work was too associated with bad news and was likely to taint any new policy or service which it wanted to implement. As Nick Frost and I have demonstrated (Frost and Parton, 2009), while it is clear that New Labour invested considerable resources in a range of new services in the broad health and welfare fields, particularly for children and families, social work was often at the margins. The emphasis was increasingly placed on a new and much broader phenomenon, *social care* in relation to services for adults and older people and *children's social care* in relation to services for children and families – the words 'social work' were hardly ever used in government publications. So, while there continued to be a demand for qualified social workers in a range of services rarely were they called social workers. The other major development which Nick Frost and I discussed was how New Labour had a much broader approach to policy and practice with children and families and that rather than have a narrow and forensic focus on child protection the focus was something much broader, 'safeguarding and promoting the welfare of children'.

However, developments in the wake of the tragic death of Baby Peter have had the effect of not only reinforcing a renewed focus upon the importance of child protection but also upon the central role of social work in this. As a consequence the government established the Social Work Task Force (2009) to investigate how both the profile and overall professional standing and skills of social workers could be improved. Following the government's acceptance of the Task Force Recommendations it then established the Social Work Reform Board to see the recommendations through to implementation. This is not to say such changes will be easy nor that they will have the hoped for outcomes, but it does demonstrate how social work has been receiving renewed official recognition and is seen as providing an important contribution to health and welfare services. These developments have received further support with the establishment by the Conservative-led Coalition government of the *Review of Child Protection* chaired by Professor Eileen Munro (Munro, 2011) which aims to overcome some of the bureaucratic impediments to good professional practice and to place professionals and professional social work judgement at the centre of a reformed child protection system.

However this renewed official interest and support for the idea of professional social work practice is far from straightforward. In particular the nature and impact of high profile child protection tragedies and scandals have been somewhat contradictory. For in the process of social work being subject to high profile and very public criticism through the scandals, the authority, legitimacy and standing of social work have been undermined. However, such scandals, particularly the case of Baby Peter, have also had the effect of reinforcing and confirming child protection as *the* central responsibility of social work. So that while other areas of practice which social work has operated in over the last forty years – such as probation, work with older people and adults, together with a whole range of family support and community based activities – have been considerably reduced, social work is seen as *the* profession for taking the central responsibilities for child protection. However, this renewed official interest and support for social work is happening at the same time as the global economy is in recession and when the government has engaged in a major attempt to cut back on a whole range of public services in an attempt to reduce the public debt within the life of the present parliament, i.e. by 2015. So, just at the time when it appears that opportunities might be opening up for the re-professionalisation of social work, practitioners and managers are being faced by increased demands, a growth in social need and major changes in the way services are organised, funded and delivered.

In this context it is worth simply reiterating something I wrote in my Preface to the first edition of this book:

> *Now more than ever it is vital that social workers recognise the need for not only handling the contemporary uncertainties and ambiguities which permeate their work, but in doing so give voice to the people with whom they work. It is not simply a question of rediscovering the importance of professional judgement but in a way which attempts to empower the users and the groups and communities with whom they work.*

(Parton, 2000: vi)

As I said then, this book provides an important contribution to the literature. For the chapters are scholarly and accessible and will prove invaluable as both an introduction to the field and as a resource for both the beginning student and the more experienced practitioner. The editors, contributors and publishers are to be congratulated and thanked for deciding to provide this second edition.

References

Frost, N. and Parton, N. (2009) *Understanding Children's Social Care: Politics, Policy and Practice.* London: Sage.

Munro, E. (2011) *The Munro Review of Child Protection: Final Report. A Child-Centred System.* London: Department for Education.

Parton, N. (2000) Preface. In Stepney, P. and Ford, D. (Eds.) *Social Work Models, Methods and Theories: A Framework for Practice.* Lyme Regis: Russell House Publishing.

Parton, N. (2011) Child Protection and Safeguarding in England: Changing and Competing Conceptions of Risk and their Implications for Social Work. *British Journal of Social Work*, 41(5) 854–875.

Social Work Task Force (2009) *Building a Safe, Confident Future: The Final Report of the Social Work Task Force.* Nottingham: Department of Children, Schools and Families.

Introduction to the Second Edition

Paul Stepney and Deirdre Ford

Social work is a complex and contested professional activity that, in the post Baby Peter (Peter Connelly) era (see Parton, 2011), has found itself subject to intense media inquiry and political scrutiny. The problems that social workers confront on a daily basis often raise issues of fundamental social and moral concern associated with human rights, independence, protection of people deemed to be vulnerable and so on. Harold Wilson (Britain's prime minister during the 1960s and 1970s) was once reported to have said that a 'week is a long time in politics . . .' It would seem that a week does not go by without social work being in the news often for all the wrong reasons. In the week preceding the writing of this introduction (early summer 2011) the national media reported the recommendations of a serious case review following the death of a three year old child in Wolverhampton, the abuse of people with learning disabilities in a Bristol care home, and the failure by various councils to provide many older people with the support that they need. These disturbing stories will all have serious implications for social workers and yet, with the exception of the child's death, the role of social work hardly received a mention. It would seem that social workers are either demonised for failing to safeguard people needing protection and held up as responsible for not tackling a variety of social problems, or they remain invisible and their work is largely ignored. We know that social workers constantly try to make a positive difference to service users' lives and support community members in a variety of ways, but this often receives insufficient public recognition. However, one of the crucial dilemmas that front line practitioners face when safeguarding vulnerable adults, as well as in child protection work, is balancing the need to be effective and evidence based, whilst seeking to promote more critical and emancipatory change. Ask practitioners to reflect on their work and they will often highlight this kind of tension. It is therefore essential that practice is informed by a clear theoretical knowledge base and appropriate range of skills, which is why the Social Work Reform Board (SWRB) in England proposed a new overarching professional standards framework for social work (DFE, 2010). However, it was also recognised that other reforms will need to be put in place to improve standards for employers, including supervision and management, enhance opportunities for continuing professional development, and progress proposals for effective partnership working.

With the workload of social workers unlikely to decrease in the foreseeable future, a situation that Moira Gibb, chair of SWRB recognised in the foreword to the 2010 report (DFE, 2010: 4) these problems look set to continue. In recently published articles one of the authors has examined the current crisis in social work and suggests that it may be presented as a choice between evidence-based practice (EBP) and critical practice (CP) (see Stepney, 2010). However, paradoxically the current predicament facing the profession may also provide the context and opportunity to achieve an alliance between EBP and CP. In particular, there is a need to balance protection measures and plans, alongside prevention strategies as part of a wider commitment to CP. In the UK the problems exposed by the death of Baby Peter, homicides committed by people experiencing mental health problems, and the widespread scandal of older people receiving inadequate levels of support, have only brought this dilemma more sharply into focus.

It is clear that the modernisation of the welfare state and recent policy reforms in mental health, child care and the personalisation of adult social care, whatever merits they have brought in the protection of 'high risk' service users, have not assisted social workers to develop more preventive community based strategies. Similar trends in the tension between child protection and family support, together with the rise of a more child focussed orientation, can be found in other European welfare states, as well as in Australia, Canada and the USA (Gilbert, Parton and Skivenes, 2011; Parton, 2007).

There is compelling evidence to suggest that, 'protection dominated' practice allied to organisational reform has not prevented the number of child deaths continuing or contributed to more effective practice (Stepney, 2010). The Coalition government's spending plans are likely to increase the pressure on front line public services to provide assistance only to those in greatest need or assessed as being high risk, thereby perpetuating the current protection orientated culture. Prevention where it is possible is more likely to be seen, especially in the UK, as a 'Big Society' issue offering scope for volunteering and self-help (Cameron, 2009). This may be seen as part of David Cameron's attempt to promote 'communitarian civic conservatism' (Blond, 2010) redirecting expectations away from the state towards the market, the family and the community.

It follows that it is clearly an extremely important time to revisit the theoretical knowledge base underpinning practice and undertake a review of social work theory and methods. This was certainly the view of the Social Work Reform Board in England in devising the professional standards framework which sets out the expectations that will be placed on social workers throughout their career (DFE, 2010: 14). It is informed by a number of core themes, including a good knowledge of the social sciences and social work practice theory, as well as clearly the capacity for critical reflection and analysis. It is against this backdrop that the second edition of the book has taken shape. It is our intention to make a contribution to the education and training of social workers in different settings across the globe, as well as to their continuing professional development. Drawing on the international literature, a major feature of the book is reflected in the contextualising of social work methods, models and theories in a global context. The book is designed to stimulate debate and critical reflection, including the application of theory to practice everywhere.

It is now more than 11 years since the publication of the first edition in December 2000 and much has happened during that time. The pace of change in social work during the first decade of the new millennium has been rapid and, as we have noted, somewhat turbulent. Tony Blair and then Gordon Brown were in residence in Downing Street for much of this period and at the time when the book was first published had strong popular appeal. Our criticism of New Labour's 'third way' modernisation project to reform the welfare state, set out in part one of the book and seen as somewhat controversial because it challenged the accepted wisdom of the day has largely been vindicated. Now we have a new Coalition government in office and true to form we have adopted a critical view of David Cameron's 'Big Society' reforms and their likely impact on social work. The 'Big Society' debate picks up on many of Tony Blair's communitarian themes, and will therefore appeal to many across the political spectrum looking for a new way forward. However, we argue that by failing to recognise growing social divisions and tackle structural inequalities its impact on disadvantaged communities is likely to be extremely limited.

It is instructive for us both to look back and recall the tentative hopes we had for the original book, based as it was on lecture notes produced for the MA Social Work degree module entitled 'Professional Practice' and taught with Frances Fleet at Exeter University. We were delighted with the response to the first edition and genuinely surprised. This is because we very much concur with Malcolm Payne who wrote in the Preface to the second (1997) edition of his bestselling, *Modern Social Work Theory* 'since the publication of the first edition, I have found out how much I did not know and understand' (Payne, 1997: xi). This encapsulates exactly how we felt as we stood and surveyed what we had produced, the assumptions we had made and the limitations we had glossed over along the way.

Structure of the book

The second edition contains a number of significant changes and is now organised into three parts. The first four chapters that make up Part One set out to establish a contextual framework that structures the debate about social work methods and thereby shapes the practice agenda. It contains much new material on the changing policy context, re-examines the role of theory, looks at the latest research evidence and considers different approaches to issues of diversity, equality and anti-racist practice. It also contains an authoritative new chapter by Malcolm Payne on rethinking the social work theory to practice debate.

The ten chapters in Part Two provide a systematic examination of different methods, models and practice theories. Although the chapters cover similar ground to the first edition, comprising both standard methods and theories alongside more hybrid models, each chapter has been updated and many have been substantially revised. As before, there are a number of contributions from established experts in the field alongside chapters from new authors. There is also a new chapter on Groupwork by Pam Trevithick, which was an obvious omission from the first edition.

The final three chapters, which comprise the new Part Three, have as a collective theme the future of practice in an international context and emphasise the global significance of the book. This section has contributions from three Australian based academics and includes a chapter on critical social work by Mel Gray, Paul Stepney and Stephen Webb; a chapter on research minded practice by Martyn Jones and importantly, a final chapter by Bill Jordan entitled 'The Big Society and Social Work: A New Direction for Practice?'

We readily acknowledge that any book on social work models, methods and theories is likely to be contested. This is inevitable especially during a time of significant policy change when the role of social work in the UK has been subjected to sustained reappraisal. Social work and social policy remain subjects of much dispute and this is reflected in the work that social workers do as well as in the practice dilemmas they encounter. However, we take this lack of consensus as both a starting point and a challenge which has stimulated us to try to develop a constructively critical perspective on the way theory can enhance and enrich practice. An important aim here is to create the conditions for critical thinking and critical reflection, as the basis for finding more creative solutions to society's problems – solutions that balance effectiveness with a commitment to social justice. This in essence is why we argue that a sound theoretical knowledge base is essential for good practice. We invite you to join us once again in our journey into the disputed world of social work methods, models and theory.

About terminology

A brief note may be helpful as these terms are used fairly loosely in everyday speech and not always applied with consistency in the social work literature. For present purposes and at the risk of oversimplification we define a theory as a framework of understanding or cluster of ideas which attempt to explain reality. In the social sciences theoretical knowledge is highly contested because different theories offer competing explanations reflecting particular values and ideological positions. The crucial point here concerns the nature of the explanation and the need to 'think theoretically'. As Neil Thompson helpfully notes we may talk of social work theory not just in relation to specific theories that explain the subject matter of social work, but 'the overall professional knowledge base that helps to shape practice' (Thompson, 2010: 4).

Theory may be sub-divided into formal and informal theory. Formal theory is to be found in published books and articles and might be said to be explicit and reflect high status knowledge and scholarship from the scientific community. Informal theory on the other hand is more implicit and reflects 'practice wisdom' that has been built up over time and derives more from experience. However, it is worth noting that both formal and informal theory remain contested and may be flawed as theoretical knowledge is often partial, provisional and value laden. What is accepted as a 'good theory' today may be shown to be inadequate and replaced by a better theory tomorrow. (For an excellent discussion see Thompson, 2010, Ch. 1).

We may sometimes wonder why something is as it is in the world or why we do things in a particular way. Such questions are useful even if they are difficult to answer and for present purposes they help us to distinguish a theory from a model. Whilst a theory attempts to explain why something is as it is, according to Thompson, 'a model seeks to describe . . . how certain factors interrelate, but it will not show why they do so' (Thompson, 2000: 22). It follows that a model tends to be more descriptive but may also be used as a tool that links theory to practice. For example, in direct work with children (a method) eco-maps may be used as a model or tool in practice, drawing upon systems theory. Here the use of an eco-map is the model or tool that links theory to practice (see Chapter 10 about Ecological Systems Theory by Peter Henriques and Graham Tuckley).

In their everyday work with service users social workers will often seek to integrate theory and practice in a meaningful way, and one way of doing this is by employing particular methods of intervention. Methods represent the more formal written accounts about how to do the job of social work (Sibeon, 1990). This occurs when theory, or a combination of theories, is made concrete and applied in practice. Where a group of theories is being discussed the term 'paradigm' may be used. This originates from the work of Kuhn (1970) to denote an approach informed by a set of related theories and beliefs about the nature of the world and the individual's place within it (Mark, 1996). For example, in Community Social Work (which is another method) 'patch models' have evolved describing how services are organised by local teams in particular communities. However, the patch model of working will not explain why services should be provided in this way. For an explanation about 'why', we need to refer to theory – in this case a paradigm consisting of systems theory, organisational and networking theory and ideas associated with community empowerment (see Stepney and Popple, 2008).

Paul Stepney, University of Tampere, Finland
Deirdre Ford, Plymouth University, UK

References

Blond, P. (2010) *Red Tory: How Left and Right Have Broken Britain and How We Can Fix it.* London: Faber and Faber.

Cameron, D. (2009) The Big Society. *Hugo Young Memorial Lecture*, London: 10 November.

Department for Education (DFE) (2010) *Building a Safe and Confident Future: One Year on.* Social Work Reform Board, London: Stationary Office (available at www.education.gov.uk/swrb/)

Gilbert, N., Parton, N. and Skivenes, M. (Eds.) (2011) *Child Protection Systems: International Trends and Orientations*. USA: Oxford University Press.

Kuhn, T. (1970) *The Structure of Scientific Revolutions.* University of Chicago Press.

Mark, R. (1996) *Research Made Simple: A Handbook for Social Workers*. Thousand Oaks, CA: Sage.

Parton, N. (2007) A Look at Contemporary Child Welfare and Practice. Editorial, *Australian Social Work*, 60, 275–277.

Parton, N. (2011) Child Protection and Safeguarding in England: Changing and Competing Conceptions of Risk and their Implications for Social Work. *British Journal of Social Work* 41(5), 874–875.

Payne, M. (1997) *Modern Social Work Theory.* (2nd edn.) Basingstoke: Macmillan.

Sibeon, R. (1990) Comments on the Structure and Forms of Social Work Knowledge. *Social Work and Social Sciences Review*, 1 (1).

Stepney, P. (2010) Social Welfare at the Crossroads: Evidence-based Practice or Critical Practice? *The International Journal of Interdisciplinary Social Sciences*, 5 (5) 105–120.

Stepney, P. and Popple, K. (2008) *Social Work and the Community: A Critical Context for Practice*. Basingstoke: Palgrave.

Thompson, N. (2000) *Theory and Practice in Human Services.* (2nd edn.) Buckingham: Open University Press.

Thompson, N. (2010) *Theorizing Social Work Practice.* Basingstoke: Palgrave.

Notes on Contributors

Avril Bellinger (previously Butler) is Associate Professor in Social Work at Plymouth University, and was awarded a National Teaching Fellowship for her contribution to education for social justice. She is the co-founder and Chair of Students and Refugees Together (START) an award-winning charity recognised for innovation in practice learning (SWAP, 2011, http://www.swap.ac.uk/getinvolved/awards.html) and cited as a good practice agency for services to refugees (Newbigging, K. and Thomas, N. (2010) *Workforce Development SCIE Guide 37. Good practice in social care with refugees amd asylum seekers*. London: SCIE). She is also director of the Centre for Practice Learning at Plymouth and has been in social work since 1971 as a practitioner, manager and teacher in both statutory and non-statutory sectors. Her research interests include creativity in social work, teaching and learning in, and for, practice, and Appreciative Inquiry as a capacity-building methodology.

Wing Hong Chui is Associate Professor in the Department of Social Work and Social Administration and Associate Dean (Undergraduate Education) of the Faculty of Social Sciences at the University of Hong Kong. He has researched and published works on youth justice, social work and criminal justice.

Lena Dominelli holds a Chair in Applied Social Sciences in the School of Applied Social Sciences and is Associate Director at the Institute of Hazards, Risk and Resilience Research at Durham University. She currently undertakes research on disasters and climate change. Alongside the wealth of experience she has as a university educator and researcher, she has worked in social services, probation and community development. She has published widely in social work, social policy and sociology. Her latest book is *Green Social Work*. She is recognised as a leading figure in social work education globally. Professor Dominelli was elected President of the International Association of Schools of Social Work (IASSW) from 1996 to 2004, and currently chairs the IASSW Committee on Disaster Interventions and Climate Change and attends UN meetings on this topic. She has received various honours from governments and universities.

Frances Fleet is now retired. She formerly worked as a probation officer in Devon, a lecturer in Social Work at the University of Exeter and a tutor for the Diploma in Probation Studies at the University of Plymouth.

Deirdre Ford is a qualified social worker and Lecturer in Social Work who for ten years combined an academic career at Exeter University with practice, working with people who have a learning disability and mental health problems, prior to taking up a full-time post at Plymouth University in 2002. She has worked extensively with service user and carer groups in both social work education and practice. Recent research interests and publications stem from practice developments related to Safeguarding Adults, and Downs Syndrome and dementia.

Peter Ford has a background in social work, counselling and family mediation, and initially qualified and worked as a probation officer. He has recently researched the development of criticality in undergraduate social work education, and his publications have addressed probation practice, safety in social work agencies, and the development of social work education, amongst other subjects. For many years he directed and taught on social work programmes at the University of Southampton. He currently uses elements of the task-centred approach in his practice as a family mediator.

Mel Gray is Professor of Social Work and Research Professor in the Research Institute for Social Inclusion and Well-being, University of Newcastle, New South Wales, Australia. She has published extensively on social work and social development. Recent books include *Indigenous Social Work around the World* (with Coates and Yellow Bird, Ashgate, 2008), *Social Work Theories and Methods* (with Webb, Sage, 2008), *Evidence-based Social Work* (with Plath and Webb, Routledge, 2009), *Ethics and Value Perspectives in Social Work* (with Webb, Palgrave, 2010), *International Social Work* – 4 volumes (with Webb, Sage, 2010), *Environmental Social Work* (with Coates and Hetherington, Routledge, 2012), *Decolonizing Social Work* (with Coates, Hetherington and Yellow Bird, Ashgate, 2012), *Social Work Theories and Methods.* 2nd edn. (with Webb, Sage, 2012) and *New Politics of Critical Social Work* (with Webb, 2010, Palgrave). Mel is Associate Editor of the *International Journal of Social Welfare*.

Peter Henriques is currently the Adoption Service Manager with Staffordshire County Council. Prior to this role Peter was a Senior Lecturer in Social Work at the University of Wolverhampton, where he established the MA Social Work Programme. His special interests include adoption and fostering policy and practice, direct work with children, practice learning and professional ethics. He has over 26 years of experience in social work as a practitioner, manager and educator. Peter has also worked as a consultant and trainer to a number of independent fostering and social care agencies.

Maggie John is a senior social worker in a long-term children and families team. Before training as a social worker she was a counsellor with Relate and has had an active interest in bringing psychodynamic perspectives to social work practice. She is an active member of the Executive Committee of GAPS (Group for the Advancement of Psychodynamics and Psychotherapy in Social Work).

Martyn Jones is a qualified social worker and Associate Professor of Social Work at RMIT University, Melbourne, where he is Associate Dean for the Human Services area within the School of Global Studies, Social Science and Planning. Previously, Martyn led the social work programmes at Deakin University, Geelong, having migrated to Australia from England where he had been teaching social work at Exeter University. His academic interests include collaborative approaches to knowledge generation and building professional and organisational research capacity in social work and human services. He continues to explore, with his co-author Heather D'Cruz, the themes of their 2004 book *Social Work Research: Ethical and Political Contexts* (Sage).

Bill Jordan worked for 20 years in the public social services, and was an activist in a poor people's movement and an advocate for disadvantaged people. He has been involved in social work education and training for over 40 years. He is the author of 28 books on social work, social policy, political economy and social and political theory. He has held visiting chairs in Amsterdam, Aalborg, Bremen, Bratislava, Budapest and Prague, and is currently Professor of Social Policy at Plymouth University.

Malcolm Payne is Policy and Development Adviser, St Christopher's Hospice, London, having been director of psycho-social and spiritual care there, and has visiting/honorary posts at Opole University Poland, Kingston University/St George's University of London, Helsinki University, Finland and Comenius University, Slovakia. For many years he was Professor and Head of Applied Community Studies, Manchester Metropolitan University. He is author of many books, including *Modern Social Work Theory* (Lyceum 3rd ed., 2005), *What is Professional Social Work* (Policy 2nd ed., 2006) and most recently *Humanistic Social Work: Core Principles in Practice, Citizenship Social Work with Older People* (Lyceum both 2011) and *Social Work in End-of-life and Palliative Care* (with Margaret Reith, Lyceum 2009)

Keith Popple is Professor and Head of Social Work at London South Bank University, UK. Previously a field worker in social services he has written widely about the relationship between 'community', social work and community development. He is joint author with Paul Stepney of *Social Work and the Community: A Critical Context for Practice* (Palgrave, 2008). Keith is a member of the Editorial Boards of the *British Journal of Social Work*, the *Community Development Journal* and the USA journal *Community Development: Journal of the Community Development Society*. The second edition of his text *Analysing Community Work: Its Theory and Practice* (Open University Press) is due to be published in 2013.

Karen Postle has a background in social work, counselling and mediation and is a Registered Social Worker. She has researched social work with adults/older people and published widely including, as joint editor with Mark Lymbery, *Social Work: A companion to learning* (Sage, 2007). Karen taught for five years at UEA, Norwich and has worked as a research advisor for INVOLVE (Public involvement in health, public health and social care research). Following early retirement she works on a sessional basis for the Universities of Southampton and Winchester and is a 'Practice Educator' and a volunteer neighbour mediator.

Brian Sheldon is Emeritus Professor of Applied Social Research, and previously Director of the Centre for Evidence-based Social Services at the University of Exeter. He has written widely on, and has conducted studies of the effectiveness of social work, and has a particular interest in the application of cognitive-behavioural methods to social and personal problems. He has recently published *Cognitive Behavioural Therapy: Research and Practice in Health and Social Care* (Routledge, 2011) and with Geraldine Macdonald, *A Textbook of Social Work* (Routledge, 2009).

Paul Stepney has recently been appointed as an adjunct Professor of Social Work and Kone Foundation Research Fellow at the University of Tampere in Finland. Prior to this he has taught at universities in Hull, Manchester, Exeter and more recently Wolverhampton, UK. For many years he worked as a community worker, generic social worker and during the 1990s combined university teaching at Exeter University with a hospital social work post. He has researched and published in the area of critical practice developing strategies of prevention alongside protection. He has published a number of articles on critical practice in Australian, UK and US journals, and has recently set up a comparative research project in two European cities to investigate these issues and explore how preventive practice might be developed. He is co-author of two books: (i) co-editor with Deirdre Ford *Social Work Models, Methods and Theories: A Framework for Practice*, (Russell House Publishing, 2000); (ii) co-author with Keith Popple *Social Work and the Community: a critical context for practice*, (Palgrave Macmillan, 2008).

Neil Thompson has held full or honorary professorships at four UK universities but is now an independent trainer, consultant and author. He has over 150 publications to his name, including over 30 books, many of them bestsellers. His latest book is *Grief and its Challenges* (Palgrave Macmillan, 2012). He has also produced a range of education and training DVDs and other learning resources (www.avenuemediasolutions.com). He has qualifications in social work, mediation, training and development and management (MBA), as well as a first-class honours degree, a doctorate (PhD) and a higher doctorate (DLitt). He edits the free monthly e-zine, *Well-being* BULLETIN (www.well-being.org.uk). In 2011 he was presented with a lifetime achievement award by the Wales branch of the British Association of Social Workers. His website and blog are at www.neilthompson.info.

Pamela Trevithick is the Visiting Professor in Social Work at Buckinghamshire New University and author of the best-selling text *Social Work Skills and Knowledge: A Practice Handbook* (OUP, 2012) which is available in five languages: Chinese, Japanese, Swedish, Spanish and Korean. She is the Chair of GAPS (Group for the Advancement of Psychodynamics and Psychotherapy in Social Work, http://www.gaps.org.uk), an organisation promoting relationship-based approaches, and psychodynamic and systemic thinking in social work.

Graham Tuckley is a Senior Lecturer in Social Work and Social Care at the University of Wolverhampton. Graham has had a long and distinguished career in social work scanning four decades. Qualifying in the early 1980s, he worked as a generic social worker, mental health practitioner and covered for many years in a very busy Emergency Duty Team. During his later years in practice he managed services for people affected by HIV and Aids. He developed his interest in academia after being a Practice Educator to numerous social work students before moving to his current teaching post. Graham is still very active and engaged in community social work and the empowerment of disadvantaged groups in the local community.

Stephen A. Webb is Professor of Human Sciences and Director of the Research Institute for Social Inclusion and Well-being, University of Newcastle, New South Wales, Australia. He is author of several books including *Social Work in a Risk Society* (Palgrave 2006) and *Evidence-based Social Work: A Critical Stance* (with Gray & Plath, Routledge 2009). He is co-editor (with Gray) of *Social Work Theories and Methods* (Sage 2008), the four-volume international reference work *International Social Work* (Sage 2010), *Ethics and Value Perspectives in Social Work* (Palgrave 2010), and the *Sage Handbook of Social Work* (for Sage, with Gray & Midgley, 2012). Webb's critical analysis *Considerations on the validity of evidence-based practice in social work* (2001, *British Journal of Social Work*, 31(1): 57–79) is the world's most cited article in the field and the most influential publication in social work over the last ten years (Hodge et al., *British Journal of Social Work*, 2011, 1–18). He is currently completing *The New Politics of Critical Social Work* for Palgrave and the 2nd edition of *Social Work Theories and Methods* for Sage.

Acknowledgements

There are many people, too numerous to mention, who have helped us to develop a better understanding of social work methods and theory. We are most grateful to all the contributors who have either revisited their earlier chapters or provided new pieces for this edition. It has been a pleasure to renew collaboration and friendships in the course of preparing this volume.

We would particularly like to thank our students and respective colleagues for their helpful comments about the first edition. We have tried to take such advice into account in planning this second edition along with the criticisms from different sources. We have gained a lot from such feedback and it has contributed to us having a clearer understanding of so many practice issues. We have been told that the first edition was too theoretical in places, or that it was too critical of policy makers. We can only plead guilty to such criticism and point out that it is difficult to strike the right balance in achieving a constructively critical perspective integrating theory, policy and research evidence. However, it is not always possible to take particular ideas or suggestions on board and we are clearly responsible for any failings that remain.

Paul would in particular like to thank colleagues from the University of Tampere in Finland, especially Anna Metteri, Tarja Pösö, Kirsi Juhila, Irene Roivainen and Pertti Koistinen from the School of Social Sciences and Humanities for their continued support, helpful suggestions and providing excellent working facilities during his many visits. Thanks are also due to Aila-Leena Matthies and Tuomo Kokkonen from the University of Jyväskylä, Kokkola University Consortium in Finland for their kindness and hospitality during his short visits and for many interesting discussions. Such visits to Finland for teaching and research have provided a stimulating environment to develop a Nordic view on the rapid pace of change in social work and reflect on the implications for developing critical models of practice. This has once again influenced the final editing of the book in many subtle but significant ways.

Deirdre would especially like to thank her brother Peter Ford for his constant support and humour, and to celebrate his scholarship and career in social work education spanning nearly forty years. Thank you to former colleagues of the Exeter University MA programme (now hosted by Plymouth University) especially Bill Jordan, and to Martyn Jones who with staff at RMIT and Victoria University, Melbourne have extended their friendship, hospitality and scholarship.

Chapter 1

An Overview of the Wider Policy Context

Paul Stepney

. . . welfare policies and practices are implicated in the production or reproduction of complex forms of social differentiation and inequality.

(John Clarke, 2000)

Under the auspices of both state and market, a vast body of disenfranchised and disengaged citizens has been constituted.

(Phillip Blond, 2010)

As we move forward into the second decade of the 21st century not for the first time social work in England finds itself at the crossroads. After the recent death of Baby Peter and other child homicides the practice of social workers, as well as doctors, health visitors, nurses and the police, has been the subject of intense media scrutiny and political inquiry (DCSF, 2009a). Given that such cases raise similar concerns as those expressed by Lord Laming during the Victoria Climbié inquiry (Laming, 2003), this has understandably led to much public anger and criticism. Practitioners find themselves caught between modernising policy reform and demanding practice realities amidst increasing levels of social exclusion and widening inequalities (Stepney, 2009). At a time of severe restraint on public expenditure political leaders of the new Conservative/Liberal Democrat coalition government are questioning whether spending on welfare represents good 'value for money' and if social workers are 'up to the job' of protecting vulnerable people. In this opening chapter an attempt will be made to explain the reasons why social work now finds itself in this unenviable predicament by situating the analysis of practice in its wider policy context.

Social work throughout the Western world now operates against a backdrop of economic globalisation where it has been restructured and reshaped by the criteria of the market concerning its performance, effectiveness and outcomes (Dominelli, 2002). The current modernisation of the welfare state began following the recession of the early 1990s, within parameters of cost containment, efficiency and affordability, and not surprisingly this has had a direct and quite dramatic impact on practice.

Social work has found itself very much in the front line of welfare reform and caught up, first in New Labour's 'third way' modernisation project and more recently in the debate about the 'Big Society'. The notion of the 'Big Society' derives from David Cameron's call for a reactivation of moral responsibility, mutuality and obligation to repair Britain's 'broken society' (Cameron, 2009). Although, as we shall see later in the chapter, there are some important differences in emphasis when such ideas are translated into policy, both Blair and now Cameron have stressed the need for opportunity (now increasingly associated with enterprise), inclusion and 'choice'. The debate has been influenced by the ideas of Phillip Blond, set out in various articles and his book *Red Tory* (Blond, 2010) designed to encourage citizens to take greater responsibility for their own welfare by promoting civic responsibility and voluntarism in the local community.

Although the call for a 'new communitarian settlement' will strike a chord with many on both the political left and right, without tackling the impact of growing structural inequalities and social divisions, David Cameron may well create a similar 'policy to practice paradox' as Tony Blair. Here the continuity in policy making is soon revealed in the way that strategies of inclusion and localism become subordinate to the management of highly differentiated and socially divided populations (Clarke, 2000). The long-term consequences for social work will clearly be the subject of much ongoing debate (and explored further in the various chapters of the book). However, in the post Baby Peter climate it is difficult to see mainstream practice being able to move beyond the current preoccupation with risk assessment, strict resource management and protection.

In the modernised welfare state the paradox of rising public expectations and growing disillusionment has pushed social work onto the defensive about the nature of its contribution to the well-being of society (Jordan, 2007) and whether it can be a force for progressive social change (Mullaly, 2007). It has found itself strategically placed at the intersection of global economic forces, national policy responses and local demands, but unable to exert much influence in any of these important domains. Its status has historically been influenced, in part, by its practitioners working with some of the most dispossessed and marginalised groups in society (Wilson, 1993). The identification of social work with poverty and disadvantage has created tensions at a time when the language of the market has permeated virtually every sphere of welfare provision. Social workers must try and resolve these contradictions and have had to embrace systems driven by financial imperatives and growing marketisation, where services targeted on the poor and most vulnerable are mirrored by high rewards for top earners in the labour market. During 13 years of New Labour in office the gap between rich and poor had widened further (JRF, 2010) creating in the process new patterns of exclusion and inequality.

Alongside the growth of what might be called 'the affordable and conditional welfare state', new user movements for change in the fields of mental health, disability and old age have now firmly established themselves. These have generated expectations about rights and empowerment which social workers have readily endorsed. However, there is a sense of irony in noting that this has occurred at a time when practitioners feel increasingly disempowered by the changing organisational culture they find themselves in (Ferguson, 2008). Moreover, service users continue to articulate their demand for enhanced rights, access to information and improved services in the political arena and have stated that they need committed social work support and workers prepared to 'go the extra mile' (Beresford and Croft, 2004; Ferguson and Woodward, 2009).

In the aftermath of the Baby Peter case a Social Work Task Force was set up to examine the current state of social work in England and identify the major obstacles to the delivery of consistently high quality practice (see www.dcsf.gov.uk/swtf). The interim report proposed a new vision and support for social work as a profession (DCSF, 2009a) and, in the final report, made 15 recommendations for change (DCSF, 2009b). However, as the executive summary made clear, ongoing government support was made conditional upon the profession accepting the need for further modernisation and reform. As the Coalition government's drastic cuts in welfare budgets begin to bite, practitioners will need to try and balance resources for crisis work to safeguard children and protect vulnerable adults with preventive work in the community (Stepney and Popple, 2008). This was a balance that went horribly wrong in the Baby Peter and Victoria Climbié cases (Laming, 2009; 2003). Recent modernising policy initiatives recognise the problem but appear to offer few constructive suggestions for creating genuinely preventative services. Worryingly, in many policy proposals (DoH, 1998; 2005) and New Deals for community regeneration, social work barely received a mention (see Stepney and Popple, 2008).

The outcome of the current reappraisal concerning the future of social work as a professional activity was in many respects predictable, with the Task Force recommendations taken up by the Social Work Reform Board (SWRB, 2010). Sooner or later the problems created by the marginalisation of prevention in protection dominated systems would come to the surface and reveal a host of fundamental tensions that can be linked to the path of policy reform (Stepney, 2006a). This follows the previous welfare reforms, first under Thatcher and then Blair, where modernisation became synonymous with a project that changed the very nature and essential character of welfare practice.

The modernisation of the welfare state had many dimensions that taken together created a new form of welfare practice, and one that demanded more from those who used its services (Jordan, 2001). Social work changed in a number of important ways:

- From practitioners having a significant degree of professional autonomy to being subject to greater technical/administrative regulation and greater organisational control (Saario and Stepney, 2009).

- From using a broad range of methods to adopting forms of intervention centred upon the management of risk (Webb, 2006).
- From practice informed by a depth of critical social science knowledge to one that utilises a broader sweep of skills-based competencies epitomised by the plethora of superficial tick box assessments (Howe, 1996).
- From locating itself within the humanitarian impulse towards betterment of the good society to mopping up the social casualties or waste products of the 'goods society' (viz. Pearson, 1975).
- From having aspirations as a force for change committed to social justice to becoming an agency of contractual regulation and control locked into meeting government efficiency targets (Harris, 2005).

In short, a complex array of 'unstable encounters' (Clarke, 2004) in times of uncertainty designed to make social work a more manageable profession.

The foundational pillars of reform were established in the 1990s by the introduction of an administrative system of care management in social care agencies and the development of competence based training. What was at stake was 'the capacity for professional discretion and judgement being replaced by routinised procedures . . . dominated by business plans and budgets' (Jones, M., 1996: 1). All provided the impetus for a process of de-professionalisation that has continued until the present day. Under care management the social worker was redesignated as a care manager, requiring a qualitatively different kind of training, or indeed little training at all. The employment of non-qualified staff to undertake much routine work and the establishment of a 'call centre' culture to process referrals at the intake stage logically followed from this.

Competence based training, now the dominant approach in UK university social work programmes, reflects a political culture which stems from the global market place and world of financial management. As Howe notes, 'Many of social work's theories and practices have become analytically more shallow and increasingly performance orientated' (Howe, 1996: 77) which, without a sustained effort to retain a critical perspective, leaves the newly trained professional ill-equipped to respond creatively to the complex needs of vulnerable people in troubled times (Parton, 1996). A further problem with competence-based training is that it leads to practice which may in turn become dismembered and de-politicised (Webb, 2006). The paradigm of competences ultimately means professional workers utilising their skills within an environment dominated by business plans and centrally determined targets, without having the autonomy or discretion to question the values which underpin it. Many of the new values from the market fit uneasily with either traditional social work values (Ferguson and Woodward, 2009) or notions of partnership, empowerment and anti-oppressive practice (Thompson, 2010).

Managerialism

One potent dimension underpinning the modernisation of the welfare state that links the state with markets, partnerships and the new consumers of public services is the concept of managerialism (Clarke *et al.*, 2000). A process of managerialisation, that begun in the 1980s, has helped to reshape public services and signifies a decisive 'shift towards managerial forms of organisational coordination' and control (*ibid*: 6). The new managerialism has helped to deliver a new set of beliefs and expectations associated with the three Es – Economy, Efficiency and Effectiveness and has supplanted or displaced the expert knowledge of the professional. The professional is no longer assumed to know what is best and professionals have had to adapt to organisational requirements and managerial priorities. Managerialism provides a solution that bridges the credibility gap between the rhetoric of needs-led services and the reality of increasingly mechanistic assessments, tighter eligibility criteria and resource driven service priorities.

The new managers, many recruited from the financial services sector, have played a central role in providing strategic leadership at a time of rapid change. This was designed to ensure broad commitment to centrally determined objectives whilst devolving responsibility to front line staff for making the organisation more user-friendly. As a concept managerialism has an ideological component that intersects global economic imperatives of the market with the local and internal working lives of staff (Jones and May, 1992).

In social work one index of the problem is the extent to which questions of equity and justice still feature in organisational mission statements but are being swamped by bureaucratic procedures and are in danger of all but disappearing from professional social work agendas. Managerial priorities now permeate almost every aspect of the care management task and enable the manager to 'scientifically' appraise performance (Jones, 2004; Pollitt and Harrison, 1992). This as we have noted has had a decisive impact on practice; for example, it was found from a study of community mental health teams in Finland that managerial control reinforced certain modes of working and excluded others (Saario and Stepney, 2009).

In many important respects managerialism has played a strategic role in overseeing the fragmentation of provision and the development of a more de-politicised practice. In so doing social work staff found it difficult to resist being co-opted into accepting 'business priorities' at the expense of professional autonomy and discretion (Harris, 2003). Moreover, this has created many schisms and tensions in local social services teams at a time of increased workloads and reduced budgets. The result, not surprisingly, has been high stress, low morale, surface compliance but a deeper mistrust about the future (Huxley *et al.*, 2005; Hadley and Clough, 1996). Thus the potential for more serious tensions erupting into conflict remains ever present. In the meantime practitioners continue to explore ways of meeting the challenge, by recording unmet need, assisting clients to appeal, and using what little discretion exists to maximise service provision within the tighter eligibility criteria which increasingly prevails in social services today (Ferguson, 2008).

Evidence of the unpromising climate created by managerial priorities shaping the outlook of front line practitioners can be found in various research studies (Saario and Stepney, 2009; Jones, 2004; Hadley and Clough, 1996). The community care reforms implemented in April 1993 represent one of the most far-reaching changes introduced into Britain's social services since they were set up in the early 1970s. In their research Hadley and Clough (1996) report that 'for all the people we interviewed the experience of change has been one of loss: the loss of being valued, the loss of having a clear purpose and hope in the future, the loss of enjoyment and, for some, the loss of a career. Almost all identified new pressures to conform' (*ibid*: 176–178). More recently despite the rhetoric of enhanced provision and choice, practice realities according to the staff interviewed by Ferguson and Woodward (2009) 'were driven by political demands for accountability and best value . . . managers control day to day practice, which is chasing numbers and targets' (*ibid*: 69).

The European dimension

Since the 1990s it has become increasingly clear that governments throughout the developed world face a vast array of common problems and overlapping issues (Clarke, 2000). What is perhaps distinctive about the situation is 'that the number, nature and severity of these problems demand solutions that are often beyond the scope of traditional forms of welfare provision' (George and Taylor-Gooby, 1996: 1). The nature and scale of the situation is worth briefly mapping out.

In very general terms the globalisation of the economy combined with the internationalisation of the nation state provides the wider backdrop to the reshaping of practice. This is not to infer that globalisation is a distinctive process producing a new world order, but rather, is the effect of different social, economic and political processes. Although such processes are commonly associated with the increasing mobility of capital, the information superhighway and so on, the effects of globalisation may be marked by partial, contradictory and highly conflictual tendencies (Clarke, 2000). Globalisation has occurred at a time when there has been a slowing down in the rise of GDP in most European nations (Eurostat, 2008) and a concomitant effort to constrain the rate of increase in public spending. As economies entered recession during the early 1990s unemployment rose and has remained persistently high in many countries even before the current global economic crisis. During this period renewed efforts were made to develop EU wide policies to tackle common economic and social problems, specifically to promote solidarity alongside subsidiarity (Lorenz, 1997).

With the enlargement of the EU, its reach as a global economic player expanded to become the second largest economy to the US producing 25 per cent of global GDP and 20 per cent of global trade, thereby acquiring the status of being an economic superpower (Schnabel and Rocca, 2007). The EU also became an important regulator of global economic activity, whilst leaving much fiscal and social policy to individual member states. Here a tension can be seen between member states adopting different approaches to policy making. Countries such as France and Germany have adopted a largely *Dirigiste* model (control by the state of economic and social affairs) designed to harmonise policies through increased regulation, whilst those like the UK adopted a more liberal Anglo/US model aimed at promoting greater market freedom through de-regulation.

If we examine the demand side of European economies we find a trend towards growing casualisation and insecurity in the labour market especially in northern Europe (Hutton, 1996). This has created an expanding sector of low paid, part-time, casualised 'junk jobs' with a disproportionately high female workforce (Esping-Andersen, 1990) more recently supplemented by migrants from Eastern Europe.

To make sense of this, we need to recognise the consequences of a situation in which international companies can locate their operations anywhere in the globe, combining technologies and human labour power in the most profitable ways. In Europe, returns to capital (dividends, profits) are at a historically high level, whilst those to labour have been declining (as a proportion of GDP) since the early 1970s. There is a surplus of unskilled labour all over the continent, but especially in the post communist countries of Eastern Europe some of whom have become members of the EU. Employers seek to use labour power 'flexibly', especially in the services sector, including human services. National governments compete for international investments as much in terms of low social costs as the high level of their social capital (education and skills of workers, trust, work ethic). The UK has led the field in 'social deregulation' and the reform of welfare systems in line with these requirements (Jordan, 1998).

Demographic changes are increasingly significant as we witness a rise in Europe's ageing population, particularly the very old, those over 80. In the EU the proportion of the over 80 population, which was 10 per cent of older people in 1960, is projected to more than double by the year 2020 to approximately 22 per cent (Eurostat, 2008). Whilst the vast majority of older people look after themselves, with support, as age increases so may disability and ill health (Bernard and Phillips, 1998). This will inevitably place additional demands on resources for health and social care at a time when other social trends suggest that the number of informal carers, especially women in northern Europe willing and able to care, will continue to fall. This is due to such factors as increasing mobility, family poverty, divorce rates and carers growing older (Cousins, 2005). Thus, there is likely to be an impending crisis in care across Europe which will require concerted action in the very near future (Österle, 2001).

It follows that the demand for welfare is set to rise given these predicted trends along with the increasing fragmentation of local communities, in both urban centres of population and rural areas. Here the articulation of need is already being expressed by a plurality of interest groups and new social movements demanding more empowering and democratic forms of provision (Stepney and Popple, 2008) and by users asserting their culturally diverse identities (Lorenz, 1997). Such demands cannot easily be satisfied by market consumerism or accommodated within existing structures at a time of severe cuts in welfare spending. The outcome paradoxically may be to perpetuate conditions of discontent, doubt, dissatisfaction and dispossession at the local level which urgently require attention (Stepney, 2010).

Welfare states throughout Europe have been subjected to unprecedented criticisms and scrutiny from across the political spectrum (George, 1996) either for being historically overgenerous and a drain on resources (Murray, 1994) or for not doing enough to tackle poverty and reduce inequalities (Lorenz, 2001). This has left social work in an ambiguous position. The ever-changing politico-economic climate presents new opportunities and dangers in exploiting the spaces and contradictions within a Neo-liberal market economy. Working with disenchanted and disaffected members of the community, on mutually negotiated terms rather than those of the market, can be a high-risk strategy. However, the rewards are likely to be significant in enhancing citizenship rights, promoting solidarity and fighting oppression, provided this can be accomplished within an enabling policy framework.

Policy responses

'In all the OECD countries, reform of welfare systems has been forced on governments by the erosion of collective institutions for protecting employment, and redistributing income providing social services' (Scharpf, 1999, cited in Jordan, 2000: iv). If the citizens of Europe face similar problems then in contrast the policy responses from governments have hitherto been marked by considerable diversity, especially in the social policy arena (Sapir, 2005). This reflects different systems of social protection or welfare state regimes. Here the work of Esping-Andersen (1990, 1996) has been extremely influential in identifying three configurations or broad clusters, which have been analysed in terms of commodification and stratification – the extent to which welfare can provide protection against the commodifying effects of the market and modify class related outcomes (Esping-Andersen, 1990). Although these have been subject to

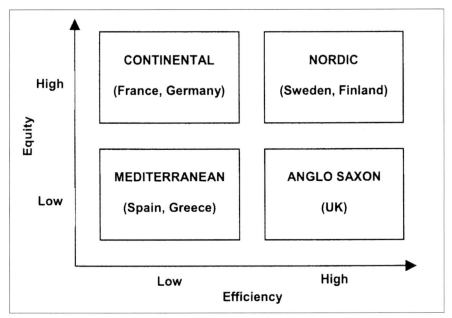

Figure 1.1 Four European social models

From Sapir (2005) adapting Esping-Andersen (1990) 3 Worlds of Welfare Capitalism – Liberal, Corporatist and Social Democratic.

some reformulation, with Sapir (2005) proposing four European social models to incorporate the Mediterranean countries, the three original typologies are worth briefly outlining as they still remain the basis for evaluating much subsequent policy change. The four models are set out in Figure 1.1, formulated by Sapir (2005) comparing welfare states on the grounds of equity and efficiency.

First, the liberal welfare states, epitomised by the USA (but with the UK in hot pursuit) have traditionally given rather ungenerous levels of social insurance benefits (retirement pensions, disability, sickness and unemployment benefits), but had extensive 'safety nets' of means tested social security benefits and tapered support for the working poor. Second, the corporatist welfare states such as Germany, have given much more generous and non-stigmatising social insurance benefits, but strongly related to employment and earnings. The downside of this is that it has both perpetuated inequalities in the incomes of those outside the labour market, and favoured men over women (who participate less in employment than in the liberal regimes of USA and UK). Third, social democratic welfare states, exemplified by Sweden and other Nordic countries, are where every citizen has a strong stake in state benefits and services, and where redistribution and universalism continue to enjoy widespread public support (Esping-Andersen, 1990).

It should be noted however, that the election of a new centre-right government in Sweden, in autumn 2006, has led to a process of modernisation of its welfare system. Sweden's Prime Minister Fredrik Reinfeldt, an admirer of Tony Blair and Bill Clinton, was elected on a platform of greater efficiency in public services and welfare reform. Hence, Sweden has now moved from a public to a more pluralist welfare regime and incorporated elements of the liberal or Anglo-Saxon model (Stepney, 2006b). A fourth social model linked to the Mediterranean countries can now be added (Sapir, 2005) where the emphasis is on employment protection for workers and social spending on retirement pensions. The family also typically plays a more central role in social support than in the other welfare regimes (Hantrais, 1999).

These regimes have responded rather differently to the challenge of globalisation and demographic change (Esping-Andersen, 1996). The liberal strategy has included those elements of social deregulation and privatisation mentioned above. The effect has been to polarise both incomes and employment opportunities, with falling real wages and a large sector of working households below the poverty line in the USA and UK. Both countries claimed to have achieved 'job miracles' in comparison with the rest of Europe, based upon a large increase in employment in the US, and a smaller one in Britain. However, in both, the growth came mainly in low paid service work, including private social care, which contributed to the need for wage subsidisation. A substantial number of these jobs have been part time, low paid and in Britain have increasingly been taken up by new migrants from Eastern Europe.

The growth in employment in social services and social care in the UK is therefore a symptom of one of the problems of this model. Ironically many of the staff administering benefits, for example, are themselves claimants of working family tax credit and housing benefit. Further, the problem of casualisation and fragmentation of employment at the bottom of the labour market, low wages and lack of incentives, have contributed to the phenomenon of households with no member in regular employment. Hence the Clinton–Blair/Brown 'welfare to work' programmes became enforcing by driving claimants into employment or training, where opportunities and incentives were lacking (Jordan, 2006). The emphasis on work as the surest route out of poverty is now being reinforced with renewed vigour by the new coalition government of David Cameron.

By contrast, in the continental regimes epitomised by Germany, unemployment rates have remained relatively high, and growth in employment has been modest. Tackling social exclusion rather than avoiding poverty is still seen as the main challenge. Social services in kind have not expanded as rapidly, and there are far fewer jobs, especially in social care. In the Scandinavian countries the 'Nordic Model of Welfare', despite reform and some retrenchment, retains a strong commitment to equality and solidarity (Kautto et al., 1999). This means that social welfare services are still extensive, and employees enjoy higher wages and better conditions than in other parts of Europe. However, they are characteristically women, and this segmentation of female employment (often part time) is increasingly seen as an unacceptable feature of the model. In the social democratic regime represented by the Nordic countries, a pluralist model is developing. However, at the present time public services for social care in Sweden and Finland still predominate; in the corporatist regimes, voluntary agencies are the main providers.

There is some evidence of convergence in northern Europe towards a more liberal and residual welfare model (Stepney, 2006b). In this Britain has rather set the pace. During the current economic crisis traditional high spending Nordic countries have begun to economise, whilst Mediterranean countries, like Greece and Spain, with socialist governments and previous EU social funding, have been forced to cut back on welfare spending. The cuts are part of the package of support from the EU and central European Bank to support their failing economies. In Britain and to a lesser extent in Germany and France, serious cuts in benefits as part of a package to reduce the budgetary deficit are now proposed along with gradual reform of pensions and increasing the age of eligibility. It is significant that these reforms have been high on the agenda of David Cameron's new Coalition government and reflect a degree of continuity with New Labour's previous programme of welfare reform. Less dramatic measures have been taken in the Nordic countries, which has slightly lowered the redistributional effect of welfare but hitherto without loss of public support or talk of 'retrenchment' (see Stepney and Popple, 2008, especially Ch. 9). Hence, this bears out the perceptive prediction that 'globalisation does not necessarily lead to convergence . . . but welfare states are now on a shared trajectory of more limited social rights' (Timonen, 1999: 255).

It is only in Central and Eastern Europe where the state is being subject to more drastic modernisation policies, in collaboration with the creation of new markets, that a significant expansion of welfare services has taken place. Both social assistance and social work have grown rapidly, in an ironic imitation of practice in the USA and UK. It is the residual 'safety nets', not the institutional features of a universal system of social protection, that have marked the transition to capitalism (Jordan, 1998; Ford and Stepney, 2003). Perhaps this was a logical step along the road that enhanced their credentials for joining the EU.

In Britain the response, in terms of social policy, can be understood as moving further down the long road of modernising the welfare state. This began during the Thatcher years, continued under Blair and the baton has now been taken up by David Cameron.

The Coalition Government's programme of welfare reform and the debate about the 'Big Society'

Red Toryism may be in 2010 what Blair's New Labour was in 1997.

(Erich Kofmel, 2009)

David Cameron has begun to mobilise a range of political interests in a project to further modernise the welfare state that links closely to the debate about the 'Big Society'. In many respects this may be a response to Tony Blair's earlier attempt to set out a similar policy path, in that it takes up many themes from New Labour's 'third way' reform programme advanced during their first term in office. The idea of the 'Big Society' is the vision which informs Cameron's call for a return to a culture of mutual responsibility and civic obligation to repair Britain's 'atomised' and 'broken society' (Cameron, 2009). The backdrop to the debate was a growing concern that the economic gains from adapting to the demands of the global market have been achieved at a significant social cost, involving a loss of community cohesion, family breakdown and a rise in anti-social behaviour, particularly gun and knife crime (Stepney, 2009). The debate has been strongly influenced and given moral thrust by the ideas of Phillip Blond, a former university theology lecturer in the Anglo-Catholic tradition of radical orthodoxy, and set out in numerous articles and his book *Red Tory* (Blond, 2010).

Blond's thesis is that there has been a 'wholesale collapse of British culture, virtue and belief' that has created a litany of social problems ranging from violent crime to family break-up and from public authoritarianism to private libertarianism. This is seen as the result of excessive market individualism working in tandem with monopoly capital during the Thatcher years combined with increasing permissiveness and an obsession with material choice. The consequences are viewed by Blond with dismay in that Britain has become 'a society with no conception of the common good held together by the anonymous forces of the market and the coercive power of the state' (Gray, 2010: 1). The *Red Tory* book is subtitled 'how left and right have broken Britain and how it can be fixed'. The book is clearly a product of its time and signifies something of a paradigm shift at the centre of British politics in the turbulent aftermath of the global recession. This may explain why it has struck resonant chords with many people across the political spectrum, disillusioned with established political positions, and looking for fresh ideas to solve what is seen as a deep-seated social and economic malaise.

Blond's solution is a blend of 'cultural conservativism and anti-market radicalism' (Gray, *ibid*: 1) that offers the basis of a radical manifesto for change. If the neo-liberal project in its present form has run its course, the question is what should replace it? The answer according to Blond is the development of 'communitarian civic conservatism' – Red Toryism for short. The Red Tory agenda can be traced back to an intellectual tradition rooted in the ideas of radical Tories such as Thomas Carlyle and William Cobbett ('rural rides'), and more recently GK Chesterton and Hillaire Belloc and the Catholic Distributive League. In 1929 the League proposed a practical alternative to what it saw as the twin evils of capitalism and socialism, fighting for the small self sufficient entrepreneur against the might of the market (Raban, 2010).

In terms of contemporary policy making the Red Tory manifesto is constructed around the themes of decentralisation, mutualism and voluntarism (Blond, 2010). When translated into action this would involve the relocalisation of the economy, recapitalisation of the poor and the revival of civic society through relations of association. In practical terms Blond has set out a raft of policy proposals that includes:

- giving employees ownership of public services,
- breaking up the big banks and creating small regional banks that would invest in social enterprises,
- enabling the unemployed to work as volunteers without loss of benefit,
- a new financial deal for the poor to encourage entrepreneurship,
- mutualising the post office (Blond, 2010; see also Respublica, 2010).

The guiding principle here is interdependence rather than individualism, where the common good would be cultivated from within and nurtured by moral regulation rather than the dictat of the state. Many of these ideas appear to stem from an attempt to recreate an idealised version of the English village in the middle ages, with Blond representing the interests of the shopkeeper, local craftsman and yeoman farmer. Services would be delivered by self-help cooperatives and social enterprises in partnership with reformed local councils, with moral authority reinforced by local influentials and the church. This conjures up an idyllic image of rural life in keeping with that created by *The Archers* on Radio 4 (Raban, 2010).

Some of these ideas were clearly attractive in principle to David Cameron and his wish to promote compassionate conservativism. However, it is doubtful whether the current conservative party would be willing to carry through many of these practical policies as they would clearly undermine the basis of its support from the city and big business. Also it is not clear how much support these ideas have amongst conservative backbenchers where the Thatcher legacy remains influential (Derbyshire, 2009). However, at the local level the Blond communitarian manifesto is seen to have much merit both ideologically as well as economically at a time of severe budgetary restraint.

The notion of the 'Big Society' has been attacked not just for an attempt to turn the clocks back and recreate the relations of the English rural village, based around the parson, postmistress and pub (Raban, 2010), but for emerging at a convenient time when cuts in public spending are likely to have a damaging effect on local services. However, without a coherent economic basis it is unlikely to have any greater impact on reducing structural inequalities and the problems that flow from them than Blair's 'third way' communitarianism.

Coalition welfare policy and the legacy of New Labour

In terms of welfare policy in general and social work in particular, the 'Big Society' debate has begun to pick up on many themes at the heart of New Labour's 'third way' modernisation project. According to Tony Blair, the 'third way' was designed to balance the freedom of the global market economy with a commitment to social justice (Blair, 1998; Stepney, 2006a). At the core of that project was the aim to transform the welfare system around work and demand 'more from those who received assistance – ''no rights without responsibilities''' – and which in exchange was predicted to improve incentives and opportunities for the poor (Jordan, 2000: iii). New Labour conducted something of a moral crusade against the poor with welfare benefits increasingly subordinate to labour market activation policies, backed up by a modest minimum wage and US style 'tough love' enforcement. Further, these elements combined in a plethora of policy initiatives, such as tax credits and various New Deals in a drive to promote responsible communities and tackle social exclusion.

It is interesting to note that social work barely received a mention in this 'third way' policy context, even if some of the language used by policy makers such as 'personal advisers' and 'packages of support' were borrowed from the profession. This reinforced the tendency for public sector social work to be used as an instrument of assessment, risk management and enforcement, rather than to support grass roots efforts at economic regeneration and social support (Parton and O'Byrne, 2000; Stepney, 2009). However, during its first term in office New Labour introduced a policy of *Modernising the Social Services* (DoH, 1998) which had some direct and important implications for social work. The White Paper was concerned with the regulation of local authorities to raise standards and meet new performance targets. As a result LA social services departments were subject to mechanisms which had been previously tried and tested in the NHS and education, including use of performance indicators, league tables and external audit. Within a few years of implementation, the policy became prescriptive and target driven reflecting a decidedly Benthamite regulatory approach with threats of penalties for non compliance (Jordan, 2000).

The social services were regularly criticised for a failure to promote independence and develop preventive strategies (Stepney, 2006a). In child care, the policy had little effect on how resources might be redirected away from statutory interventions towards more effective protection linked with family support (Stepney, 2009). It led to the perpetuation of protection dominated practice but without the necessary quality of evidence, local knowledge and resources that was required to be effective (Parton, 2007). This was crucially missing in both the Baby Peter and Climbié cases (Laming, 2003; 2009).

New Labour appeared determined to continue many of the Thatcherite populist themes, under a banner of social inclusion, including appeals to the middle ground of British politics. And by appeasing the popular prejudices of middle England, Tony Blair's 'Third Way' became pre-occupied with clearing the streets of the underclass, with surveillance and control, with a battery of targets for welfare practitioners to meet that constrained and redirected professional judgement, and latterly with 'respect' and tackling anti-social behaviour rather than a genuinely new social contract rooted in justice and empowerment. This is the policy legacy which the coalition government of David Cameron has inherited.

In May 2010 the coalition government set out a radical set of welfare reforms. The new work and pensions secretary, Ian Duncan Smith, described the present benefit system as 'bust' and suggested that many people on benefits view those who take up job offers as 'bloody morons' (Wintour, 2010: 1). He proposed a drastic simplification of the benefit system promising to make it financially worthwhile for unemployed people to come off benefits to work, raising the state retirement age to 66 and to curtail universal benefits enjoyed by the middle classes. On the latter point, the plan to controversially cut child benefit for higher rate tax payers had also been announced provoking a backlash from many working mothers. The public reaction and media commentary was mixed as many of the reforms were viewed as necessary at a time of severe budgetary restraint. The response from the Labour opposition was somewhat muted given that many of the reforms, such as moving people off incapacity benefit and into work had begun under New Labour.

The continuity in policy with New Labour signifies a further tactical retreat from universal provision, accompanied by a redirection of expectations away from the state towards the market, the family and the community. The Coalition government's programme of welfare reform starting with the benefit system, allied to promoting the 'Big Society', makes a virtue of such change. The reality is that this will undoubtedly place a greater burden on informal carers, many of whom are women, at a time when they are subject to competing pressures in the labour market, the family and community (Stepney and Popple, 2008). In one sense this might be said to accord with the principle of subsidiarity, where seeking support from the state is seen as a last resort (Spicker, 1991). However, this may be a convenient and cheap policy option at a time of budgetary restraint when the family is under pressure and the community is subject to the forces of fragmentation and division. The result in the UK is growing alienation, division and exclusion.

An important factor here which social workers will encounter in their daily working lives is the increasing feminisation and racialisation of poverty in a welfare society linked to new patterns of exclusion (Williams and Johnson, 2010). In the past there was a lack of clear policy response to tackle this problem which meant that women had to rely on social security benefits or the labour market (or both) for income maintenance. In the new millennium, New Labour began to not only 'think the unthinkable' but translate this into policy with the abolition of Lone Parent premiums in income support alongside the various New Deals designed to push people into the formal labour market. Arguments about benefit dependency and social responsibility, first deployed against black single mothers in the US, informed much of New Labour's 'tough love' welfare policy. The coalition government appear destined to make a virtue of this approach in the name of economic necessity alongside mutual responsibility and participation by persuading people to take greater responsibility for their own welfare.

However, we know that women form the basis for developing many networks of care and support in the community (Stepney and Popple, 2008) and such resources need to be acknowledged and developed rather than exploited. The consequences of ignoring this role will have serious social consequences, as a recent EU report made clear by highlighting Britain's poor record on child poverty and children's well being (Bradshaw *et al.*, 2006). The call by David Cameron for a 'new communitarian settlement' underpinning the debate about the 'big society' will strike a chord with many across the political spectrum, but without tackling the problem of growing social divisions and structural inequalities its impact will be limited. In the new millennium neo-liberals may have lamented the passing of Thatcher and Blair but they have found Blond and Cameron's 'Big Society'. Consequently, social work continues to have an important role to play in supporting all marginalised groups to tackle poverty and fight oppression at the local level, whilst responding to pressures to become more effective in safeguarding children and protecting the vulnerable. The problems and potential associated with demonstrating effectiveness whilst promoting greater social justice are explored in the next chapter.

References

Beresford, P. and Croft, S. (2004) Service Users and Practitioners Reunited: The Key Components for Social Work Reform. *British Journal of Social Work*, 34(1) 53–68.

Bernard, M. and Phillips, J. (1998) *The Social Policy of Old Age*. London: Centre for Policy on Ageing.

Blair, T. (1998) *The Third Way: Politics for the New Century*. Fabian Pamphlet 588. London: The Fabian Society.

Blond, P. (2010) *Red Tory: How Left and Right Have Broken Britain and How We Can Fix it*. London: Faber and Faber.

Bradshaw, J., Hoelscher, P. and Richardson, D. (2006) An Index of Child Well-being in the EU. *Journal of Social Indicators*, 80(1) 133–177.

Cameron, D. (2009) The Big Society. *Hugo Young Memorial Lecture*, London: 29 November.

Clarke, J. (2000) A World of Difference? Globalisation and the Study of Social Policy. In Lewis, G., Gewirtz, S. and Clarke, J. (Eds.) *Rethinking Social Policy*. Sage.

Clarke, J. (2004) *Changing Welfare, Changing States: New Directions in Social Policy*. London: Sage.

Clarke, J., Gewirtz, S. and McLaughlin, E. (Eds.) (2000) *New Managerialism New Welfare?* London: Sage.

Cousins, M. (2005) *European Welfare States: Comparative Perspectives*. London: Sage.

Department for Children, Schools and Families (2008) *Analysing Child Deaths and Serious Injury Through Abuse and Neglect: What Can We Learn? A Biennial Analysis of Serious Case Reviews 2003–2005.* Research Report DCSF-RR023, London: HMSO.

Department for Children, Schools and Families (2009a) *Social Work Task Force: Facing up to the Task.* (Interim Report, July 2009) London: HMSO.

Department for Children, Schools and Families (2009b) *Social Work Task Force: Building a Safe, Confident Future.* (Final Report, November 2009) London: HMSO.

Department of Health (1998) *Modernising the Social Services.* London: HMSO.

Department of Health (2005) *Independence, Well-being and Choice: Our vision for the future of Social Care for Adults in England.* London: HMSO.

Derbyshire, J. (2009) The NS Profile: Phillip Blond. *New Statesman*, 19th February.

Dominelli, L. (2002) *Anti-Oppressive Social Work Theory and Practice.* Hampshire: Palgrave.

Esping-Andersen, G. (1990) *The Three Worlds of Welfare Capitalism.* Cambridge: Polity Press.

Esping-Andersen, G. (1996) *Welfare States in Transition.* London: Sage.

Eurostat (2008) *Europe in Figures: Eurostat Yearbook 2007–2008.* Luxembourg: EU Commission. (www.europa.eu.int/comm/eurostat)

Ferguson, I. (2008). *Reclaiming Social Work: Challenging Neo-Liberalism and Promoting Social Justice.* London: Sage.

Ferguson, I. and Woodward, R. (2009) *Radical Social Work in Practice: Making a Difference.* Bristol: The Policy Press.

Ford, D. and Stepney, P. (2003) Hospital Discharge and The Citizenship Rights of Older People: Will the UK Become a Test-bed for Eastern Europe? *European Journal of Social Work*, 6(3) 257–272.

George, V. (1996) The Future of the Welfare State. In George, V. and Taylor-Gooby, P. (Eds.) Op. cit.

George, V. and Taylor-Gooby, P. (Eds.) (1996) *European Welfare Policy.* Basingstoke: Macmillan.

Gray, J. (2010) Red Tory, by Phillip Blond, Book Review, *The Independent*, 2nd April.

Hadley, R. and Clough, R. (1996) *Care in Chaos: Frustration and Challenge in Community Care.* London: Cassell.

Harris, J. (2003) *The Social Work Business.* London: Sage.

Harris, J. (2005) *Modernised Social Services in the UK: Franchised Social Work in the McMunicipality.* Paper presented at conference: The changing place of municipal social work in Finland in the 21st Century, Tampere, Finland: University of Tampere.

Hantrais, L. (1999) Socio-demographic Change, Policy Impacts and Outcomes in Social Europe. *Journal of European Social Policy*, 9(4) 291–309.

Howe, D. (1996) *Surface and Depth in Social Work Practice.* In Parton, N. (Ed.) Op. cit.

Hutton, W. (1996) *The State We're In.* Vintage.

Huxley, P., Evans, S., Gately, C., Webber, M., Mears, A., Pajak, S., Kendall, T., Medina, J. and Katona, C. (2005) Stress and Pressures in Mental Health Social Work: The Worker Speaks. *British Journal of Social Work*, 35(7) 1063–1079.

Jones, A. and May, J. (1992) *Working in Human Service Organisations: A Critical Introduction*. Melbourne, Cheshire: Longman.

Jones, C. (2004) The Neo-Liberal Assault: Voices From The Front Line of British Social Work. In Ferguson, I., Lavelatte, M. and Whitmore, E. (Eds.) *Globalisation, Global Justice and Social Work*. London: Routledge.

Jones, C. and Novak, T. (1993) Social Work Today. *British Journal of Social Work*, 23: 195–212.

Jones, M. (1996) *Bridging the Worlds of Professionals, Managers and Users in the Personal Social Services: Culture, Politics and Partnership*. Proceedings of Crisis in the Human Services Conference, Cambridge, September.

Jordan, B. (1998) *The New Politics of Welfare: Social Justice in a Global Context*. London: Sage.

Jordan, B. (2001). Tough Love: Social Work, Social Exclusion and the Third Way. *British Journal of Social Work*, 31, 527–546.

Jordan, B. (2006) Public Services and the Service Economy: Individualism and the Choice Agenda. *Journal of Social Policy*, 32(10) 143–162.

Jordan, B. (2007) *Social Work and Well-being*. Lyme Regis: Russell House Publishing.

Jordan, B. with Jordan, C. (2000) *Social Work and the Third Way: Tough Love as Social Policy*. London: Sage.

Joseph Rowntree Foundation (2010) *Monitoring Poverty and Social Exclusion 2010*. annual report (www.jrf.org.uk/publications/monitoring-poverty-2010).

Kautto, M., Heikkilä, M., Hvinden, B., Marklund, S. and Ploug, N. (Eds.) (1999) *Nordic Social Policy: Changing Welfare States*. London: Routledge.

Kazi, M. (2003) *Realist Evaluation in Practice*. London: Sage.

Kofmel, E. (2009) *Phillip Blond's "Respublica" Think Tank and Radical Orthodoxy*. Sussex Centre for the Individual and Society, University of Sussex.

Laming, Lord (2003) *Report of the Inquiry into the Death of Victoria Climbié*. London: HMSO.

Laming, Lord (2009) *The Protection of Children in England: A Progress Report*. 12 March, London: HMSO.

Lorenz, W. (1997) *Social Work in a Changing Europe*. Keynote address and paper presented at an International Conference, Culture and Identity: Social Work in a Changing Europe, Dublin.

Lorenz, W. (2001) Social Work Responses to New Labour in Continental European Countries. *British Journal of Social Work*, 31, 595–609.

Mullaly, B. (2007) *The New Structural Social Work*. Ontario, Canada: Oxford University Press.

Murray, C. (1994) The New Victorians . . . and the New Rabble. *Sunday Times*, May 29th.

Österle, A. (2001) *Equity Choices and Long-Term Care Policies in Europe*. Aldershot: Ashgate.

Parton, N. (Ed.) (1996) *Social Theory, Social Change and Social Work*. London: Routledge.

Parton, N. and O'Byrne, P. (2000) *Constructive Social Work*. Basingstoke: Macmillan.

Parton, N. (2007) A Look at Contemporary Child Welfare and Child Protection Policy and Practice. Editorial. *Australian Social Work*, 60(3) 275–277.

Pearson, G. (1975) *The Deviant Imagination.* Basingstoke: Macmillan.

Pollitt, C. and Harrison, S. (1992) *Handbook of Public Services Management*. Oxford: Blackwell.

Raban, J. (2010) Cameron's Crank. *London Review of Books* (22nd April) 32(8) 22–30.

Respublica (2010) Thinktankcentral: Thatcher Failed Says Self-styled Red Tory, Phillip Blond as he Launches Twenty Policy Ideas (http://conservativehome.blogs.com/thinktankcentral/2010/03/thatcher-failed-says-selfstyled-red-tory)

Saario, S. and Stepney, P. (2009) Managerial Audit and Community Mental Health: A Study of Rationalising Practices in Finnish Psychiatric Outpatient Clinics. *European Journal of Social Work*, 12(1) 41–56.

Sapir, A. (2005) *Globalisation and the Reform of European Social Models*. Breugel Policy Brief, Brussels (www.breugel.org/opublic/publication/)

Schnabel, R. and Rocca, F. (2007) The Next Superpower? The Rise of Europe and its Challenge to the United States. Lanham, MD: Rowman and Littlefield.

Scharpf, F. (1999) *Governing on Europe: Effective and Democratic?* Oxford: Oxford University Press.

Social Work Reform Board (2010) *Building a Safe and Confident Future: One Year on.* (Progress report from Social Work Reform Board, December) London: HMSO.

Spicker, P. (1991) The Principle of Subsidiarity and the Social Policy of the European Community. *European Journal of Social Policy*, 1(1).

Stepney, P. (2006a) Mission Impossible? Critical Practice in Social Work. *British Journal of Social Work*, 36(8) 1289–1307.

Stepney, P. (2006b) The Paradox of Reshaping Social Work as 'Tough Love' in The Nordic Welfare States. *Nordisk Socialt Arbeit*, 26(4) 293–305.

Stepney, P. (2009) English Social Work at the Crossroads: A Critical View. *Australian Social Work*, 62(1) 10–27.

Stepney, P. (2010) Social Welfare at the Crossroads: Evidence-based Practice or Critical Practice? *The International Journal of Interdisciplinary Social Sciences*, 5(5) 105–120.

Stepney, P. and Popple, K. (2008) *Social Work and The Community: A Critical Context For Practice*. Basingstoke: Palgrave.

Thompson, N. (2010) *Theorizing Social Work Practice.* Basingstoke: Palgrave.

Timonen, V. (1999) A Threat to Social Security? The Impact of EU Membership on the Finnish Welfare State. *Journal of European Social Policy*, 9(3) 253–261.

Webb, S. (2006) *Social Work in a Risk Society.* London: Palgrave.

Wilson, R. (1993) *Poverty, Powerlessness and Dispossession: A Personal Guide.* BBC2 programme, March 21st.

Wintour, P. (2010) Coalition Government Sets Out Radical Welfare Reform. *The Guardian*, 26th May, 1.

Williams, C. and Johnson, M. (2010) *Race and Ethnicity in a Welfare Society.* Buckingham: Open University Press.

Chapter 2

An Introduction to Social Work Theory, Practice and Research

Paul Stepney

My view is that theory is too important to be left to theorists.

(Neil Thompson, 2010)

To show no interest in theory is to travel blind.

(David Howe, 1987)

A text which invites the reader to embark on a journey of exploration into the world of social work methods must necessarily address the central problem of relating theory to practice, and consider how research may influence such a debate. However, a word of caution is in order, especially as anyone seeking neat explanations or simple answers is soon likely to become frustrated. The nature of the relationship between theory, practice and research is far more complex than it may first appear and it is doubtful whether it is fully understood (Sawdon, 1986; Thompson, 2010). In this chapter, and the following chapter by Malcolm Payne, we will endeavour to demystify the nature of theory and explore how it can be used in an informed, reflective and practical way to enhance social work practice. Further, we will try to show how the relationship between theory and practice can help us to understand different approaches to social work research.

The starting point adopted here is to risk stating the obvious by acknowledging that theory has the potential to enhance our understanding and thereby contribute to more *informed* practice (Thompson, 2010; Coulshed and Orme, 2006). It does this by providing the essential 'raw material' or building blocks that can be used as a basis for critical thinking and action (Thompson, 2000). Coulshed (1991: 8) has highlighted one of the unstated assumptions in the debate by reminding us that 'whether we recognise it or not, theoryless practice does not exist; we cannot avoid looking for explanations to guide our actions, whilst research has shown that those agencies which profess not to use theory offer a non problem solving, woolly and directionless service'. Nonetheless as Thompson (2010: 6) notes 'the fallacy of theoryless practice remains widespread' and so the apparent invisibility of theory needs to be exposed, so that such myths might be challenged and the significance of theory brought out and critically examined.

Whilst the connections between theory and practice are clearly important, and the potential for creative thinking quite considerable, this is something which it would seem the vast majority of practitioners (not to mention academics) find difficult to make. The end result is all too often muddled thinking, confusion or a process hampered by various bugbears (explored more fully by Malcolm Payne at the beginning of the next chapter). It is therefore little wonder that in the face of such an 'imaginary monster' we become prone to giving up and quietly eject complex theoretical concepts from our mental maps about practice. Theory in turn becomes rationalised and reinterpreted as 'unnecessary baggage' that complicates the picture too much, something the hard-pressed and streetwise practitioner can well do without. This inevitably creates a serious theory to practice gap.

The debate highlights the tension between two very general models of practice. The first draws on a notion of practice which presents the social worker as a kind of maintenance mechanic with stress on such qualities as technical competence, hard skills and knowledge of procedures and the law. The alternative view suggests that social work has more in common with the art of gardening (organic of course) which emphasises the need to achieve sustainable growth and change through a process of critical exploration and development. Davies (1994: 205) has put the case extremely well for the social maintenance approach arguing that it is a crucial, but rather undervalued role. He suggests that 'for the practice of social work, a knowledge of the social sciences is less crucial than training in basic skills'. Variations on the social gardening model have been proposed by a number of writers in both social work and adult education (Freire 1972; Knowles 1973). For example, this approach could be found in the post-Barclay vision of community social work that emerged during the 1980s and revealed in the development of decentralised services organised in small neighbourhood teams (Stepney and Popple, 2008: 115).

Not surprisingly much of social work is likely to be somewhere in between these two poles and adopt elements of both as an aid to carrying out the core tasks of assessment, care planning, problem solving and so on. In fact the position adopted here is that both models are important and can contribute to producing the well rounded practitioners that service users look for and have a right to expect. For this a wide range of theoretical knowledge, research evidence as well as the skills and ability to engage in inquiry based learning will be needed. Consequently, it is contingent upon us to find some fresh links and connections between basic competence (the bedrock of effectiveness), critical inquiry and theory.

The meaning of 'theory': different approaches to producing knowledge and competing views of reality

The term 'theory' is sometimes placed in inverted commas to denote that it is a contested concept. At the risk of oversimplification, a theory may be defined as a 'framework of understanding or cluster of ideas that attempt to explain reality'

(Stepney and Ford, 2012: xi). In the social sciences, theories tend to be contested because they offer competing explanations that reflect different approaches to knowledge (epistemology) and reality (ontology), as well as revealing particular values and ideological positions. To understand this it is necessary to explore these different approaches to knowledge and competing views of reality in greater depth.

The basis of much controversy lies in the demise of earlier versions of positivism (where the purpose was to find general laws based upon scientific measurement and observation to identify 'social facts' or 'truths' to explain an 'objective reality'). Thomas Kuhn, Karl Popper and others challenged the view that knowledge could be based on 'social facts', as absolute truths. Scientific knowledge could not achieve absolute certainty, as observation is theory driven, contextually significant, value laden and operates according to cultural convention (Kuhn, 1970; Popper, 1959). Theoretical knowledge is at best probabilistic and provisional – what is known today may have to be modified and replaced tomorrow. The world or social reality cannot be known independent of theoretical constructs and ideological representations, consequently, there is no such thing as certain truth. Hence, if truth and certainty are not attainable then we have to choose between competing theories or paradigms (cluster of theories).

In a classic sociological text Berger and Luckmann (1971) explored this issue and proposed that there is no single objective reality but a number of competing realities based on different forms of knowledge and experience. If one accepts this then it follows that there is no such thing as 'social facts and truths waiting to be discovered and measured' (as positivist approaches have always maintained), rather knowledge is mediated through different frameworks of understanding and shared views of reality, which have to be actively constructed. This view of reality draws upon an epistemological approach that is referred to as interpretivism. This emphasises the process of human understanding and interpretation rather than the 'social facts' approach associated with positivism. If we turn to ontological considerations then Berger and Luckmann's position is relativist and may be termed social constructivism, which can be distinguished from other philosophical positions in the social sciences (in particular, objectivism associated with positivism). Finally, just to confuse things further, if we move along the 'ontological continuum' we find that there is another important position called realism. This is set out in Figure 2.1:

Realism shares with positivism the view that the scientific methods of measurement of the natural sciences can be usefully applied to the social sciences. Realism is premised on the belief that there is an objective reality (rather than multiple constructs) that is independent of our knowledge and understanding of it (Sayer, 2000), but unlike positivism takes a more constructivist position in relation to the interpretation of individual experience. The advantage here is that realism allows for a more critical view of knowledge, which it sees as provisional

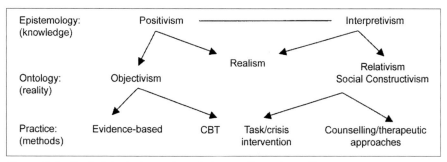

Figure 2.1 Basic links between knowledge, reality and practice

and shaped by dominant social structures. Hence, critical realism 'seeks to be sensitive to the multiple realities of subjective experience, but views these within the context of dominant structures' (Stepney, 2009: 18). The implication of this is that the epistemological and ontological position we adopt, concerning what constitutes theories of knowledge and reality, will influence our choice of methods.

This has potentially some quite profound implications for social work theory and practice. In social work many of our ideas are borrowed from the social sciences, philosophy, law and so on, which means that inevitably our theoretical knowledge base is very broad. It also needs to be recognised that such ideas may be at a highly abstract level of analysis, quite speculative and fiercely contested (Parton, 1996).

Sociology, psychology and social policy, the new social sciences, whatever merits and insights they bring, do not offer any neat and consistent theory about human behaviour. This places them towards the interpretivist or realist positions. It follows that whilst academics can usefully debate such theoretical dilemmas the practitioner can only afford such luxuries if they bring tangible benefits and lead to positive outcomes. Consequently, over time, abstract theory from the social sciences has been subject to a process of professional adaptation and refinement. In the case of social work, as it slowly developed in the US and Europe, it gradually and hesitantly established a professionally derived body of knowledge. This is an unfinished project and clearly subject to ongoing change and reformulation reflecting the results of empirical research and scholarship. It is also an attempt to span the divide between the personal and the political explaining how our thoughts about the social world connect with individual feelings and experience. This is set out in Figure 2.2 below.

Thompson (2010) makes a useful distinction between formal and 'informal theory'. Formal theory derives from the social sciences and implies 'rational thinking, distance and objectivity which contrasts with feelings and the living reality of social work encounters' (Coulshed and Orme, 1998: 7). Hence, it is now convenient to refer to formal theory from the social sciences once it has been

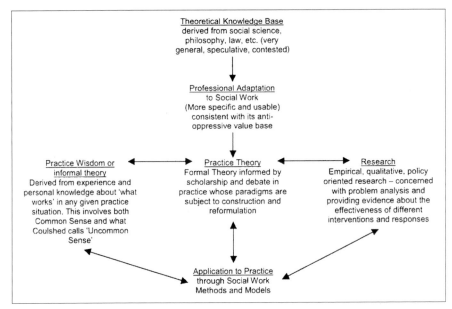

Figure 2.2 From the abstract knowledge and theory to social work methods

adapted for use in social work as practice theory. This is not to infer that such knowledge is fixed or unproblematic and devoid of internal contestation and dispute, but represents a genuine attempt to combine reading and research to create a more usable and accessible knowledge base.

However, practice theory also derives its applicability and resonance from other less elevated and recognisable sources, in particular knowledge and experience of what might work in any given situation. If we do this then experience suggests what is likely to happen. This may be referred to as informal theory, although some writers refer to this kind of knowledge as practice wisdom, which is built up over time and passed on through word of mouth about doing the job. Others refer to this as working class knowledge to denote how the views of service users get absorbed into the professional culture. A more popular description might be just to call it common sense.

'Informal theory' or common sense dressed up?

The notion of common sense contains a certain paradox: it is something which in a general sense is very real and compelling, with the potential for wide application, yet remains essentially quite personal and idiosyncratic. The end result is that common sense becomes riddled with ambiguity and is one of those concepts which tends to be all things to all people. Thus in recognising its strength and capacity for infusing practice theory with everyday knowledge about experience 'at the sharp end' of life, we also need to recognise weaknesses and limitations. For example, common sense may descend into parochialism, popular prejudice and worse which has led Coulshed to suggest that we may need to harness common sense with 'uncommon sense' (Coulshed, 1991).

The reason for this is that common sense may reflect highly discriminatory and racist attitudes which clearly need to be exposed and challenged. For example, social workers sometimes encounter racism amongst people who comment on the decline of their neighbourhood by saying 'this used to be a nice area before they came . . .' and prefixing it with 'its only common sense'. Clearly this kind of reaction is informed by particular values which need to be challenged with a very different kind of common sense. Here we are concerned with the less visible but common experience of oppression which has roots in perpetuating existing social divisions on the basis of race, class, gender, or disability in local communities. Of course, these two kinds of common sense may not be easily reconcilable, which indicates why it is important that taken for granted knowledge and popular assumptions be subjected to the same critical analysis and scepticism as would be applied to more formal types of knowledge. The methods we employ in practice will need to do all this and more.

Practice theory and critical reflection

Practice theory, as has been noted, will be subjected to a range of influences not least a practitioner's self-reflection about what the job entails. In this sense theory will need to be reflexive and adaptable to changing practice constructions. Conversely, reflection is the way practitioners weigh up the possibilities in any given situation and evaluate the extent to which existing theory is adequate (Payne, 2002, 2005). This is closest to what Schön referred to as having a 'reflective conversation with the situation' (Schön, 1983). We all implicitly do this much of the time but often without having the space to record the content or process involved.

However for reflection to become meaningful and significant for practice it will need to be translated into positive action. Here Thompson draws our attention to Kolb's (1984) model of experiential learning which encourages both reflection and active experimentation (Thompson, 2000). The model has four stages:

- **concrete experience** – which includes all life experiences, not just formal training.
- **reflective observation** – standing back and considering the significance of the experience.
- **abstract conceptualisation** – considering broader and deeper issues which stem from reflection. According to Thompson this involves 'hypothesis formation' as we try and place the experience in a wider context.

- **active experimentation** – where new learning begins as we put our abstract concepts into practice.

The cycle can then begin again as active experimentation becomes the next concrete experience to reflect upon (Thompson, 2000: 5–6).

Payne (2002, 2005), drawing on the work of Fook (2002), identifies three ways of thinking associated with being a reflective and critical practitioner. He suggests that *reflective thinking* is essential and becomes the basis for 'thinking things through', while *reflexive thinking* complements this by 'taking into account many different perspectives on a situation' and aids the application of theory to new situations. Finally, *critical thinking* will be required to question accepted wisdom and where necessary find solutions that promote change beyond the scope of the existing social order (Payne, 2005: 32).

Clearly reflection must be placed in its appropriate social/cultural, economic and political context amidst competing ideas about the role of social work, which are taken up below. Since the very nature of social work is contested, practice theories provide a useful framework for reflecting on the nature of the task, alternative courses of action, underlying assumptions, predictions about possible outcomes and what Sheppard (1995) has referred to as the problem of 'disconfirming evidence'. Here as elsewhere critical reflection may help us to avoid jumping to superficial conclusions, based upon tradition and routine (Coutts-Jarman, 1993) which support the three Cs – Conformity, Consensus and Convention. Given the foregoing, 'critical reflection' also signifies a 'melting pot' in which values play a prominent part. The responsive, creative and critical practitioner will need to be morally as well as conceptually fluent.

Locating social work methods and developing a structure for practice

It is argued that social work methods are informed by a very broad spectrum of ideas, formal theoretical knowledge and what might be referred to as informal theory or practice wisdom. And to deconstruct particular approaches requires considerable energy and skill. Hence, it is hardly surprising to find that the end result is a continuously evolving map of different methods and models. These can usefully be conceptualised in terms of a two dimensional diagram first proposed by Burrel and Morgan (1979). Social thinkers since Marx have argued that society can be understood in terms of a tension between the forces of change and stability, and the extent to which subjective experience contradicts objective reality. These were combined by Burrel and Morgan (1979) as set out in Figure 2.3.

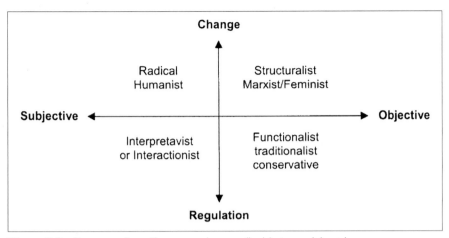

Figure 2.3 Four paradigmatic approaches applicable to social work

This generates the four paradigms in Figure 2.3 which have subsequently been reworked and applied to social work by various writers (Rojek 1986; Sawdon 1986; Howe 1987).

The second diagram, Figure 2.4 below, displays the general orientation which might be taken by the social worker operating within a particular paradigm.

There are at least three problems which can be identified when using such a model. First, it is doubtful whether each of the methods currently in use can be equated with a particular paradigm. Whilst some may fit quite well, for instance

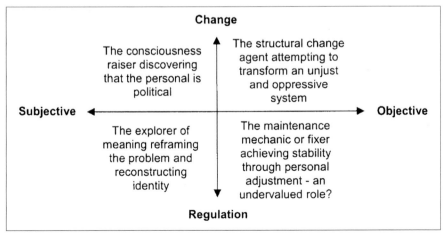

Figure 2.4 The general orientation of the practitioner operating within a particular paradigm

critical social work within a paradigm of objective or structural change (Stepney, 2010), others remain problematic. One of the reasons for this is that many methods are concerned with both regulation and change, which in practice are not mutually irreconcilable. Second, some methods such as community social work and ecological approaches derive from a number of different but interdependent traditions which cannot adequately be located without adding further dimensions to the model. Third, such models might be seen as reductionist and social work is hopefully more than the sum of its component parts.

Notwithstanding these criticisms such a model may still be useful provided we recognise that it represents broad clusters and a general theoretical orientation rather than a template for innovative practice. The view proposed here is that mapping our practice in this way can still be helpful as an initial starting point which confirms broader patterns and opens up possibilities for combining methods in a clear yet constructive way (Coulshed and Orme, 2006). As Coulshed notes, 'if we have a variety of tools in our workbag, we are more able to offer a service which is determined by client need rather than our own' (Coulshed, 1991: 9).

However attractive and compelling it is to contemplate the integration of theory and practice, Sheldon reminds us of the many obstacles that can get in the way of achieving it (Sheldon, 1978). At least three problems can be identified. Firstly, 'theory' and 'practice' originate from two different sub-cultures, one academic and the other work based, and tensions are likely to re-emerge when points of dispute arise. Secondly, the social work curriculum encourages an eclectic, supermarket approach where all theories are treated as potentially of equal status and value. Thirdly, the professional culture of social work has hitherto not embraced a strong research tradition and this means that few opportunities exist for staff to conduct routine empirical evaluations of their work.

These criticisms have in part been answered by developments identified in the previous section, alongside the search for greater effectiveness in social work. This element is central to the movement for evidence-based practice, epitomised by the work of Brian Sheldon, and the establishment of research centres at a number of universities including Stirling, Huddersfield and Exeter to name but three. Such centres were established specifically to promote a culture of evaluation and research minded practice in the personal social services. New courses in research methods have also been incorporated both within initial training as well as on post qualifying programmes. It is therefore appropriate to address the question of research in the final sections of the chapter.

Social work research and the evaluation of practice

In very general terms research is about 'seeking knowledge for a purpose' (D'Cruz and Jones, 2004: 5) according to certain scientific principles and values. At its simplest it is concerned with finding answers to specific questions as a form of inquiry. What distinguishes research from other forms of inquiry is that it should be done in a 'systematic, disciplined and rigorous way ... making use of appropriate research methods and designs' (Becker and Bryman, 2004: 14). The choice of research questions and methods of inquiry will clearly be influenced by both epistemological and ontological considerations and can be located within the general philosophies and theories of the social sciences. Practice based research and evaluation, whatever its aims and limitations, come within this framework.

Research has the capacity to influence and enrich the theory to policy/practice debate and in so doing contribute to better quality interventions and services. In the past this process was sometimes referred to as experimental social policy (Smith, 1975) or action-research (CDP, 1977), although it can also be found in mainstream research designs and evidence-based approaches. However, for this tradition to enhance practice will require rational, open and democratic policies to be put in place to ensure that research is part of a process of critical inquiry rather than become the handmaiden of cost control. Used wisely, research has the potential to be used as a 'basis for critical review and reflection, including comparison of different ways of providing similar services, an analysis of factors which influence quality and a pointer to unintended or unexpected outcomes' (Cheetham, 1998: 26). One way of realising this potential is to develop an integrated model of practice evaluation, combining the three perspectives of accountability, critical knowledge production and development (Chelimski, 1997). This would facilitate a way of meeting two crucial requirements for practice: the need for criticality alongside effectiveness (Stepney and Rostila, 2011) and revealed in the debate between critical practice and evidence-based practice (Stepney, 2010 and explored further in the chapter by Gray, Stepney and Webb).

In discussing practice evaluation it should be recognised that the relationship between research and practice is problematic in several respects. This can be illustrated from the many well-funded and influential projects in the field of child care, child protection and safeguarding (Packman et al., 1986; Cleaver and Freeman, 1995; Packman and Hall, 1998; Rutter, 2006). These have formed the basis of Department of Health guidelines and local authority policies in this field, which have become increasingly prescriptive over time. In this they have tended to serve the purpose of top down managerial imperatives and reinforce organisational control, thereby restricting the scope for professional initiatives and judgement. However, on one point all these studies have agreed: the importance of the quality of the relationship between social worker, parents and children. This repeated finding contains something of a paradox. First, it is not always clear how researchers have reached informed conclusions from their methodology, as it sometimes seems more of a post-hoc policy. Second the prescription it entails is often vague and generalised, in terms of honesty and good faith, rather than specific methods. In other words, an emphasis on good practice is often undermined by considerable fogginess about how this is recognisable and how it can be achieved.

During recent years practitioners have begun to alter the balance concerning their participation in the research process and practice-based research has slowly advanced (Fuller and Petch, 1995). Various developments are significant here including improvements in methodologies which are more responsive to the needs of practitioners; a certain amount of methodological synthesis and pluralism; and increasing collaboration between practitioners and researchers (Shaw and Gould, 2001; Kazi, 1998). It is often necessary, as Karvinen (1999: 282) reminds us, to develop a range of research strategies which 'should be sensitive enough to uncover not only general tendencies, but also contextual particularities'. Nonetheless, social work still faces some formidable theoretical and ideological hurdles if practitioner/ researchers are to combine evaluation concerned with effectiveness with a broader commitment to emancipatory change and social justice (Stepney and Rostila, 2011; Shaw, 1998). One such hurdle where progress is being made relates to tackling methodological disputes or paradigm wars (Pawson and Tilley, 1997).

There is evidence to suggest that unsurprisingly in a market economy marketised assumptions frequently exert an influence on the research agenda (Stepney and Rostila, 2011). It follows that this may encourage a higher value to be placed on hard, empirical, outcome based methodologies, which are seen to be objective and neutral, rather than softer qualitative approaches, action-research or policy orientated studies (Webb, 2001). The scientific validity of randomised controlled trials and quasi experimental designs is not disputed here, although their usefulness in social science research is more contentious (Usher, 1997). However, the value placed on alternative methodologies often involves making a political as well as a professional judgement. Significantly, qualitative methods may allow for more empowering and reflective evaluations of practice (Shaw and Gould, 2001; Shaw, 1998). Consequently we need to make the epistemological and ontological criteria for exercising such judgements about methodology more explicit (D'Cruz and Jones, 2004; Thompson, 2000).

Towards a manifesto for practice evaluation

In a telling contribution to the debate, Shaw challenges much conventional wisdom by calling on social workers to develop 'a critical, reflective and enabling practice' anchored in an exploration of how experienced practitioners evaluate their work. He suggests that this offers a valid foundation for building on existing expertise rather than importing 'off the shelf' research designs (Shaw, 1998). Clearly much here depends on the quality of the experienced practitioner and their capacity to reflect critically and abstract from individual practice examples to general theory and back to another real situation (Pawson and Tilley, 1997). Notwithstanding the problems inherent in identifying good practice and distinguishing it from 'convincing stories' about practice, Shaw (1998) draws up a manifesto for evaluation in practice and suggests that social workers should be encouraged to:

- Exploit the potential of reflective methods to reflect hard on both process and outcomes.
- Make their theoretical assumptions explicit, including taken for granted knowledge about culture, identity, class, gender, disability etc.
- Get close to service users' experiences, and respect these as authentic accounts of resilience in the face of oppression.
- Develop genuinely participatory and dialogical forms of evaluation as critical inquiry (Freire, 1972).
- Ground research evaluation strategies in different practice theories and methods of intervention (214–215).

Whilst Shaw makes a strong case for practitioners developing qualitative methods, such as participant observation, life histories and focus group work, a convincing case can be made for an integrated approach referred to above, drawing upon the work of Chelimski (1997). This would utilise mixed method designs reflecting a degree of methodological pluralism and, for example, draw on critical theory as part of a critical realist approach to identify the causal mechanisms at work that produce a range of individual outcomes in the context of dominant structures (Stepney and Rostila, 2011; Kazi, 2003; Pawson and Tilley, 1997). This has the potential for combining experimental rigour, to discover what works for whom in what context, with user participation towards more emancipatory practice. The challenge as always with a pluralistic and integrated approach is to create a research design which conveys a sense of explanatory synthesis with ontological coherence.

Responding to uncertainty

Another problem in constructing a valid framework or manifesto for practice evaluation is the degree of uncertainty and unpredictability which permeates much of the terrain of social work. Thompson (2010: 186) makes reference to this in explaining the basic tenets of existentialist theory and practice with 'the recognition that human existence is characterised by constant change . . . and thus a degree of uncertainty'. One of the implications of this is that before embarking on a new piece of work we should expect the unexpected and predict the unpredictable. Flexibility has always been the key to the social worker's survival if not success, but the challenge is to use this purposefully in a world where there are few benchmarks of truth and certainty. What is at stake here is social work's capacity to operate effectively in situations of uncertainty, especially for its clients, who remain amongst the most marginalised and excluded groups in society.

There have been two broad responses to the problem of uncertainty. One embraces a discourse of competences (CCETSW, 1996) the other reflective practice (Thompson, 2010; Payne, 2005). The issue here is whether the latter can be adequately developed within a paradigm dominated by the former.

The development of competence-based training, at both qualifying and postqualifying level, and its influence on practice emerged during the early 1990s following a succession of child abuse scandals. The various inquiry reports highlighted deficiencies in training and agency procedures. Both have been addressed through the language of competences permeating professional agendas. However, this response was a reaction to wider global pressures and the new market in welfare to try and maintain reliable standards in an uncertain world. It also answered the call for improvements in services and enhancing consumer choice. What is more problematic is deciding in what sense competence-based approaches may be empowering and the extent to which they reinforce managerial control (Adams, 1998). Further, it has been argued that they undermine the movement towards anti-oppressive practice (Dominelli, 1996).

Adams identifies six major criticisms of competence-based approaches including arguments that they are more suited to work in stable, bureaucratic organisations rather than the organic milieu of social work; they fragment practice into artificially discrete elements; they are outcome-based and encourage convergent and mechanistic thinking; they concentrate exclusively on measurable aspects of job performance; and they overemphasise techniques and skills at the expense of values and critical reflection (Adams, 1998: 258). The result may be analogous to what Pearson once described as welfare technicians reducing complex socio-political issues to a series of technical tasks, such that the problems of politics become the problems of administration (Pearson, 1975; Habermas, 1978).

If social workers are going to be trained to 'approach each situation respectful of difference, complexity and ambiguity' (Parton and Marshall, 1998: 246), as well as provide a competent level of service, then it is the capacity for critical inquiry and reflection that must be enhanced. Critical inquiry as we have noted above can be developed by practitioners becoming more research minded and policy orientated, and importantly, integrating these elements into their practice. Developing discerning powers of critical reflection are essential if social work is to combine effectiveness in its traditional helping and care management role with a commitment to social justice and empowerment (Lishman, 1998; Stepney, 2006).

Conclusion – theory, practice and research in an age of uncertainty

The terrain which social workers occupy and traverse is contested, uncertain and marked by considerable political conflict (Payne, 2005). The contradictions and dilemmas that practitioners encounter in their daily work reflect this tension, which is why a sound theoretical framework, knowledge of policy and research mindedness are essential for good practice. In this chapter an attempt has been made to demystify the nature of theory, and use the knowledge of the social sciences to explore the theory to practice debate. We have also examined how theory is important for understanding social work research and the evaluation of practice. Social work in its international context (Midgley, 1997) draws on such a framework and develops in areas where sometimes other professionals might fear to tread, for example, supporting oppressed minorities and promoting human rights of all marginalised groups. The increasing demand for new knowledge and a critical approach to its application is consistent with this tradition.

It follows that we need to approach social work theory in a concrete yet practical way so that it can be used with confidence and skill. This will be the starting point and challenge taken up by Malcolm Payne in the next chapter.

References

Adams, R. (1998) Social Work Processes. In Adams, R., Dominelli, L. and Payne, M. (Eds.) *Social Work: Themes, Issues and Critical Debates*. Basingstoke: Macmillan.

Becker, S. and Bryman, A. (2004) *Understanding Research for Social Policy and Practice: Themes, Methods and Approaches.* Bristol: The Policy Press.

Berger, P. and Luckmann, T. (1971) *The Social Construction of Reality.* Harmondsworth: Penguin.

Burrell, G. and Morgan, G. (1979) *Sociological Paradigms and Organisational Analysis.* London: Routledge.

CCETSW (1996) *Assuring Quality: in the Diploma in Social Work – 1. Rules and Requirements for the DipSW.* (second revision) London: CCETSW.

CDP (1977) *Gilding the Ghetto: The State and the Poverty Experiments*. London: Home Office, National Community Development Inter-project Team.

Cheetham, J. (1998) The Evaluation of Social Work: Priorities, Problems and Possibilities. In Cheetham, J. and Kazi, M. (Eds.) *The Working of Social Work.* London: Jessica Kingsley.

Chelimski, E. (1997) The Coming Transformations in Evaluation. In Chelimsky, E. and Shadish, W.R. (Eds.) *Evaluation for 21st Century. A Handbook.* Thousand Oaks: Sage. 1–26.

Cleaver, H. and Freeman, P. (1995) *Parental Perspectives in Supervised Cases of Child Abuse*. London: HMSO.

Coulshed, V. (1991) *Social Work Practice: An Introduction.* (2nd edn.) Basingstoke: Macmillan.

Coulshed, V. and Orme, J. (1998) *Social Work Practice: An Introduction.* (3rd edn.) Basingstoke: Macmillan.

Coulshed, V. and Orme, J. (2006) *Social Work Practice: An Introduction.* (4th edn.) Basingstoke: Palgrave Macmillan.

Coutts-Jarman, J. (1993) Using Reflection and Experience in Nurse Education. *British Journal of Nursing*, (2).

Davies, M. (1994) *The Essential Social Worker: A Guide For Positive Practice.* (3rd edn.) Aldershot: Arena.

D'Cruz, H. and Jones, M. (2004) *Social Work Research: Ethical and Political Contexts.* London: Sage.

Dominelli, L. (1996) De-professionalising Social Work: Anti-oppressive Practice, Competences and Postmodernism. *British Journal of Social Work*, 26, 153–175.

Fook, J. (2002) *Social Work: Critical Theory and Practice*, London, Sage.

Freire, P. (1972) *Pedagogy of the Oppressed*, Harmondsworth, Penguin.

Fuller, R. and Petch, A. (1995) *Practitioner Research: The Reflective Social Worker.* Buckingham: Open University Press.

Habermas, J. (1978*) Knowledge and Human Interests.* London: Heinemann.

Howe, D. (1987*) An Introduction to Social Work Theory.* Aldershot: Wildwood House.

Karvinen, S. (1999) The Methodological Tensions in Finnish Social Work Research. In Karvinen, S., Pösö, T. and Satka, M. *Reconstructing Social Work Research.* SoPhi., Jyväskylä, Finland: University of Jyväskylä Press.

Kazi, M. (1998) Putting Single-case Evaluation into Practice. In Cheetham, J. and Kazi, M. (Eds.) *The Working of Social Work.* London: Jessica Kingsley.

Kazi, M. (2003) *Realist Evaluation in Practice.* London: Sage.

Knowles, M. (1973) *The Adult Learner: A Neglected Species.* Houston: Gulf Publishing.

Kolb, D. (1984) *Experiential Learning.* Englewood Cliffs NJ: Prentice-Hall.

Kuhn, T. (1970) *The Structure of Scientific Revolutions*. (2nd edn.) Chicago: University of Chicago Press.

Lishman, J. (1998) *Personal and Professional Development.* In Adams, R., Dominelli, L. and Payne, M. (Eds.) (1998) *Social Work: Themes, Issues and Critical Debates.* Basingstoke: Macmillan.

Midgley, J. (1997) Social Work in International Context. In Reisch, M. and Gambrill, E. *Social Work in the 21st Century.* USA: Pine Forge Press.

Packman, J., Randall, J. and Jaques, N. (1986) *Who Needs Care? Social Work Decisions about Children*. Oxford: Blackwell.

Packman, J. and Hall, C. (1998) *From Care to Accommodation.* London: HMSO.

Parton, N. (Ed.) (1996) *Social Theory, Social Change and Social Work*. London: Routledge.

Parton, N. and Marshall, W. (1998) Postmodernism and Discourse Approaches to Social Work. In Adams, R., Dominelli, L. and Payne, M. (Eds.) *Social Work: Themes, Issues and Critical Debates.* Basingstoke: Macmillan.

Pawson, R. and Tilley, N. (1997) *Realistic Evaluation.* Thousand Oaks: Sage.

Payne, M. (2002) Social Work Theories and Reflective Practice. In Adams, R., Dominelli, L. and Payne, M. (Eds.) (2002) *Social Work – Themes, Issues and Critical Debates.* (2nd edn.) Basingstoke: Palgrave.

Payne, M. (2005) *Modern Social Work Theory.* (3rd edn.) Basingstoke: Palgrave.

Pawson, R. and Tilley, N. (1997) *Realistic Evaluation.* Thousand Oaks: Sage.

Pearson, G. (1975) *The Deviant Imagination.* Basingstoke: Macmillan.

Popper, K. (1959) *Objective Knowledge.* Oxford: Clarendon Press.

Rojek, C. (1986) *A Way of Being.* London: Routledge.

Rutter, M. (2006) Is Sure Start an Effective Preventive Intervention? *Child and Adolescent Mental Health*, 11(3) 135–141.

Sawdon, D. (1986) *Making Connections in Practice Teaching.* Heinemann: NISW.

Sayer, A. (2000) *Realism and Social Science.* London: Sage.

Schön, D. (1983) *The Reflective Practitioner: How Professionals Think in Action.* New York: Basic Books.

Shaw, I. (1998) Practising Evaluation. In Cheetham, J. and Kazi, M. (Eds.) *The Working of Social Work.* London: Jessica Kingsley.

Shaw, I. and Gould, N. (2001) *Qualitative Research in Social Work.* London: Sage.

Sheldon, B. (1978) Theory and Practice in Social Work: A Re-examination of a Tenuous Relationship. *British Journal of Social Work*, 8(1) 1–22.

Sheppard, M. (1995) *Care Management and the New Social Work: A Critical Analysis.* London: Whiting and Birch.

Smith, G. (1975) Action Research: Experimental Social Administration. In Lees, R. and Smith, G. *Action Research in Community Development*. London: Routledge.

Stepney, P. (2006) Mission impossible? Critical Practice in social work. *British Journal of Social Work*, 36(8), 1289–1307.

Stepney, P. (2009) English Social Work at the Crossroads: A Critical View. *Australian Social Work*, 62(1) 10–27.

Stepney, P. (2010) Social Welfare at the Crossroads: Evidence-based Practice or Critical Practice? *The International Journal of Interdisciplinary Social Sciences*, 5(5) 105–120.

Stepney, P. and Ford, D. (Eds.) (2000) *Social Work Models, Methods and Theories: A Framework for Practice.* Lyme Regis: Russell House.

Stepney, P. and Popple, K. (2008) *Social Work and The Community: A Critical Context For Practice*. Basingstoke: Palgrave.

Stepney, P. and Rostila, I. (2011) Towards an Integrated Model of Practice Evaluation Balancing Accountability, Critical Knowledge and Developmental Perspectives. *Health Sociology Review* (Australia) 20(2) 133–146.

Thompson, N. (2000) *Theory and Practice in Human Services.* (2nd edn.) Buckingham: Open University Press.

Thompson, N. (2010) *Theorizing Social Work Practice.* Basingstoke: Palgrave.

Usher, R. (1997) Introduction. In McKenzie, G., Powell, J. and Usher, R. *Understanding Social Research Perspectives on Methodology and Practice.* London: Falmer Press.

Webb, S. (2001) Some Considerations on The Validity of Evidence-Based Practice in Social Work. *British Journal of Social Work* 31(1) 57–79.

Chapter 3

Rethinking the Social Work Theory to Practice Debate

Malcolm Payne

Theory: irrelevant, disconnected, inapplicable?

Practitioners have three main bugbears about using social work theory in practice. The first is irrelevance. Articles and books about theory seem engaged in debates in complicated and pretentious language about fine distinctions between different ideas, which never seem to come to any resolution. None of this seems designed to help practitioners with useful things that they can do in practice. Indeed, some of the complexity seems just to be saying something obvious that you already knew, but in tortuous language.

The second bugbear is disconnection from practice realities. Most theory is about psychological or social ideas which may be interesting and might help practitioners with setting general aims in their work. However, in practice when you have to do a community care assessment or decide whether a child is being abused, legal and agency requirements (the forms that need to be completed) and written procedures tell you (if not always clearly) what you have to do: how does the theory help?

The third bugbear is application. There are many competing social work theories discussed in textbooks, mostly drawn from psychological and sociological ideas. You are expected to follow complicated procedures. Theories are also highly generalised, so that they do not tell you much about mental illness, or older people or children. How do you decide which to use, or can you put several of them together? How do you remember what it says you should do? Then, how do you connect it to the issues the particular user group and community that you and your agency have to work with?

A bugbear, if you look it up in a dictionary, did not originally mean an irritating difficulty: it meant an imaginary monster to frighten children and hence an object of mystery and apprehension. My argument in this chapter is that you can approach social work theory in a concrete and practical way and, if you do, you will find that using theory is essential in working with and respecting the autonomy of service users and clarifying your accountability to your agency. My starting point is, then, to suggest an approach to dealing with social work theory that demystifies it, so that you can use it with confidence rather than apprehension.

In order to do this, I argue that you do have to get involved in a certain amount of theoretical complexity, and I move on to disentangling some of the complexities of social work theory and explaining how you might deal with them. I hope this will help to remove some of the bugbears for you. Finally, I look at various ways in which you can adapt practice theory to use it in a practical way.

Approaching social work theory

The approach to theory

There are many different theories set out in texts such as this one. They are often complex, so you cannot know and understand them all in detail. Therefore, you have to choose between them, either selecting one for general purposes or for a particular case or making a combination of them. This means developing enough grasp of the theories that you come across to make a reasonable decision about whether you want to select them for a more detailed look. I have set out my approach to doing this in social work theory in Box 1.

***

Box 1 Approaching social work theories

1. The basic idea
2. Prescription – practical actions it tells you to do
3. Where the theory comes from
4. Connections with other theories
5. Prohibitions – actions it tells you not to do

***

The first thing I do, when I approach a social work theory, is to identify its basic idea. This says what it is useful for and distinguishes it from other competing theories. Usually you can get hold of this basic idea fairly readily. It can help you decide whether it is relevant at all to you and your practice. Understanding the basic ideas of different theories also allows you to use one theory to criticise another. This may help in writing student assignments about theories. It also helps in practice, because it highlights the theory's advantages and downsides and points to gaps between theories.

The second aspect of my approach to a theory is to pick out the main practical actions that it tells you to do. This gives you an immediate clue about useful things that might help you with what you need to do in your practice. Doing this also makes the theory clearer, as it explains how its practice prescriptions follow from the main ideas.

Most social work theories emerged from work with a particular experiment or user group. The third action to take is to find out where the theory came from and places where it is used: mental health or children and families work for example. This tells you whether it is particularly fitted for working with the user group that you practise with.

The fourth action in this approach is to see a theory's connections with other theories, or its opposition to other theories, so that you can see what ideas you can use together and what you have to keep separate. You can then work with your supervisor, practice educator or colleagues to see how to use theories together in an organised way.

The fifth aspect of understanding a theory is to ask what it tells you *not* to do; its prohibitions. This is almost as important as its prescriptions, because it makes the limitations of the theory clear.

How not to use social work theory

There is one main rule: do not use a social work theory as a matter of personal choice. For ethical and practical reasons, service users should give informed consent to what you are doing together, so therefore they have to know what you are doing and why. This requirement is included in most codes of professional practice (Payne, 2010) because most people that you serve are entitled to be in control of deciding what will benefit them and what might be unhelpful. The 'informed' aspect of informed consent makes it the responsibility of the social worker to explain it in ways that allow service users to understand the choices and make the right decision. Therefore, you have to know your aims in using the theory, how it might work to their benefit and any problems they might experience. The practical reason for getting informed consent from service users is that if they agree to what you intend to do, they are more likely to contribute to making it work. Also, for reasons of professional standards and quality, your colleagues and agency should know what ideas you are using and the particular combination of ideas you have put together. These should be tested out with your colleagues and supervisor.

Working with service users' informed consent is another reason why you need to have a firm grasp of at least the basic idea of a theory: you will have to explain what you want to do and why. There is some evidence that using theory explicitly by talking it through with service users helps practitioners to think clearly about their overall aims and engage their user, while dealing with all the complications of practice (Secker, 1993). When it comes down to using particular processes, you need to be able to explain the detail of the theory's prescriptions, so you need the detail as well. Obviously to give service users choice, to put them in control of what you are doing or at least to give them some influence or rights in how social work affects them, you have to understand the theory of what you are doing well enough to be able to explain why evidence and an organised system of thought says that it should be helpful to do what you are proposing to do.

As well as your accountability to service users, you also have accountability to your colleagues and your agency. This is particularly important where you are being eclectic or where you are starting with a new theory. For example, perhaps you have been on a course about solution-focused practice. This is a well-accepted psychological therapy, but has only been patchily adopted in most social work agencies. Your supervisor and colleagues need to know that you are trying out something new and that you might be doing something that they or service users might not expect and so that other people can answer questions about it that come their way. If it turns out to be useful, they also need to learn from what you are doing.

Dealing with complexity

Using this fairly practical approach to deciding whether a theory will help you still leaves an immense amount of complexity to deal with in journals and books about theory. How do we deal with this? I argue in this section that first we need to understand that everything we do has a theory, sometimes hidden or unspoken, and to use it we need to think through how much detail we need to understand.

Informal and tacit theory

Everything that everyone does, including social work practice, is based on theory but the theory on which a particular action is based may be tacit or informal. Tacit theory is the ideas that we know, but it is unspoken. For example, English people usually know how to make a cup of tea, learning it in our families. We know how it works without learning the underlying physics and chemistry. When my American daughter-in-law started work in a legal office in London, however, she had to come for a lesson in English tea-making to give her the confidence required to be part of the rota for making tea at work. Such situations make you aware just how much tacit theory is around in our everyday lives.

Informal theory may be spoken about, but it has not been worked out, expressed in an organised way, supported by evidence and argument and published formally in articles or textbooks. Acknowledging the existence of tacit and informal theory accepts the reality that people are influenced by many different ideas and by their own life experience, not only by academic and professional theories. Payne and Askeland (2008) discuss a Norwegian analysis that distinguishes in professional understanding between our 'life-historical' knowledge that we acquire informally, our professional knowledge that we gain through practising our profession and scientific or formal knowledge that is researched and written down. We interpret and refine each of these aspects of professional understanding as we use them in practice. While these various sources of practice understanding influence each other, there is a constant process of interpretation and adaptation of ideas between them. Scientific knowledge becomes practical through successful interpretation, while practice ideas become scientific through being expressed as general practice theory and being tested through empirical science.

The theory-practice relationship

The relationship between theory and practice, therefore, is complex and constantly changing. There are three main questions:

- Which has priority as a source: practice or theory?
- How is practice theory validated by scientific research, intellectual debate or practice debate?
- What is the role of organisational, political and social constraints on practice?

We can't just decide that psychodynamic or empowerment theory is in principle a good thing, and that we should use it. We have to ask questions about 'good thing for what purpose?' and 'can it be adapted to be used in a social care agency with our responsibilities?' I argued above, in discussing how not to use social work theory, that we should not do this on our own, but through working with our supervisors and team and gaining the understanding and consent of service users we are working with.

So most people would agree that social work theory is both formal and informal, tacit and explicit and it mainly uses ideas from other academic fields, but they have to be adapted properly and selected to be relevant to the agency responsibilities.

How much depth do you need?

Detailed theoretical formulations are partly about completeness in setting out an argument in favour of a theory: this helps you to think through the reasons for accepting or rejecting it either in general or in a particular case and justifying it to your agency manager and service users. The detail is also partly about exposition of how to use it: giving you a handbook to consult when you are learning what to do, which can put aside once you have a firm grasp of a theory. There will be some theory that, once you are clear about the basic idea, that you can be sure will or will not help you in your present role. To make this decision, there are two questions to ask. First, do you need or want to study the theory in depth?

Needing to go in deep is about requiring more detail to use the theory in your practice; wanting to have greater understanding of it is partly about personal interest or wanting completeness in this area of your life or practice. But depth of understanding is only partly about personal interest: needing depth of knowledge about a theory may come from teamwork with colleagues, being effective with service users or developing academic understanding.

Teamwork with colleagues may lead you to need more depth of understanding if you are working in a specialist area. For example, if you work in a mental health crisis intervention team, your colleagues might actively use crisis theory and have a clear conception of the stages of a crisis and the appropriate actions at each stage. To communicate effectively among team members and be clear with service users, all members of the team need to reach a similar level of understanding.

Being effective with users is another aspect of needing to develop an in-depth understanding of a theory. You can often use the basic idea of theories to inform a general approach to a case, but if you are trying to disentangle complicated situations to help people to move forward over a period, you are likely to need a more detailed understanding of stages of action. For example, many people understand that the basic idea of task-centred practice involves clarifying a problem, then setting out on a programme of tasks to resolve it (Marsh and Doel, 2005). Simply doing this might help systematise your practice. However, detailed study would show you that you should start by getting users to prioritise the problems and agree the order of priority with you. It would also tell you that it works well if you share the tasks so that you do some and they do others, and what you each do depends on the achievement of the other person. Both of these points, prioritising and sharing, help to keep both users and practitioners motivated and on track. We are more likely to carry out a task if we have given it priority in our own mind, and if someone else is relying on us to keep our part of the bargain. You could have worked out these points from your common sense and understanding of human beings. But you don't have to, because the theoreticians have worked it out for you (and many other helpful points), set it all down in an orderly fashion in textbooks and, in the case of task-centred theory, have tested it out in research to confirm that it is helpful (see Chapter 7).

You may question whether improved academic understanding is as necessary as teamwork and being effective with service users. However, completing academic assignments is a way of learning, getting ideas into your mind in a clear way so that you can use them. This carries on after you are a student. Your professional commitment might well lead you on to further academic study, to go in deep because you are interested in the detail either to build up your store of knowledge and understanding or, more practically, to satisfy yourself that you have a full grasp of the ideas and can use them skilfully.

Intersectionality as an example

Take, for example, the theory of intersectionality (Murphy *et al.*, 2009). Your first reaction might be that this is a pretentious and quite possibly unfamiliar word, what can it mean in practice? So we go through 'the approach'.

The basic idea of intersectionality is that many people (particularly many users of social work services) are part of not just one but several oppressed minorities or social groups. For example, think about an older woman, who is lesbian, disabled and black. Because all these aspects of identity are present in one person, they intersect. That is, they don't just add up (for example, the more minorities you are part of, the more troubled you are), and one does not trump the others (for example, black is the most oppressed so the others don't count). Instead, they all count and they interact in complicated ways depending on your life chances and social experiences. This is different from anti-discrimination or anti-oppression theories, which concentrate on the disadvantages of discrimination and oppression that you suffer because of your minority identity. These theories find it hard to cope with multiple minority identities, so intersectionality is a useful addition to them.

Now consider the other points of the approach. Point two, the practical application is looking at someone in a minority and working out in detail how the different aspects of their minority identities interact. This might really help you to work with, say, a young woman in care who is troubled by her identity, but will probably not be a big issue when doing a community care assessment on a white older woman. Point three, this is a sociological idea that has been around for half a century. It comes from sociologists working on ethnicity and the position of minorities, trying to understand how different minority identities interacted. During the first decade of the 21st century, social work academics have become interested in it because it helps you to handle some of the complexities of working with people from minorities who experience uncertainties about their identity. Explanations based on intersectionality are likely to be sociological rather than looking at, for example, psychological conflicts or preventing behavioural problems arising from identity conflicts. Point four, it connects with feminist and anti-discrimination theory, so ideas from these theories and perhaps critical theory might help you to use intersectionality. It is also a postmodernist theory, because it emphasises the variability of identity, so related theories such as narrative ideas or solution-focused practice might help you to explore intersectionality with someone. On the other hand, it is about social interpretations of experience, so using cognitive-behavioural or task-centred theory with it is likely to be impractical because these focus on the details of behaviour change, and psychodynamic theory, which focuses on managing internal psychological drives, is likely to be theoretically inconsistent with intersectionality. Point five, intersectionality theory tells you not to make assumptions about how different minority identities intersect. For example, our older, disabled, black woman might be helped in getting her family to accept her need for help by their shared strong black identity and experience of discrimination. Another woman with the same set of identities intersecting might find that the religious faith connected with her black identity inhibits relationships with her family because they reject her sexuality, but helps her connect with a secularist group of disabled people.

After working through 'the approach' with intersectionality, you might decide to take a fuller interest if you have your own concerns about identity, or you work a lot with people with minority identities. Otherwise, it might apply to some situations that you deal with, but you may prefer to put it back on the shelf and focus on something else. You could get it down again if your job or your personal position changes.

Do you need to know how the theory developed?

After you've thought about the depth you need to explore, the second question to ask as a way of guiding you about the amount of detail you need to absorb is: do you need to know the process of development of a theory? Social work theories do not spring fully formed from the theorist's mind. They are usually created as a reaction to or improvement on other ideas. Alternatively, they may be an interpretation for social work of a practice theory or of a set of ideas that the author of the theory has found in psychology or sociology. They may then be tested out in their original setting, presented, argued over, improved, interpreted for use in other settings, renewed by other ideas and so on. This is the process going on in social work journals and competing books that some readers find frustrating and confusing. Eventually, though, there is a fairly well-established formulation of the theory available for practitioners to use.

Most practitioners have no need to bother with this process; they just need to pick up the presently agreed formulation, if possible suitably adapted for their user group or agency, and use it. If this produces problems for them in practice, they may need to adapt it further, or return to question one and go in deep to find alternative formulations that suit them better. On the other hand, if you are using theories where the debate is white hot at the moment, you may want to go on courses and join specialist groups to get involved in the debate.

This is academic involvement as part of your professional life that again helps to get ideas clear and firmly lodged in your mind. You are probably going to need to do this throughout your career as knowledge develops and you change your job. For example, when I began work in palliative care social work nearly a decade ago, I only had a very general and out-of-date idea of the theory and research on working with dying and bereaved people, picked up over the years. I had to read the latest editions of the books I had read some years previously and some of the latest texts to lead me back into the ideas that are currently used in palliative care social work practice. For example, I had learned about stage theories of bereavement, which say that people go through a series of stages in their reaction when someone important to them dies. But I found that these had been amended, because research which showed that people generally went through similar emotions in the same order had been superseded. Later studies showed that while the emotions were often present, they sometimes came all together or in a different order (Reith and Payne, 2009). Also, some research had shown that 'dual process' theories were an important consideration (Stroebe and Schut, 1999); these say that people switch between different reactions, sometimes focusing on their loss and sometimes looking to the future and getting on with reorganising their lives.

Complex language and jargon

The complexity of the detail in theory, once you get beyond the basic idea, is not the only complexity that many people find troublesome when they are faced with dealing with theory. One of the bugbears is that many theories, or the debates about them, are put into high-flown language and detailed linguistic distinctions that make you lose the will to live. All of this is hard to follow and creates a jargon that you either use as a mantra without really understanding it or you have to abandon because using the terms of the theory would make no sense to the normal people that you work with. Another problem is that the jargon of many theories seems to over-complicate everyday language that we all understand. Some of it seems like deficit language, which insults the dignity of service users too; it applies some insulting jargon word to their behaviour and problems. It may seem better to stick to simple everyday ideas, which you can explain properly to service users.

'The approach' helps here too. If we can understand the basic idea behind the distinctions being made in theoretical debate, we can often work out whether we need it in this case, how to use it and how not to use it.

As an example, we can look at the term 'resistance', a word in ordinary use but also important in psychodynamic and in critical theory. In everyday talk, resistance means refusing to do something that someone else wants you to do; it implies a rebellious attitude. Suppose you are asked to assess Mrs Jones, an older woman, for community care services. Her family and healthcare professionals think she is unsafe living alone and really needs to be in a care home. This seems like an entirely reasonable suggestion, but she keeps coming up with objections. Sooner or later, someone is going to label her 'resistant', a potentially demeaning psychological interpretation of her refusal.

But, if we understand the theories fully, is this piece of jargon actually being used correctly? We can delve into the detail to see. Critical and radical theory suggests that social structures in society rooted in the economic system persistently enable people who already have power in society to gain further social advantages and prevent people from having access to fair resources to live their life in the way that they want. Mrs Jones fits this picture: really good community care services that she could have at home would be fine for her, but budget constraints designed to favour generously low taxation for well-off people favour the cheaper option of a care home. So should we permit or encourage her resistance? The argument for doing so says that if lots of similar older people also protested, the state would be forced to change socially unjust policies in favour of greater equality of power. Many people complain, however, that critical or radical theory seems to lead to over-simplified proposals like this. Encouraging her protests might leave Mrs Jones without services, labelled as a difficult old woman whose obstructiveness absolves social workers and government from doing anything about her needs. It does not protect and help Mrs Jones as an individual, but places her at risk, in favour of some distant political or social change that might never arrive.

But this is an over-simplified understanding of critical theory. It proposes that social justice will only be achieved if people who are concerned about social inequalities come together to resist trends in society that lead to social oppression. This is a long-term process, in which individual actions have a place, but have to be carried out as part of the shared movement towards change, with an awareness of the political and social implications of their resistance. Mrs Jones is not in this position; she is not part of a wider movement, from which she would gain support in her actions, and she is responding to her personal preferences for care arrangements rather than a general social objective. It would be different if she were part of a local community organisation that campaigns for older people to have greater choice in care and that supports its members through cooperation and community support in remaining in their own homes. A social worker could help to stimulate and enable such an organisation, but also only as part of collective local action; these things are never achieved alone. In the absence of this, critical theory tells us that the state (through social workers) must respect and listen to its citizens, and try to mediate between everyone to meet needs in a mutually supportive way. The social worker would therefore look for ways of engaging family members and professional colleagues to arrive at a way of going forward that would be acceptable to Mrs Jones. Encouraging individual resistance in the absence of collective support and engagement is not correct use of the critical interpretation of resistance.

Psychodynamic theory is, perhaps, the source of the implied diminishment of Mrs Jones's actions by saying that they are part of some psychological failing. But again, is this an appropriate theoretical usage or a mistaken application of poorly understood jargon? Delving into the theory, resistance in psychodynamic theory is a defence mechanism. Defence mechanisms are irrational reactions that protect important unconscious drives. If this were psychodynamic resistance, we would see irrational behaviour from Mrs Jones, which would she would be unaware of. It would be pushing her to behave like this because of some deep-seated reaction to a problem in her past, perhaps over-controlling or abusive parents. Mrs Jones's resistance is not like this: professionals or family members might not like the fact that she does not want to do what they want, but it is perfectly clear that she is actively resisting, so it is not unconscious behaviour, such as somehow never getting around to something she knows is important. Also, if we are open-minded about her views, she does have a rational case for her arguments. So in psychodynamic terms, she is not being resistant, and it is wrong to label her so.

Mrs Jones's behaviour is an example of why it is useful to understand the complexities of the professional language and ideas we are using. If we are not careful, we oversimplify the ideas and fail to respect service users by giving them inappropriate theoretical labels.

Is theory ideological?

An ideology is a body of beliefs associated with a particular political or social philosophy. The main reason why some people think that social work theories should not be ideological is the view that, since they are supposed to be practically useful, they should be backed by evidence of their effective outcomes rather than by arguments about philosophy or belief. Hidden behind that is an equally ideological view about what is acceptable support for a theory: should there be empirical evidence that it is successful in achieving its outcomes, or should it merely be interesting and well-argued?

There are two main points to make about these criticisms of ideology. The first is that there is value in a guide to action, such as a social work theory, being intellectually coherent, well-argued and consistent. Making sure that the ideas involved in a theory are explicit and well-developed contributes to its validity and helps to convince practitioners and the people to whom they are accountable that it is appropriate to use a particular theory. In turn, this helps practitioners justify themselves.

The second point is that all ideas are ideological to some degree; complaints about ideology often conceal an opposing ideology. For example, behavioural criticisms that psychodynamic theory is empirically untestable rely on an ideology that a particular model of how knowledge is developed is the only way of understanding human life.

Using theory in practice

In this section, I move on to ways in which we can use theoretical ideas in practice.

Agency procedures and guidelines

The theory that social work texts describe seems to be very distant from your agency's procedures: which is more important? The answer to this question is: both are important, but they try to achieve different things. Procedures tell you how the agency organises its social work, not how to do it. For example, its forms and instructions tell you what should be covered in an assessment, and perhaps whom to contact, but not how you should interact with people to find it out. You are expected to know that, and you know it from the skills and theory you were taught in social work courses.

For example, my employer, St Christopher's Hospice, has a policy, procedures and guidelines on suicide. The policy says, in brief, that we aim to prevent our service users from committing suicide and explains why. This is not obvious; committing suicide is legal, so the organisation needs to justify its policy. The main justification is that the hospice helps people dying with advanced illnesses, a high proportion of whom suffer serious anxiety or depression. But they can live a good quality of life with the best treatment, so we should prevent them from committing suicide in order that they can get the treatment to live happily again for the remainder of their life, even if it is short. The procedures then set out what to do if someone tells you they are thinking of committing suicide; there are people you have to notify, so that they can take action. Finally, the guidelines, written by a working party of psychiatrists and social workers, suggest some questions you might ask to assess the risk, based on the research on the best questions to ask. According to the risk judgement that you make, the guidelines offer various alternative actions to help someone who is thinking of suicide. Neither formal nor informal theory can tell you the agency's policy or the procedure to follow when someone is thinking about suicide; this has to be local to the agency, with its particular responsibilities. The guidelines are closest to theory, but even they do not tell you how to engage with someone who is thinking about suicide or how to help them; they give you useful information from a specialist that you apply according to your skills and the theory of interaction with service users that you are using.

Adapting theories

Can you adapt theories to suit your purposes, or should they be used as they were written? There are two objections to the adaptation option. The first is that it leads to inconsistency and error, like the confusions about resistance that we looked at earlier. Unless you understand the theory in its complexity, you may miss important factors, or only partially use the ideas. The second objection is that adaptation risks misusing a theory. You aim to work in a strengths-based way but because of inevitable compromises with colleagues' different views of appropriate practice, lack of resources in the agency and conflicts with agency procedures or legal demands, you miss some of the basic requirements. Rapp and Goscha's (2004) analysis of the research on strengths-based case management in mental health, for example, suggests that an effective model of practice is often compromised by not providing enough staff and leadership to implement it properly in the way that research shows is effective.

Despite these objections, not all theory is of a kind that aims to give you a detailed set of prescriptions for practice; this is one of the reasons that some theories seem like ideologies rather than practical guidance for action. Feminist theory, for example, is most often presented as a set of ideas. You take them on and follow through their implications for how you see the issues that service users face. The important thing is to engage with and interpret the ideas to work in the situations you are faced with; the framework of ideas gives you confidence and a direction for your practice.

Critical reflection

The critique of adaptation suggests, therefore, that we need to examine our use of theory to make sure we are doing it properly, and apply the 'idealogical' theories. The idea of critical reflection helps you with this. Using it, however, also carries theoretical and ideological implications (Fook and Gardner, 2007). This is because adapting theory by using critical reflection makes clear that, in realistic daily practice, set theoretical prescriptions have to be altered by circumstances.

The main processes of critical reflection are set out in Box 2.

Box 2 Main elements of reflection

- Experience – you identify an important experience that occurred in your work.
- Reflection – you follow an organised process for thinking about the experience.
- Action – as a result of your reflection, you devise appropriate actions to move forward in the work that you are doing.

(*Source*: Jasper, 2003; Payne, 2005, Ch 2; 2009)

The whole point about this is that you focus down on specific events, rather than looking at what you are doing in the round. You might use theory in any of these three processes. For example, you might use theory to decide which experience from a number of possibilities is the most important, and to work out why it is so important. You could also use theory to guide your reflection by asking yourself what different theories might tell you about the experience. In the action phase, you might use a theory to tell you what action follows from the assessments of the experience that you have made.

Reflection can lead to the development of theory. Collecting examples of reflections about various experiences might help you to discover aspects of a theory that are not working for the service users you are working with. You could then publish an adaptation to a theory. More likely, in everyday practice, you share with colleagues and find similar experiences; as a result you can adapt agency procedures that use the theory.

What is the critical element of reflection about? There is quite a lot of debate about this issue (White *et al.*, 2006). First, critical thinking is different from critical reflection. With critical thinking, you are trying to avoid taking ideas about the situation for granted. For example, a fourteen year-old girl with a record of delinquency is living with foster carers, but not obeying their rules about the time to come home every night. You could put this down to rebellious behaviour typical of teenagers or suspect that there is a risk of drug abuse or further delinquency.

But these informal theories are common assumptions about the risks to young women, rather than a thought-through analysis of the detail of her attitudes and problems, so you would discard them as starting assumptions. Critical reflection means a process of reviewing evidence and understanding of these situations in general and the factors involved with this young woman in particular, and setting out a balance sheet of arguments for and against various explanations and decisions, before working out what action you would take. In particular, looking at concrete evidence of what happened in particular examples of behaviour might give you a firmer basis for thinking through what is happening.

The second point about critical reflection is that it uses theoretical positions that avoid taking for granted the social order, that is, the existing assumptions in society about who has the power to define, both formally and informally, the social rules that we all follow. So when, as social workers, we are asked to enforce a social convention, we ask whose interests that social convention benefits. For example, are we more likely to take children away for their own protection from their parents at birth with families from minority ethnic groups or lower socio-economic groups than we are from the ethnic majority or higher socio-economic groups? If so, does that contribute to maintaining socially-approved views about child-rearing rather than helping families to implement the reasonable alternatives that come from their culture or social environment? By asking these sorts of questions, we might still decide to secure the child's protection, but we will also have checked that our reasons for doing so are well worked out and based on evidence of what is best for the benefit of the child, rather than just falling into line with a conventional view about what is good for children.

Conclusion

The main argument that I have been putting forward in this chapter is that apparent irrelevance, disconnection from reality and difficulty in applying practice theories can be managed by taking a practical approach to them. We cannot know everything, we must choose and we must adapt. So the question is not: 'should we reject practice theories?' but: 'how do we use them in a practical way?'

I presented an approach to grasping the basic idea of a practice theory and whether it might be useful to you in your agency. Then, I emphasised that you should not go through this selection process as an individual, but work with colleagues and with service users to check out ideas that seem relevant. By this means, individual social workers can gain the contribution of their teams and supervisors to how they use theory, remain accountable for their practice and gain the informed consent of the users they work with.

Although in many cases a grasp of the basic idea of a theory is enough to decide whether it is appropriate for use in a particular job or with a particular service user, I also argued that once you are using a practice theory, it is essential to have a detailed understanding of it and how it is supposed to work. Much of the detailed infrastructure of theoretical development in the social work literature need not detain us in everyday practice, but to avoid making mistakes that disadvantage or disrespect the people we work with, we do need a good understanding of the requirements of our theoretical approach and of its concepts.

Finally, I have suggested that theory needs adaptation to make it practical, and we need to connect it with agency procedures and reflect critically on what we are doing to make sure that theory informs but does not overpower our daily practice.

References

Fook, J. and Gardner, F. (2007) *Practising Critical Reflection: A Resource Handbook*. Maidenhead: Open University Press.

Jasper, M. (2003) *Beginning Reflective Practice*. Cheltenham: Nelson Thornes.

Marsh, P. and Doel, M. (2005) *The Task-Centred Book*. London: Rouledge.

Murphy, Y., Hunt, V., Zajicek, A.M., Norris, A.N. and Hamilton, L. (2009) *Incorporating Intersectionality in Social Work Practice, Research, Policy, and Education*. Washington, DC: National Association of Social Workers.

Payne, M. (2005) *Modern Social Work Theory*. (3rd edn) Basingstoke: Palgrave Macmillan.

Payne, M. (2009) Critical Reflection and Social Work Theories. In Adams, R., Dominelli, L. and Payne, M. (Eds.) *Critical Practice in Social Work*. (2nd edn) Basingstoke: Palgrave Macmillan: 91–104.

Payne, M. (2010) *Humanistic Social Work: Core Principles in Practice*. Basingstoke: Palgrave Macmillan.

Payne, M. and Askeland, G.A. (2008) *Globalization and International Social Work: Postmodern Change and Challenge*. Aldershot: Ashgate.

Rapp, C.A. and Goscha, R.J. (2004) The Principles of Effective Case Management of Mental Health Services. *Psychiatric Rehabilitation Journal*, 27(4): 319–333.

Reith, M. and Payne, M. (2009) *Social Work in End-of-life and Palliative Care*. Bristol: Policy Press.

Secker, J. (1993) *From Theory to Practice in Social Work: The Development of Social Work Students' Practice*. Aldershot: Avebury.

Stroebe, M. and Schut, H. (1999) The Dual Process Model of Coping With Bereavement: Rationale and Description. *Death Studies* 23(3): 197–224.

White, S., Fook, J. and Gardner, F. (Eds.) (2006) *Critical Reflection in Health and Social Care*. Maidenhead: Open University Press.

Chapter 4

Anti-Racism and Social Work

Deirdre Ford

My mum is Polynesian and my dad is white, the kids at school call my mother names like, skivvies, slave bride, and spoon face. Sometimes I wish that my mum wouldn't come into school.

(Sandhu, 2004)

Research undertaken by the Institute of Race Relations reveals 'new and emerging geographies of racism' (Burnett, 2011) accompanying globalisation and significant demographic changes in rural communities and towns. 'New migrants' including migrant workers from Eastern Europe have sought employment in the UK following the expansion of the European Union (Phillips, 2010). People seeking asylum have been 'dispersed' by the Home Office to areas often with high levels of unemployment, poverty and deprivation, posing further challenges for them if they are granted leave to remain. Numbers of Gypsies and Travellers have also increased in some of these areas in recent years where they have encountered discrimination by local councils. Terrorist activity and government steps to promote homeland security (the 'war on terror') have fuelled Islamophobia (Bhatti-Sinclair, 2011). This is the context for a chapter which revisits social work's commitment to anti-racist practice. It stems from the knowledge that racism is a daily reality in the lives of many people with whom social workers are engaged, as well as a shared belief that 'now is not the time to abandon commitments to fighting racism' (Singh, 2011).

Human rights and social justice serve as the motivation and justification for social work action. In solidarity with those who are disadvantaged, the profession strives to alleviate poverty and to liberate vulnerable and oppressed people in order to promote social inclusion.

(International Federation of Social Workers (IFSW), 2000)

The IFSW declaration affirms the pursuit of social justice as a core value for the profession. Social justice features in the draft *Standards of Proficiency* proposed by the profession's new regulator in the UK, '6.1: Be able to work with others to promote social justice' (HPC, 2011). Dominelli maintains that 'anti-oppressive practice, with its value commitment to the realisation of social justice, is one variant of a range of emancipatory approaches to social work'. (Dominelli, 2002: 4). As a corollary to social justice, anti-oppressive perspectives have been influential in social work theory and practice during the last two decades, informed in turn by Marxist, feminist and radical ideologies. Anti-oppressive practice seeks to challenge dominant power relations by confronting social divisions and the processes of categorisation that sustain structural inequality. It exposes the intersectionality (see Chapter 3) that results in 'the layering of oppressions within individual experience' (Williams, 1999: 220). Challenging discrimination and oppression will involve political activity and distributive justice:

> *It could be argued that the concept of discrimination derives from political analyses of fair/unfair distribution of goods and services within a given system, while the notion of oppression derives from political analyses of structural patterns of mistreatment.*
>
> (Harlow and Hearn, 1996: 102)

Terminology can cause some confusion as the phrase 'anti-oppressive practice' is often regarded as synonymous with 'anti-discriminatory practice'. In this vein Dalrymple and Burke (2006) review definitions of anti-oppressive practice and take their lead from Phillipson (1992) by regarding anti-discrimination as the legal, specific means to challenge discrimination, one that is complementary to anti-oppressive practice but in a limited way. Thompson, meanwhile, makes the link between discrimination as 'the process (or set of processes) that leads to oppression. To challenge oppression it is therefore necessary to challenge discrimination' (Thompson, 2001: x).

Critics may question whether anti-oppressive practice can ever overcome power differentials inherent in the professional relationship with service users (Sakamoto and Pitner, 2005). It is also charged with promoting binary, oppositional discourses by virtue of the prefix 'anti' which is universally disliked. Other criticisms of anti-oppressive practice (AOP) are summarised by McLaughlin:

> . . . *firstly that AOP was ideologically driven and was itself oppressive, secondly that it focused on 'trivial' issues of language and terminology and thirdly that it was a top down divisive approach that was detrimental to the black struggle against racism.*
>
> (McLaughlin, 2005: 289)

Nevertheless anti-oppressive practice has done much to broaden understanding of oppression to encompass its diverse forms including racism. Anti-racism is an approach that seeks to identify and understand the processes through which racism operates, whether overtly or in more insidious ways (Phillipson, 1992). It examines how these processes are sanctioned by, and within, institutions. Thus it locates social work as a form of state activity, and applies the overall analysis to local practice (Dominelli, 1997). Anti-racist practice has encouraged resistance against other forms of oppression and has mobilised individuals and groups in pursuit of its political aims (Bhatti-Sinclair, 2011). It requires practitioners to understand that race is a social construct or ideology in which myths abound, the products of biological essentialism over centuries serving structural inequality.

Power

Central to the anti-oppressive framework and to anti-racist theory is the concept of power. Studies of empowerment informed by the writings of Freire (1972), Lukes (1974) and, latterly, Foucault (1977) have challenged the radical view that power is wholly negative, reconceptualising the complexity of power relations as shifting and contextualised (Fook, 2002). Issues of power in social work are largely problematised, nevertheless, and merit further attention and vigilance in the anti-racist project (Williams, 1999). Anti-racist practice is necessarily concerned with inequalities that stem from the exertion of power, whether structurally or at the level of the individual. Gould offers an analysis, which sanctions the importance of theorising anti-racism in this way in order to develop practice (Gould, 1992; quoted in Baldwin, 1996). Gould identifies four dimensions or modalities of power:

> The 'behaviouralist modality' engages us in the identification of prevailing interests in decision-making processes. The 'non-decision-making modality' notes the way in which powerful groups can deny access to resources through negating the interests of disadvantaged groups. The modality which rests on the theory of hegemony describes the way in which conflict can be pre-empted through compromise on minor issues, and the creation of belief systems which are internalised by disadvantaged people. In the poststructuralist modality, power is described as being exercised through 'forms of knowledge which define and proscribe human identity'.
>
> (Baldwin, 1996: 25)

New ideologies emerge from specific social structures and power relations (Husband, 1991). By employing 'dominant discourses, scientific and professional, racist ideology constantly seeks to obscure, and naturalise relations of dominance' (Singh, 2000: 8). The Macpherson Report regarding the murder of Stephen Lawrence endorsed the declaration of social work's statutory authority in 1991 that racism is endemic in the institutions of British society (Macpherson, 1999; CCETSW, 1991). McLaughlin (2005) cautions that since then, however, the state has itself mainstreamed and 'institutionalised' what were once radical positions by seeking to own charges of structural racism with promises of inquiry and change. Anti-oppressive practice in this arena is seen as no longer in contention with the state but rather is in danger of domestication, reverting to a focus on individual behaviour such as the use of language, rather than challenging the structures of society that perpetuate racism. Phillips (2009) meanwhile argues against the term 'institutional racism', preferring the phrase 'systemic bias' with attention to class to describe the more subtle processes of discrimination and inequality through which is power is exerted.

Identity and difference

Having survived charges of 'political correctness' from the New Right (a term employed to divert attention from any form of unpalatable truth), anti-racist social work continues to face challenges from within the profession itself. Gilroy's earlier criticisms of municipal anti-racism were rightly influential and, as Humphries observes, beset social work education (Gilroy, 1990; Humphries, 1997). Not least of these were the 'crucial ambiguities' that contribute to the confusion surrounding the meaning of racism, as well as the failure to make links between racism and other social divisions (Humphries, 1997). Social work in counties such as Devon and Cornwall described as some of the most homogenous in England (Burnett, 2011) where service users are not perceived to be characterised by ethnic diversity, has struggled to maintain its emphasis on anti-racist practice (Baldwin, 1996; Phillips, 2010). Despite the changing demographies noted earlier, the response that 'there is no problem here' documented in the Jay Report of 1992 persists as a feature of the South West peninsula (Jay, 1992; Dhalech, 1999; Sandhu, 2004). As many writers have commented, the absence of clear definitions of racism rooted in the lived experiences of black and minority ethnic people, not only served the agenda of the Right. It reduced anti-racist practice to the level of concern for language and representation instead, culminating in the notorious Race Awareness Training (Sivanandan, 1991; McLaughlin, 2005). As a consequence of these factors practitioners uninformed by black perspectives have avoided discourses of race and thus marginalised the discrimination experienced by black and minority ethnic people at both personal and institutional levels. Misconceptions surrounding cultural relativity and fears of encountering accusations of racism have also undermined a readiness to intervene. Particular avoidance strategies are fully recognised by Dominelli (1997), and result in the practices described in the Smith Report on the Probation Service (Smith, 2000). In contrast, social workers whose knowledge and understanding are shaped by narratives of racism might be better disposed to embrace formulations of identity and difference. Identity politics, premised on the idea of identity that is constructed dialogically and through intersubjectivity, concerns the politics of recognition. Fraser maintains, however, that identity politics has been responsible for the misrepresentation of culture rather than redistributive justice, leading to an oversimplification and reification of group identity and interaction across social divisions (Fraser, 2000). It can be regarded as a form of 'strategic essentialism' invoking the identities which are themselves the consequences of oppression (Phillips, 2010) and diverting attention away from the material causes of oppression.

In mitigation, ideas of diversity, identity and difference accord not only with the complexities enshrined in personal constructs of self (Somers, 1994; Lloyd, 1998). They are also congruent with traditional aspects of the profession's value base that commend respect for persons and individual self-worth (Biestek, 1961; BASW, 2002). 'Black' as an organising term is troublesome in this context; nevertheless its history and significance are well documented. Black as a political category has represented not only shared experiences of racism and marginalisation but also resistance amongst groups characterised by ethnic diversity and difference (Hall, 1992). Sivanandan describes how black as a 'political colour' was deconstituted, however, by multiculturalism (Sivanandan, 1991). Moreover, people identifying with 'ethnically distinctive and exclusive professional and political groups' contested black identity as a broadly inclusive term, acceptable to Asian and Chinese populations (Husband, 1992: 94; Bhatti-Sinclair, 2011). Neither in binary opposition to white oppression does it serve the experiences of white populations such as Roma people from Eastern Europe, for example, facing discrimination in the UK. Such political constructs employed to strengthen and mobilise oppressed groups are further undermined by the flagrant individualism of market principles perpetuated by the Coalition government in the UK which devalues collectivist approaches and 'interpersonal connection' (Furlong and Wight, 2011).

Cultural sensitivity is an important feature of contemporary anti-racist practice (Laird, 2008), rejecting any form of categorisation that implies homogeneity and fixed identity. It precedes the idea of 'cultural competence', which has gained considerable momentum in recent years among health professions and latterly social work. Cultural competence is defined as 'a set of congruent behaviors, attitudes, and policies that come together in a system, agency or among professionals that enable effective interactions in a cross-cultural framework' (Cross *et al.*, 1989, cited in Harrison and Turner, 2011: 3).

Originally conceived to improve practice with black and minority ethnic people, cultural competence has been extended in social work to include groups identified by other social inequalities at risk of exclusion. Research by Harrison and Turner reveals how in practice it symbolises 'a respect for difference and inclusion of marginalised groups and individuals' (2011: 14). Models of cultural competence encourage practitioners to develop awareness of their own cultures, values, beliefs and worldview, respect for cultural differences, knowledge of different cultures, and cross-cultural skills (NASW, 2001; Laird, 2008). Similar to other social constructionist analyses, cultural competence has attracted criticism that it does not take account of the power relations central to anti-racist practice and the understanding of how inequality is structured by such means (Williams, 1999). With a multi-cultural lens racism is seen to be 'levelled' alongside other forms of oppression and racial inequalities are denied or ignored. Cultural competence has been accused of reinforcing stereotypes and promoting 'othering', presupposing that practitioners themselves represent the dominant culture (Phillips, 2010). It is dismissed as a skill that can be learnt and the language of 'competence' is contested (Furlong and Wight, 2011; Harrison and

Turner, 2011). Cultural competence has also been challenged for its emphasis on the development of cultural knowledge in order to work with diversity rather than adopting an approach of 'not-knowing' and encouraging critical awareness (Kapuscinski, 2008; Ben-Ari and Strier, 2010: Furlong and Wight, 2011). Proponents of cultural competence, however, maintain that far from simply perceiving cultural differences as 'exotic' and essentialist, the practitioner begins with a critical dialogue about their own worldview as a basis for working cross-culturally. Reflection on their own cultural location and difference relative to others is regarded as essential in order to recognise their own racist views and assumptions (Laird, 2008). Phillips (2010) meanwhile argues for understandings of race and racism that are temporal and contextual. The practitioner is required to 'de-naturalise and de-centre' their own cultural location in order to develop 'reflective self-scrutiny' (Furlong and Wight, 2011).

New racism

The significance of culture within anti-racism is not unproblematic. Race as an artificial construct aligned with biological determinism was discredited by its association with fascism, specifically Nazi theories of eugenics. Thereafter the discourse of race appropriated culture as an immutable set of characteristics that neatly upholds the nation state, through notions of difference. This process was termed 'new racism' (Barker, 1981). Husband records the ease with which the New Right moved to perceptions of 'alien', inferiority and ethnocentrism. In defining nation through culture the New Right inevitably define 'different' as 'alien' (Husband, 1991: 64). Culture could then serve as a smokescreen to obscure race and racist ideology that constructs difference on the basis of ethnicity as racially inferior (Patel, 1995; Thompson, 2001). As noted, so-called ethnically sensitive practice, shaped by stereotypical assumptions, that did not extend beyond a preoccupation with differing religious practices and diet, served to de-contextualise the position of black people as service users. The intersection of race, gender and class were ignored together with the material and emotional impact of racism. As the backlash against anti-racism engendered by the New Right was designed to maintain inequalities of power by trivialising, and detracting from anti-racist activity, so new racism supported mutually exclusive concepts of nationality and citizenship epitomised by the Apartheid system of South Africa (Gilroy, 2000). In this scheme the defence of culture and tradition is perceived as natural, as 'common sense'.

Gilroy is confident, however, that 'the era of New Racism is emphatically over' (Gilroy, 2000: 34) and he continues to argue that the politics of race is increasingly irrelevant for many. His concern is to denature and deconstruct race, to find a different political language and a new way of conceptualising the relationships between groups of people which inevitably would dispense with terms like 'anti-racist practice'. In a region like the South West, however, it is too soon to relinquish anti-racism:

> Racism does exist within Cornwall . . . The effects of racism on young people are, at present, largely ignored by many organisations and at times the blame is put back onto BME (black and minority ethnic) groups by agencies stating that racism is not an issue in Cornwall as 'there are too few BME people'. This type of attitude blames members of BME communities for racism.
>
> (Sandhu, 2004: 3)

With regard to social work, the paradox that finds black people under-represented as service users in receipt of preventive social care but over-represented in systems of social control is well documented (Skellington, 1996; Thompson, 2001). Owusu-Bempah provides a powerful illustration of how social work unwittingly colludes with the processes of racism in pathologising individuals to the neglect of inequalities that are induced by the system. Efforts to bolster the self-concept of black children in the care system epitomise the failure to address the more significant impact of racism on the life chances of black people (Owusu-Bempah, 1997).

> If racist consequences accrue to institutional laws, customs or practices the institution is racist whether or not the individuals maintaining those practices have racist intentions.
>
> (Jones (1993) cited in Patel, 1995: 29)

Maintaining the commitment to anti-racism

Anti-oppressive practice developed in tandem with new social movements organised around the rights of women, black, and disabled people. Dominelli describes how initially it represented a critique of practice as a function of middle-class values (Dominelli, 1994; Lloyd, 1998). Despite its radical aims it is hardly surprising, however, that anti-oppressive social work has failed to address the inequalities within welfare provision outlined above. Located within organisational and bureaucratic structures that espouse white liberal values, social work's potential for political action is constrained and subject to competing claims (Williams, 1999). Professionalism is identified by some writers as a barrier to developing broader structural approaches 'or non-individualistic ways of working' (Lloyd, 1998: 715). 'Being political is synonymous with being unprofessional' in public sector services where professional detachment and its function in maintaining power relations are accepted uncritically (Husband, 1991: 66). The challenge to the profession in this instance is to develop a concept of professionalism that sanctions and affirms the political dimension to practice in pursuit of social justice (Ferguson and Lavalette, 2006).

Social workers employ casework methods which do not invite challenges to the social structures that discriminate against service users. The imposition of care management on social work practice has magnified these difficulties. Consumerist values, while conducive to assessments and services that are ethnically sensitive, discourage a more radical approach to social care characterised by notions of social justice and inclusion. The equivocal nature of a liberal welfare state that seeks to promote the freeplay of the market economy, while retaining a centralised system of power and control, is one which finds expression in the delivery of community care. Commenting on social work in Vietnam former BASW director Clive Walsh writes:

> It is about enabling and transacting with individuals at a community level: something we have lost. Our community care is about economics. Theirs is about care. Ours says we can no longer afford dependency. Theirs simply says people must be helped.
> (Walsh, 1996)

In contrast, however, Lloyd examines the opportunities afforded by new configurations of power and the changing contexts for practice (Lloyd, 1998). Her endorsement of community development as a model for anti-oppressive practice is a reminder that black communities and groups have continued to gain political influence (Husband, 1991; Dhalech, 1999; Bhavnani, 2005). Lloyd argues that the contract culture can be harnessed to create 'new alliances between professionals and the communities in which they work' (*ibid*: 723). Above all, this analysis aims to confront successive governments from a position of strength, whereby anti-oppressive practice is defined and theorised in the context of the changes that result from globalisation. With reference to social divisions Williams takes up the point:

> What is needed, therefore, is a more precise analysis of theories of interconnection or intersection; a more rigorous look at how anti-racist approaches and the more illusive 'black perspectives' connect within the framework of anti-oppressive practice.
> (Williams, 1999: 226)

This need for a more holistic approach based on understanding the complexity of racism in association with other social inequalities is supported by research undertaken by Bhavnani et al. (2005).

While the issue of 'black perspectives' is not uncontentious (Sivanandan, 1991; Humphries, 1997), the development of a black perspectives agenda has been crucial to the development of anti-racism (Singh, 2000: 14). Black perspectives represent the means to progress debates surrounding identity, commonalities of experience and the structural factors that perpetuate oppression. In affirming the histories of black people and challenging dominant white modes of thought, they underpin emancipatory practice. The presence of people seeking asylum and refugees in a region like the South West exposes the prevalence of racism in all sectors of society. Yet the 'invisibility' of racism, allied with underreporting of racial incidents and inadequate systems of ethnic monitoring, perpetuate the 'No problem here . . .' myth, as does the race-blind approach adopted by many agencies (Henderson and Kaur, 1999; Burnett, 2011). Thus while practitioners fail to recognise that racism is 'a structural phenomenon with a long history and ideology, developed and applied at a number of levels', the profession is not ready to relinquish anti-racist social work in favour of more positive-sounding constructs (Patel, 1995: 18). In this climate, surrendering 'anti-racism' as a practice principle will permit the survival of 'race' as a construct that sanctions oppression. Its demise will fuel the lingering denials that racism does exist and is endemic in social institutions.

References

Baldwin, M. (1996) White Anti-racism: Is it Really 'No Go' in Rural Areas? *Social Work Education*, 15(1) 18–33.

Barker, M. (1981) *The New Racism*. London: Junction Books.

BASW (British Association of Social Workers) (2002) *Code of Ethics for Social Work.* Birmingham: BASW.

Ben-Ari, A. and Strier, R. (2010) Rethinking Cultural Competence: What Can We Learn from Levinas? *British Journal of Social Work*, 40(7): 2155–2167.

Bhatti-Sinclair, K. (2011) *Anti-Racist Practice in Social Work.* Basingstoke: Macmillan.

Bhavnani, R., Mirza, H.S. and Meetoo, V. (2005) *Tackling the Roots of Racism: Lessons for Success.* Bristol: The Policy Press.

Biestek, F. (1961) *The Casework Relationship*. London: George Allen and Unwin.

Burnett, J. (2011) *The New Geographies of Racism.* London: Institute of Race Relations.

CCETSW (1991) *One Small Step Towards Racial Justice.* London: CCETSW.

CCETSW (1996) *Assuring Quality: in the Diploma in Social Work – 1. Rules and Requirements for the DipSW* (second revision). London: CCETSW.

Dalrymple, J. and Burke, B. (2006) *Anti-Oppressive Practice: Social Care and the Law.* (2nd edn.) Buckingham: Open University Press.

Dhalech, M. (1999) *Challenging Racism in the Rural Idyll.* Final Report of the Rural Race Equality Project. National Association of Citizens' Advice Bureaux.

Dominelli, L. (1994) *Anti-Racist Social Work Education*. Paper presented at 27th Congress, International Association of Schools of Social Work, Amsterdam, July.

Dominelli, L. (1997) *Anti-Racist Social work.* (2nd edn.) Basingstoke: Macmillan.

Dominelli, L. (2002) Anti-oppressive Practice in Context. In Adams, R., Dominelli, L. and Payne, M. (Eds.) *Social Work: Themes, Issues and Critical Debates* (2nd edn.). Basingstoke: Palgrave Macmillan.

Ferguson, I. and Lavalette, M. (2006) Globalisation and Global Justice: Towards a Social Work of Resistance. *International Social Work*, 49(3) 309–318.

Fook, J. (2002) *Social Work Critical Theory and Practice.* London: Sage.

Foucault, M. (1977) *Discipline and Punish: The Birth of the Prison*. London: Penguin Books.

Fraser, N. (2000) Rethinking Recognition. *New Left Review*, 3: 107–120.

Freire, P. (1972) *Pedagogy of the Oppressed*. Harmondsworth: Penguin.

Furlong, M. and Wight, J. (2011) Promoting 'Critical Awareness' and Critiquing 'Cultural Competence': Towards Disrupting Received Professional Knowledges. *Australian Social Work*, 64(1) 38–54.

Gilroy, P. (1990) The End of Anti-racism. In Ball, W. and Solomos, J. (Eds.) *Race and Local Politics*. London: Macmillan.

Gilroy, P. (2000) *Between Camps*. Harmondsworth: Allen Lane.

Hall, S. (1992) New Ethnicities. In Donald, J. and Rattansi, A. (Eds.) *'Race', Culture and Difference*. London: Sage.

Harlow, E. and Hearn, J. (1996) From Rhetoric to Reality: Historical, Theoretical and Practical Complexities in Educating for Anti-discriminatory and Anti-oppressive Social Work. In Ford, P. and Hayes, P. (Eds.) *Educating for Social Work: Arguments for Optimism*. Aldershot: Avebury.

Harrison, G. and Turner, R. (2011) Being a 'Culturally Competent' Social Worker: Making Sense of a Murky Concept in Practice. *British Journal of Social Work*, 41(2): 333–350.

Health Professions Council (HPC) (2011) *Consultation on Draft Standards of Proficiency For Social Workers in England.* http://www.hpcuk.org/aboutus/consultations/index.asp?id=124 Accessed Oct 2011

Henderson, P. and Kaur, R. (Eds.) (1999) *Introduction: Rural Racism in the UK. Examples of Community-Based Responses*. London: Community Development Foundation.

Humphries, B. (1997) The Dismantling of Antidiscrimination in British Social Work: A View from Social Work Education. *International Social Work*, 40(3): 289–301.

Husband, C. (1991) 'Race', Conflictual Politics, and Anti-racist Social Work: Lessons from the Past for Action in the '90s. In Northern Curriculum Development Project (No. 1) *Setting the Context for Change*. Leeds: CCETSW.

Husband, C. (1992) Racism, Prejudice and Social Policy. In Coombe, V. and Little, A. (Eds.) *Race and Social Work: A Guide to Training*. London: Routledge.

International Federation of Social Workers (2000) *Definition of Social Work*. http://www.ifsw.org/f38000138.html Accessed Oct 2011.

Jay, E. (1992) *Keep Them in Birmingham: Challenging Racism in South West England*. London: Commission for Racial Equality.

Kapuscinski, R. (2008) *The Other*. London: Verso.

Laird, S. (2008) *Anti-Oppressive Social Work: A Guide for Developing Cultural Competence*. London: Sage.

Lloyd, L. (1998) The Post- and the Anti-: Analysing Change and Changing Analyses in Social Work. *British Journal of Social Work*, 28(5) 709–727.

Lukes, S. (1974) *Power: A Radical View*. London: Macmillan.

Macpherson, W. (1999) *The Stephen Lawrence Inquiry*. Cm. 4262-1. HMSO.

McLaughlin, K. (2005) From Ridicule to Institutionalization: Anti-oppression, the State and Social Work. *Critical Social Policy*, 25(3): 283–305.

National Association of Social Workers (2001) *NASW Standards for Cultural Competence in Social Work Practice*. Washington: NASW.

Owusu-Bempah, J. (1997) Race. In Davies, M. (Ed.) *The Blackwell Companion to Social Work.* Oxford: Basil Blackwell.

Patel, N. (1995) In Search of the Holy Grail. In Hugman, R. and Smith, D. (Eds.) *Ethical Issues in Social Work*. London: Routledge.

Phillips, C. (2010) White, like who? Temporality, Contextuality and Anti-Racist Social Work. *Critical Social Work*, 11(2): 71–88.

Phillips, T. (2009) The G2 Interview: Decca Aitken Meets Trevor Phillips. *The Guardian* 23 February.

Phillipson, J. (1992) *Practising Equality: Women, Men and Social Work.* London: CCETSW.

Sakamoto, I. and Pitner, R. (2005) Use of Critical Consciousness in Anti-Oppressive Social Work Practice: Disentangling Power Dynamics at Personal and Structural Levels. *British Journal of Social Work*, 35(4), 435–452.

Sandhu, M. (2004) *No Problem in Cornwall.* Report of the Anti Racism Project, Young People Cornwall.

Singh, G. (2000) *Developing Black Perspectives in Practice Teaching.* Conference and Research Findings. London: CCETSW.

Singh, G. (2011) Social Work's Anti-Racist Journey. *Community Care*, 2 March.

Sivanandan, A. (1991) Black Struggles Against Racism. In Northern Curriculum Development Project (No. 1) *Setting the Context for Change*. Leeds: CCETSW.

Skellington, R. (1996) *'Race' in Britain Today* (2nd edn.) London: Sage.

Smith, G. (2000) *Thematic Inspection Report. Towards Race Equality 2000. HM Inspectorate of Probation.* London: HMSO.

Somers, M. (1994) The Narrative Constitution of Identity: A Relational and Network Approach. *Theory and Society*, 23, 605–649.

Thompson, N. (2001) *Anti-discriminatory Practice.* (3rd edn.) Basingstoke: Macmillan.

Walsh, C. (1996) The Ties that Bond us Across the World. *Professional Social Work*. BASW Sept.

Williams, C. (1999) Connecting Anti-racist and Anti-oppressive Theory and Practice: Retrenchment or Reappraisal? *British Journal of Social Work*, 29(2), 211–230.

Part Two: Social Work Methods Re-evaluated

Chapter 5

Psychodynamic Thinking in Social Work Practice

Maggie John and Pamela Trevithick

This chapter provides an account of what is meant by the term 'psychosocial social work practice', using a case vignette to describe its importance and relevance in direct practice. It begins with brief coverage of the history of the influence of psychoanalysis on social work in the United States and United Kingdom. The chapter then identifies a number of key psychoanalytic concepts and how these can be applied in ways that illuminate our understanding, and our ability to work safely and effectively, with the situations regularly encountered in practice. The link between theory and practice – and the contribution that psychoanalytic theory can offer in situations of complexity – is illustrated with reference to a case scenario.

Psychoanalysis and social work

The application of Freudian ideas in social work was one of the earliest attempts to put forward a theory and practice that could enable practitioners to understand and to address the situations and problems presented in social work. It was an approach that was particularly influential in the 1960s and early 1970s in the USA and UK, and has been described in different ways, such as, a *psychoanalytically-informed approach* to social work (Riggs *et al.*, 2009), *psychodynamic casework* (Kenny and Kenny, 2000: 30), *social* casework (Perlman, 1957; Timms, 1964), *psychodynamic approach* (Brearley, 2007) or as *psychosocial work* (Coulshed, 1991: Howe, 2002). Within these different terms, the emphasis given to *external* factors (*socio*), alongside those elements that reflect an individual's *internal* world (*psycho*) can vary but often not markedly. For example, Brearley's (2007) account of a *psychodynamic approach* places an emphasis on relationships:

> *Psychodynamic thinking is predominantly concerned with certain key relationships, namely those between the self and significant other people, past and present experience, and inner and outer reality, with simultaneous focus on both the actual*

relationship and those built up internally from experience and with special emphasis on the processes of these relationships and interactions.

(Brearley, 2007: 86–87)

From a slightly different perspective, Howe's account of *psychosocial work* places a greater emphasis on the social environment:

. . . by psychosocial we mean that area of human experience which is created by the interplay between the individual's psychological condition and the social environment. Psychosocial matters define most that is of interest to social work, particularly people who are having problems with others (parents, partners, children, peers and professionals) or other people who are having a problem with them. There is a simultaneous interest in both the individual and the qualities of their social environment.

(Howe 2002: 170)

The term *psychodynamic thinking* is used in this chapter. However, all psychoanalytically-based approaches attempt to understand the extent to which psychological and social or systemic elements are at play within a given situation – their causes and manifestations – and how we might work creatively and collaboratively with whatever understanding has been gained. Psychodynamic thinking is an attempt to understand what is happening and why at the level of the individual and wider system, and what needs to be done.

The history of psychoanalytic ideas in social work

United States of America

The history and impact of psychoanalytic ideas in Britain tended to be more generalist whereas in the United States this influence led to the development of a number of distinct practice theories and approaches. The most important theory to be developed in relation to social work was ego psychology (E.G. Goldstein, 1995), a theory and practice that was influenced by the work of Anna Freud on the role of the ego, described in *The Ego and the Mechanisms of Defence* (A. Freud, 1937). Ego psychology focuses on the ability of the ego to adapt to reality and how the ego can be supported and strengthened in its efforts to function (Hartmann, 1958; Parad, 1958; see Chapter 6). Other important theories were also related to social work including: crisis intervention (Parad, 1965); self psychology (Kohut, 1985); transactional analysis (Berne, 1961); psychosocial theories of human development (*Eight Stages of Man*) (Erikson, 1959) and the psychological and social theories that emerged from the Frankfurt School, particularly the work of Fromm (1942) and Marcuse (1956). It is interesting to note that Carl Rogers (1951; 1961), a clinical psychologist and founder of client-centred therapy, was influenced by the work of Freud. Also, Maslow (1954) acknowledged the intellectual debt he owed to Freud. However, both Rogers and Maslow were critical of some aspects of Freudian ideas and went on to advance different theories. In terms of social work education, the link between people's inner and outer worlds in psychosocial practice was promoted on social work training courses in a number of US colleges, influenced by the writings of Hollis (1964) and Perlman (1957) and other theorists.

United Kingdom

In the United Kingdom, 'a psychoanalytic approach to social work' (Brearley, 2007) did not give rise to the development of distinct practice approaches. This was mainly because the post-war period saw a preoccupation in social work with organisational changes associated with the development of the welfare state. However, some theories that were developed in the USA crossed the Atlantic although it is difficult to identify with any certainty the extent to which UK front-line practitioners adopted and adapted psychoanalytic theory. Some commentators have suggested that in the 1950s and 1960s, social work became increasingly associated with a form of casework that reflected a psychoanalytic or psychosocial orientation (Coulshed, 1991: 10). This is likely to be true in relation to some areas of practice more than others. For example, in the area of mental health and child guidance clinics, psychodynamic ideas could be seen to flourish during this period but even in these contexts, there may have been a tendency for social work to be overly influenced by psychiatry or to adopt an unquestioning view of 'classical psycho-analytic theory' (Timms, 1997: 724). Burnham argues that whilst academic publications may indicate that psychoanalytic ideas were highly influential, this should not be taken to reflect 'what social workers actually did' (Burnham, 2011). Where psychosocial ideas tended to flourish with less orthodoxy, and in ways that were more innovative, was in the voluntary sector – in organisations such as the Richmond Fellowship, Family Welfare Association, and some children's charities, such as the National Society for the Protection of Children (NSPPC).

However, by the late 1960s and early 1970s, psychoanalytic ideas in UK social work came under considerable attack from a number of different quarters. For example, some supporters of 'radical social work' criticised psychodynamic thinking for a 'tendency to explain social problems in terms of individual inadequacy or pathology' (Brearley, 2007: 81) in ways that neglected social and political influences on the problems people faced. Also, the 'expert' status and pathologising attitude adopted by some psychodynamically-oriented practitioners was seen by some as 'a form of policing the poor' (Coulshed, 1991: 10). It is true for all practice approaches that good ideas or theories in the wrong hands can easily go astray. A different challenge emerged in the early and mid 1970s from the USA, put forward by Reid and Epstein (1972) and Fischer (1973) who took issue with Freudian-based methods and the effectiveness of social casework. These criticisms cleared the path for the introduction of new approaches, such as the *unitary approach* (H. Goldstein, 1973), which incorporated systemic thinking with a focus on individual concerns, and *task centered casework* (Reid and Epstein, 1972), which outlined a structured, time-limited and problem focused approach that has a strong evidence base and measurable outcomes (see Chapter 7).

British Independent Group

An influence that had a more indirect impact on social work, and one that is often overlooked, is the contribution made by what is termed the *British Independent Group* within psychoanalysis – sometimes also referred to as *the British School of Psychoanalysis* (Kohon, 1986) or the *Middle Group* because of the middle position it held between factions that were associated with Melanie Klein and Anna Freud within the British Psycho-Analytical Society. Prominent figures in the *Independent Group* included Winnicott, Fairbairn, Guntrip, Balint and others. The work of this independent group is associated with the term *object relations* – a body of theory that rejected Freud's sexual drive theory and argued instead that human beings are primarily motivated to seek satisfying relationships with other people. Klein's work was also commonly identified as fundamental to the development of object relations theory, and Bowlby's (1979) research and writing on *attachment* – and the importance of the infant developing close and protective relationships with their parents or primary care-giver – similarly highlighted the importance of object relating in human growth and development. The impact of object relations theory in social work at this time tended to be most evident in work with children, particularly child guidance clinics, but its influence has continued to be influential in therapeutic communities, in the therapeutic work undertaken at the London Tavistock Clinic (now the Tavistock Centre) and the organisational research and consultancy provided by the Tavistock Institute.

The relationship as central to a psychosocial approach

According to Parton, the emphasis placed on the relationships and relating in the work of writers from the *Independent Group*, particularly Winnicott and Bowlby, provided social work with an important 'theoretical orientation' (Parton, 2008: 257). In fact, social work was one of the first professions to highlight the importance of the relationships that are created with service users and other significant individuals, a point emphasised in the seminal text by Coulshed:

> While it is true that people do not come to social work looking for a relationship, and while it is no substitute for practical support, nevertheless social workers are one of the few groups who recognise the value of relating to others in a way which recognises their experience as fundamental to understanding and action.
>
> (Coulshed, 1991: 2)

The importance of the relationships or 'working alliance' that we work to build could be said to constitute one of the few areas where considerable agreement among social workers can be found and is a subject that has been the focus of a number of publications (Biestek, 1961; Howe, 1998; Ruch et al., 2010; Trevithick, 2003). The particular contribution that a psychosocial perspective adds is an acknowledgement that as well as external factors, internal processes motivate human behaviour. The greater the trust, sense of safety, openness and understanding that is evident in the relationship that is created, the greater the likelihood that an individual will be able to understand, acknowledge and come to terms with areas of truth or reality that have previously been rejected or denied. For these internal processes to be part of the dialogue we create, it is essential for us to recognise and work with unconscious processes, that is, 'what is not said, cannot be said or can only be spoken of indirectly' (Davy and Cross, 2004: 4). We now turn to look at some key psychoanalytic concepts that enable a deeper analysis of the complexities of human experience.

Key psychoanalytic concepts

In the following section, a number of key concepts are defined. The focus of psychoanalysis, like that of social work, is to gain some understanding of people's inner and outer worlds, including their capacity to relate. It is this understanding that is needed to inform different aspects of social work practice – observation, the assessment process, decision-making and action. Within this process, a central feature of psychoanalytic theory is a recognition of unconscious states – a concept that Freud did not 'discover' but one that he systematically investigated as a key feature of mental life. The terms central to Freud's early thinking include:

> Conscious (Cs) – described by Freud as 'immediate data'. This refers to all thoughts, feelings and sensations of which we are aware at a given moment.

> Preconscious (Ps) – describes 'thoughts which are unconscious at the particular moment in question but which are not repressed and are, therefore, capable of becoming conscious' (Rycroft, 1972: 122).

> Unconscious (Ucs) – describes the 'mental processes of which the subject is not aware' (Rycroft, 1972: 172). Freud highlighted the 'logicality and irrationality of the unconscious, its allusive, distorted quality, the fact that it is not located in time or space and is communicated symbolically rather than in words' (Brearley, 2007: 88).

From 1920 onward, Freud introduced different structural distinctions in the form of id, ego and superego. In this conceptualisation, the id represents most unconscious, primitive instincts and impulses; the superego represents the 'conscience' of the mind – the place where rules, moral codes, taboos and censorship are harboured to control behaviour, often based on internalised representations of parental/authority figures. The *ego* is characterised as the conscious and reasoning part of the mind, where its primary function is to negotiate with external reality (sometimes called *reality-testing*) and to make decisions. It represents the organised parts of the psyche, in contrast to the unorganised, and passion-driven *id*, and moralising *superego*.

The importance of defences in social work

An important representation of unconscious states is evident in the unaware defences that people adopt in order to protect the ego – or the self – from thoughts, feelings or actions that are felt to be threatening (Jacobs, 2010: 110). All human beings have defences some of which are conscious and intentional strategies or behaviours that people adopt to achieve a particular aim. However, other defences are unconscious, that is, they are protective reactions or behaviours that for the most part lie beyond our immediate awareness and control. For example, events may be forgotten or *repressed* in order to protect us from memories that would produce anxiety if they became conscious (Reber *et al.*, 2009: 679), such as feelings of guilt or shame. Or defences can distort what is remembered, which means it can be difficult to gain an accurate picture of experiences and events. It is worth remembering that the greater the wounding that an individual has experienced, the greater the level of defensiveness that is likely to be triggered. Thus, it is the most defensive people who greatly need our help, but any offer of help can run the risk of being *resisted* because the same defences that are designed to protect the individual can also block the opportunity for helpful contact to be made (Trevithick, 2011). Given the understanding and sensitivity that is required, it is unhelpful and possibly damaging to confront defences head-on because they emerge in response to anxiety. Therefore, a more appropriate and helpful approach involves attempting to understand the nature of the anxiety and its cause:

> A key to understanding defences is the concept of anxiety. Anxiety is ubiquitous to human nature. It is at times intolerably painful and can seriously affect a person's ability to function normally. The greater the degree of anxiety in relation to a person's tolerance and ability to manage it, the more will there be a need to construct defences against it . . . Individuals as they grow through life develop a repertoire of defensive strategies to protect themselves from the impact of their most painful experiences and the nightmarish anxieties to which these give rise.
>
> (Brearley, 2007: 88)

At this point, it is worth noting that anxiety can easily be confused with feelings of fear because they often accompany one another. However, Reber *et al.* remind us that fear has a known object and, therefore, can be identified and talked about whereas anxiety describes a more generalised emotional state, where the sense of threat or danger cannot be easily recognised (2009: 48).

The defensive armoury that people develop can be seen in the level of resistance encountered. Some resistance, opposition or defiance is conscious and appropriate to the situation, but in this chapter our focus is on the manifestation of unconscious *resistance* that becomes evident when unacceptable thoughts, feelings or experiences are encountered. Resistances can be weak or strong and describe the extent to which an individual allows another person to understand them in ways that make 'unconscious processes conscious' (Rycroft, 1972: 142). Again, this work involves enabling people to understand the negative impact that defences and resistances occupy.

Having provided an account of some important concepts in psychoanalysis, we now want to change the focus of this chapter in order to highlight the relevance of these and other concepts when related to a case scenario. This scenario was described by a practitioner in a case discussion group, which we later followed up with a tape-recorded session where the practitioner was invited to consider 'how psycho-analytic concepts could be applied to a typical social work event'. The practitioner's comments are indicated in italics and so too are the psychoanalytic concepts that we cover. Appropriate changes have been made to protect the anonymity of the individuals involved. For example, the initial child protection investigation – which related to a serious incident perpetrated by the mother's previous partner – has not been covered in the scenario presented in order to illustrate other points.

Case scenario – A Child Protection Case Conference

The case conference was well attended, with nine professionals present – together with both parents who had recently separated. The atmosphere was uneasy. Child protection concerns about the children were in the balance. De-listing was an option but signs of progress were needed to reassure the professionals in attendance. However, the mother presented as scatty and confused. This seemed to have the effect of galvanising various professionals to step in with statements of clarification and robust advice. At one point the chairperson homed in on the mother and challenged her vigorously about her approach to running the family home, which was described by one professional as 'close to squalid'. In response, the mother unconvincingly commented that she 'muddles along and most things get done one way or another' but this fell far short of an adequate response. Concerns were not allayed. Instead there was a sense that this 'just wasn't good enough'. The challenge continued, without leaving a stone unturned and eventually the mother was in tears. I was aware of feeling uncomfortable throughout this process, as it seemed so unnecessary. I was also aware that this was an uncharacteristic intervention by the chairperson, who is usually very supportive of family members at child protection conferences which can be so daunting.

For the next few days, I found myself mulling over the conference, and feeling agitated about the mother's vulnerability. What came to mind was my knowledge of the family history. The mother was both intelligent and articulate. However, she had a poor relationship with her father, who she described as emotionally cold and critical, and who constantly communicated his disapproval of her.

The hypothesis that kept emerging for me was whether the conference had been an enactment of that relationship, with the mother falling into the role of vulnerable child-victim persecuted by a harsh parental figure (conference chairperson). I kept this tentative thought in mind in my subsequent work with the mother, and we talked about her tendency to portray herself as less competent than she really is and the benefits of coming across as 'scatty and confused'. These conversations were not always easy. I often felt provoked by the mother's somewhat contrived ineffectiveness, which could be exasperating and leave me feeling inappropriately punitive towards her.

As the work progressed, we linked these moments, and the situations where the mother seemed to be setting me up to be critical, to her need to re-experience events in relation to her father. My work focused on the need to avoid all invitations to retaliate or to be punitive when being set up to criticise, and the mother's work focused on trying to identify the feelings that were being re-enacted that led her to invite criticism and disapproval. This same desire to re-enact criticism was also evident in the criticism that the mother levelled at one of her five children – a daughter aged eleven. The mother was unable to own her critical behaviour towards this child but comments from the school indicated a concern that the child was showing signs of depression.

Reflective practice

Practitioner's commentary: During this case conference, my overall sense was one of unease and incongruity. Both indicated to me that unconscious processes were at play. I felt I was witnessing the mother sabotaging the outcome of the conference by unnecessarily generating further anxiety in the professional group. This sabotage came to a head with the chairperson launching something of an attack on the mother and the mother dissolving into tears. Although the children were taken off the 'at risk' list, I felt that the reactions that were played out in the case conference warranted thinking about in greater depth before the work with this family was closed. When thinking about reflective practice, the starting point for me is an openness to use of self. It establishes the 'third position', that of participant observer, where the transference and counter transference mobilisations are registered and thought about rather than acted out.

The following account outlines the transference and counter-transference thoughts and feelings that were evident in the case conference and later in the practitioner's work with the mother in question. Transference and counter-transference are summarised as follows:

> *Transference.* Transference occurs in every human relationship. It describes our ability to transfer onto others an emotion or pattern of relating that have their roots in the past and to re-experience these unconscious feelings in the present. These transferred feelings can be positive in character, and induce feelings of trust and safety. However, a *negative transference* can also occur, where more hostile feelings of hatred, jealousy and mistrust are passed on – a situation experienced by most social workers at some point in their career. Both negative and positive transference can lead us to feel or react to other people inappropriately (Howe, 2008: 167).

> *Counter-transference.* There are two forms of counter transference. The first is seen as positive and describes our ability to be open and receptive to the transferred feelings of others. Reactions that accurately reflect another person's thoughts and feelings can be enormously valuable as an aid to understanding. A second form of counter transference involves the emotions that we bring into our contact with other people that are based on our own unresolved fears and fantasies from the past (Heimann, 1950). These can blur or distort our sense of reality and perception of events.

In the scenario, the openness of the practitioner to *transference* is evident in the practitioner's awareness of being 'set up' to re-enact the mother's unresolved feelings from the past, where the practitioner was being invited to become, in fantasy, the mother's 'cold and critical' father. This same feeling may have been successfully transferred, and acted out, by the conference chairperson. The practitioner's awareness of her *counter-transference* is evident in her ability to pick up and take in the feelings of vulnerability that the mother expressed, which the practitioner understood to be a defence that was being deployed by the mother in order to avoid taking charge of her life and the kind of responsibilities that a fully functioning adult is expected to carry. The practitioner felt that anxieties about being criticised or 'getting it wrong' could be driving the mother's behaviour. The use of *denial* and *avoidance* was also evident in the mother's refusal to 'own' her destructive and critical attitude toward her eleven-year-old daughter. The practitioner's exploration of the benefits gained by the mother in coming across as 'scatty and confused' could link to the concept of *secondary gain*, that is, when a particular behaviour is used to give practical advantages. In this case scenario, the *gain* is the 'immediate freedom from emotional discomfort' (Bateman *et al.*, 2010: 105) – a discomfort that is located in the mother's struggle or resistance to fully embrace the responsibilities of adulthood. A different way to conceptualise the mother's reaction would be to consider *regression*, that is, whether she was demonstrating an abandonment of 'more usual adult responsibilities' and 'regressed to more child-like and dependent ways of behaving' (Bateman *et al.*, 2010: 36). The following account illustrates the 'depth explanations' (Howe, 1996: 92) that this case required:

> **Practitioner's commentary:** *I found myself reflecting on the roles that had been played out in the case conference – that of victim and perpetrator – and how the mother's relationship throughout her childhood with a cold and critical father might be repeating itself within the dynamic of this family. Two issues of concern remained with me. First, the extent to which the mother's childhood experiences were impacting on her relationship with her daughter and second, the extent to which the mother was in a position to actively protect her children from abuse if again threatened by a future partner and what changes were needed for her to provide long term security for the children.*
>
> *Somewhere there was a critical voice and somewhere there was a hurt child, somewhere there was abusive power and somewhere there was helpless passivity. Had the mother internalised the critical voice of her father into a harsh and unforgiving superego, and was she then projecting the unbearably painful feelings of guilt and shame outside herself? Drawing on the psychoanalytic concepts of splitting and projection, my hypothesis was that these polarised positions all belonged to the mother's internal world, but that she was unable to integrate them without anxiety.*

The practitioner's comment about whether 'the mother internalised the critical voice' is a reference to *internalisation*, that is, 'the acceptance and adaptation of beliefs, values, attitudes, practices and standards, etc. as one's own' (Reber *et al.*, 2009: 395). This concept is similar to *introjection* which can be both a defence and a feature in normal development. This describes a process where the functions of the external world – located 'out there' – are absorbed symbolically, or in fantasy, and replaced by an imagined object that is internalised and brought 'inside' (Colman, 2009: 389). For example, the *super-ego* is formed by introjections of parental values and those of other authority figures. If introjection describes what we take in, projection describes what we give out. *Projection* is one of the most common and potentially damaging defences and is evident when people falsely attribute an intolerable, unacceptable or unwanted thought, feeling, action, or attribute onto someone or something else. In this defence:

> *Projected aspects of oneself are preceded by denial, that is, one denies that one feels such and such an emotion, has such and such a wish, but asserts that someone else does.*
>
> (Rycroft, 1972: 126)

It is a defence that most social workers experience – both in terms of negative and idealised projections – and often involves some form of criticism or condemnation. For example, in social work, projections can lead to our becoming what I term 'a reliable hate object', that is, someone who is rendered the target of negative projections on the basis that we are considered to be safe enough to bear, survive, understand and work with these projections without retaliating. In a similar way, it is possible for positive attributes to be projected on to an idealised individual although when the *idealisation* bubble bursts or breaks down, as often it will, this can 'give way to rage and hatred' (Greenson, 1973: 344). Projections almost always accompany splitting and denial.

Like projection, *splitting* is an important concept in psychoanalysis. It involves a *disassociation* from reality by separating out the self (splitting of the self) or objects (splitting of the object) into 'good' and 'bad', often in response to conflicts that lead to *repression*, where an individual forgets and also forgets what is forgotten, or dissociates or disconnects from feelings that feel dangerous to his or her psychic well-being. In many ways, splitting can be seen as a feature of normal behaviour – as a way of managing two competing elements – but in its extreme form it can become highly problematic if there is no integration of 'good' and 'bad' parts:

> *Social workers often find themselves on the receiving end of splitting when clients compare them with other workers, for example, talking of the health visitor in glowing terms while scathingly criticising the social worker.*
>
> (Brearley, 2007: 89)

An example of a more extreme form of splitting is evident in the concept of *identification with the aggressor* which describes how a person can identify, appropriate and adopt the aggression and violence they have experienced by adopting the attributes and behaviour of the aggressor. This defence was identified by Anna Freud (1936):

> *. . . faced with an external threat . . . the subject identifies himself* [sic] *with his aggressor. He may do so either by appropriating the aggression itself, or else by physical or moral emulation of the aggressor, again by adopting particular symbols of power by which the aggressor is designated . . . The behaviour we observe is the outcome of a reversal of roles: the aggressed turns aggressor.*
>
> (Laplanche and Pontalis, 1973: 208–209)

It is the concept of splitting and identification with the aggressor that is a feature of the hypothesis put forward by the practitioner in the following comment:

> **Practitioner's commentary:** *If she owned her own critical voice, she would feel identified with her cruel father and, therefore, she worked hard to locate this aspect of herself in the chairperson (and at other times, any authority figure), whilst remaining unaware of her own treatment of her daughter. Evacuating all her power left her feeling depleted and weak – a vulnerable*

child-self that was devoid of the necessary competence and confidence for parenting – but at least this was preferable to feeling that she was a monster.

The 'location of aspects of herself in the chairperson' is a reference to Melanie Klein's concept of *projective identification*. Projective identification has similar features to counter-transference and can sometimes be confused with the concept of *projection*, described earlier in terms of falsely attributed intolerable feelings to other people (Colman, 2009: 607). In the case conference scenario, projective identification describes how the chairperson was mobilised by the mother to adopt the role of aggressor, thereby re-enacting her earlier experience of being a victim and, at the same time, evacuating the mother's own feelings of aggression. It is the uncharacteristic behaviour that people adopt – and often in an extreme form – that can indicate that the practitioner has become mobilised by another person to act on their behalf. It is a situation that can mean that the worker, once mobilised, can fail to notice and to respond appropriately to dangerous or threatening situations, such as those encountered in child protection or where the possibility of suicide is evident. The importance of this concept can be found in the writing of Mattinson (1975) on supervision, who gives the example of a social worker communicating or responding to their supervisor in ways that are highly unusual and uncharacteristic of that practitioner – as if mirroring a particular feature of the service user-practitioner relationship, such as intense anger, hopelessness, powerlessness or despair that the practitioner has picked up.

Although the practitioner was working from a number of hypotheses, her thinking remained open to being corrected, challenged or refuted in the light of new information (Trevithick, 2012):

> **Practitioner's commentary:** *Drawing on the hypothesis of the mother's identification with the father-aggressor, yet also remaining open to new thoughts which may lead me to refute my hypothesis, I ensured that the focus of my work with the family over the next few months addressed moments where the mother appeared either stressed out or dogmatic with her daughter, or authoritative and confident in her role, trying all the time to pull the two positions closer together. My intention was to help the mother recognise both aspects of her personality but to re-script them into legitimate and functional components of her self, leading to a degree of containment (the depressive position) rather than the need to resort to projective defences.*

In the above commentary, two important psychoanalytic concepts are mentioned: containment and the depressive position. *Containment* is based on Klein's concept of projective identification and describes a situation where 'one person in some sense contains a part of another' (Hinshelwood, 1991: 246) in ways that relieve and transform the original anxiety into something more tolerable and bearable. The modified feeling is then taken in – or introjected – and what is also taken in is the realisation that anxiety can be contained or relieved by another person. One of the features of unmanageable anxiety is the inability to integrate thinking and feeling. In the work of Bion (1962) containment can help to enable this link to be made. For Bateman *et al.* it is a skill that involves:

> . . . *positive reinforcement, working positively with defences, helping with coping, reframing problems, judicious use of transference and counter-transference as important techniques. Holding and containing involves the capacity to do nothing, 'to be with'* . . . *the patient (person)* . . . *and to give positive reinforcement with encouraging remarks.*
>
> (Bateman *et al.*, 2010: 116–117)

The ability to cope with *ambivalence*, that is, the ability to allow for loving and hating the same person, is referred to in Kleinian terminology as the *depressive position*. Before the *depressive position*, the infant is said to deal with his or her destructive impulses, and anxieties about being left alone and not surviving, by splitting and projection (*paranoid-schizoid position*). The paranoid-schizoid position is an attempt to keep separate contradictory or ambivalent feelings. At this early stage in development, the infant feels it is impossible to simultaneously love and hate the same person. However, in time the infant comes to realise that the mother (carer) who nurtures and frustrates is the same person, that is, that the same person can have both good and bad features. In this conceptualisation, working through the paranoid-schizoid position in this way leads to a concern for the other and a desire to repair any imagined damage the child believes they have caused. This is known as the depressive position. Brearley describes this transition as follows:

> *Winnicott (1984: 100) helpfully described it (depressive position) as 'the development of the capacity for concern' and saw it as a stage toward maturity and reciprocity. The inevitable conflict between love and hate for the same person is not bypassed by the 'either/or' strategies of splitting and projection, but rather by tolerating the ambivalence involved and working through the realistic regrets towards a sense of reparation. There is recognition and acceptance that significant other people may sometimes let us down, but that this is not an ultimate disaster.*
>
> (Brearley, 2007: 89)

If these 'positions' and transitions are inadequately worked through, it can lead to a situation where the inability to tolerate deeply painful feelings results in an acting out, rather than a working out, of unresolved, painful feelings which is a situation that is suggested in the mother's behaviour towards her daughter. For the practitioner, the destructive feelings being communicated by the mother toward her daughter constituted a re-enactment of the mother's painful childhood experiences and a situation that the practitioner felt it necessary to address:

Practitioner's commentary: *At an appropriate point, we agreed that it would be helpful to involve the daughter in the sessions which involved thinking carefully to ensure that this work was child-focused. It centred on inviting the daughter to give feedback to her mother and to describe her feelings during this process. At the same time, my work focused on containing the mother's feelings of guilt and blame during this interaction.*

I was aware that the mother was an adult but that child parts of her inner self could be active, sometimes undermining her parenting, and yet insisting on being seen. Her own attachment to her father had been ambivalent and, in turn, she was unawarely or unconsciously reproducing the conditions of this ambivalence in her relationship with her daughter. For this mother to continue to react defensively could be a recipe for trouble but I felt that a different, more creative outcome was possible if the focus could be on different roles and identifications.

To have been able to offer psychotherapy would have been desirable but in terms of the contribution that social work could provide, I felt that enabling the mother to understand and to become more aware of the internal and unconscious processes that appear to be driving her actions could be powerful and empowering – and perhaps ultimately determine how this family managed itself.

What is highlighted in the above account is the practitioner's capacity to contain the anxieties of both the mother and daughter in ways that enabled difficult feelings to be expressed and felt. An assumption that is evident in this account, and central to psychodynamic thinking, is the extent to which understanding, particularly self-understanding, can be therapeutic and central to the change process. Understanding why a person might need to keep unwanted feelings at bay can be the first step to realising that certain feelings have a history, that others were involved in that history and, perhaps most importantly, that feelings can be changed. They need not be a life sentence. A central feature of the practitioner's account is the extent to which she used theory to illuminate her understanding and also how aspects of her own emotional experience were used to help her 'think through' the factors at play as a feature of reflective professional practice:

Practitioner's commentary: *It would have been easy to withdraw from this family after the conference, given that the concerns for the children's safety had diminished. I could have concluded that the mother would always be the same and, in response to the feelings of irritation and frustration that her behaviour engendered in me, I could have acted out my part in the drama, as sometimes happens, by cancelling appointments or giving her short shrift during minimal visits. This could have confirmed the mother's world view that people did not care about her and confirmed her projected sense of being a victim of external aggression.*

However, I would also have felt dissatisfied and the 'burn out' familiar to social workers would have gone up a notch. Instead the intervention attempted to promote emotional fluidity and flexibility – creating the conditions for growth and change – by providing sufficient insight for the family to avoid repeating the same patterns of behaviour and, perhaps inevitably, finding themselves being re-referred. This was achieved partly by my refusal to act out the role of aggressor and at the same time allowing the projection and the mother's hatred of me – yet knowing throughout that I had the strength and intellectual and emotional understanding to survive her attacks. Without this understanding and engagement with the emotional processes at play in this family, the intervention could have been perfunctory and counter-productive, possibly creating the conditions for the mother to regress into the role of passive victim to such an extent that she neglected the children's needs, again putting them at risk. It is interesting that this more in-depth analysis of this case was not evident in the initial referral, which focused on a previous partner's abuse of the children, but emerged only through the process of working with the family. It was my decision to work on the underlying issues, supported through discussion in supervision, that enabled the mother to act protectively and to provide longer term security for the children. This case is now closed and no further concerns have been identified.

The importance of wider social factors

This chapter has focused on the mother's 'inner' world but in doing so, we do not underestimate the impact of the 'outer' world and the environmental or social influences that affect a person's life and sense of emotional well being. As human beings, we are shaped by – and shape – our social world, although not all people have equal capacity to shape their world. Those experiencing high levels of social disadvantage, and those who are highly defended psychologically are likely to be less engaged in this shaping process in positive ways than other people who are more resilient. It is the interplay between a person's psychological condition and their social environment that is the focus of social work – and the fact that 'social workers are concerned with troublesome aspects of the client's environment' (Kenny and Kenny, 2000: 36). Other chapters in this volume examine the wider social environment.

Conclusion

This chapter has looked at the history of the influence of psychoanalysis on social work, both in the United States and United Kingdom and, using a case scenario, has described and applied a number of key psychoanalytic concepts in order to highlight the importance of psychoanalytic thinking in social work. It seems appropriate to end with a final comment from the practitioner whose work is described in this chapter:

> **Practitioner's commentary:** I hope that this case study has illustrated how psychoanalytic concepts can be applied to a typical social work event, such as a child protection conference. This work has not meant that I have been involved in providing some kind of therapy, but what it does illustrate is the extent to which my practice is psychoanalytically-informed, and how this perspective helps me to make sense of my observations and intuitions.

References

Bateman, A., Brown, D. and Pedder, J. (2010) *Introduction to Psychotherapy: An Outline of Psychodynamic Principles and Practice.* 4th edn. London: Routledge.

Berne, E. (1961) *Transactional Analysis in Psychotherapy.* New York: Grove Press.

Biestek, F.P. (1961) *The Casework Relationship.* London: Allen and Unwin.

Bion, W.R. (1962) *Learning from Experience*. London: Heinemann.

Bowlby, J. (1979) *The Making and Breaking of Affectional Bonds.* London: Tavistock.

Brearley, J. (2007) A Psychoanalytic Approach to Social Work. In Lishman, J. (Ed.) *Handbook of Theory for Practice Teachers.* 2nd edn. London: Jessica Kingsley.

Burnham, D. (2011) Selective Memory: A Note on Social Work Historiography. *British Journal of Social Work*, 41: 5–21.

Colman, A.M. (2009) *A Dictionary of Psychology.* 3rd edn. Oxford: Oxford University Press.

Coulshed, V. (1991) *Social Work Practice: An Introduction.* 2nd edn. Basingstoke: Macmillan/BASW.

Davy, J. and Cross, M. (2004) *Barriers, Defences and Resistance.* Maidenhead: Open University Press.

Erikson, E.E. (1959) *Identity and the Life Cycle: Selected Papers*. New York: International Universities Press.

Fischer, J. (1973) Is Casework Effective? A Review. *Social Work*, 1: 107–110.

Freud, A. (1937) *The Ego and the Mechanisms of Defence.* London: Hogarth Press and The Institute of Psychoanalysis.

Fromm, E. (1942) *The Fear of Freedom.* London: Kegan Paul.

Goldstein, E.G. (1995) *Ego Psychology and Social Work Practice.* 2nd edn. London: Free Press.

Goldstein, H. (1973) *Social Work Practice: A Unitary Approach*. Columbia, SC: University of South Carolina Press.

Greenson, R.R. (1973) *The Technique and Practice of Psychoanalysis*. 2nd impression. London: Hogarth Press and The Institute of Psychoanalysis.

Hartmann, H. (1958) *Ego Psychology and the Problem of Adaptation*. (Translated by David Rapaport). London: Imago Publishing.

Heimann, P. (1950) On Counter-transference. *International Journal of Psycho-Analysis*, 31: 81–84.

Hinshelwood, R.D. (1991) *A Dictionary of Kleinian Thought.* 2nd edn. Northvale, NJ: Aronson.

Hollis, F. (1964) *Casework: A Psychosocial Therapy.* New York: Random House.

Howe, D. (1996) Surface and Depth in Social Work Practice. In Parton, N. (Ed.) *Social Theory, Social Change and Social Work.* London: Routledge.

Howe, D. (1998) Relationship-based Thinking and Practice in Social Work. *Journal of Social Work Practice*, 16: 2, 45–56.

Howe, D. (2002) Psychosocial Work. In Adams, R., Dominelli, L. and Payne, M. (Eds.) *Social Work: Themes, Issues and Critical Debates.* 2nd edn. Basingstoke: Macmillan.

Howe, D. (2008) *The Emotionally Intelligent Social Worker.* Basingstoke: Palgrave Macmillan.

Jacobs, M. (2010) *Psychodynamic Counselling in Action.* 4th edn. London: Sage.

Kenny, L. and Kenny, B. (2000) Psychodynamic Theory in Social Work: A View From Practice. In Stepney, P. and Ford, D. (Eds.) *Social Work Models, Methods and Theories.* Lyme Regis: Russell House Publishing.

Kohon, G. (Ed.) (1986) *The British School of Psychoanalysis: The Independent Tradition.* London: Free Association.

Kohut, H. (1985) *Self Psychology and the Humanities: Reflections on a New Psychoanalytic Approach.* New York: Norton.

Laplanche, J. and Pontalis, J-B. (1973) *The Language of Psycho-Analysis.* London: Hogarth Press.

Marcuse, H. (1956) *Eros and Civilization: A Philosophical Inquiry into Freud.* London: Routledge & Kegan Paul.

Maslow, A.H. (1954) *Motivation and Personality.* New York: Harper and Row.

Mattinson, J. (1975) *The Reflection Process in Casework Supervision.* London: The Tavistock Institute of Medical Psychology.

Parad, H.J. (Ed.) (1958) *Ego Psychology and Dynamic Casework.* New York: Family Services Assoc. of America.

Parad, H.J. (Ed.) (1965) *Crisis Intervention: Selected Readings.* New York: Family Services Assoc. of America.

Parton, N. (2008) Changes in the Form of Knowledge in Social Work: From The 'Social' to The 'Informational?' *British Journal of Social Work*, 38(2), 253–269.

Perlman, H.H. (1957) *Social Case Work: A Problem-Solving Process.* Chicago: University of Chicago Press.

Reber, A.S., Allen, R. and Reber, E.S. (2009) *The Penguin Dictionary of Psychology.* 4th edn. London: Penguin.

Reid, W.J. and Epstein, L. (1972) *Task Centered Casework.* New York: Columbia University.

Riggs, D.W., Delfabbro, P.H. and Augoustinos, M. (2009) Negotiating Foster-Families: Identification and Desire. *British Journal of Social Work*, 39(5): 789–806.

Rogers, C.R. (1951) *Client-Centered Therapy: Its Current Practice, Implications and Theory.* Boston: Houghton Mifflin.

Rogers, C.R. (1961) *On Becoming a Person: A Therapist's View of Psychotherapy*. Boston: Houghton Mifflin.

Ruch, G., Turney, D. and Ward, A. (Eds.) (2010) *Relationship-Based Social Work: Getting to the Heart of Practice*. London: Jessica Kingsley.

Rycroft, C. (1972) *A Critical Dictionary of Psychoanalysis.* Harmondsworth: Penguin.

Timms, N. (1964) *Social Casework. Principles and Practice*. London: Routledge.

Timms, N. (1997) Taking Social Work Seriously: The Contribution of the Functional School. *British Journal of Social Work*, 27(5): 723–737.

Trevithick, P. (2003) Effective Relationship-Based Practice: A Theoretical Exploration. *Journal of Social Work Practice*, 17: 2, 173–186.

Trevithick, P. (2011) Understanding Defences and Defensive Behaviour in Social Work. *Journal of Social Work Practice*, 25: 4, 389–412.

Trevithick, P. (2012) *Social Work Skills and Knowledge: A Practice Handbook.* 3rd edn. Maidenhead: Open University Press.

Chapter 6

Crisis Intervention as Common Practice

Wing Hong Chui and Deirdre Ford

Introduction

In day-to-day practice, it is not surprising that social workers and human services workers come into contact with people in states of crisis. Almost every individual, in one way or another, experiences crises at times in their own lives and participates in the crises of others at different stages in life (Calhoun *et al.*, 1976; Robinson, 1979; Stephen and Woolfe, 1982; Young, 1983; Hoff, 1995; Walsh, 2006; Thompson, 2011). While some may cope with crises on their own, others may seek help from family members and friends or turn to professionals for practical and emotional support. Encountering various forms of crisis such as domestic violence, physical illness, suicidal ideation, and personal loss is generally recognised as one of the integral parts of direct practice within the range of social work settings. The manifestation and characteristics of a crisis, however, vary from one to another, so that there is no consensus regarding what constitutes a crisis. Additionally, crisis situations generally require immediate responses from practitioners and managers alike to give advice and to arrive at decisions within a short period of time. As such, crisis work may provoke anxieties and induce a sense of helplessness amongst trained workers, not to mention those who are inexperienced and not prepared for it. A sound knowledge of the concepts and principles of crisis theory therefore is important in order to take up the challenges, along with service users, of confronting crises, and avoiding the less satisfactory outcome of mere 'crisis survival' (Thompson, 1991, 2011). While there is no one prescription for dealing with crises, crisis intervention is seen as one of several therapeutic models that offers a clear framework for understanding the salient features of crises and principles to guide intervention. According to Ewing:

> *Social scientists speak of crisis intervention as a conceptual model for understanding human adjustment, family dynamics, and even organisational development. Community mental health workers view it variously as a strategy for the prevention of mental disorder and psychiatric hospitalisation, a form of short-term psychotherapy, a model for community consultation, and as a rationale for new self-help and paraprofessional programmes.*

> (Ewing, 1978: 3)

One assumption of this model is that every person has a potential for growth and an ability to grow from the experience. What social workers can do is to facilitate those who are in distress so that they can discover and develop coping strategies to meet life demands. In this respect, crisis intervention 'represents a strengths approach because it underscores the possibility of client growth even in horrible situations' (Walsh, 2006: 273). Caplan (1964), Carkhuff (1969), Rapoport (1970), Shneidman (1972) and Golan (1974) amongst others proposed that the right kind of minimal intervention during a brief crisis period can achieve a maximum effect. Another pragmatic argument in favour of crisis services in the last two decades, particularly in the British context, is that budget cuts and pressures on resources place emphasis on the great value of employing 'brief' therapies or time-limited intervention rather than traditional longer term psychotherapy (Monach and Monach, 1993). By no means do we argue that crisis intervention itself provides us with all solutions to sophisticated crisis contexts but it is a mode of brief treatment for the immediate threats imposed on an individual, and if necessary, follow-up services can and should be provided after the critical moment.

The concepts and development of crisis theory, which derived from the practice of psychiatry in America, have been written about extensively since the 1960s (Lindemann, 1965; Parad, 1965; Rapoport, 1970; Golan, 1978; Ewing, 1978; Burgess and Baldwin, 1981; Roberts, 1990; Thompson, 1991; Coulshed and Orme, 1998; Payne, 2005; Walsh, 2006). There is an abundance of literature to illustrate how crisis intervention has been applied in relation to service users such as older people with dementia (Marshall, 1990; Thompson, 1991, 2011; Parker, 1992); people who are dying or bereaved (Berman, 1978; Sharer, 1979; Burgess and Baldwin, 1981; Smith, 1982; McConville, 1990; Hillman, 2002); suicidal clients (Lewis *et al.*, 1990; Jobes *et al.*, 2005); people who misuse substances (Cocores and Gold, 1990; Gilliland and James, 1997); victims of violence and their abusers (Bard and Ellison, 1974; Warner, 1979; Kilpatrick and Veronen, 1983; Petretic-Jackson and Jackson, 1990; Roberts and Dziegielewski, 1995; Hillman, 2002; Roberts and Roberts, 2005); and those with health related and mental health related problems (Robinson, 1979; Hess and Ruster, 1990; Mitchell, 1993; Burgess and Roberts, 2005). Admittedly most of these are American texts and it is questionable whether crisis intervention is still regarded as an important model of social work practice in Britain. It is timely therefore to revisit the concepts of crisis intervention and to illustrate how it can be applied in practice with the person-in-crisis.

This chapter has eight sections. Relying on social work and health literature, the first and second sections deal with the concepts of crisis and the basic assumptions underlying this time-limited crisis intervention approach. The third section briefly summarises different phases or stages of crisis intervention in helping service users work through traumatic events. Sections four to eight examine how crisis intervention can be used constructively with people and communities who suffer acute crisis as a result of large-scale accidents or disasters.

Defining crisis

> *A crisis refers to . . . A crisis occurs when . . . A crisis affects . . . Crisis has been viewed as . . .*
>
> (Umana *et al.*, 1980, cited in O'Hagan, 1986: 14)

Any attempt to look for a universal definition of crisis is doomed to failure (Langsley *et al.*, 1968; Umana *et al.*, 1980; Thompson, 1991, 2011). O'Hagan for instance recognises that the term 'crisis' is indeed elusive and vague in its meaning and is subject to personal interpretation:

> *A set of circumstances or conditions which constitute a crisis for one individual, may not do so for another. An unmanageable problem may render Mr Smith in a state of panic, and may be a matter of indifference to Mrs Brown. The sight of a spider could provoke a massive phobic reaction which we may justifiably call a crisis for the person concerned, whilst the birth of a mentally handicapped child may be perfectly manageable determinants, and it is easy to understand why many of the pioneers gave up the task of definition.*
>
> (O'Hagan, 1986: 14)

Another similar explanation offered by Johnson is that 'crisis' and 'stress' are commonly used interchangeably by practitioners and students alike, and indeed there should be a distinction between the two terms:

> *Stress by itself isn't crisis: not even severe stress. Nor is a stressful event like job loss or illness a crisis, although such an event may precipitate a crisis. In some cases, an event that triggers a crisis in one person may scarcely even affect another. So much depends on the person's feelings about the situation, as well as their ability to cope with it at that time. The same situation occurring at another time in the person's life may not upset them unduly.*
>
> (Johnson, 1979: 15–16)

Thus it is important to be aware that different people may think of a crisis in many different ways and the cornerstone in understanding the nature and impact of a crisis situation depends largely on the feelings, perceptions and responses of an individual. Social work practitioners thus need to be open-minded and sensitive in order to understand the immediate concerns and worries of those involved rather than rigidly classifying crises according to the practitioners' frame of reference (Specter and Claiborn, 1972; Sebolt, 1972; Cohen and Nelson, 1983; Parker, 1992). While there are many definitions of crisis and crisis may be perceived in different ways according to different experiences, most of them entail a negative connotation and certainly interpret crisis as a form of danger and destructive force to individual and social functioning. Some examples are as follows:

> *Crisis results from impediments to life goals that people believe they cannot overcome through customary choices and behaviours.*
>
> (Caplan, 1964: 40)

Crisis is a subjective reaction to a stressful life experience, one so affecting the stability of the individual that the ability to cope or function may be seriously compromised.
(Bard and Ellison, 1974: 68)

Crises are personal difficulties or situations that immobilise people and prevent them from consciously controlling their lives.
(Belkin, 1984: 424)

A crisis brings about a temporary state of disorganisation in which people experience disruption of their normal functioning and, due to the inability to cope, they can become frustrated, distressed and angry. A number of authors such as Aguilera and Messick (1982), Young (1983), Thompson (1991, 2011), Roberts and Dziegielewski (1995) and Payne (2005) however draw attention to the positive dimension in viewing crisis by borrowing ideas from the two Chinese characters – *Wei Chi* – that represent the word 'crisis'. These two characters indicate the presence of both 'danger' and 'opportunity', and literally mean the possibility of growth and impetus for change. Aguilera and Messick further emphasise that crisis can be seen as a turning point for better or worse in the person's well being:

Crisis is a danger because it threatens to overwhelm the individual or their family, and it may result in suicide or psychotic break. It is also an opportunity because during times of crisis individuals are more receptive to therapeutic influence.
(Aguilera and Messick, 1982: 1)

At the point of crisis, it may be easier to admit that problems are beyond control and to be more receptive to change if defences collapse. Thus this gives a person a chance to look for new skills to meet demands in living (Gilliland and James, 1997). Recognising crisis as a turning point, the primary aim of crisis work is 'not simply to minimise the harm of a crisis, to 'cut losses', but rather to maximise the positive potential of crisis' (Thompson, 1991: 28). Another key term related to crisis theory and practice is 'homeostasis'. It refers to 'self-regulation and the need to preserve a balance: in this case in affective (emotional) and cognitive (thinking) function which is dependent upon an individual's coping mechanisms' (Parker, 1992: 44). In the normal course of events every individual attempts to maintain a steady state of feeling and being, mostly by utilising customary methods of problem solving or defence mechanisms:

The principle of homeostasis is borrowed from physiology and is defined by the need to preserve stable chemical or electrolyte balances within the body necessary to sustain life. When the balances are upset, self-regulatory mechanisms are triggered that help to return these balances to healthy levels for the individual.
(Burgess and Baldwin, 1981: 24)

Nonetheless, no one is immune to crises and at times our homeostatic equilibrium or normal functioning is disrupted for various reasons. Janosik (1984) opines that every crisis, whether universal or idiosyncratic, is accompanied by disequilibrium or disorientation. Heightened emotions, affective discomfort, cognitive confusion, and a sense of helplessness and powerlessness are often experienced. In this respect, it is essential for crisis workers to be sensitive to the signs of upset, enabling service users to understand the causes of crises and to arrive at a healthy process of recovery or restoration. What are the events that produce stress and vulnerability? At the outset it should be emphasised that every crisis is a unique experience and yet attempts have been made to generalise possible factors to explain crisis situations. According to Rapoport, 'a crisis is an upset in a steady state caused by hazardous events' (1970: 276) and, broadly speaking, hazardous or precipitating events can be experienced by an individual as a loss, a threat or a challenge. Nonetheless, Rapoport provides a rather vague definition of these three domains:

> *A threat may be directed to instinctual needs or to an individual's sense of integrity or autonomy. A loss may be that of a person or an experience of acute deprivation. A challenge may be to survival, growth, mastery, or self-expression.*
>
> (Rapoport, 1970: 277)

Loss, threat and challenge result in differing affective reactions: for example loss often produces anger and protest. Threat may result in anxiety, fearful anticipation and uncertainty. Challenge may produce feelings of hopeful anticipation but at the same time panic may be experienced. In contrast, a simpler way of classifying crisis has been offered by Gilliland and James (1997), Coulshed and Orme (1998) and Payne (2005). There are two basic types of crisis in general terms, namely developmental (or maturational) crises and accidental (or situational) crises. While developmental crises can usually be anticipated and are seen as a normal part of human development and maturation such as pregnancy, marriage, retirement and ageing (Erikson, 1977), accidental crises are either unexpected or tragic events such as sudden bereavement, loss of health, hospitalisation and accidents. Butler and Elliott (1985) outline foreseeable changes to both external and internal patterns of living and in turn these natural crisis points to life transitions will induce periods of upset which call for readjustments. Given the fact that most developmental crises can be expected there is huge scope for social workers in prevention work. On the other hand, crisis intervention such as that undertaken by rape crisis services, women's refuges and suicide prevention centres should be readily available in the community to handle those unforeseen situational crises (Coulshed and Orme, 1998).

Basic assumptions of crisis theory and practice

> *Understanding the variations and sequences of emotions, with the accompanying defences, is at the heart of crisis intervention.*
>
> (Cohen, 1990: 284)

This section aims to revisit the theoretical base and assumptions of crisis intervention. The major conceptual development of crisis theory and practice is attributed to the work of Erich Lindemann, Gerald Caplan, Lydia Rapoport and Howard Parad (Ewing, 1978; Roberts, 1990). Golan uses ten statements to summarise the basic tenets of crisis theory, as shown below (Golan, 1974; 1978).

Tenets of crisis theory

1. An individual (or family, group, or community) is subjected to periods of increased internal and external stresses throughout their normal life span which disturb their customary state of equilibrium with their surrounding environment . . . The hazardous event may be a single catastrophic occurrence or a series of lesser mishaps which have a cumulative effect.
2. The impact of the hazardous effect disturbs the individual's homeostatic balance and puts them into a vulnerable state.
3. A precipitating factor can bring about a turning point, during which self-righting devices no longer operate and the individual enters a state of active crisis, marked by disequilibrium and disorganisation.
4. As the crisis situation develops, the individual may perceive the initial and subsequent stressful events primarily as a threat . . . as a loss of a person or an ability . . . or as a challenge to survival, growth, or mastery.
5. Each of these perceptions calls forth a characteristic emotional reaction that reflects the subjective meaning of the event to the individual.
6. Although a crisis situation is neither an illness nor a pathological experience and reflects a realistic struggle to deal with the individual's current life situation, it may become linked with earlier unresolved or partially resolved conflict.
7. The actual state of active disequilibrium, however, is time-limited, usually lasting up to four to six weeks.
8. Each particular class of crisis situation seems to follow a specific sequence of stages which can be predicted and mapped out.
9. During the unravelling of the crisis situation, the individual tends to be particularly amenable to help.
10. During the reintegration phase, new ego sets may emerge and new adaptive styles may evolve, enabling the person to cope more effectively with other situations in the future. However, if appropriate help is not available during the critical interval, inadequate or maladaptive patterns may be adopted which can result in weakened ability to function adequately later on.

(Extracted and modified from Golan, 1974: 500–501)

Put simply, a crisis reaction will involve shock, emotional responses and resolution in the reconstruction of a new equilibrium. Other than basic crisis theory, Janosik (1984, also cited in Gilliland and James, 1997) acknowledges that contemporary crisis intervention strategies are drawn from psychoanalytic theory, systems theory, adaptational theory and interpersonal theory. One major assumption of psychoanalytic theory is that early childhood fixation is the major reason for turning an event into a crisis, and this theory argues for the importance of gaining access to the unconscious and past emotional traumatic experiences to understand a person's crisis. Using systems theory may not only enable the helping professional to conceptualise the wider conflicting processes impinging on a specific circumstance but also to look at the crisis event in the total social and environmental settings (Haley, 1976; O'Hagan, 1986; Cormier and Hackney, 1987; Parker, 1992). With reference to adaptational theory, both maladaptive behaviours and adaptive behaviours are learned, and when applied to crisis work, the person in crisis should be encouraged to replace maladjusted functioning such as negative thoughts and destructive defence mechanisms with new, self-enhancing ones by reinforcing their successful experiences (Gilliland and James, 1997). Finally, interpersonal theory (Rogers, 1977) places a great emphasis on the value of promoting a sense of internal control and enhancing the personal self-esteem of those who have lost confidence and are self-defeating as a consequence of experiencing acute crisis. This can be achieved by employing counselling techniques such as unconditional positive regard, empathy and genuineness in the helping process (Thorne, 1992; Howe, 1993). Thus crisis intervention is often regarded as an eclectic approach that generously comprises ideas and concepts from a number of psychological and developmental theories. Thompson (1991, 2011) is rightly critical of traditional crisis theory, not least for its dissociation from the structural factors of oppression and its reliance on clinical terms which serve to pathologise the individual experiencing trauma. A community oriented approach to the theory however enables a reappraisal of the crisis response to be made with due regard for the cultural values of a society, its belief systems and the socio-economic factors that might shape reactions. Cohen for instance draws attention to the experience of immigrant families in the United States in the aftermath of disaster (Cohen, 1990). Broader perspectives can be gained from 'community crises' which are considered in the second part of the chapter.

Process of crisis intervention

In the light of the basic assumptions of crisis theory and practice, two models conceptualise the process of crisis work. They are Caplan's three phases of crisis (1961) and Roberts' seven stages of working through crises (1990). Both appear to see crisis as having a structure which can be broken down into specific phases or stages for intervention. In practice, these phases are not clear-cut or mutually exclusive. Moreover, they are unlikely to proceed in a linear sequence. Nevertheless, the models provide a direction for social work practice and have particular relevance for intervention but their use requires practitioners' sensitivity and flexibility in relation to the actual crisis situations and individuals' responses to crises. Caplan's three distinct phases are:

1. the impact stage
2. the recoil stage
3. adjustment and adaptation

(1961, cited in Thompson, 1991, 2011)

Generally speaking, an onset or initial phase of a crisis is initiated when a hazardous event results in a state of confusion and disorientation from increased internal or external stress. During the impact phase the first and most important concern of a crisis worker is to attend to the immediate effect and perception of the crisis on an individual. This involves the person in crisis in defining the nature of problems openly and examining the detrimental effects of a crisis on himself or herself. Getting to grips with issues arising from the situation is one means of encouraging participation right at the beginning of the intervention process. Young (1983) provides a list of three main intervention activities in the impact phase, which are the management of heightened emotions, the restructuring of the crisis situation and the activation of coping responses. Given that the stage is usually short, these three activities may need to be addressed at the same time. Quick reactions and intense counselling work may also be required. The second phase of crisis intervention is called the recoil stage. It occurs when the individual attempts to use customary coping mechanisms to regain a state of equilibrium but these attempts to cope fail. As mentioned before, the experience of failure leads to a period of upset and disorganisation. Thompson (1991: 10) reports that 'physical symptoms can also feature at this stage of the crisis process, such as fatigue, headaches, stomach disorder'. The final phase of crisis intervention is adjustment and adaptation which is also a stage of 'breakthrough or breakdown' (Thompson, 1991, 2011) or a crisis integrative phase (Young, 1983). This phase is particularly important simply because it involves the individual and a practitioner working together to confront crises and evaluate these experiences or results of the actions which have been taken.

> *Basically, the integrative phase is concerned with accepting or assimilating the implications of the crisis into the individual's life. Integrative activities include working through:*
> * *Current issues which continue to appear and demand attention throughout the crisis resolution phase.*
> * *Past issues associated with the current crisis which have arisen and underlying past issues that are being reawakened.*
> * *Implementing the decisions and actions initiated in the restructuring process.*
> (Young, 1983: 42)

Once new coping mechanisms have been developed, the crisis has been resolved and normal functioning is resumed. However, the pace of integrative work should take into account a number of factors such as the individual's readiness and motivation, and the availability of both tangible and intangible resources. Termination needs to be dealt with explicitly, and an evaluation is very useful in consolidating the gains of crisis intervention, reinforcing the experience of handling crises and discussing how this experience can be transferable into the future. Further to Caplan's model, Roberts' (1990) seven stages of crisis intervention are also of practical use when working with individuals who have experienced accidental crisis. The stages are:

1. Assessing lethality and safety needs which aims to tease out the perception and meaning of crisis on an individual.
2. Establishing rapport and communication by showing acceptance of and genuine respect for those who receive help.
3. Identifying the major problems or the precipitating events and old ineffective coping methods that cause intense emotion and distress.
4. Dealing with feelings and providing support by active listening and facilitation of expression in a safe environment which is conducive to self-disclosure.
5. Exploring possible alternatives by examining the past, less adaptive responses to the crisis events and defining what are more adaptive coping behaviours to resolve them.
6. Formulating an action plan by restoring cognitive functioning and giving positive reinforcement for the willingness to face problems and commitment.
7. Providing follow-up by making referrals or informing of the availability of crisis work in the future.

(Roberts, 1990; 1991)

Among the limitations of crisis intervention (Payne, 2005; Thompson, 1991, 2011; Kanel, 2007) it should be noted that the response of different ethnic groups to the crisis event will be culturally determined. For example in Chinese philosophy excessive emotions are considered harmful to the balance of Yin and Yang causing poor health. In this context an individual would habitually suppress their emotions in the onset phase at the optimal point for intervention, and thereby mask the true nature of the crisis. Nevertheless the framework can be employed effectively to relieve emotional distress and offset stress-related disorders in the long term. Walsh (2006: 294) concludes that 'the process of assessment and planning in crisis intervention will become more appropriately client centred as social workers develop broader guidelines for understanding the crisis experiences of different cultural groups'.

Crisis intervention, social work and disaster recovery

Sadly the 'decade of disasters' that charted the end of the 20th century in Britain has been eclipsed by international events heralded by the destruction of the twin towers of the World Trade Centre – '9/11' – in 2001. The intervening decade has been marked by both man-made and natural disasters: Bali, Madrid and London terrorist bombings in 2002, 2004 and 2005, the Asian Tsunami of 2004, Hurricane Katrina that took an estimated 1,836 lives in Louisiana in 2005, the 2008 Sichuan earthquake in China, earthquakes in Chile and Haiti in 2010, and the earthquake and tsunami in Japan in March 2011. Conflict associated with major civilian casualties, displacement and migration of populations (Sudan, Iraq, Afghanistan) must also feature in this litany. In the light of these events local authorities across the globe now plan for the impact of 'catastrophic incidents' on their own nationals, alongside preparation for local emergencies (Muma and Jokinen, 2008; Devon County Council, 2011). Likewise national government responses to disasters occurring overseas parallel the measures implemented by local governments dealing with domestic incidents (Murray, 2003). However, The National Audit Office (2006) review of the experiences of UK nationals affected by the Asian Tsunami identified variable and inconsistent support and information for survivors seeking repatriation, or relatives desperate for news (Bisson *et al*. 2011). What has emerged from all of these emergencies is the recognition that an immediate, co-ordinated and humane response is vital.

Whilst not in the same league as the floods and loss of life in countries such as Pakistan in 2010 and again in 2011, communities in the UK have also withstood local emergencies caused by flooding (Boscastle in 2004, Hull and Evesham in 2007, Cockermouth in 2009). As well as climatic hazards and extreme weather conditions caused by snow and ice, local councils now routinely address incidents such as major gas leaks and explosions, fire, chemical spills and oil pollution off the coast, diseases in livestock notably foot-and-mouth disease and swine flu (Devon County Council, 2011). Following a devastating series of disasters that included the Hillsborough stadium tragedy and the Lockerbie plane bombing, the Allen Report (Allen, 1991) recommended that social services departments should be the lead agency in the welfare response with designated roles and responsibilities for other local authority agencies and voluntary organisations. The report recommended a holistic, coordinated and proactive approach to emergency planning through the creation of welfare-related plans and protocols, as well as the activation of a range of support services after the crisis event. At a time when public sector cuts are placing local government under extreme financial pressure the capacity to respond even to the day-to-day needs of local populations is undermined (see Chapter 1). It is questionable, therefore, whether resources will always be available to plan and train for disaster recovery – that event which may never happen. Similarly the contribution of social workers has been scrutinised in terms of their training and ability to respond to trauma and grief (Murray, 2003). In the context of such debates this section of the chapter charts the themes and developments that characterise a decade of crisis intervention in the wake of disaster. It surveys the role of social workers in national and international arenas. The argument is made that social workers can, and do make a significant contribution to crisis intervention and disaster recovery. As state controlled services fail to deliver and communities have to find their own solutions (Ferguson and Lavalette, 2006), we maintain that the profession of social work is well-placed to support the individuals, groups and communities caught up in the catastrophes and emergencies that are a fact of life in the new millennium.

Community resilience

Roberts asserts that 'crisis intervention has become the most widely used time-limited treatment modality in the world' (2005: 6). Since the last edition of this book crisis intervention for disaster recovery has changed considerably and has become increasingly sophisticated. The Civil Contingencies Act 2004 provides a comprehensive framework for emergency planning and civil protection in the UK, replacing Civil Defence regulations. As 'Category One' responders, local authorities are required to assess the risk of an emergency occurring and to prepare emergency plans. The Act incorporates a wide-ranging definition of emergency as any event or situation which presents a serious threat to human welfare or the environment, and 'war or terrorism which threatens serious damage to the security of the United Kingdom' (*Great Britain Civil Contingencies Act* 2004). New terminology populates planning and preparation guidance, epitomised by 'capabilities' (a military term denoting the capacity to respond to and recover from a particular threat or hazard) and 'resilience'. There is considerable emphasis on community preparedness and resilience. Local resilience forums are a requirement of the 2004 Act, comprising representatives from 'blue-light' emergency services, local authorities, the health service, environment agency and other partners. As well as dealing with the aftermath of an emergency, the task of these forums is to ensure that all services and organisations work together to establish and maintain effective multi-agency plans. The government's view of community resilience is that it is 'about communities and individuals harnessing local resources and expertise to help themselves in an emergency, in a way that complements the response of the emergency services' (Cabinet Office, 2011: 4). Community resilience is a familiar concept to social workers (Chapter 11; Whelan *et al.*, 2002; Norris *et al.*, 2008) and introduces another dimension to crisis intervention. Rowlands (2007) asserts that strengthening and building resilience is key to effective social work responses in disaster situations. Following Hurricane Katrina, for example, the Red Cross model of establishing shelters, described by McCulloch, provided social workers with the opportunity to facilitate community organisation:

> *It turned out that all the shelters were requesting social workers exclusively. Social workers were considered to be most useful to shelter staff and evacuees because we knew how to negotiate systems and work with people effectively.*

(McCulloch, 2011: 149)

Social workers also played a similar, vital role during, and after the terrorist attacks in New York (Gillen, 2003). A pre-emptive approach to disaster mitigation through community work is suggested by Mathbor (2007). Strengthening social capital and building capacity at a local level are regarded as crucial processes for developing community resilience. Adopting the principles of radical social work, Pentaraki (2011) advocates community-based models of social work to promote community organisation and development post-disaster in collaboration with grassroots action groups.

Working at the macro-level

These writers contribute to a burgeoning literature that identifies the profession's ability to work at 'micro' and 'macro' levels in crisis situations (Marlowe, 2009; Thompson, 2011). It is now widely recognised that social inequalities and injustice are exposed by crisis events (Mathbor, 2007; Priestley and Hemingway, 2007). Dominelli (2010) argues that poverty must be acknowledged as the greatest human-made form of disaster. Poorer coastal communities have certainly experienced the worst effects of recent earthquakes and tsunamis, for example (Shaw and Goda, 2004; Busaspathumrong, 2007) and there is a close correlation between disasters, poverty and the environment. The vulnerability of people in the margins of society is compounded by the exploitation of environmental resources and unplanned urbanisation in dangerous locations such as unstable slopes and flood plains. The 'urbanisation' of disasters will be inevitable as urban populations grow at an unprecedented rate.

> *More than 1 billion people today live in appalling conditions in urban areas and their numbers are growing. And it is mostly this population – whose basic needs are not always provided for – that is at most risk from cyclones, floods, earthquakes, infectious diseases, crime, fires, and transport and industrial accidents.*

(International Federation of Red Cross and Red Crescent Societies, 2010: 11)

Disaster risk will also increase with the impact of climate change, not least due to weather and climatic hazards, environmental degradation, reductions in water and food availability (UN International Strategy for Disaster Reduction, 2008).

Again communities whose resources are already depleted by poverty and unemployment experience its impact most keenly. Incorporating macro perspectives into the theory and practice of crisis intervention is essential for social work, therefore, in the pursuit of social justice for communities affected by disaster (National Association of Social Workers, 2011; Thompson, 2011). A sinister development at the macro level is that of 'disaster capitalism', exposed by the work of Naomi Klein who speaks of the 'ranking of life' in the capitalist project whereby 'race and money buy survival' in disasters (Klein, 2007). Lavalette and Ioakimidis (2011) temper Klein's argument effectively with examples of how communities have resisted attempts by corporate elites to exploit disaster situations. Nevertheless crisis-oriented social work at this level must be vigilant alongside communities against 'social shocks', a term employed by Klein (2007, cited in Lavalette and Ioakimidis, 2011). Land grabs by property developers displacing local villagers in post-tsunami Sri Lanka illustrate how governments can be duplicitous in allowing social shocks to occur (Leckie, 2005).

The acknowledgement that post-disaster responses can compound and exacerbate the problems confronting individuals and their communities represents another theme in the literature. Rowlands quotes Ife in warning of the 're-emergence of colonialist attitudes' that can accompany 'expert' help from outside and undermine the capacities of local communities to support themselves (Ife, cited in Rowlands, 2007: 119). This is reflected in the experiences of Irene Fraser in Sri Lanka who commented that 'post-tsunami life seemed like a corporate take-over' due to the influx of international aid agencies and 'emergency experts' (Fraser, 2005: 40). Coordinating organisations to *respect* community capacities and strengths is a significant task of relief work. Developing this theme, in his critique of trauma-focused treatment perspectives for people who are refugees Marlowe describes how problems of resettlement, especially unjust social policies and social disadvantage, can cause more psychological distress than the initial experiences of fleeing war and persecution (Marlowe, 2009). Again westernised models of psychosocial support are often privileged over social networks, indigenous forms of healing and the resilience of people who have lived through trauma. Working in crisis situations, such as those brought about by armed conflict, has caused relief agencies represented by the Sphere Project to recognise this potential for disaster response to sometimes have adverse, rather than mitigating consequences:

> In collaboration with affected communities and authorities, we aim to minimise any negative effects of humanitarian action on the local community or on the environment.
> (The Sphere Project, 2011)

Sphere reports that there is 'a growing conceptual and operational focus on local and national responses with the awareness that affected populations must be consulted' (The Sphere Project, 2011). An important feature of both disaster preparedness and crisis intervention must include an acknowledgement of the natural strengths of the individuals and communities affected by the event (Rowlands, 2007; Saleebey, 2008). Collaboration and partnership are features of successful crisis intervention with individuals and their communities (Teater, 2010; Thompson, 2011).

Human rights

The International Red Cross and Red Crescent Movement together with other non-governmental organisations established the Sphere Project in 1997. Its aim is to provide minimum standards for humanitarian assistance in response to disasters and to improve accountability for aid. The phrase 'humanitarian aid' or assistance has gained prominence in international crisis work to denote intervention that has a firm foundation in human rights. As noted earlier, human rights violations can occur following natural disasters due to the forced relocation of communities with loss of ownership of land and property, discrimination in the provision of aid and access to support. Other forms of infringement are 'sexual and gender-based violence; loss of documentation; unsafe or involuntary return or resettlement' (UN Inter-Agency Standing Committee, 2006). Without a rights-based response, natural hazards can quickly become socially created human disasters that impact disproportionately on socially excluded groups. Priestley and Hemingway (2007), for example, draw parallels with the social model of disability to reveal how post-disaster, disabled people may be doubly disadvantaged due to the loss of independence and even destitution as networks of support break down and care-givers are lost. They observe that when resources are scarce, disability may be viewed negatively and lead to further exclusion even when the impairment is newly acquired due to the hazardous event itself. This is recognised in the UK where emergency plans must consider the welfare of 'vulnerable people' known to the local authority as part of disaster preparedness. People who are deemed to be vulnerable or isolated should be contacted during an emergency to see if they need assistance. The term 'vulnerable' is challenged, however, by a concern for human rights that focuses disaster preparedness on 'disabled people's resilience and agency in mobilising personal resources or social networks', rather than victimhood (Priestley and Hemingway, 2007: 35). It has been argued that in the UK a rights-based approach increasingly characterises support for people affected by disasters (Eyre, 2003). Emergency plans must comply with domestic equality legislation to ensure that no-one with 'protected characteristics' under the Equality Act 2010 is discriminated against or further disadvantaged by actions taken post-disaster. Responders must respect individuals' human rights. The discourse of rights is not reflected in government guidance, however, which simply defines humanitarian assistance as:

> Those activities aimed at addressing the needs of people affected by emergencies; the provision of psychological and social aftercare and support in the short, medium and long term.

(Department of Culture, Media and Sport, 2011.13)

Nevertheless it is acknowledged that a number of public inquiry reports in the UK, not least the MacPherson report on the murder of Stephen Lawrence in 1999 and the inquiry into the Ladbroke Grove rail disaster in 2000, have had a significant influence in promoting a rights-based approach, in association with the Human Rights Act 1998.

Social work and disaster recovery

Crisis intervention can be related to the cycle of stages that occur during a disaster. Prior to impact, the emphasis is on community preparedness, mitigation and prevention, as noted earlier, to build disaster-resilient communities. Secondly, the time during the impact when the disaster strikes is shaped by immediate relief and disaster responses. Post impact refers to the period immediately after the event prior to the beginning of recovery. Recovery and reconstruction follow with disaster survivors working toward restoration of their pre-disaster state. Finally future risk reduction and prevention should complete the cycle. Emotional responses to disaster, comparable with a staged model of loss, include 'heroism' characterised by altruism to ensure the immediate survival of self and others, followed by the 'honeymoon' phase that draws together people with a shared understanding who experienced the disaster. Disillusionment may then occur as media interest wanes along with the sense of community engendered among survivors, and the crisis agencies withdraw. Criticism of crisis responses, blaming and scapegoating represent attempts to gain control in this phase. Recovery and reconstruction are assisted by rebuilding, memorial events and anniversaries (American Red Cross, 1992, 1993, cited in NASW, 2011). Building on understanding of these psycho-emotional factors, in the aftermath of '9/11' Roberts developed the ACT model of crisis intervention. He offers a three-stage framework of Assessment, Crisis Intervention and Trauma Treatment, while acknowledging that like similar stage theories and methods, it should be applied flexibly rather than as a rigid linear sequence (Roberts, 2002). The ACT model integrates assessment methods and tools with Roberts' seven stages of crisis intervention outlined above, and a ten-step protocol for acute traumatic stress management (ATSM) developed by Lerner and Shelton (2001). The latter refer to traumatic stress as 'a normal reaction to an abnormal event' in order to distinguish it from post-traumatic stress disorder. They describe the stages of ATSM as follows:

1. **Assess the situation for danger** towards self and others with a view to moving people away from a dangerous location and avoiding further exposure to trauma.
2. **Consider the mechanism of injury**, how people may have been affected physically, and/or emotionally through witnessing gruesome incidents, for example.

3. **Evaluate the level of responsiveness** of the individual who may be exhibiting the symptoms of 'emotional' shock and failing to respond to what has occurred. It is important to recognise that lack of responsiveness may be an adaptive process to cushion the individual from the true nature of the disaster.
4. **Address medical needs** and ensure that treatment is provided by trained emergency medical responders wherever possible.
5. **Observe and identify** people who have experienced or witnessed the event for signs of emotional or traumatic stress. There may be individuals who experience emotional stress simply as a result of exposure to someone who has been directly affected.
6. **Connect with the individual** by introducing yourself and clarifying your role. Build rapport through simple questions such as 'How are you doing?' and non-verbal communication.
7. **Ground the individual** by reviewing the facts of what has occurred and encouraging the person to talk about how they experienced the event, including physiological and behavioural responses. Lerner and Shelton (2001) advise that this process can disrupt 'negative cognitive rehearsal' or repetitive thoughts about the event that might be harmful. If it is possible, reassure the person that they are safe now.
8. **Provide support** using empathic listening skills to understand and convey respect for the individual's thoughts and feelings. Strive to understand their perceptions of the traumatic event.
9. **Normalise the response** by validating the person's experience and helping them to understand how people typically respond in these circumstances. Many organisations such as Disaster Action and local authorities in the UK provide information about common emotional responses to crisis events to reassure those affected that their reactions are to be expected.
10. **Prepare for the Future** by reviewing what has occurred, 'bringing the person to the present', talking about events that may occur in the future, and making referrals to available resources as needed.

(Lerner and Shelton, 2001)

Roberts' integrative model emphasises the importance of assessment combined with a strengths approach in determining treatment planning and decision-making for the individual in a crisis state (Roberts, 2002). Most people are resilient and do recover from a traumatic event through their own resources. While urgent medical needs and physical safety must be prioritised, however, it is argued that for some, crisis intervention to address the psychological effects of a disaster can prevent acute traumatic stress reactions from developing into a longer-term stress disorder. Critical incident stress debriefing sessions for groups of those affected by the crisis are advocated by some services, typically within 72 hours of the event occurring (Muma and Jokinen, 2008; Morrison, 2007). Criticisms levelled at this method, however, are that warning people of emotional reactions they might expect may increase the likelihood of those symptoms occurring. Moreover, a focus on psychological issues and counselling may divert individuals from mobilising their own social networks and the resources of faith communities, for example (Marlowe, 2009). Crisis intervention should be characterised, therefore, by culturally sensitive support.

Conclusion

The substantial body of literature identified at the beginning of this chapter testifies to the rapid development of crisis intervention skills and knowledge in recent decades. Planning for disaster has precipitated the growth of effective inter-agency co-operation and training. From such levels of co-operation developments might be usefully extended to other arenas where multidisciplinary practice is essential to service delivery. Within this framework social work is well placed to contribute to progress. Just one example where social work has much to offer is that of relationships. By virtue of the magnitude of the event and needs of those involved, relationships between survivors or victims and workers differ in terms of intensity and duration from those proscribed by conventional professional boundaries. A relation-based approach might be regarded as a particular attribute of professional practice in this context (Ruch et al., 2010). With regard to the development of the theoretical model, community work described in Chapter 11 and anti-oppressive practice can inform the understanding of crisis in relation to community. Indeed in the context of globalisation and technical advancement a broader analysis of crisis must provide the focus for intervention. Both the Lockerbie disaster and the terrorist attacks in America illustrate the way in which the communities of several countries are suddenly linked by just one event. It is expedient therefore that social work has a responsibility to promote its considerable expertise and skills in the practice of crisis intervention and to engage with other professions in the relief of emotional distress following a disaster.

References

Aguilera, D.C. and Messick, J.M. (1982) *Crisis Intervention: Theory and Methodology.* (4th edn.) St Louis, MS: C.V. Mosby.

Allen, A.J. (1991) *Disasters: Planning for a Caring Response – Report of the Disasters Working Party.* London: HMSO.

Bard, M. and Ellison, K. (1974) Crisis Intervention and Investigation of Forcible Rape. *The Police Chief,* 41(May): 68–73.

Belkin, G.S. (1984) *Introduction to Counseling.* (2nd edn.) Dubuque, IA: William C. Brown.

Berman, L.E. (1978) Sibling Loss as an Organiser of Unconscious Guilt: A Case Study. *Psychoanalytic Quarterly,* 47: 565–587.

Bisson, J.I., Lewis, C., Howlett, M., Corallo, D., Davies, E. and Norris, V. (2011) Perceived Support and Psychological Outcome Following the 2004 Tsunami: A Mixed Methods Study. *The Psychiatrist*, 35: 283–288.

Burgess, A.W. and Baldwin, B.A. (1981) *Crisis Intervention Theory and Practice: A Clinical Handbook.* Englewood Cliffs, NJ: Prentice-Hall.

Burgess, A.W. and Roberts, A.R. (2005) Crisis Intervention for Persons Diagnosed with Clinical Disorders Based on the Stress-crisis Continuum. In Roberts, A.R. (Ed.) *Crisis Intervention Handbook: Assessment, Treatment and Research.* (3rd edn.) New York: Oxford University Press.

Busaspathumrong, P. (2007) The Role of Social Workers and Social Service Delivery During Crisis Intervention for Tsunami Survivors. *Journal of Social Work in Disability and Rehabilitation*, 5: 3–4, 127–137.

Butler, B. and Elliott, D. (1985) *Teaching and Learning for Practice.* Aldershot, Hants: Gower.

Cabinet Office (2011) *Strategic National Framework on Community Resilience.* http://www.cabinetoffice.gov.uk/content/community-resilience Accessed Oct 2011.

Calhoun, L.G., Selby, W. and King, H.E. (1976) *Dealing with Crisis: A Guide to Critical Life Problems.* Englewood Cliffs, NJ: Prentice-Hall.

Caplan, G. (1961) *An Approach to Community Mental Health.* New York: Grune and Stratton.

Caplan, G. (1964) *Principles of Preventive Psychiatry.* New York: Basic Books.

Carkhuff, R.R. (1969) *Helping and Human Relations: A Primer for Lay and Professional Helpers* (Vol. 2). New York: Holt, Rinehart and Winston.

Cocores, J.A. and Gold, M.S. (1990) Recognition and Crisis Intervention Treatment with Cocaine Abusers: The Fair Oaks Hospital Model. In Roberts, A.R. (Ed.) *Crisis Intervention Handbook: Assessment, Treatment and Research.* Belmont, CA: Wadsworth.

Cohen, L.H. and Nelson, D.W. (1983) Crisis Intervention: An Overview of Theory and Technique. In Cohen, L.H., Claiborn, W.L. and Specter, G.A. (Eds.) *Crisis Intervention.* (2nd edn.) New York: Human Sciences Press.

Cohen, R.E. (1990) Post-disaster Mobilisation and Crisis Counseling: Guidelines and Techniques for Developing Crisis-oriented Services for Disaster Victims. In Roberts, A.R. (ed.) *Crisis Intervention Handbook: Assessment, Treatment and Research.* Belmont, CA: Wadsworth.

Cormier, L.S. and Hackney, H. (1987) *The Professional Counselor: A Process Guide to Helping.* Englewood Cliffs, NJ: Prentice-Hall.

Coulshed, V. and Orme, J. (1998) *Social Work Practice.* (3rd edn.) London: Macmillan.

Department for Culture, Media and Sport (2011) *Humanitarian Assistance Strategic Guidance. Building capability to look after people affected by emergencies.* London: Cabinet Office.

Devon County Council (2011) *LRF Combined Agencies Emergency Response Protocol.* http://www.devon.gov.uk/caerp_v6.0_05.03.11_-2.pdf Accessed Oct 2011.

Dominelli, L. (2010) *Social Work in a Globalizing World.* Cambridge: Polity Press.

Erikson, E. (1977) *Childhood and Society.* London: Fontana.

Ewing, C.P. (1978) *Crisis Intervention as Psychotherapy.* New York: Oxford University Press.

Eyre, A. (2003) Disaster Survivors and Bereaved Are Being Listened to Better. *Society Guardian*, 6 March.

Ferguson, I. and Lavalette, M. (2006) Globalisation and Global Justice: Towards a Social Work of Resistance. *International Social Work*, 49: 3, 309–318.

Fraser, I. (2005) Small Fish Trampled in Post-Tsunami Stampede. *Forced Migration Review*, 39–40.

Gillen, S. (2003) New York State of Mind. *Community Care*, 11 September.

Gilliland, B.E. and James, R.K. (1997) *Crisis Intervention Strategies.* (3rd edn.) Pacific Grove, CA: Brooks/Cole.

Golan, N. (1974) Crisis Theory. In Turner, F.J. (Ed.) *Social Work Treatment: Interlocking Theoretical Approaches.* New York: The Free Press.

Golan, N. (1978) *Treatment in Crisis Situations.* London: Free Press.

Great Britain Civil Contingencies Act 2004: Elizabeth II. Chapter 36 (2004) London: HMSO.

Haley, J. (1976) *Problem-solving Therapy.* New York: McGraw-Hill.

Hess, H.J. and Ruster, P.L. (1990) Assessment and Crisis Intervention with Clients in a Hospital Emergency Room. In Roberts, A.R. (Ed.) *Crisis Intervention Handbook: Assessment, Treatment and Research.* Belmont. CA: Wadsworth.

Hillman, J.L. (2002) *Crisis Intervention and Trauma: New Approaches to Evidence-based Practice.* New York: Kluwer.

Hoff, L.A. (1995) *People in Crisis: Understanding and Helping.* (4th edn.) San Francisco: Jossey-Bass.

Howe, D. (1993) *On being a Client: Understanding the Process of Counselling and Psychotherapy.* London: Sage.

International Federation of Red Cross and Red Crescent Societies (IFRC) (2010) *World Disasters Report.* http://www.ifrc.org/en/publications-and-reports/world-disasters-report/ Accessed Oct 2011.

Janosik, E.H. (1984) *Crisis Counseling: A Contemporary Approach*. Monterey, CA: Wadsworth Health Sciences Division.

Jobes, D.A., Berman, A.L. and Martin, C.E. (2005) Adolescent Suicidality and Crisis Intervention. In Roberts, A.R. (Ed.) *Crisis Intervention Handbook: Assessment, Treatment and Research.* (3rd edn.) New York: Oxford University Press.

Johnson, R. (1979) Recognising People in Crisis. In Robinson, J. (Ed.) *Using Crisis Intervention Wisely.* Horsham, PA: International Communications.

Kanel, K. (2007) *A Guide to Crisis Intervention.* (3rd edn.) Belmont, CA: Thomson Brooks/Cole.

Kilpatrick, D.G. and Veronen, L.J. (1983) Treatment for Rape-related Problems: Crisis Intervention is not Enough. In Cohen, L.H., Claiborn, W.L. and Specter, G.A. (Eds.) *Crisis Intervention.* (2nd edn.) New York: Human Sciences Press.

Klein, N. (2007) *The Shock Doctrine: The Rise of Disaster Capitalism.* London: Allen Lane.

Lavalette, M. and Ioakimidis, V. (Eds.) (2011) *Social Work in Extremis. Lessons for Social Work Internationally.* Bristol: The Policy Press.

Langsley, D.G., Pittman, F.S., Machotka, P. and Flomenhaft, K. (1968) Family Crisis Therapy: Results and Implications. *Family Process*, 7: 753–759.

Leckie, S. (2005) The Great Land Theft. *Forced Migration Review*, 15–16.

Lerner, M.D. and Shelton, R.D. (2001) *Acute Traumatic Stress Management*, New York: The American Academy of Experts in Traumatic Stress.

Lewis, R., Walker, B.A. and Mehr, M. (1990) Counseling with Adolescent Suicidal Clients and their Families. In Roberts, A.R. (Ed.) *Crisis Intervention Handbook: Assessment, Treatment and Research.* Belmont, CA: Wadsworth.

Lindemann, E. (1965) Symptomatology and Management of Acute Grief. In Parad, H.J. (Ed.) *Crisis Intervention: Selected Readings.* New York: Family Service Association of America.

Marlowe, J. (2009) Conceptualising Refugee Resettlement in Contested Landscapes. *The Australasian Review of African Studies*, 30: 2, 128–151.

Marshall, M. (Ed.) (1990) *Working with Dementia.* Birmingham: Venture Press.

Mathbor, G.M. (2007) Enhancement of Community Preparedness For Natural Disasters: The Role of Social Work in Building Social Capital For Sustainable Disaster Relief and Management. *International Social Work*, 50: 3, 357–369.

McConville, B.J. (1990) Assessment, Crisis Intervention, and Time-limited Cognitive Therapy with Children and Adolescents Grieving the Loss of a Loved One. In Roberts, A.R. (Ed.) *Crisis Intervention Handbook: Assessment, Treatment and Research.* Belmont, CA: Wadsworth.

McCulloch, M.S. (2011) Worker's Eye View of Neoliberalism and Hurricane Katrina. In Lavalette, M. and Ioakimidis, V. (Eds.) *Social Work in Extremis. Lessons for Social Work Internationally.* Bristol: The Policy Press.

Mitchell, R. (1993) *Crisis Intervention in Practice.* Aldershot: Avebury.

Monach, J. and Monach, J. (1993) Crisis Intervention: No Panacea: A Voluntary Organisation Perspective. *Practice*, 6: 3, 181–192.

Morrison, J.Q. (2007) Social Validity of the Critical Incident Stress Management Model for School-based Crisis Intervention. *Psychology in the Schools*, 44: 8, 765–777.

Muma, P. and Jokinen, A. (2008) Crisis Intervention in Finland. *Bereavement Care*, 27: 1, 10–12.

Murray, R. (2003) We Need a Register of People Who Can Help Support The Bereaved. *Society Guardian*, 2 March.

National Association of Social Workers (NASW) *Policy statement: Disaster.* http://www.socialworkers.org/pressroom/events/911/disasters.asp Accessed Oct 2011.

National Audit Office, assisted by the Zito Trust (2006) *Review of the Experiences of United Kingdom Nationals Affected by the Indian Ocean Tsunami.* London: National Audit Office.

Norris, F.H., Stevens, S.P., Pfefferbaum, B., Wyche, K.F. and Pfefferbaum, R.L. (2008) Community Resilience as a Metaphor, Theory, Set of Capacities, and Strategy for Disaster Readiness. *American Journal of Community Psychology*, 41: 127–150.

O'Hagan, K. (1986) *Crisis Intervention in Social Services.* London: Macmillan.

Parad, H.J. (Ed.) (1965) *Crisis Intervention: Selected Readings.* New York: Family Service Association of America.

Parker, J. (1992) Crisis Intervention: A Framework for Social Work with People with Dementia and their Carers. *The Journal of Care and Practice*, 1: 4, 43–57.

Payne, M. (2005) *Modern Social Work Theory.* (3rd edn.) Basingstoke: Palgrave Macmillan.

Pentaraki, M. (2011) Grassroots Community Organising in a Post-Disaster Context: Lessons For Social Work Education From Ilias, Greece. In Lavalette, M. and Ioakimidis, V. (Eds.) *Social Work in Extremis. Lessons for Social Work Internationally.* Bristol: The Policy Press.

Petretic-Jackson, P. and Jackson, T. (1990) Assessment and Crisis Intervention with Rape and Incest Victims: Strategies, Techniques and Case Illustrations. In Roberts, A.R. (Ed.) *Crisis Intervention Handbook: Assessment, Treatment and Research.* Belmont, CA: Wadsworth.

Priestley, M. and Hemingway, L. (2007) Disability and Disaster Recovery. A Tale of Two Cities? *Journal of Social Work in Disability & Rehabilitation*, 5: 3–4, 23–42.

Rapoport, L. (1970) Crisis Intervention as a Mode of Treatment. In Roberts, R.W. and Nee, R.H. (Eds.) *Theories of Social Casework.* Chicago: University of Chicago Press.

Roberts, A.R. (1990) An Overview of Crisis Theory and Crisis Intervention. In Roberts, A.R. (Ed.) *Crisis Intervention Handbook: Assessment, Treatment and Research.* Belmont, CA: Wadsworth.

Roberts, A.R. (Ed.) (1991) *Contemporary Perspectives on Crisis Intervention and Prevention*. Englewood Cliffs, NJ: Prentice-Hall.

Roberts, A.R. (2002) Assessment, Crisis Intervention and Trauma Treatment: the Integrative ACT Intervention Model. *Brief Treatment and Crisis intervention*, 2: 1, 1–21.

Roberts, A.R. (Ed.) (2005) *Crisis Intervention Handbook: Assessment, Treatment, and Research.* (3rd edn.) New York: Oxford University Press.

Roberts, A.R. and Roberts, B.S. (2005) A Comprehensive Model for Crisis Intervention with Battered Women and their Children. In Roberts, A.R. (Ed.) *Crisis Intervention Handbook: Assessment, Treatment and Research.* (3rd edn.) New York: Oxford University Press.

Roberts, A.R. and Dziegielewski, S.F. (1995) Foundation Skills and Applications of Crisis Intervention and Cognitive Therapy. In Roberts, A.R. (Ed.) *Crisis Intervention and Time-limited Cognitive Treatment.* Thousand Oaks, CA: Sage.

Robinson, J. (Ed.) (1979) *Using Crisis Intervention Wisely.* Horsham, PA: International Communications.

Rogers, C.R. (1977) *Carl Rogers on Personal Power: Inner Strength and its Revolutionary Impact.* New York: Delacorte.

Rowlands, A. (2007) Training for Disaster Recovery. *Journal of Social Work in Disability & Rehabilitation*, 5: 3–4, 109–126.

Ruch, G., Turney, D. and Ward, A. (2010) *Relationship-based Social Work: Getting to the Heart of Practice.* London: Jessica Kingsley.

Saleebey, D. (2008) *The Strengths Perspective in Social Work Practice.* (5th edn.) Harlow: Pearson Education.

Sebolt, N. (1972) Crisis Intervention and its Demands on the Crisis Therapist. In Specter, G.A. and Claiborn, W.L. (Eds.) *Crisis Intervention.* New York: Behavioral Publications.

Sharer, P.S. (1979) Supporting Survivors of Unexpected Death. In Robinson, J. (Ed.) *Using Crisis Intervention Wisely.* Horsham, PA: International Communications.

Shaw, R. and Goda, K. (2004) From Disaster to Sustainable Civil Society: The Kobe Experience. *Disasters*, 28: 1, 16–40.

Shneidman, E. (1972) Crisis Intervention: Some Thoughts and Perspectives. In Specter, G.A. and Claiborn, W.L. (Eds.) *Crisis Intervention.* New York: Behavioral Publications.

Smith, C.R. (1982) *Social Work with the Dying and Bereaved.* London: Macmillan.

Specter, G.A. and Claiborn, W.L. (Eds.) (1972) *Crisis Intervention.* New York: Behavioral Publications.

Stephen, M. and Woolfe, R. (1982) *Coping in Crisis: Understanding and Helping People in Need.* London: Harper and Row.

Teater, B. (2010) *An Introduction to Applying Social Work Theories and Methods.* Maidenhead: Open University Press.

The Sphere Project (2011) *Humanitarian Charter and Minimum Standards in Humanitarian Response.* http://www.sphereproject.org/ Accessed Oct 2011.

Thompson, N. (1991) *Crisis Intervention Revisited.* Birmingham: PEPAR Publications.

Thompson, N. (2011) *Crisis Intervention.* Lyme Regis: Russell House Publishing.

Thorne, B. (1992) *Carl Rogers.* London: Sage.

Umana, M.S., Gross, S.J. and McConville, M.T. (1980) *Crisis in the Family: Three Approaches.* New York: Gardner.

UN Inter-Agency Standing Committee (2006) *Protecting Persons Affected by Natural Disasters: IASC Operational Guidelines on Human Rights and Natural Disasters.* Washington: Brookings-Bern Project on Internal Displacement.

UN International Strategy for Disaster Reduction (2008) *Briefing Note 01 – Climate Change and Disaster Risk Reduction.* Geneva: UN ISDR.

Walsh, J. (2006) *Theories for Direct Social Work Practice.* Belmont, CA: Brooks/Cole.

Warner, C.G. (1979) Comforting and Caring for the Rape Victim. In Robinson, J. (Ed.) *Using Crisis Intervention Wisely.* Horsham, PA: International Communications.

Whelan, J., Swallow, M., Peschar, P. and Dunne, A. (2002) From Counselling to Community Work: Developing a Framework For Social Work Practice With Displaced Persons. *Australian Social Work*, 55: 1, 13–33.

Young, K.P.H. (1983) *Coping in Crisis.* Hong Kong: Hong Kong University Press.

Chapter 7

Task-Centred Practice in Challenging Times

Peter Ford and Karen Postle

Introduction

The first part of this chapter comprises an outline of the rationale for and operation of task-centred practice. The chapter then discusses factors which could hinder staff from effectively undertaking task-centred practice. It draws on research undertaken by one of the authors (Postle, 1999), which, while dated, nonetheless remains relevant to the current context of heavily bureaucratised practice in work with both children and adults. This research is also generalisable to all fields of practice beyond solely its focus of work with older people. Where it is not possible to refer to the people with whom social workers work simply as 'people', we have usually termed them 'clients'. This term, while acknowledged as problematic, we see as no less so than terms such as 'user', 'consumer' or 'customer'.

Perhaps one reason for the enduring popularity of task-centred practice amongst social workers is that, unlike several other practice models, it was developed within and for social work, originating from research into social work practice. It is also one of the major contributions made by the profession and academic discipline of social work to all those who use their interpersonal skills to help others resolve problems, and its elements are widely used (frequently without acknowledgement) in areas ranging from counselling to education. It is a model of practice that not only derives from research, but lends itself to research, insofar as it embodies the setting of goals whose achievement is easily measured. Consequently the model has been developed and refined through numerous empirical studies in the past forty years.

Task-centred practice is consistent with social work values, in that it has the potential to be person-centred and empowering. However, in our experience, it may not always be fully understood and in consequence can be misused; we have fairly frequently encountered social work students describing instances where they have told people what to do, without negotiating, as 'using the task-centred approach'. This can even include insisting that something happens as a condition of specific social work action (such as a child not being taken into care).

Used appropriately, task-centred practice is essentially a clear and practical model that can be adapted for use in a wide range of situations. Its two most important characteristics are that it is focussed on *problem-solving*, and that it is *short-term* and *time-limited*. These characteristics help to define the situations in which it may usefully be applied.

A focus on problem-solving

The approach is designed to help in the resolution of difficulties that people experience in interacting with their social situations, where internal feelings of discomfort are associated with events in the external world. These *psychosocial problems* can be very diverse, ranging from relationship difficulties to a lack of material resources. Research into the effectiveness of task-centred practice has indicated that the model is effective when applied to a specific range of problems, characterised by Reid (1978) as follows:

- Problems of interpersonal conflict (e.g. within families, or work situations).
- Dissatisfaction in social relations (e.g. amongst young adults newly alone away from home).
- Problems in dealings with formal organisations.
- Difficulties in role performance (e.g. in becoming partners, parents etc.).
- Problems of social transition (in moving from one role or situation to another).
- Reactive emotional distress (e.g. illness, bereavement).
- Problems in securing adequate material resources.
- Behavioural problems.

It is essential to note that the corollary of the model's known effectiveness in addressing problems in these eight specified areas is that it should not be used in situations not listed here.

Time limits

Planned short-term work is one of the defining characteristics of task-centred practice, which originated from some well-known research into the relative benefits of brief and extended casework conducted by William Reid and Ann Shyne in the late 1960s (Reid and Shyne, 1969). This and later studies suggest that the outcomes of short-term time-limited work are at least as good as those of long-term open-ended work. For this reason alone task-centred practice soon became popular within Britain's new Social Services and Social Work Departments when the model was first promulgated in the early 1970s; for agencies inheriting the traditions of psychosocial casework, an approach with fixed time limits to social work involvement offered obvious cost benefits. In the cost-cutting climate that prevails forty years later, effective, short-term, evidence-based interventions are more relevant than ever.

There are other benefits to planned short-term work. Client and social worker alike need to put immediate energy into the work, because time is limited. The dangers of social work effectiveness becoming dependent on the worker/client relationship, which may or not work out, are minimised in the short-term. The research of Reid and Shyne and others indicates that when change does occur in the context of interpersonal work, it tends to happen earlier rather than later in the process.

For all these reasons the proponents of task-centred practice advocate a limit of six to twelve sessions. For situations where further work is indicated, a fresh contract for a further round of work can be made; it is important that the time boundaries are not unthinkingly extended and that, as in any piece of work, careful consideration is given to why the work is being extended, rather than just letting it 'drift'.

General characteristics of task-centred practice

In addition to the key features of a focus on problem-solving and the use of time-limits, the task-centred model is distinguished by:

- The selection of a target problem from the problems presented.
- The use of tasks to address the selected problem.
- Continued review and negotiation between client and social worker.

Task-centred work is a *process*, in which client and social worker work together through five sequential phases. The first three phases (**problem exploration, the selection and prioritisation of target problems**, and **goal-setting, task identification and contract-making**) usually occupy perhaps two interviews, at the end of which some initial tasks will have been set. Work then moves into the fourth phase, **working to implement the tasks**, which includes a review of the outcomes of the initial tasks and the effect they have had on the identified problems. If the original tasks have been successful in addressing the problems, fresh tasks may be agreed; if they have not, then the reasons for this will be discussed. Some difficulties may be resolved easily, others may require tasks in their own right, and still others may demand a wholly new overall task strategy. During the third and fourth phases, the main focus will be on the planning of tasks that clients will perform themselves. The final session **bringing the work to an end** lays emphasis on what the client has learned and achieved; all the work is reviewed. In practice the imminence of the ending will have been mentioned several times already, so that the entire process is experienced as time-limited. We now set out the five phases in more detail.

Phase one – Problem exploration

Getting started – initial explanations

Task-centred practice is characterised by mutual clarity; the client should be as clear as the social worker about the processes that will be followed, in order to participate fully in the work. This characteristic of clarity is generally absent when the task-centred model is misused, and so clients are likely to be unsure about the process or feel compelled into agreeing with what the worker suggests or, worse, tells them to do. So explanations are important; but this does not mean that task-centred work begins with a lengthy and detailed introduction to the approach. Explanation can be done incrementally, as the first phase develops. It is important that by the end of this first phase, the client is clear that he or she is participating voluntarily in a time-limited process, with distinct phases, that will engage him or her as well as the worker in activities that will aim to resolve some, at least, of the problems presented.

The processes of problem exploration and assessment

The next element of the initial phase of task-centred practice is problem exploration. Reid defined problems as 'unmet or unsatisfied wants as perceived by the client' (1978). The problems to be addressed may be established in various ways, the most obvious being their identification by the client. Alternatively, they may emerge in the course of discussion between social worker and client. Less commonly, the worker may take the lead in identifying problems; in this situation the worker must take care not to detract from the client's unique expertise in their understanding of their individual situation (see Smale *et al.*, 1993 and Smale *et al.*, 2000). However problems are identified, it may be the task of the worker to formulate them clearly and in a mutually acceptable form.

All this of course assumes that the client has a problem or problems which they wish to address. If they need the worker's help in formulating the problem, then the worker in turn must first ascertain not only 'What is the problem?' but also 'For whom is this a problem?' Social work agencies, in adopting 'procedural' models of working (Smale *et al.*, 1993 and Smale *et al.*, 2000) generally prioritise their own agendas, most often that of resource allocation, above resolving the problems of the people with whom they engage, and social workers using this model need to be clear that their clients own the problems being addressed; what is a problem for the agency may not necessarily be a problem for the client.

The process of problem exploration will then entail the answering of a series of questions:

- What happens, typically, when this problem occurs?
- How often does it happen?
- How serious is it for the client?
- How did it begin?
- What has the client done to resolve it?
- How well did these efforts work?

Task-centred practice may not succeed unless there are changes in the contextual factors that influence, and are influenced by, the problem. So it is also necessary to establish the context in which problems are occurring:

- What causative factors exist in the surrounding context?
- What are the obstacles to problem-solving work?

- Who else is involved and in what ways?
- What resources can be invoked to help?

The answers to these various questions will provide the data for the cognitive process of assessment. Assessment is no longer, as it once was, an activity in which the 'expert' social worker uses professional knowledge to make judgments about others. In contemporary social work, it should be a reciprocal process in which social worker and client exchange information and expertise in the course of a dialogue; this 'Exchange Model', set out by Smale, Tuson and their colleagues in 1993, and further elaborated in 2000, is entirely compatible with the framework of task-centred practice.

As a further check on the suitability of task-centred practice for the problems identified, they should be classified against the list of eight problem types set out in the introduction to this chapter; if they cannot be placed within this framework then it is unlikely that the model will be effective. Finally, three useful tests at this point are:

- Does the client acknowledge the problem and wish to work on it?
- Is the client in a position to work on the problem, with the social worker as his or her agent?
- Is the problem framed in specific, limited and explicit behavioural terms?

Phase two – The selection and prioritisation of target problems

A 'target problem' is one which both worker and client acknowledge, and which they explicitly agree will become the focus of their work together. It will be based on the client's initial wants, but may have changed and developed in the process of problem identification. Commonly there will be a series of problems presented and discussed, and when this happens they will need to be ranked in the order of their importance to the client. This ranking will facilitate the deciding of which problems need to be addressed first. There are several ways in which this can be done, and the choice of approach depends on what works best for each client. Priestley and McGuire, for example, advocated the construction of 'Problem Checklists' using flip-chart sheets (1978). Milner and O'Byrne suggest a 'Problem Scale' which facilitates exploration of the interconnectedness of various problems (2009).

Phase three – Goal setting, task identification and contract making

Problem statements and setting goals

Following the identification and ranking of target problems, the first problem to be tackled will need to be framed within a 'problem statement'. The way in which a problem is framed and defined is crucial in motivating both client and social worker. It should be stated in a manner which reflects the concerns of the client but does not at the same time make it seem overwhelming and incapable of solution; instead the statement should foster constructive problem-solving work, for example by reflecting how the client might behave differently in order to obtain what they want. Goals may be included within the problem statement, if the parties concerned are ready to engage in the goal-setting process.

Tasks

In task-centred work, a task is defined as a 'planned problem-solving action'. There are three broad classes of task, the most important of which comprises tasks undertaken by a client between sessions. Secondly there are tasks undertaken by the worker between sessions, sometimes in partnership with the client. The third class comprises tasks undertaken within a session.

Task-centred practice is designed to enhance the problem-solving skills of participants, so it is important that tasks undertaken by clients involve elements of decision-making and self-direction; we must reiterate that this process is not about telling people what to do. The model can only be empowering for clients if they understand the purpose of the agreed task and how it is likely to affect the target problem. If the work goes well then they will progressively exercise more control over the implementation of tasks, ultimately enhancing their ability to resolve problems independently.

Tasks may be undertaken individually, on a shared basis among two or more people, or reciprocally; reciprocal tasks involve two people in an exchange of tasks.

Generating and choosing task ideas

The generation of new problem-solving ideas is a key feature of the task-centred approach; the creativity of this process can simultaneously break through the depressing failure of previous problem-solving efforts and motivate the participants with a sense of optimism. Ideas for possible tasks can be elicited through systematic discussion or through lively conversation eliciting the spontaneous generation of ideas. Although the worker will usually start the process, all participants will be invited to join in, for example in family work. Ideas may be based on past problem-solving attempts. Questions can be used to clarify what might be done.

The notion that practitioners are the primary and expert source of ideas for tasks is unhelpful and detracts from the concept of people being experts in their own/their families' lives. This does not, however, negate the ways in which social workers do use their expertise and these are helpfully summarised in Smale *et al.* (2000: 152–153). Nevertheless the task-centred model does highlight the potential for clients to generate their own suggestions and the need to allow plenty of space for this. Commonly, accounts of successful task-centred practice feature situations where social worker and client have worked together to identify and develop task ideas. Such examples appear to succeed because both parties are strongly motivated from the start of the process, and are able to reinforce each other's motivation. Shared motivation is an essential element in task-centred practice and, if this is compromised for any reason, such as when someone feels ground down by the pressures and stresses they are facing in coping with their children, then the approach may not work. When people are able to feel motivated, the determination to address their problems brought by the client at the beginning is built up and encouraged. For this very reason, it is essential that the initial tasks proposed are feasible and offer a reasonable chance of success. Although the task-centred approach contains mechanisms for recovering and learning from failed tasks, it is most effective when its problem-solving methods succeed from the outset. So it is better to start with modest tasks that are achievable than attempt larger tasks where the risk of failure is greater.

The process of task generation may have produced several ideas and possibilities; when this happens the selection of appropriate initial tasks to address the target problem will need some care. The criteria of likely success, relevance to the target problem and participants' motivation should assist this selection process.

Establishing incentives and motivation for task performance

As we have just noted, motivation is very important in this approach. The task-centred model is founded on the notion that the individual's propensity to engage in tasks is motivated by the unsatisfied wants that constitute the problem. In order to undertake a task, the person must want something that they do not have. The task may not, of itself, satisfy the want, but the person must see it as a step in that direction. Such incentives provide the initial motivation for task performance.

If the initial task has a successful outcome and produces movement towards a desired goal, then motivation is reinforced. This feedback provides incentives for the next stage, which may be a similar task or perhaps a more difficult one. Failures may also be motivating, but this is not the case for everyone and it is important not to, albeit inadvertently, set people up to fail. For example, the initial exploration may have missed a lack of motivation. Nevertheless, analysis of what went wrong can also generate ideas for new and different tasks. Throughout the work, mutual clarity is essential. The client needs to understand the process, and the social worker needs to understand the client's priorities, goals and motivation. Their confidence should be ascertained, their strengths and abilities identified, and learning from past successes as well as failures should be discussed.

Role-played rehearsals may be useful in approaching daunting tasks. Large goals may be reduced to more attainable sub-goals.

Planning the details of task implementation

Most tasks require a degree of detailed planning. Take a task as seemingly simple as 'Bob will call the dentist to make an appointment'. Bob has not been to the dentist for many years. He fears that his acutely painful toothache may be caused by undiagnosed cancer of the mouth, and his consequent anxiety is so great that he has been unable to pick up the telephone. But while he does nothing, he fears that his condition is worsening. He does not know whether he is still registered with the dental practice, and those who now work there are strangers to him. He has very little money and fears that the free National Health Service dental treatment (in the United Kingdom) associated with his benefits may no longer apply, leaving him with a bill he cannot pay. So the necessary planning involves working out, in detail, when he will make the telephone call, what he will say about his toothache and what enquiries he will make about his registration and the costs of treatment. His motivation to address the task needs to be reinforced so that it is greater than his overwhelming anxiety. In discussion with his social worker, Bob agrees firstly that they will role-play the telephone call together and secondly that, if he is happy with the role-play, he will then make the actual call, a few days later, from the social work office with his social worker alongside him. This is an anonymised real-life example. 'Bob' made the call, it wasn't cancer, he got treatment, and his confidence in his own problem-solving abilities was increased in direct proportion to the reduction in his anxiety level.

Planning involves not only preparing for the task, but also learning the skills of how to plan. It reinforces the importance of the task, increasing the likelihood that the client will remember it and attempt it. The role of the social worker at the task planning stage is to ask questions:

- How will this task be done?
- Who will do what?
- What is needed for this task to be attempted with good prospects of success?
- What skills (e.g. assertiveness) need to be developed, perhaps through coaching?

The degree of detail required in planning is a matter of judgment for the worker. In the example just given, an overtly simple task needed breaking down and planning in considerable detail; in other situations this will not be necessary. In all cases the worker should aim to stimulate the client's thinking about the task to be done. At the same time, there should be allowance for the possibility that the client may appropriately modify the task or even substitute a better one; the task-centred model, despite its order and clarity, can be adapted in many ways, and one of the present authors recalls William Reid himself advocating flexibility in its application, at a seminar in the early years of the model's development.

Simulating and rehearsing tasks

Plans of any kind are more likely to succeed if they can be tried out first. Many task plans can be rehearsed beforehand using role-play or other kinds of simulation exercise. The role-play of a simple telephone call was an important element in the case example given above, in which the social worker played the role of dentist's receptionist and the client played himself. This could have been preceded by, for example, the two roles being reversed, enabling the worker to model the task behaviour desired. Different approaches and scenarios can be tried out in this way. The model is explicitly educational, enabling the client to rehearse and learn new problem-solving skills; it is in all senses pedagogical.

Anticipating potential obstacles to task performance

In the task-centred approach, obstacles are defined as impediments preventing clients from solving their problems. Obstacles may obstruct specific task plans, or more generally they may impede all kinds of problem solutions. In our example of Bob, the obstacle was chronic, intense and growing anxiety, and this was hindering both the specific task plan and more general attempts to improve the situation. An obstacle may itself be a target problem – in which case the chosen strategies would not necessarily differ from those adopted if it were no more than an impedance. In our case, anxiety was not the target problem; nevertheless, the simple task strategy of making a call was designed to reduce some of the anxiety, and achieved this modest aim.

It is good practice to try and anticipate how potential obstacles will be tackled. A useful technique in this regard is to ask 'What if . . .?' questions:

- 'What if Bob finds out that he does not qualify for free dental treatment?'
- 'What if Bob discovers that he does have a malignant condition?'

The answers to 'What if . . .?' questions can promote discussion of how to resolve obstacles. An even simpler question is for the social worker to ask the client 'What might go wrong with the tasks?' This 'anti-sabotage' procedure can sometimes uncover potential obstacles that no-one had thought of. Or the discussion can invoke the history of previous problem-solving efforts, which may be associated with failure and need to be reframed as learning opportunities.

Summarising, task agreement and contracts

Before the planning session ends, the social worker and client will need together to review and summarise the task plan. This is especially important when the plan is complex, when there are several tasks, when several people are involved, or when the task performers are children. Useful techniques at this point include the production of written task plans for all parties, perhaps as part of a written contract, or the worker simply asking the client to present their version of what the plan is; this can, of course, be reciprocal, and the client may ask the worker what he or she will be doing to contribute to the plan.

The end of this phase of task-centred work is often marked by the making of a contract between worker and client. A contract is essentially an agreement to work together in order to resolve the stated problem or problems, and to achieve any specified goals. At this point it is essential that the client agrees explicitly and voluntarily to undertake the task. This should not be omitted amidst all the other matters being discussed and nor should silence be assumed to imply consent; social workers often work with involuntary clients (Trotter, 2004) in fields such as child protection, youth offending and safeguarding adults. In situations such as these it is important to identify and focus on areas which allow scope for the client's voluntary participation. The actual contract may be verbal or written, using the client's words as far as possible, and it may include a detailed task plan. Written contracts may be perceived as formal, but have the merit of being easy to review later on.

Phase four – Working to implement the tasks

Implementation of tasks between sessions

There is not a great deal to say about this self-evident phase, but that is not to deny its importance. Its success will depend on all the groundwork undertaken in the previous phases of the process. Clients may go away and work on their agreed tasks on their own, or with others. Social workers similarly may work on their agreed tasks; for example, the worker's tasks may include advocacy on behalf of the client. Or both may work together on the tasks. Some of the North American literature on task-centred practice uses the sporting metaphor of 'coaching' to describe the role of the practitioner at this stage, attributing significant expertise to the worker. Whilst this idea may not accord fully with the notion of the client as expert, the image of the 'coach' does embody ideas of encouragement and support which are entirely consistent with good practice, and thereby consistent with the Smale et al.'s 'Exchange' model (2000). This does not necessarily imply practitioner and client spending considerable time working together; telephone calls can provide useful contacts during this period.

Intermediate review of tasks and problems

The central period of working on planned tasks will be punctuated by regular, planned review meetings. The first purpose of these sessions is to assess progress in the implementation of agreed tasks. This progress will be a measure of any changes achieved, in relation both to the target problems and to the problem-solving abilities of the client. Successful task accomplishment, or progress in that direction, will be praised. Failed tasks may be met with an empathic response from the worker. If the agreed tasks were not attempted, then a discussion of the reasons for this will be necessary. Obstacles to task performance may need further consideration; for example, it may be necessary to review how far those involved are able to be/still motivated to work on their tasks. This review of tasks often leads on to the generation of ideas for the next task.

The second function of review sessions is to review changes in target problems. This is likely to involve continuing exploration of the problem, including its frequency and severity, and the client's impression of any changes that are happening as a result of the work, or other factors. Discussion of this area can be assisted by using questions, such as:

- Was it an appropriate/feasible task?
- How much change has occurred?
- Is it sufficient – for the client? For the social worker?
- How durable is the change likely to be?
- What factors have caused the change?
- What has the task work contributed to the change?
- Does analysis of the change suggest a shift in the focus of the work?

The analysis of change resulting from task-centred work can assist the empirically-oriented practitioner in evaluating the effectiveness of their practice. Exploration of the changing dynamics of the target problem is a process that began in the first phase of the model, continues through this intermediate stage and will be concluded in the final review.

Following the review of tasks undertaken and changes in target problems, a number of possibilities appear:

- If it is agreed that enough has been achieved and there are no other problems pressing, then the work may be concluded by moving directly into the final phase.
- Alternatively, if there has been sufficient change in the prioritised target problem, the work may move on to the next problem, revisiting phase three above.
- A third possibility is to continue working on the first target problem through new or revised tasks.
- Finally, the review may suggest that it is inappropriate to continue using the task-centred approach.

Phase five – Bringing the work to an end

Concluding session

The ending of the process of task-centred work will have been anticipated in the first sessions, when social worker and client together agreed on time limits for the work. In the intermediate sessions the worker will have reminded the client of the time remaining. The agreed time limits are not absolutely rigid. If the successful completion of a task has led to the successful resolution of a problem, then the work may be concluded early. Alternatively, the participants may agree on an extension of the agreed time limits where further work looks likely to improve the outcome. In such cases they should contract to meet for a small number of additional sessions, usually no more than four.

Final task and problem review

As with the intermediate sessions, the final session begins with a review of task accomplishments, which leads into a review of progress made in addressing the target problems. This final problem review should be made with as much attention to detail as the original problem exploration in phase one; in addition, any progress made will be evaluated. Useful questions at this point may be:

- What was the problem like at the outset?
- What changes have since occurred?

Such questions facilitate an evaluation that is realistic, rather than unduly positive or negative. Written material may also be helpful at this point, for example the records of the social worker or any written contracts made earlier.

Review of accomplishments and problem-solving skills

In the final session it is important to acknowledge what clients have accomplished, in order to reflect back and reinforce what they have achieved. In Bob's case, he commented that it had been important that he, rather than his social worker, had called the dentist. Although he had been afraid to make the call, the fact that he had done it increased his confidence in attending the ensuing dental appointment, an event which he had also feared. In this way the review of accomplishments can lead directly into the identification of improved problem-solving skills. The worker should help the client to generalise these skills, so that they may be applied to future problems, including problems not addressed in the work just undertaken.

Future plans

As a general rule, the conclusion of social work intervention should be prospective as well as retrospective; there should be discussion, not only of what has happened, but what is likely to happen in the future. Problems may continue to exist, or they may recur. So, finally, client and worker together will consider how the former will address problems in the future, on the basis of positive accomplishment and the learning of improved problem-solving skills. If the task-centred model has been employed effectively, both the client and the social worker will emerge from the process with enhanced abilities in their respective situations.

We have now set out the essential elements of the task-centred practice in a form that students have told us they find helpful. For further ideas on learning about the model, Chapter 5 of Marsh and Doel's very helpful textbook (2005) may usefully be consulted.

Obstacles to implementing task-centred practice

This part of the chapter uses research to examine some obstacles which persist in current practice with adults and which militate against the effective use of task-centred practice. Both the model itself and many of our comments are equally applicable to social work with young people and families. We consider: the core nature of the client/worker relationship, the focus on risk, dependence upon personalisation (see, for example, Carr and Robbins, 2009) as a model of service delivery in response to problems, and finally the time-limited nature of current practice with adults. We would argue that, where relevant, it remains possible to use a task-centred approach in work with adults and also in work with children and families. Although this argument could be applied to a wide range of social work practice methods, some of which are explored elsewhere in this book, we suggest that it is particularly pertinent to task-centred practice because its time-limited, planned and contract-based approach appears superficially to fit well with the nature of current practice.

The core nature of the client/worker relationship

Task-centred practice, like any other social work method, cannot be applied on its own and is dependent upon the worker's use of self in the development of a relationship with the person with whom they are working. The use of self, however described, is widely recognised as important and integral to social work (England, 1998; Howe, 1996; Wilson et al., 2011).

Postle's research, undertaken with social workers working with older people, showed that, although these workers were continuing to use themselves skilfully in their work, they frequently commented on their loss of opportunity for this, feeling that such work was being squeezed out by the increase in bureaucratic tasks which they had to undertake (Postle, 2001: 2002). In the 1990s, the introduction of care management increased a sense of demoralising bureau-cratisation (Lymbery, 2005) and this does not seem to have lessened with the recent inception of personalisation where, despite early promises, paperwork appears still to be disproportionate. One social worker, describing the impact of personalisation, expressed this change in her work thus, summing up what many others have expressed:

> *One of the reasons I chose to leave local authority employment was because I wanted to spend more time with the actual people I was supporting.*

(Dunning, 2011)

This clearly echoes these earlier comments from a team manager in Postle's research on care management:

> *There just isn't the time for them to be giving of themselves in the way that they were . . . I'm not putting down the counselling, but it's got to be seen as something apart from what we do . . . we should actually be purchasing counselling skills, buying them in from a secondary provider.*

In interviews with social workers engaged in care management, they variously referred to 'client-centred stuff, counselling', 'listening', 'spending time', 'using yourself', 'therapy', 'support', and work 'beyond the package'. This element of their work, the emotional labour, can be seen as core to the social work task (Gorman and Postle, 2003), whatever form that task may take, and essential to the successful application of any social work method. Yet it was such work which care managers felt under pressure to reduce and which became regarded, as one care manager described it, as 'undercover' work. There are similar concerns that it will be squeezed out under the operation of personalisation (Lymbery and Postle, 2010).

Postle observed a trainer running an in-house course who asked whether staff found that people always told them something really important right at the end of a visit or several visits. The students agreed that this was often the case and the trainer's advice, clearly given with the intention of helping the students to reduce their time pressures, was to tell the client to 'Tell me the problem sooner' instead of leaving it until the last five minutes. This comment relies on a bureaucratic, linear and procedural approach to the work, in which the worker can fit the client to their schedule rather than working at the client's pace, thus enabling and empowering them to participate on a more equal basis in the work. An alternative approach to that suggested by the trainer can be found in the classic work of Biestek, and appears closer to the nature of the practice which social workers were saying that they now found difficult because of the increasingly bureaucratic nature of their work:

> *The function of the caseworker is principally to create an environment in which the client will be comfortable in giving expression to his feelings. The skill to create this environment is much more important than the skill of asking stimulating questions. In fact, the latter skill will be ineffective without the permissive atmosphere.*

(Biestek, 1961: 40)

The function which Biestek describes, while clearly never universally present in social work, is nonetheless a crucial starting point for working with someone to determine the problem issues which could be resolved by use of task-centred practice. However, if this element of developing a relationship is subsumed by process-driven approaches such as have become prevalent in most fields of work (see, for example, Munro, 2011) the resultant tendency will be to look for short-term, quick-fix forms of working, as indicated by the trainer's comment above. Hence there is a risk that, in trying to use task-centred practice, social workers would not take time to work alongside the client to determine the problem to be addressed or that they may, indeed, see policy-driven agendas as the sole or predominant task.

In contrast to procedurally-driven approaches, Munro (2011) offers substantial recognition of the professional expertise of social workers. The comment in Paragraph 3.6 of the Review that 'many parents experiencing problems . . . were not offered any help' would suggest that social workers offering a problem-centred approach might be welcomed by such parents. It remains a concern that many social workers experience difficulty in using and/or articulating their use of theoretical models and in using their skills in their practice due to the pressures of their work context (McDonald *et al.*, 2008). Hence the potential for using task-centred work in all areas of practice may remain undeveloped while the client-worker relationship remains primarily a procedural one.

The focus on risk

Social workers operate in a prevailing climate of risk, reflecting the heightened sense of risk in the society in which they work (Beck, 1992; Giddens, 1991; Postle, 2002; Webb, 2006). This is a society concerned with the actuarial calculation of risk and its reduction or elimination, and yet one in which new risks become increasingly difficult to manage (Giddens, 1991; Ginsburg, 1998; Parton, 1996). Much social work, particularly assessment, focusses on the extent to which someone is at risk and, indeed, this governs the 'eligibility criteria' for a service (Harding, 1997) and features widely in consideration of how a balance is struck between autonomy and protection in discussing individual budgets (Lymbery and Postle, 2010). At the same time, many staff perceive a considerable risk of, at least, complaints and, at worst, litigation against themselves or their Local Authorities, and their work is increasingly circumscribed by concerns about risks related to health and safety. Concurrently, however, the speed of work throughput does not give staff time properly to evaluate and monitor risk, or spend time with people or their carers working on ways to reduce it. Such approaches could well include using task-centred practice to enable people to find and use strategies for risk reduction. This was how one team manager in Postle's research summarised her dislike of this approach:

I don't like the 'quick in and out, do the assessment, do the review, close it' type of approach where you focus on delivery of care . . . I feel quite strongly that, if someone goes out and does an assessment and identifies a number of risk factors and the person is neutral, or even a bit resistant, about having help, I don't feel we should say, 'There's nothing we can do'.

Hence the focus on risk militates against seeing or hearing and then working with anything which is not an issue of serious risk. In our example given earlier, were Bob considering an individual budget for his care, his need to visit his dentist might well not have been identified as a problem or, if it was, it may have been seen as something which there was little or no time for his social worker to work with him to resolve, because the focus would be on completing necessary paperwork. Coupled with the process-driven nature of the work, this emphasis on risk makes it very hard for professionals to work beyond immediate presenting problems:

As a local authority social worker I became disillusioned with the implementation of personal budgets and found that more and more my role was filled with sitting in front of the 'risk panel' – fondly named the "Dragons' Den" – trying to justify why Mr Smith chose not to go to a day centre and wanted to go fishing instead.

(Dunning, 2011)

Dependence upon individualised and bureaucratised responses to problems

Contemporary social workers work within a society in which universalising notions of consensus have largely collapsed (Harvey, 1989). This contrasts with the collectivism more easily identifiable with the modernist origins of the UK welfare state and with the social democracy of the 'old left' (Giddens, 1998). Although social workers' work has over time reflected both individualism and collectivity, the care management approach described by the SSI Guidance in the 1990s located the care manager as an expert in a procedural model of assessment which did *not* afford expertise in their situation to the person being assessed (SSI and SWSG, 1991a; 1991b; 1991c; Smale *et al.*, 1993; Smale *et al.*, 2000). The newer 'person-centred' approach of personalisation has promised to involve the users of services more in their assessments but there is a focus on individualised responses rather than co-operative or collective approaches (Lymbery and Postle, 2010). Anecdotally, personalisation appears to be generating as much bureaucracy as the care management model it supersedes!

Social workers historically have tended to work in individualised ways with people, looking at individual solutions to individual needs, rather than considering the broader picture of what could benefit a community and, in turn, the individual. This individualised approach was exemplified in Postle's observation of a social worker's visit to an elderly woman, where the worker discussed whether the woman's shopping could be done for her by a volunteer. This would be cheaper than the current arrangement where the woman went shopping with a paid carer, which she preferred, because it enabled her to choose goods herself. This was constructed as this woman's problem, rather than one which many elderly people experience and which, with a less individualistic approach, a more co-operative and community-based style of working, time for the social worker to think creatively and a less market-driven environment, could be resolved differently. In this context, the radical neo-Marxist approach of Ferguson *et al.* (2002) offers a refreshing contrast to that of the neo-Liberal consensus, as also does the service user perspective advocated over many years by Beresford and colleagues (see for example Beresford *et al.*, 2011). Both help us to lift our heads from a concentration on individualistic or procedurally-driven approaches to consider what works for people using services themselves, including ways in which social workers may reclaim the political role which has been largely absent in their work for some years (Postle and Beresford, 2007).

Where there is a concentration on the bureaucratic aspects of the job, invariably generated or exacerbated by individualised approaches, and anxiety about completing these tasks, social workers will have difficulty concentrating on wider aspects of work, encompassing preventative or community-based work. This individualism is compounded by the degree and form of specialisation and fragmentation in work with both adults and children, which presents a response to people's situations and problems which segments and compartmentalises them, militating against opportunities for collective work. The emphasis on assessments of individuals, rather than of individuals in their situations, means that a holistic picture of their environment is not obtained (Smale *et al.*, 1993, 2000). The lack of this broader picture curtails enhancement of the client's or their wider network's problem-solving capacities, thus making it difficult to use an approach such as task-centred practice, which relies on the widest possible exploration of problems, a field from which to generate and choose task ideas and, above all, on the person's own expertise in their situation in order to correctly identify how their problem-solving capacity can be enhanced (Smale *et al.*, 2000).

The time-limited nature of current practice

When discussing the focus on risk, Postle's research noted that there was a tendency for the nature of the work to be, as the team manager quoted above described it, 'quick in and out, do the assessment, do the review, close it'. Her comments fit with notions of dealing with 'core business' only, an approach which had come to dominate the way social workers continue to work, particularly as resources tighten (Lymbery and Postle, 2010). As the same team manager said:

> *I'm increasingly hearing managers say, 'That's not our job' and, 'We're not going to get involved with **that** because we do **this**' and it's sort of setting boundaries around*

a very small area of work. The lines of demarcation are being put in quite wrongly, I think.

Although, of course, social work intervention should always be focussed, concentration on core business, together with other public sector management orthodoxies such as decentralisation and devolution, can be very effective in helping organisations to be strategic and to meet goals. The goals may, however, become short-term because these are the easiest ones against which outputs and performance can be measured. Such orthodoxies do not have the capacity to enable organisations or managers to deal with complexity and uncertainty (Clarke and Newman, 1997). Considering that the core business of social work could be defined as dealing with social problems characterised by their complexity and uncertainty, it becomes apparent that the adoption of such orthodoxies might prove problematic. In discussing how care managers, as they then were, might get job satisfaction, another team manager's comments epitomise this change of emphasis from quality to output:

> *Perhaps people need to get their job satisfaction from quantity rather than quality and perhaps you need to think, 'Wow! I helped x number of people' rather than, 'I have helped Mrs. So and So over the last six months' which I think, really, is where we're at.*

Prior to the introduction of personalisation, the operation of care management meant that the initial worker was unlikely to remain involved and there was little opportunity to develop a relationship, however brief, with the person. At the time of writing, the nature of the social work role in personalisation is unclear (Lymbery and Postle, 2010). If it does not encompass scope for building and working within a relationship with the client, then the involvement of an individual social worker with the client will continue to be too brief even for the use of a time-limited model like task-centred practice. Similarly, if the lessons of the Munro Review, alluded to above, and the work of authors such as White (see, for example, White, 2008) are not heeded, then work with children and families affords equally limited scope for effective and appropriate use of the model.

We have noted that regular review is central to task-centred practice. In operating care management, because workloads were very high, once cases were closed, reviews of care packages were either very delayed or not done. As one team manager observed:

> *My view would be that you're much safer to say, 'I set up the services. The care management process is that that's what happens and then we review it in six months time.' And that, to some extent, provided those reviews are carried out, unfortunately they're not, but I mean if those reviews were carried out, then to all extents and purposes, we've done the job that we're paid to do.*

Although the care management process was intended to encompass reviews, the volume of work prevented these from being done. Hence the time-limited nature of the work precluded the possibility of the checks on implementation needed for task-centred practice to be effective. The person's case would be likely to have been closed to monitoring/review long before the manager could ascertain and review their progress with the task. This lack of review is a feature in much social work practice because time pressures, workloads and concentration on other, often procedural tasks militate against it. It is, however, a vital component of successful task-centred practice.

Conclusion

This chapter has outlined the model of task-centred practice which, as we have shown, serves as an enduring and very valid approach to supporting people's problem-solving capacities in ways which are person-centred and potentially empowering. We have then moved to consider some of the obstacles in using the model appropriately in the current context of social work practice, with all the challenges which that presents.

Writing this at a time of draconian cuts in Local Authority and, in turn in many instances, voluntary sector funding, it is hard to remain optimistic but it is to be hoped that social workers will find ways to rise to the challenges presented and continue to counter procedurally-driven and risk-focussed ways of working which militate against the use of proven models such as this.

Graham Tuson

Readers will see that we have cited Graham Tuson's work and, as this book was going to press (January 2012), sadly we learned that he had died. We have always considered that the work which he and Gerry Smale did on models of assessment made an invaluable and lasting contribution to social work education and practice. Knowing Graham as a colleague and an educator, we found him inspirational and insightful with a sharp intellect and a keen wit. He had a knack for enabling people to question what's all too often taken for granted in social work and to fully understand the complexity of the task.

References

Beck, U. (1992) *Risk Society: Towards a New Modernity*. London: Sage.

Biestek, F. (1961) *The Casework Relationship*. London: George Allen and Unwin.

Beresford, P., Fleming, J., Glynn, M., Bewley C., Croft, S., Branfield, F. and Postle, K. (2011) *Supporting People: Towards a Person-Centred Approach*. London: Policy Press.

Carr, S. and Robbins, D. (2009) *The Implementation of Individual Budget Schemes in Adult Social Care.* Research Briefing 20, London: Social Care Institute for Excellence.

Clarke, J. and Newman, J. (1997) *The Managerial State*. London: Sage.

Dunning, J. (2011) How Bureaucracy is Derailing Personalisation. *Community Care*, 31 May.

England, H. (1998) *Social Work as a Profession: The Naïve Aspiration*. Southampton: CEDR, Department of Social Work Studies, University of Southampton.

Ferguson, I., Lavalette, M. and Mooney, G. (2002) *Rethinking Welfare: A Critical Perspective.* London: Sage.

Giddens, A. (1991) *Modernity and Self-Identity. Self and Society in the Late Modern Age*. Cambridge: Polity Press.

Giddens, A. (1998) *The Third Way: the Renewal of Social Democracy*. Cambridge: Polity Press.

Ginsburg, N. (1998) Postmodernity and Social Europe. In Carter, J. (Ed.) *Postmodernity and the Fragmentation of Welfare*. London: Routledge.

Gorman, H. and Postle, K. (2003) *Transforming Community Care: A Distorted Vision.* London: BASW/Venture Press.

Harding, T. (1997) *A Life Worth Living: The Independence and Inclusion of Older People*. London: Help the Aged.

Harvey, D. (1989) *The Condition of Postmodernity: An Enquiry into the Origins of Social Change*. Oxford: Blackwell.

Howe, D. (1996) Surface and Depth in Social Work Practice. In Parton, N. (Ed.) *Social Theory, Social Change and Social Work.* London: Routledge.

Lymbery, M. (2005) *Social Work with Older People: Context, Policy and Practice*. London: Sage.

Lymbery, M. and Postle, K. (2010) Social Work in the Context of Adult Social Care and the Resultant Implications for Social Work Education. *British Journal of Social Work*, 40: 8, 2502–2522.

McDonald, A., Postle, K. and Dawson, C. (2008) Barriers to Retaining and Using Professional Knowledge in Local Authority Social Work Practice with Adults in the UK. *British Journal of Social Work*, 38: 7, 1370–1387.

Marsh, P. and Doel, M. (2005) *The Task-Centred Book.* London: Routledge.

Milner, J. and O'Byrne, P. (2009) *Assessment in Social Work.* Basingstoke: Palgrave MacMillan.

Munro, E. (2011) *The Munro Review of Child Protection: Final Report – A Child-centred System.* London: Department for Education.

Parton, N. (1996) Social Work, Risk and the Blaming System. In Parton, N. (Ed.) *Social Theory, Social Change and Social Work*. London: Routledge.

Postle, K. (1999) *Care Managers' Responses to Working Under Conditions of Post-modernity.* PhD thesis, University of Southampton.

Postle, K. (2001) The Social Work Side is Disappearing. I Guess it Started with us Being Called Care Managers. *Practice*, 13: 1, 13–26.

Postle, K. (2002) Working Between the Idea and the Reality – Ambiguities and Tensions in Care Managers' Work. *British Journal of Social Work*, 32: 3, 335–351.

Postle, K. and Beresford, P. (2007) Capacity Building and the Reconception of Political Participation: A Role for Social Care Workers? *British Journal of Social Work*, 37: 1, 143–158.

Priestley, J. and McGuire, P. (1978) *Social Skills and Personal Problem-Solving*. London: Tavistock.

Reid, W.J. (1978) *The Task-centred System*. New York: Columbia University Press.

Reid, W.J. and Shyne, A.W. (1969) *Brief and Extended Casework*. New York: Columbia University Press.

Smale, G., Tuson, G. and Statham, D. (2000) *Social Work and Social Problems: Working Towards Social Inclusion and Social Change*. Basingstoke: Macmillan.

Smale, G., Tuson, G. with Biehal, N. and Marsh, P. (1993) *Empowerment, Assessment, Care Management and the Skilled Worker*. London: HMSO.

SSI and SWSG (1991a) *Care Management and Assessment. Practitioners' Guide*. London: HMSO.

SSI and SWSG (1991b) *Care Management and Assessment. Summary of Practice Guidance*. London: HMSO.

SSI and SWSG (1991c) *Care Management and Assessment. Managers' Guide*. London: HMSO.

Trotter, C. (2004) *Working with Involuntary Clients: A Guide to Practice*. London: Sage.

Webb, S. (2006) *Social Work in a Risk Society*. Basingstoke: Palgrave MacMillan.

White, S. (2008) Drop the deadline, *The Guardian*, 19 November 2008 available at: http://www.guardian.co.uk/society/2008/nov/19/child-protection-computers-ics accessed 5/9/11.

Wilson, K., Ruch, G., Lymbery, M. and Cooper, C. (2011) *Social Work: An Introduction to Contemporary Practice*. 2nd edn. London: Pearson Education.

Chapter 8

Cognitive-Behavioural Methods in Social Care: A Look at the Evidence

Brian Sheldon

Choosing an approach

This is a book providing different perspectives on the tasks of staff working in the personal social services within which committed advocates are invited to make a case that a given model or approach has something to offer. Having written my first papers on behavioural approaches in 1978 I cannot escape the charge of standing commitment myself, and in any case this is usually seen as a 'good thing' in our discipline. However, I have long been suspicious of method, or theory-led explanations as to how untoward or troublesome social circumstances, or thoughts or feelings or behaviour, arise in the first place and what might best be done about them (Sheldon, 1978a; Sheldon and Macdonald, 2009, Ch 7). My misgivings are as follows:

1. Epistemology (the study of knowledge and its development) is replete with examples of large-scale theorising (Marxism, psychoanalysis, feminism – I have nothing against the latter stance, only against the lax research methods often employed). These products purport to be able to explain virtually *everything*, but tend also to require that our critical faculties be disengaged, the better to tune into broader waveband insights derivable from emotion and values; or proponents engage in the *pre-emptive disqualification* of critics to preserve the faith. Nevertheless, living in anxious circumstances as we do, we have tended to prefer these: but at a price I would say, both to our clients and to the intellectual development of our discipline.

2. Developing 'crushes' on favoured theories or approaches sometimes induces us to dis-attend either to inconsistencies *within* them (why should only some kinds of trauma be hard to recover from memory when most people who have suffered bad experiences have great trouble forgetting the fact? (Webster, 1996)) or to logical inconsistencies *between* them and other theories. The inescapable problem is, however, that if Bowlby and Erikson are right about major influences on child development (from the research I don't think they are) then Klein, Freud and Piaget must be wrong; if Skinner is right (he is powerfully *somewhat* right I think) then Piaget and Vygotsky are wrong: the significant events, the discernible stages and the timescales proposed are all different. Thus, ideas which contradict each other should not be plonked down next to each other on 'salad bar' training

courses. This practice is usually referred to as *eclecticism*: another allegedly 'good thing'. *Considered* eclecticism is an altogether different matter, providing that we have established rules for the considering, which we haven't quite (see below).

3. The standard approach to such problems within social work has been to adopt a relativist position; ensuring that words like *right, wrong*, or *science* are encased in 'don't really mean this literally but can't think of another word to capture the complexity behind what I'm trying to argue' inverted commas. Postmodernism (I think the term postrationalism more accurate) has given a further boost to this idea of no fixed position from which to evaluate either theories, or results derived from empirical research (Webb, 2001; Sheldon, 2001). To challenge this idea Sokal and Bricmont (1998) published a spoof postmodernist view of relativity theory in *Social Text.* The paper was full of complex physics mixed together with philosophical nonsense. It was taken very seriously and much debated in top French philosophical journals. The attempts at cognitive-dissonance reduction and face-saving which followed disclosure provide us with a wonderful, negative-image template of the skills necessary for critical thinking when evaluating evidence (Gambrill, 1997, 2012; Macdonald and Sheldon, 1998). Nor is this only a game for physical scientists and philosophers. Some time ago, a colleague and I published an April Fools Day spoof in *Community Care*. It advertised a course based on a new American Social work theory. The course details were full of quasi-biological references to 'semi-permeable membranes' surrounding the client's 'osmotic motivational system' etc. There was considerable interest; requests for block booking reductions were received, and we were forced to leg it with quiet dignity. Couldn't happen today, of course. Last April's proposal for a National Flipchart Archive received a stern rebuff.

These are not remarks about gullibility, but do point to a rather naïve appetite for the novel and the all-explanatory. But human beings are *very* complicated and we have been studying each other for a long time, so such things are (necessarily) hard to come by. Well no, there isn't any fixed or privileged position from which to observe, and we do indeed always influence what we are trying to measure. Also, people *react* to knowledge of observation, and we have a strong tendency to find what we expect or have been told to find as the following, chastening example from another, rather more secure field shows. There was once much controversy about the precise number of human chromosome pairs per cell in the human body. Some 12-year-olds can now tell you that it is 23, but in the 1920s staining and microscope slide preparation techniques left the matter in some doubt. In 1923, the eminent American zoologist, Theophilus Painter, pronounced that there were 24 pairs. This authoritative conclusion was repeated in textbooks over the next thirty years alongside photographs clearly showing (had anyone bothered to count) only 23 pairs. The power of argument from authority, the power of routine 'givens' and the power of peer-group pressure are all revealed in this case and we have many equivalent examples in our own field (Sheldon, 1987; Sheldon and Macdonald, 2009 Ch 2).

I do not think I am contradicting myself in the paragraph above, because it is scientific method that has induced us to become constructively paranoid about trusting unaided judgement, and because science (without the little inverted commas) is our best hope if we are to allow for, compensate for, and control out as far as possible this set of well understood human tendencies to jump to conclusions and stick to them, and readily to countenance what accords with our existing views, and not what does not. Therefore, the logical starting point for any consideration of how best to select a remedial approach to any given set of difficulties is to consider (a) what it presumes about the aetiology (the growth and development pattern) of the problems, and whether there is robust research to support a particular view; and (b) then to consider what is known, at what level of methodological rigour, about previous attempts to help *via* the application of given methods to particular circumstances and histories. In other words, we must learn to review the evidence for what we do *before* we do it, and not just to respond routinely or reflexively as we go along, and justify this later. Therefore, I make use of and teach cognitive behavioural approaches because of the extent and the quality of the evidence, including evidence of limited effects in some areas, and not just because I am used to it. Because I used to be used to some *very* different methods (psychoanalysis), implanted by a professional training course which seemed positively to favour the unlikely and the bizarre – sadly the experience is still to be had.

The above prescription takes us on to the idea of evidence-based practice as a unifying concept for all of the foregoing. Evidence-based approaches have the following features:

- Optimal bias-reduction regarding our preferential use of research in practice, on the '*what* is known depends on *how* it is known' principle formulated by Bacon in 1604. 'Studies and theories are not created equal' about sums up this point (Sackett *et al.*, 1996; Sheldon, 1978b).
- The explicit selection of intervention methods based upon 'current best evidence'.
- A requirement that practitioners explicitly debate with clients and with each other regarding why a particular approach looks like a good bet, and then to monitor and evaluate results as rigorously as possible (Sheldon and Chilvers, 2000; Sheldon and Macdonald, 2009). Not a new idea, but one which is gathering force within our discipline. Staying power is now the challenge.

The proposition before us then, is that would-be helpers should be more discerning in their selection of research and theory for use in practice, and learn to prefer findings from 'studies of good quality' (DoH, 1994). What exactly does this mean? Before trying to answer this question let me enter the proviso that there is no single methodological approach that is always better than others, it all depends on what we are trying to find out. In short, some methodological approaches give us more secure results in some fields. All empirical investigations can make a contribution providing what is being claimed in the way of results and practical implications is plausibly attributable to what was done to produce a hoped-for change, and could not equally be due to collateral influences. Thus, one does not need (nor could one ethically set up) a randomised controlled trial (RCT) to find out what it is like to be a child within the public care system. In-depth, largely qualitative interviews with children and carers is the most revealing approach, particularly if based on large, random, stratified samples of respondents (because children come into care for different reasons, have different problems, and are placed in different circumstances). However, if on the basis of signposts from qualitative research of this kind we decide to follow a particular course of action to try to find our way towards better than typical outcomes, we *do* need an RCT or two, or better still, a systematic review of RCTs (Sheldon and Macdonald, 2009; Littell, 2008). Despite much debate in academic circles about whether experiments are the only fruit, they are, in the British social care field, as rare as blue oranges (see MacDonald and Kakavelakis, 2004 for an example).

Thus, regarding *intervention* research, there *is* a very definite hierarchy (not just a continuum) of methods which produce higher or lower levels of *attributive confidence* (i.e. address through their procedures the question: are these differences due to that programme within the boundaries of a five in a hundred, or a one in a hundred, statistical chance ($p > 0.05$; $p < 0.01$) that they are not?). Here is what this methodological hierarchy looks like:

Figure 8.1 Methodological procedure and attributive confidence

Methodology	Procedure	Attributive confidence
Systematic review of *randomised controlled trials, or meta-analysis* of *controlled trials:* These look at effect sizes from comparisons of one approach with another standard or routine intervention, or with nothing, across many studies of the same type. (see Littell, 2008 on the pitfalls).	The pre-publication of a search strategy (usually involving both electronic databases and the hand-searching of journals) against specific inclusion and exclusion criteria. These cover issues regarding relevance and methodological sufficiency. Exhaustive search of data-sources, an unvarnished presentation	These studies maximise bias reduction, so much so that almost always the effect size (degree of comparative benefit) against hard outcome indicators is reduced in comparison with other methodologies. If well conducted they provide our most secure results. If producing negative outcomes, then they are

	of results and implications, and regular up-dating are other hallmarks.	still *very* valuable in advising what *not* to do.
Single experiments: Comparing the effects of an intervention with an attention, placebo control, or other-treated group, since attention and belief in the expertise of helpers also have strong effects. Best of all (but rare) are studies with three conditions compared: no intervention, standard intervention, and test intervention.	Random allocation to two or more groups (within which good-sized samples iron out differences between recipients). One group then receives an as consistent as possible exposure to the intervention under test. The other receives non-specific attention or another service. Outcomes are assessed against specific quantitative outcome indicators (e.g. readmission to hospital, recidivism). Such findings can be backed up by standardised qualitative tests.	Maximal bias reduction, but single studies can sometimes be errant (either positively or negatively). Standardising (that is making as uniform as possible) the intervention 'ingredients' poses problems, but large samples help to average out intervention differences. Sub-analysis of service-provider variations can also help to reduce this problem. Differential dropout rates require particular attention.
Single experiments with a non-intervention control group: Since many services never reach potential beneficiaries anyway opportunities to exploit rational controls abound. It is randomisation that causes ethical difficulties.	Random allocation of subjects; some get an as consistent as possible exposure to a given approach and others are left to their own devices.	Very substantial bias reduction properties, but does not tell us how far any differences between groups are due to specific approaches under test or non-specific attention factors. Replications or even concordant findings from quasi-experimental or pre-post studies (see below) increase plausibility.
Narrative reviews: These are not usually as exhaustive as systematic reviews and tend to have weaker inclusion and exclusion criteria. Can	Authors draw up a list of topics which they wish to search e.g., 'social work in general hospitals', 'supported housing for learning disabled people'	Suffers from the problem of 'convenience samples' i.e. sources readily available to the authors, and from a higher possibility of partiality or

also contain research using different methodologies. In such cases findings should be 'layered' i.e. it should be possible to see what results come in what proportion from which methodologies.	and then track down likely sources and look for emergent trends and implications.	selective perception than where a tight, pre-published protocol is in place. Nevertheless, worthwhile summaries, sometimes coming close to later, more systematic reviews in their conclusions for less cost and labour. A good starting point for something more rigorous.
Quasi-experimental studies: These are comparison studies but without random allocation, therefore we can never be sure that we are comparing like with like, though case-matching helps moderately to increase confidence. A comparison of different service patterns in different settings.	The effects of a particular service pattern used in one location, or with one set of clients. These are compared with a similar group who are not receiving the intervention – usually on a pre-post basis.	An underused investigative method since it compares the results (usually pre and post) between areas where an approach is in use with a comparable area where it is not. Very useful for use in social services where different services are routinely introduced in one area and not in another. Cross contamination can be a problem.
Pre-post tests: Sometimes known as time series designs, these procedures compare problems and gains on a before and after basis in a single sample.	Baseline, i.e. pre-intervention (preferably standardised) measures are taken in key problem areas prior to service (see Fischer and Corcoran, 2007 for an accessible manual). They are then repeated at the end of the programme for comparison purposes.	Most evaluations in social services are post-only (see below) and so it is difficult to calculate the value added. This approach takes 'snapshots' of functioning on a before and after basis. Nevertheless it cannot determine the extent to which any improvements which occur are due to the mere passage of time (maturational factors)

		or to other collateral factors.
Post-test only: This approach reviews outcomes only, without the benefit of specific pre-intervention (baseline) measures. Client opinion studies fall into this category.	Ideally the sample is chosen against criteria of need, type and extent of the problem. The intervention is made, and then measures of the outcomes are made.	These studies are often rich in qualitative detail about what it is like to be on the receiving end of services, addressing 'why?' and 'how?' questions more than 'how much?' ones. However, a common problem is representativeness. Do the respondents in the sample reflect the range of service users and problem characteristics? Random sampling of populations helps here and should be routine in social services as part of the service planning process.
Single case designs: Largely quantitative measures (though there is no reason why standardised qualitative measures should not be included) applied to single cases.	Measures are taken on a before and after (AB design) or before/after/follow-up basis (ABA designs) or even in experimental form (ABAB designs) where interventions are baselined, the intervention made, then withdrawn, then reinstated and differences noted. Mainly used in behaviour therapy, though there is no reason why this should be so, providing that case-specific behavioural change in line with the aims of a given approach are pre-specified.	Should be more widely used by practitioners whatever the intervention method in use. Enables staff and clients to assess progress and adjust accordingly. Routine in cognitive-behavioural approaches.

How well does the range of techniques known collectively as cognitive behavioural therapy (CBT) match up to these standards? Well, a very curious thing happened recently in this field. The editor of one of its most prestigious journals seemed to be arguing for *less* research. When academics call for less of anything but government interference, we should sit up and take notice! The argument ran: 'we really have little need of further experimental work on the comparative effectiveness of cognitive behavioural therapy'. He is right: the multidisciplinary literature contains over 5000 empirical examples, the vast majority producing clinically significantly positive results against comparisons with either no intervention or with other commonly employed methods (Hollon and Beck, 2004; Sheldon, 2010). These results add up to the fact that, within this literature, in respect of a wide range of demanding problems, virtually no other approach ever does better (Benton and Schroeder, 1990; Bergin and Garfield, 1994; Lambert, 2004; Sheldon, 2011). This is true on a smaller scale in our own field (Reid and Hanrahan, 1981; Sheldon, 1986; Macdonald and Sheldon, 1992; Macdonald and Winkley, 2000). The editor went on to observe that further training and dissemination work ought now to be our priority. To which sensible view I would only wish to add the rider that these approaches are sometimes used by psychologists and American clinical social workers against rather discrete problems in somewhat protected settings. There are some examples to the contrary (see Scott, 1989; Sheldon, 2010, 2011; Hudson and Macdonald, 1988) but extending the use of CBT to routine, community settings (where things are a whole lot messier) is undoubtedly the next challenge for our discipline. However, looking at where we are now, how well does the approach meet the criteria for evidence-based practice outlined above? Here are some arguments in support of the fact that it does so very well:

1. There is a very large regularly replicated body of empirical research on how problems arise in the first place as a result of maladaptive learning or through learning deficits (see Pavlov, 1927; Skinner, 1953; Bandura, 1969; Sheldon, 2011 for a review).
2. There is a close 'logical fit' (the best predictor of positive outcomes in effectiveness research) between these 'nature of' studies and the body of techniques which constitute the CBT approach. In other words, there are no general purpose approaches based loosely on theoretical assumptions in this field, rather, specific methods are indicated as a result of empirical investigations of the causes of problems.
3. This research on 'nature of' and 'what to do about' questions relies much more on experimental and quasi-experimental methods (as we have seen, the strictest tests of professional good intent) than is typical across the helping professions.
4. Users of CBT approaches are trained to be explicit about what they are trying to achieve, and help is offered in a contractual way, based upon informed consent

(BABCP, Code of Ethics 2010). If anything, having favoured quantitative rigor for so long, we now lack good, representative, qualitative research on the experience of being a client with whom these approaches are being tried. However, where we have such findings, they are rather positive. Indeed, looking at the comparative research regarding other approaches, a fair conclusion would be that although clients are willing to consider all sorts of arguments (from the plausible to the fanciful) about the *origins* of their difficulties, they turn into CBT fellow travellers when it comes to the evaluation of *outcomes*. Is there more or less aggression? Can they do useful things that would have been very unlikely prior to intervention? Do the children now regularly go to school? Has deliberate self-harm reduced or disappeared, wherever such problems originally came from?

5. Any idea that CBT might be useful for a few minor, easy to target problems must simply be abandoned in the light of the empirical evidence. There are now reviews and compilations of evidence based largely on experimental studies showing successful application in fields such as:

- Depression (Gloaguen *et al.*, 1998).
- Schizophrenia (Jones *et al.*, 1998; Falloon, Boyd and McGill, 1984; Sheldon, 2010).
- Challenging behaviour in children (Carr, 2000; Sheldon, 2010; Macdonald and Winkley, 2000).
- Learning disabilities (Bennett and Gibbons, 2000).
- Post-traumatic stress disorder (Van Etten and Taylor, 1998; NICE, 2005).
- Multi-faceted problems which generally come the way of social care staff (Scott, 1989; Cigno and Bourne, 1999; Sheldon, 2010).

6. Central to this form of practice is the use of single-case experimentation. That is, of employing quantitative alongside qualitative measures of change against which progress or its absence can be monitored. In short, a rigorous form of case management, making use of hard outcome indicators, is firmly in place (see Figure 8.3 for an example).

7. The idea that CBT approaches rob therapeutic encounters of their humanity and flexibility is a defensive myth. The cognitive and the behavioural literatures are full of discussions of relationship skills, motivation building approaches and so forth (Sheldon, 2011; Sheldon and Macdonald, 2009). Moreover, a number of studies suggest that clients positively prefer an explicit 'recipe' to follow where help is on hand to cook it. However, although such process factors deserve our close attention, they do not always constitute a *sufficient* condition for change. There is always the possibility, as so often reported upon in the early effectiveness studies of social work (Gibbons *et al.*, 1978) that however well regarded we may be for our settee-side manner, we sometimes do little manifestly to affect problems. An ethical as well as a technical issue, surely?

If any readers have been harbouring 'get on with it, Sheldon' thoughts during the foregoing discussions, then I am unrepentant, since I consider that *all* proposals as to what busy practitioners should do more or less of should be accompanied by a review of the evidence to back up the advice. Put another way, should not authors and teachers have to (as maths teachers used to urge) 'show their working out, not just their answers?'

This work done, we are now free to look at research on learning and how it might be applied to our interventions, for however routine and relaxed the contacts, that is what they are.

Classical conditioning and its therapeutic derivatives

I.P. Pavlov won his Nobel Prize for his work on the *physiological* processes of digestion. Interestingly, the word in italics is often presented in publishers' proofs as *psychological* – a good example of higher-order classical conditioning at work – since Pavlov is now associated above all with his contributions to psychology. He and his colleagues embarked upon a project to map the range and the effects of conditioned reflexes from a sense of frustration, because no matter how great the care they took to control the circumstances in which they conducted their experiments, certain psychological phenomena always interfered. In other words, the laboratory animals developed associations and anticipations about food, as they do in ordinary domestic life. These effects fascinated Pavlov, who saw them as a challenge to scientific method. Pavlov's procedure (the right pictures will be in your head as a result of classical conditioning) was to collect saliva directly from the cheek gland of a dog held in place by a harness, in a soundproofed laboratory. Now, and I will say this only once, the purpose of presenting animal experiments is to get the 'psychological grammar' right. There is nothing in this chapter that does not apply equally well to human beings (see below). Here is the sequence:

1. A tone is sounded no salivary response occurs. (*Neutral stimulus: NS*).
2. The tone is sounded and meat powder is deposited into a dish in front of the animal or directly into its mouth. The dog produces salivary flow as a matter of innate reflex. (*Unconditional stimulus: UCS*). This procedure is repeated several times.
3. The tone is presented without the meat powder and salivary flow occurs to this stimulus alone – the dog has learned a new response. (*Conditional stimulus: CS*)
4. Stimuli resembling the CS will tend to produce a similar reaction. Spend ten seconds imagining you are licking half a lemon (you are now salivating in response to marks on paper).

Classical conditioning is then, a pattern of *stimulus association* learning. Stimuli impinge in *clusters*, there are spatial and temporal connections (features of place, circumstances and time) which throughout evolutionary history it has been useful for animals (and humans) to respond to interchangeably since one, or one class, might predict the likelihood of the other. Thus anything that might reliably signal the possibility of satisfaction of a basic drive, or the avoidance of danger, and so prepare us for what may ensue, conveys an advantage on the 'better-safe-than-sorry' principle, literally vital in evolution. In the case of salivation this operates by ensuring that the elapsed time between first prospect and food energy being available for use (via the action of the enzyme Ptyalin breaking down large glucose molecules) is shortened, as is the feeding episode during which we would once have been vulnerable to predation. In the case of learned fear-reactions the advantages operate through the fight/flight mechanism of the body changes in muscle tone, heart rate, blood pressure and blood clotting speed, sweating, breathing rate, pupil size, and so forth, all of which prepare us for more effective escape or for combat. However, while it is useful to remind ourselves of the power of fierce drives and emotions, it is a mistake to forget the powerfully pleasurable feelings which (through the limbic system in the brain) exert a telling influence on our behaviour and thinking. Praise from an admired friend or mentor can, for example, produce such warm feelings that all our day-to-day doubts and worries are washed away. It has long been known that the brain contains dedicated centres for pleasure as well as for pain (Olds, 1956). The biochemistry of all this is not our particular concern but the environmental effects most certainly are, since decision-making, our own and that of our clients, is not the desiccated intellectual process represented in some textbooks on cognition. It is powerfully influenced by emotion, by chains of conditioned predispositions, and by intrusive memories of past successes and failures (see Damasio, 1994, for a full treatment of the role of emotion).

Let us turn now to a human experiment in this field, that of Watson and Rayner (1920). These pioneers were keen to see whether Pavlov's results applied in cases of unreasonable fear and anxiety. The study was called 'Little Albert' in parody of Freud's celebrated 'Little Hans' case of alleged castration anxiety.

Sorry, but I can't resist this aside: Little Hans was analysed (by post) using his father as intermediary, and Freud's interpretation of the fear was basically Oedipal – the animal representing strong and possibly dangerous masculinity, pawing the ground between the boy and his mother. This interpretation ignores two interesting facts (a) that most horses in nineteenth-century Vienna would be mares or geldings, and (b) that Hans' fear began after a large brewer's dray horse collapsed and died in the shafts next to him (too simple to be considered significant).

The procedure, which would nowadays have gotten everyone concerned into trouble under the Children Act, was as follows. The six-month-old Albert was placed in a play pen and introduced to a tame white rat (NS – no reaction beyond curiosity occurred). A fire gong was then struck loudly (UCS) every time the animal was introduced. Next the animal (CS) was repeatedly released *without* the accompanying noise, but it still gave rise to fear and avoidance reactions. The child had learned a new fear (a conditioned response, CR) purpose-built in the laboratory. Two clinically important phenomena were demonstrated in Watson and Rayner's work. The first is *generalisation*. Pavlov noted from his experiments that anything resembling the CS would eventually, in chain-like fashion, come to produce the same CR. Little Albert came proportionately to fear a whole range of similarly furry objects bearing decreasing resemblance to the original CS. But, sauce for the goose, something interesting has happened in later discussions of the experimental procedure:

- The extent of the generalisation was exaggerated to include Rayner's fur coat.
- The fact that the stimulus conditions had to be reinstated as Little Albert began naturally to desensitise is rarely mentioned.
- Albert was never treated for his artificially induced fear (simple desensitisation would have done the trick) and his mother took him away (Harris, 1979).

The temptations with this nice story, not very threatening to the main findings, but interesting in a 'post modern' sort of way, lie in the way in which it has been embroidered regarding generalisation. However, we see this phenomenon of stimulus generalisation in our own cases, where clients have had a bad experience in one setting but adverse responses have spread to a wide range of vaguely similar circumstances. This is a notable feature of post-traumatic stress disorder (Joseph *et al.*, 1995;) and of social phobias, leading to increasing withdrawal.

Moving out of the laboratory, here is a case example from my own practice (Sheldon, 2010):

Case example

Mrs Wood, aged 40, was referred to the social services department for 'support' by her somewhat exasperated family doctor. In his view, Mrs Wood suffered from agoraphobia, a 'dependent personality', and a number of other poorly specified 'personality difficulties'. Knowing how to motivate social workers, the doctor also said that he had some worries about Mrs Wood's young son, because not only had she barely left the house in the previous three years, but very little had been seen of this child. Stimulus conditions reliably associated with being grilled before a child abuse inquiry (UCS). Mrs Wood described herself as always having been 'a nervous person'. She recounted stories about dismounting from her bicycle as a child whenever a car came up behind her, going some distance out of her way to avoid a yappy dog; feeling very shy and conspicuous as a teenager, and so forth – a range of normal-enough fears, but noteworthy in their combination and extent. She also reported a strong and persistent fear of hospitals and of all medical encounters, probably stemming from her mother's bloodcurdling accounts of the birth of her younger sister, and from worship in a Christian sect which, let us say, had 'issues with blood'.

Mrs Wood became pregnant 'by accident', comparatively late in life. In order to persuade her to have the baby in hospital, the doctor had played up the dangers of a home confinement, raising her already high level of anxiety about the birth. One hot summer's day, when she was seven months pregnant, Mrs Wood had fainted while crossing a footbridge spanning a small river near her home. 'I was sure I was going to fall in, and when I came round, people said an ambulance was on the way and I panicked. People were trying to hold me down, covering me with clothing.' She fought to get free: 'I knew I had to get away, I got very upset, and eventually I persuaded someone to see me home. When I got in I was shaking all over. I shut and bolted the doors, back and front . . . I was sure that the ambulance was going to call at the house . . . I hid out of sight of the windows . . . and eventually (it took about an hour) I calmed down, and sat waiting for my husband to come home from work.' 'Catastrophic' or even 'paranoid' thoughts of this type are an important feature of panic reactions.

Mrs Wood had her baby at home, against medical advice, painfully, but without serious complication. She tried to go out several times after that but never got further than the front garden, or if at night, as far as the front gate. She reported the following feelings at each attempt: 'Shivering, awful feelings in the pit of my stomach; pounding heart; light-headedness.' In the daytime everywhere seemed 'very bright and stark'. She felt conspicuous out in the open, 'almost as if I might be struck down'. Her breathing felt loud in her ears and her biggest fear was that she would collapse again.

If we examine this case in the light of classical conditioning theory, the following pattern emerges:

- Mrs Wood may have possessed a predisposing personality for strong fear reactions (see Claridge, 1985; Mcguffin, Owen and Gottesman, 2004). Certainly her accounts of her earlier life showed her to be eminently conditionable to a range of not objectively threatening circumstances.
- Against a background of heightened anxiety about pregnancy, dreading the thought of the possibility of having to go into hospital, Mrs Wood experienced a traumatic incident (UCS) which aroused in her a powerful fear reaction (*unconditional response: UCR*).
- This incident, when paired with the previously neutral stimulus of the footbridge and other stimuli associated with being out of doors (CSs), produced a conditioned response to these stimuli. Even after the incident itself had passed, the pregnancy was over, she was perfectly well, and the

crowd no longer in sight, she still experienced fears and catastrophic images associated with this context.

- Mrs Wood reported that her panic state was made worse by the attempts of would-be helpers to restrain her until the ambulance came. Natural escape behaviour was prevented, thus intensifying her fear.
- This conditioned fear response quickly generalised to virtually all outdoor circumstances, even though objectively they barely resembled the circumstances of her collapse. Furthermore, every time Mrs Wood tried to go out of doors she was punished for the attempt by her powerful emotions (setting up a 'fear of fear' reaction): even though she saw such feelings as annoying and irrational.
- Cognitive factors played a part in maintaining Mrs Wood's avoidant reactions. Her strong emotions influenced her thought patterns, and vice-versa. When asked about what she thought would happen if she tried to confront her fears, she responded with typically 'catastrophic' views: 'I'd die and then my child would be on his own' etc. Thus, these hypotheses were very rarely tested out, and avoidance reactions continued to predominate ('relief conditioning').

Intervention methods: slow exposure and systematic desensitisation

The applicable evidence in such cases strongly favours exposure therapy and systematic desensitisation (slow exposure). Such approaches are also useful in cases where strong and unreasonable fears which do not amount to full-scale phobias, but which nevertheless seriously interfere with life satisfaction, are concerned. Current estimates suggest that such problems are experienced by one in 12 of the population as a whole, and are further concentrated in social services caseloads. There is a genetic predisposition.

Here is an outline of the approach (systematic desensitisation) used with Mrs Wood. There are two kinds of systematic desensitisation: *in vivo* (live practice); and *imaginal*, a cognitive approach using the same principles but employing imagination rather than direct exposure. Both forms have the same four therapeutic ingredients:

1. A graded hierarchy of anxiety-producing stimuli (see Figure 8.2).
2. A relatively slow rate of progression through the stages of this hierarchy, the pace being dictated by the need for a lowering of anxiety to occur before the next item is approached.
3. A counter-conditioning element in the form of deep muscle relaxation. This was always an effective technique (Bandura, 1969; Emmelcamp, 1994) and rapid exposure methods are only coming to supersede it on the grounds that they are more efficient – if one can persuade clients to co-operate, that is.

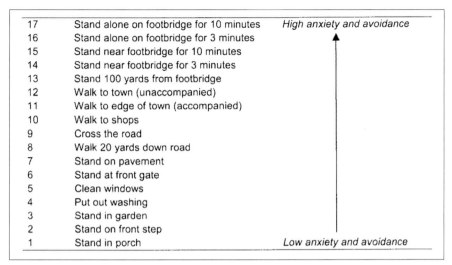

17	Stand alone on footbridge for 10 minutes	*High anxiety and avoidance*
16	Stand alone on footbridge for 3 minutes	
15	Stand near footbridge for 10 minutes	
14	Stand near footbridge for 3 minutes	
13	Stand 100 yards from footbridge	
12	Walk to town (unaccompanied)	
11	Walk to edge of town (accompanied)	
10	Walk to shops	
9	Cross the road	
8	Walk 20 yards down road	
7	Stand on pavement	
6	Stand at front gate	
5	Clean windows	
4	Put out washing	
3	Stand in garden	
2	Stand on front step	
1	Stand in porch	*Low anxiety and avoidance*

Figure 8.2 Contact with fear-provoking stimuli (Sheldon, 2011)

Mrs Wood was taught progressive relaxation and deep breathing *in situ* during the assignments contained in Figure 8.2. Sometimes she was accompanied by a student social worker, and sometimes deliberately not. If the next step looked too large, the progression from one to the other could be bridged by spending longer completing the earlier task. The procedure was labour-intensive but short term, and in fact this client never did make it across the footbridge during the course of the programme. She said firmly that she could easily go to town another way so that it was not a real problem. However, she reported at follow-up that she *had* at last conquered this fear. Following a row with her husband about his over-solicitousness, she had felt particularly determined about the issue and had marched to the bridge and stood trembling on it for ten minutes: amateur counter-conditioning, but effective, and wonderful solace for family therapists.

4. The cognitive components in this case (not separate, but woven in) were (a) psycho-education on the nature of anxiety; (b) the idea of undertaking little experiments and attending to what *actually* happens. Discussion of the fact that the anxiety always reduces after a while.

Operant conditioning

The more we learn about child development, the more we are forced to abandon the environmental determinism of the 1960s and acknowledge the active, experimenting, contribution of children themselves. Much of child development 'unfolds' from within. Very young babies show signs of a strong urge to explore, to *operate upon* (hence the word 'operant', not a fancy new term, it's in *Hamlet*,

Act III) and to manipulate their environments (see Donaldson, 1978 for a sensible, *thin* book). Such activities rapidly attract consequences of a positive, an aversive, or a relief-producing kind. Some of these consequences just happen, e.g. reaching out and touching something hot; some we deliberately organise, e.g. in withdrawing attention from bad behaviour. Thus, from the earliest years, by accident and by design, human beings are exposed to sets of *contingencies* (if you . . . then . . .) which experiences amount to a sub-Darwinian process of the natural (and unnatural) selection of behaviour patterns. Some sequences are 'stamped in', others 'stamped out' (Thorndike, 1898). Nothing new here, and once again the contribution of behavioural psychology has taken the form of carefully charting the dynamics of this way of acquiring new responses. The towering contribution is that of the American psychologist B.F. Skinner (1953, 1971) whose project was to develop an entire psychology without reference to interior goings on (if you are thinking of rats now, do remember that this is a *Pavlovian* reaction). Let us start with Skinner's animal experiments just to get the sequence clear. He gave his name to a glass-sided box equipped with a food dispenser and a release lever or disc which the animal (usually rats or pigeons: never both) could operate from the inside. All other factors are under the control of the experimenter. Here is a summary of Skinner's procedures:

- A hungry rat or pigeon (never both) is placed in a glass-sided box with a food release lever or disc, and engages in exploratory (operant) behaviour, eventually bumping into the lever and hitting the jackpot. The animal tries this again and clumsy initial operation quickly gives way to expert tapping or pecking. The rat's unlikely behaviour (for a rat) has been *positively reinforced* and so it is repeated, or rather the other way around. It has learned a new pattern of behaviour. Thus, *a positive reinforcer is a stimulus which strengthens, amplifies, or increases the rate of a behavioural sequence that it follows.*
- Next imagine a Skinner box with a wire grid for a floor, capable of delivering an irritating and continuous level of shock *until* an encounter with the lever turns this off for a period. As in the previous case the rat spends a lot of time operating the respite lever. This process is called *negative reinforcement*. It also leads to an *increase* in new behaviour, but with the object of *removing* an aversive set of conditions. Thus *a negative reinforcer is a stimulus the contingent removal of which strengthens, amplifies or increases the frequency of the behaviour pattern which led to it.*
- Next consider a situation where depressing the lever in the Skinner box leads every time to a loud noise. Such behaviour is decreased, probably extinguished, under these conditions. The animal quickly learns an avoidant reaction. Thus a *punishing* stimulus *decreases* or *extinguishes a behaviour pattern which it follows*.

Here are a couple of case vignettes from my own practice which show reinforcement contingencies at work:

- A lonely man with a serious drink problem who had learned that brushes with the police after altercations in public houses usually resulted in his daughter coming to stay with him until he was 'better'. More disorderly behaviour broke out.
- A 12-year-old boy who felt that his needs came a poor second to his parents' troubles, discovered, by accident (operantly), that a random, peer-inspired episode of fire-setting leading to a visit from the police, had the effect of jerking his father out of the depressed state he had been in since a serious industrial accident, and produced some concern for *him.* More fires broke out.

Intervention methods: contingency management

Evidence suggests that the most effective methods in such cases of maladaptive learning are based on *contingency management*, i.e. changing reinforcement patterns to ensure that useful, pro-social behaviour attracts reinforcement, and

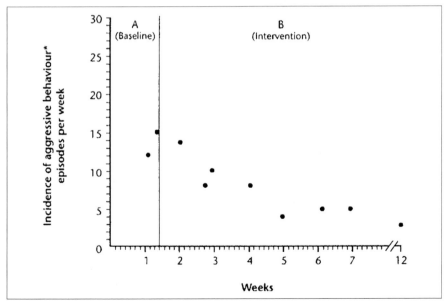

*Operationally defined as: shouting at mother or passers by in the street; threatening mother or members of the public; swearing, pushing or throwing objects; acting out macho fantasies in play.

Figure 8.3   A differential reinforcement for other behaviour, plus response-cost scheme to control aggressive behaviour in a nine-year-old boy

that negative, self defeating, anti-social behaviour does not. In case these terms seem a little Orwellian, giving rise to 'who is to decide about these things' feelings, well, at a political level, I agree. But in most day-to-day cases the distinction is obvious. There is, after all, nothing admirably rebellious about setting fire to neighbours' property to attract the attention of your depressed, physically disabled father, and there is nothing dissidently incorrigible about getting plastered and attacking people so that your daughter will abandon her own family to come and look after you; there are simply better ways to live. So, these issues remain, awkwardly, matters of informed judgement and debate. Here is an example of the application of contingency management (sometimes called differential reinforcement) techniques to a problem.

From the age of six onwards Kenneth's behaviour had been a cause for concern to his mother and his teachers. He was aggressive to other pupils, swore at his mother, and on a few occasions, when shopping, had run through the supermarket pushing trolleys into people. His general demeanour was aggressive and he liked to dress in combat gear and have his hair cropped in military style. Following the departure of his father (an army PE instructor) from whom he got most of this behaviour, Kenneth's mother made a determined effort to change his conduct. At the time of the referral to a child and family guidance clinic she recounted that she had spoken to him at length about her embarrassment at his behaviour, tried to bribe him, and, as a last resort, used physical punishment: all to no avail. The approach of the social worker emphasised the need for consistency. Most of what had been tried before had been tried for short periods, the mother giving up and moving on to something new if an approach proved ineffective in the short-term, producing an intermittent negative reinforcement effect. The differential reinforcement programme used in this case contained the following features:

1. The identification of, and positive reinforcement of, low-probability behaviours somewhat incompatible with shouting, swearing and aggressive or embarrassing behaviour in the street while away from school. Those chosen were improved school attendance; small-scale domestic tasks; regular attendance without incident at an after-school club; reduced incidence of shouting and swearing etc. The reinforcers used were street credible stickers signifying a build-up of credit towards significant purchases, e.g. training shoes, football kit, plus collateral reinforcement in the form of praise.
2. An ultra-reliable set of sanctions for adverse behaviour, based on deprivation punishments, e.g. staying indoors; time out for 15-minute intervals – terminable by a believable apology after five; loss of screen privileges.
3. Basic assertion training for, and rehearsal of, typical incidents with the mother – the key part of the programme as it turned out. Progress came fairly quickly once the mother had grasped the idea of consistency and had learned to respond

to *current* behaviour rather than memories of yesterday's. The child remained at home, which was once an outcome in serious doubt, and a more regularised contact scheme was established with the father who grudgingly supported the scheme

Vicarious learning and modelling

Probably the most distinctive feature of CBT is that its practitioners do not rely upon verbal influence alone, but seek to *demonstrate* more adaptive, more skilful, and one hopes, more effective approaches to problems. Many of the difficulties which come our way are due to *learning deficits*, that is, to serious gaps in the behavioural repertoires of individuals. For example: how to manage difficult behaviour from a child; how to negotiate about rather than fight over conflicts of interest; how to cope with living again in the community after a period in a psychiatric unit; how to be calmly and rationally assertive when put upon. Solutions to these problems are largely a matter of social skills, which may not have been acquired naturally. Vicarious learning can account for the following patterns of change:

1. The second-hand acquisition of completely new *sequences* of behaviour. Remember adolescence when, being stalled somewhere between childhood and adulthood most of us experimented cavalierly with strange new ways of walking, dressing, talking, and so forth, mostly gathered from others or from images in the media (yes, you did). Such behavioural symbols of changing identity are tried on, kept, adapted, or discarded according to the internal (emotional) and external behavioural payoffs they produce. The problem is that sometimes there are no suitable models available (e.g. of how to walk away from trouble without loss of face) and so learning deficits accrue which threaten development.

2. Emotional reactions can also be learned vicariously. As children we learn what to fear by watching others behave fearfully, or how to cope by watching others approach threatening circumstances calmly.

3. Thought patterns, more particularly problem-solving styles, can be acquired by watching how others deal with challenges and then inferring (not always accurately) what processes of mental computation and interpretation led them to a given course of action.

Case example

A middle-aged man in a fairly serious state of depression, who had been made redundant three times in two years, had worked out a survival plan based upon observations of others not made redundant. His chosen models had allegedly 'kept their heads down' and survived. Yet on every occasion of loss of employment the reasons given to him were that he appeared to lack initiative, made only a minimal contribution to the team to which he belonged, and was more concerned with the inconsequential details of his own tasks. The approach used, with some success in that he has been off anti-depressants for over 12 months and is increasingly well-regarded at work, was based upon the modelling and rehearsal of a more pro-active, assertive approach in situations identified by him as threatening. He found the approach artificial at first, describing it as 'not real'. The response was that it might come to feel real with practice, which it did. Most social skills begin life as 'role play' to start with (think back).

Such modelling and social-skill training programmes should be organised according to the following common stages:

1. Identifying specific problems resulting from gaps in the client's behavioural repertoire, and deciding what new patterns of behaviour could be developed to fill these.
2. Dividing the target responses into their component parts (for example, coming into a room full of people (you don't have to *be* confident, just to *act* confidently); deciding who to stand next to and what to say; introducing oneself; non-verbal responding; getting in on the conversation, and so forth).
3. Identifying with clients any patterns in their thinking (images and inner speech) which may encourage misinterpretation of the motives of others or avoidance responses, e.g. 'people are looking at me, they can tell I don't belong here'.
4. Demonstrating to clients what a competent performance might look like; rehearsing any problematic parts of the sequence or going through it slowly and deliberately, emphasising options and decision points.
5. Developing more complex performances by chaining together different sequences.
6. Gradually introducing difficulties likely to be found in real life as the client becomes more able to cope with its vicissitudes (for instance, not getting an immediate answer when trying to be friendly; meeting increased persistence after saying no to something).
7. Supervising practical assignments on which clients report back.

Example of a group approach

The transfer of clients from psychiatric units back into the community was, and is, fraught with difficulties. Usually, if at all, the fears and worries of clients are handled individually. However, many of these sources of anxiety are held in common by them. I was once involved in running a group for about-to-be discharged patients who were encouraged first to identify their worries, then to discuss the extent to which they might be concentrating on and over-reacting to fears and neglecting sources of support, and then to rehearse ways of approaching difficult situations *via* role-play, sometimes with video feedback. This project had both cognitive, modelling, and live-practice desensitisation elements, and was thought very useful by participants at the evaluation stage (Social Skills Inventory; Self-esteem Scale – see Fischer and Corcoran, 2007). Outcome studies in this field point to modelling as an effective technique providing that it focuses on explicitly defined behavioural deficits. The results from more general-purpose programmes are less good.

Cognitive factors and methods

Here are the factors and their associated approaches to which the cognitive therapy literature suggests that we should attend in cases where we suspect that negative thinking is impeding attempts to improve functioning:

- *Selective Perception*. Perception is no camera-like activity in which sense data is recorded, then later 'developed' and looked at on a screen in the head. It is an active, constructive process strongly influenced from the outset by our brains overriding raw sensory data, and is strongly influenced by past experience. Thus we are all capable of not attending to things which later look obviously important (see any child abuse inquiry report) or of over-concentrating on negative stimuli and favouring pessimistic interpretations. This is a particular problem in cases of depression, low morale, anxiety states and regarding challenging behaviour in children. The approach used in CBT constitutes a friendly, persistent, but logical, evidential challenge to such distortions, and encourages clients to test out less defensive, less pessimistic ideas in a controlled way.

- *Attributions*. Human beings search actively for meaning when confronted by complex stimuli. We seek to attribute causality (sometimes making mistakes) as we try, like amateur scientists, to evaluate potential threats, rewards, or sources of relief. Attributive cognitions fall into two main patterns: the external (circumstantial) and the internal (dispositional). The typical direction of causal attribution tends to vary with personality, with experience, with regularly encountered contingencies, and according to emotional state. It may be that some of us are statistically more likely to look to our environments for explanations of our failures; some of us are more likely to blame ourselves. The same can be said of our successes. Generally speaking, women are statistically more likely to look outwards for explanations of success and inwards for explanations of failure. As you might have guessed, the situation is reversed for men (Brown, 1986, Ch 9). Social workers often encounter individuals whose patterns of self blaming or self-excusing cognitions seem implausibly uni-directional. Here are a couple of case vignettes:
  - A young woman, worried and preoccupied by memories of persistent sexual abuse in childhood, who felt that she 'must' have done 'something'

to encourage her stepfather, and 'must' have enjoyed the 'games' at the time, making her a bad person.

– A client with a string of different psychiatric diagnoses to her name, living in a hostel, who attributed the sound of nearby laughter to cruel jokes being made at her expense, and silence in the house to a wish by her critics that they should not be overheard when discussing her failings. Thus she could never win.

- *Dichotomous Thinking*. Clients with a string of bad experiences behind them sometimes seek the temporary security of completely good versus completely bad views of their problems, and, initially present non-negotiable appraisals and attributions regarding these to staff trying to help them. For example: 'He's *just* like his father and he'll never change, it's *in* him' (as in the case in the section on operant conditioning). In such cases exponents of CBT try to establish the idea of a *continuum* of possibilities, along which small down-payments of change against a more realistic plan might become acceptable if little experiments begin to show useful gains.

In the research literatures of psychotherapy, social work and clinical psychology, two strong trends have been visible for some time:

1. That the elements of a focused, fairly intensive, task-centred, quasi-behavioural approach, within which due regard is paid to the problem of translating new understandings into behavioural change, are strongly associated with positive outcomes (Reid and Hanrahan, 1981; Sheldon, 1986; Macdonald and Sheldon, 1992; Lambert, 2004).

2. That problems which have behavioural components (virtually all do) but which are also strongly rooted in, or maintained by, internal factors such as mood and thought patterns, respond well to approaches which seek to analyse, make clear, and test out in reality the perceptions, beliefs and patterns of negative, self-defeating cognition which lead to avoidance, disengagement and, eventually, alienation.

Case example

Mrs M (44) was referred for CBT and 'social support' by her psychiatrist. The research findings discussed above closely encapsulate the sad and threatening life events that she encountered:

- She was an adopted child (probably her intended role was to thaw out a frozen marriage).
- She was raised in a distant, arm's-length way.
- She later had two violent marriages herself.
- She was raped.
- She suffered the loss of her 18-year-old daughter in a car accident and had to make the decision to switch off the life-support machinery.

She later, understandably, had occupational difficulties, made worse by the current, 'if officially ill, stay away; if officially well, come in and perform to standard' policies which pass for 'human resources management'.

Scores on the Hamilton and Beck Depression Inventory Scales showed her to be in the most serious 1 per cent of cases, with suicidal ideation a daily preoccupation. Medication made her sleepy and unable to function. She was therefore likely to alternate between feeling that nothing mattered much, and occasional bursts of agitation: 'Like being on your way somewhere important but 'dozing off at the wheel'' she said. The cognitive component of work with Mrs M concentrated on the following factors:

1. That she had a brittle sense of gratitude towards her adoptive parents – 'they told me I was special because they *chose* me, but then they sent me to a boarding-school three miles down the road and didn't often have me home'. As an adolescent she kicked over the traces, this behaviour leading to expulsion from school. In her parents' view, and note, in *hers*, this amounted to ingratitude. Similarly, that her interest in her natural mother's fate amounted to a 'betrayal of trust'.

2. That her early sexual experimentation ('I knew how to get boys to give me what I wanted': *Social worker*: 'What was that?' *Answer*: 'Attention, affection') was the result of 'bad blood'.

3. That her desire to find a 'strong man or two' who would protect her – which led to two violent relationships (the attractive macho behaviour was not supposed to be brought home) – was a result of her 'stupidity'.

4. That she should have performed some routine checks on the state of her daughter's car (e.g. tyre pressures, brakes) before she set off on her fatal journey, even though she had absolutely no mechanical expertise.

5. That the person who followed her and raped her had 'had his fuse lit' by her, and that she should have known better what flirting would lead to.

6. That getting better meant abandoning her daughter's cherished memory and 'moving on' without her, and so would constitute another betrayal. The approach used was to persuade her to take her daughter's love and the memories of her with her throughout life. She seized upon the idea.

7. That her present, loving partner, whom she thought 'too kind for his own good', was only displaying sympathy or at best short-term love, and would leave her when he found out more about her (they are now happily married).

The behavioural components in this case were based on the idea of 'scheduling pleasant events' against a desensitisation hierarchy (see Chapter 7). The principle here is to encourage reality testing (i.e. will the meal with friends really be a disaster; will the movie *really* not be enjoyable; will trips to the keep-fit club *really* not result in weight loss; will confiding in your partner *really* distance him more than will the 'partner-management scheme' currently in place; does bad, manipulative sex with previous partners mean that nothing more meaningful is possible with someone quite different?).

Obstacles to the use of cognitive behavioural approaches by social services staff

The primary function of the Centre for Evidence-based Social Services (of which I was Director) was dissemination of existing research and its implications for practice and service development. It was thus a rational conclusion that as part of our output, staff should receive training in CBT. This view was supported by findings from a large questionnaire exercise (n = 1226) conducted by the Centre (see Sheldon and Chilvers, 2000) within which respondents gave high priority to items regarding initiatives that would improve their 'knowledge of effective intervention methods'. Incidentally, they were virtually all professionally qualified. Accordingly, we conducted eight three-day courses plus case-project work, a follow-up day, and some on-site support in the interim for staff from 16 social services departments. This project involved 274 professional grade staff, and given that every phase was subject to evaluation (*via* anonymous questionnaires) it is a training research project in its own right. Here are our findings from the exercise:

1. All courses were substantially oversubscribed. The high point was 217 applications for 40 places within seven days of advertising, with other courses attracting potential applicants on an average 4:1 ratio for the places available.
2. Questions as to prior knowledge of cognitive behavioural methods revealed the following: although virtually all participants had *heard of* the approach only a small minority had received any training in it at all on their qualifying courses. Subsequent departmental training courses never touched the subject, being concerned largely with compliance with new administrative procedures and 'initiatives'.
3. Therefore, we find ourselves in a position where possibly the most effective approaches to a wide range of problems within the remit of social services are less likely to be taught than other approaches with a far less substantial record of effectiveness. But let us turn now to what happens when staff do get training in these methods. If we take as our quality standard the last two columns on the right of Figure 8.4, then we have an 87.7 per cent rating of satisfaction and an 87.2 per cent level for relevance. As indicated earlier, these courses also contained a project phase, in which staff were asked to apply what they had learned to a case and produce assessment and evaluation data on this work. However, of the 274 staff involved, only 85 (31 per cent) came back with case material showing that they had been able to apply these methods. The course tutors issued an amnesty on this at the end of the training, inviting people who might not have an opportunity to use the approach to attend anyway and to tell us why this was so. These staff identified the following obstacles to implementation (in rank order):

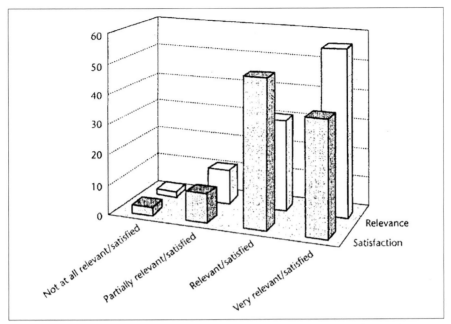

Figure 8.4 Satisfaction with and perceived relevance of CBT training (n = 231)

1. Pressure of work – but then one has to ask what was being done instead? The answer appeared to be increasing amounts of risk-management work (child care and mental health workers) and accountability exercises (all).

2. That therapeutic work is discouraged in some authorities, which have regimes which determine that even qualified staff spend most of their time assessing cases and then trying to find 'external providers' who might provide limited help on a tight budget.

3. CBT work usually requires short-term but intensive involvement with clients and their families; this, we are told is also discouraged by present conventions, within which clients *either* receive glancing, problem-containing contact when crises occur, or longer term 'drip feed' support if their needs are largely practical and foreseeable (which many are not). Inadequacy of resources is one aspect of this problem. However, the point remains that if we do not intervene in timely fashion, using effective approaches, then we only get these cases later, in direr circumstances, when most therapeutic possibilities have evaporated.

More recent training experiments, featuring greater workplace contact with staff during the project phase improved case-study completion rates by 15–20 per cent. So, get some training. (I can provide it if you get stuck – profbsheldon@ mbechippenham.co.uk).

Conclusions

I have tried in this chapter to bring together arguments about the need for the principles of evidence-based practice to inform our selection of approaches. We have also examined together the research track record of CBT methods, and, *via* case examples and references to other research, looked at their relevance to parts of the social care field. My main conclusion is, therefore, that here is a body of knowledge and techniques, directly applicable to mainstream practitioners, with an unrivalled record of effectiveness, which have been rather self-defeatingly neglected. Further, and to my continuing amazement, most qualifying courses do not teach these to their students (if you are a student and this is so on your course, make a fuss). If we look for reasons as to why this is the case, then the prime contenders are the continual so-called reforms and reorganisations of social services, which have pushed anything but high-eligibility-threshold, problem *containment* aside (a very expensive way to run a service, by the way.) At the same time there has been a dumbing down of social work education during recent years (see Macdonald and Sheldon, 1998) and an ever expanding incorporation of political fads and fashions into an already crowded curriculum: 'never mind the quality, feel the *width*'.

However, if we look at recent political developments, in child care, mental health, and rehabilitation services for elderly people, then it is obvious that some new opportunities for something more rational and more effective (bankers permitting) are available – other professions are taking them, note. If you are content with the idea of virtual reality social work, or being the equivalent of a call centre employee, you need do nothing, your existing terms and conditions will be renewed automatically.

Finally remember the wise words of Arron Beck (1976) to his depressed patients: *If you don't have plans for yourself, you will quickly become part of someone else's.*

References

Bacon, F. (1605) *The Advancement of Learning.* (1965, G.W. Kitchen Ed.) London: Dent.

Bandura, A. (1969) *Principles of Behavior Modification.* New York: Holt, Rinehart and Winston.

Beck, A.T. (1976) *Congitive Therapy and the Emotional Disorders.* New York: International Universities Press.

Bennett, D.S. and Gibbons, T.A. (2000) Efficacy of Child Cognitive-behavioral Interventions for Anti-social Behavior: A Meta Analysis. *Child and Family Behavior Therapy,* 22: 1, 1–15.

Benton, M.K. and Schroeder, H.E. (1990) Social Skills Training with Schizophrenics: A Meta-analytic Evaluation. *Journal of Consulting and Clinical Psychology,* 58: 6, 741–747.

Bergin, A.E. and Garfield, S.L. (Eds.) (1994) *Handbook of Psychotherapy and Behavior Change.* (4th edn.) Chichester: John Wiley and Sons.

British Association for Behavioural and Cognitive Psychotherapies (2010) *Code of Ethics.* revised, Cambridge University Press.

Brown, R. (1986) *Social Psychology.* New York: Free Press.

Carr, A. (2000) (Ed.) *What Works With Children and Adolescents.* London: Brunner Routledge.

Centre for Evidence-based Social Services (1999) *Annual Report.* University of Exeter.

Cigno, K. and Bourne, D. (1999) *Cognitive Behavioural Social Work in Practice.* Aldershot: Arena.

Claridge, G. (1985) *Origins of Mental Illness.* Oxford: Blackwell.

Damasio, A.R. (1994) *Descartes; Error: Emotion, Reason and the Human Brain.* New York: Grosset Putnam.

DoH (1994) *A Wider Strategy for Research in the Personal Social Services.* London: HMSO.

Donaldson, M. (1978) *Children's Minds.* London: Fontana Press.

Emmelcamp, P.M. (1994) Behaviour Therapy with Adults. In Bergin, P.E. and Garfield, S. *Handbook of Psychotherapy and Behaviour Change.* Chichester: John Wiley.

Falloon, I.R.H., Boyd, J.L. and McGill, C.W. (1984) *Family Care of Schizophrenia.* New York: Guilford Press.

Fischer, J. and Corcoran, K. (2009) *Measures for Clinical Practice: A Sourcebook. Vols. 1 and 2* (3rd edn.) New York: The Free Press.

Gambrill, E. (1997) *Social Work Practice: A Critical Thinker's Guide.* Oxford: Oxford University Press.

Gambrill, E. (2012) *Propaganda in the Helping Professions.* New York: Oxford University Press.

Gibbons, J.S., Butler, J., Urwin, P. and Gibbons, J.L. (1978) Evaluation of a Social Work Service for Selfpoisoning Patients. *British Journal of Psychiatry*, 133: 111–118.

Gloaguen, V., Cottraux, J., Cucherat, M. and Blackburn, I.M. (1998) A Meta-analysis of the Effects of Cognitive Therapy in Depressed Patients. *Journal of Affective Disorders*, 49: 1, 59–72.

Gough, R. (1993) *Child Abuse Interventions.* London: HMSO.

Gould, R.A., Otto, M.W., Pollack, M.H. and Yap, L. (1997) Cognitive Behavioral and Pharmacological Treatment of Generalised Anxiety Disorder: A Preliminary Meta-analysis. *Behavior Therapy*, 28: 285–305.

Harris, B. (1979) Whatever Happened to Little Albert? *American Psychologist*, 34: 151–160.

Hollon, S.D. and Beck, A.T. (2004) Cognitive and Cognitive-behavioural therapies, in Lambert, M.J. (Ed.) *Handbook of Psychology and Behaviour change*, Chichester: Wiley

Hudson, B.L. and Macdonald, G.M. (1988) *Behavioural Social Work.* London: Macmillan.

Jehu, D. (1967) *Learning Theory and Social Work.* London: Routledge and Keagan Paul.

Jones, C., Cormac, I., Mota, J. and Campbell, C. (1998) Cognitive Behaviour Therapy for

Schizophrenia (Cochrane Review) In *The Cochrane Library*, Issue 1, 2000. Oxford: Update Software.

Joseph, S., Williams, R. and Yule, W. (1995) Psychosocial Perspectives on Post-traumatic Stress. *Clinical Psychology Review*, 15: 515–544.

Lambert, M.J. (Ed.) (2004) *Bergin and Garfield's Handbook of Psychotherapy and Behavior Change.* (5th edn.) Chicago: John Wiley and Sons.

Littell, J.H. (2008) Evidence-based or Biased? The Quality of Published Reviews of Evidence-Based Practices, *Children and Youth Services Review*, 1299–1317.

Lu, S.H. (2001) *China, Transnational Visuality, Global Postmodernity.* Stanford, CA: Stanford University Press.

Macdonald, G.M. and Kakavelakis, I. (2004) *Helping Foster Carers to Manage Challenging Behavior: Evaluation of a Cognitive-Behavioral Programme for Foster Carers*, Centre for Evidence-Based Social Services. University of Exeter.

Macdonald, G.M. and Sheldon (1992) Contemporary Studies of the Effectiveness of Social Work. *British Journal of Social Work*, 22: 6, 615–643.

Macdonald, G.M. and Sheldon, B. (1998) Changing One's Mind: The Final Frontier? *Issues in Social Work Education*, 18: 1, 3–25.

Macdonald, G.M. and Winkley, A. (2000) *What Works in Child Protection?* Basingstoke: Barnardo's.

McGuffin, P., Owen, M.J. and Gottesman, I.I. (Eds.) (2004) Psychiatric Genetics and Genomics. *Genes, Brain and Behavior*, 3: 186.

National Institute for Clinical Excellence (2005) *Post traumatic Stress Disorder (PTSD). The Management of PTSD in Adults and Children, in Primary and Secondary care.* Clinical Guideline 26, London: National Collaborations Centre for Mental Health.

Olds, J. (1956) Pleasure Centre in the Brain. *Scientific American*, 195: 105–116.

Pavlov, I.P. (1927) *Conditioned Reflexes: An Investigation of the Physiological Activity of the Cerebral Cortex.* Translated and Edited by Anrep, G.V. London: Oxford University Press.

Reid, W.J. and Hanrahan, P. (1981) The Effectiveness of Social Work: Recent Evidence. In Globerg, E.M. and Connolly, N. (Eds.) *Evaluative Research in Social Care.* London: Heinemann Educational Books.

Sackett, D.L., Rosenberg, W.M., Gray, J.M., Haynes, R.B. and Richardson, W.S. (1996) Evidence-based Practice: What it is and What it isn't. *British Medical Journal*, 312: 7203, 71–72.

Scott, M. (1989) *A Cognitive Behavioural Approach to Clients' Problems.* London: Tavistock.

Sheldon, B. (1978a) Behavioural Approaches in Social work, *Social Work Today*, 4.9, 5.9.

Sheldon, B. (1978b) Theory and Practice in Social Work: A Re-examination of a Tenuous Relationship. *British Journal of Social Work*, 8: 1, 1–22.

Sheldon, B. (1983) The Use of Single Case Experimental Designs in the Evaluation of Social Work. *British Journal of Social Work*, 2: 1.

Sheldon, B. (1986) Social Work Effectiveness Experiments: Review and Implications. *British Journal of Social Work*, 16: 223–242.

Sheldon, B. (1987) The Psychology of Incompetence. In Drewry, G., Martin, B. and Sheldon B. (Eds.) *After Beckford: Essays on Child Abuse.* Egham, Surrey: Royal Holloway and Bedford New College.

Sheldon, B. (1989) *Studies of the Effectiveness of Social Work.* PhD Thesis, University of Leicester.

Sheldon, B. (2001) The Validity of Evidence-based Practice in Social Work: A Reply to Stephen Webb. *British Journal of Social Work,* 31: 801–809.

Sheldon, B. (2011) *Cognitive Behavioural Therapy.* 2nd edn. London: Routledge.

Sheldon, B. and Chilvers, R. (2000) *Evidence-based Social Services: Prospects and Problems.* Lyme Regis: Russell House Publishing.

Sheldon, B. and Macdonald, G.M. (1999) *Research and Practice in Social Care: Mind the Gap.* Centre for Evidence-based Social Services, University of Exeter.

Sheldon, B. and Macdonald, G.M. (2009) *A Textbook of Social Work.* London: Routledge.

Skinner, B.F. (1953) *Science and Human Behaviour.* New York: Macmillan.

Skinner, B.F. (1971) *About Behaviourism.* Eaglewood Cliffs, NJ: Prentice Hall.

Sokal, A. and Bricmont, J. (1998) *Intellectual Impostures.* London: Profile Books.

Sweet, A.A. and Loizeaux, A.L. (1991) Behavioral and Cognitive Treatment Methods: A Critical Comparative Review. *Journal of Behavior Therapy and Experimental Psychiatry,* 22: 3, 159–185.

Thorndike, E.L. (1898) Animal Intelligence: An Experimental Study of the Associative Processes in Animals. *Psychological Review,* Monograph 2.

Van Etten, M.L. and Taylor, S. (1998) Comparative Efficacy of Treatments for Post-traumatic Stress Disorder: A Meta-analysis. *Clinical Psychology and Psychotherapy,* 5: 124–126.

Watson, J.B. and Rayner, R. (1920) Conditional Emotional Reactions. *Journal of Experimental Psychology,* 3: 1–14.

Webb S.A. (2001) *Some Considerations on the Validity of Evidence-based Practice in Social Work.* British Journal of Social Work, 31, 57–79.

Webster, R. (1996) *Why Freud was Wrong: Sin, Science and Psychoanalysis.* London: Fontana Press.

Chapter 9

Counselling and Contemporary Social Work

Avril Bellinger and Frances Fleet

> *. . . we grew together,*
> *Like to a double cherry, seeming parted,*
> *But yet an union in partition;*
> *Two lovely berries moulded on one stem . . .*
>
> (Shakespeare, *A Midsummer Night's Dream*, III: II. lines 208–211)

This is a good time to be reviewing the relationship between counselling and contemporary social work. At the time of writing, social work in England is emerging from a period of managerial and bureaucratic control in which the definition of social work had been conflated with state agency function (Lavalette and Ioakimidis, 2011). The public view of social work is dominated by media accounts of child protection failures and students often express surprise at the range of settings and activities that are open to them when qualified. A change of government provides an opportunity for the profession to reposition itself in relation to the state. A major review of social work education, provision and management (DfE, 2010), establishment of a social work college and change of registration body from the General Social Care Council to the Health Professions Council in 2012 create opportunities for a focus on relationship and social justice to come to the fore. Such a development is strongly supported by global initiatives in which the 2010 World Congress on Social Work and Social Development identified the importance of relationship as one of four priorities for the coming decade (IFSW, 2010). The effects of structural and political developments are dealt with in more detail elsewhere in this volume. This chapter about counselling is written as a focus on relationship-based practice.

The efficient and equitable delivery of services demands a very different set of skills from those envisaged by students entering the profession wanting to work therapeutically with people (Hugman, 2009). On the other hand the social work literature repeatedly affirms the vital importance of counselling skills (Brearley, 1995; Payne, 1995; Brown, 2005; Seden, 2005; Ruch *et al.*, 2010). We would argue that safe and effective practice relies on a well-developed capacity to develop therapeutic alliances within whatever organisational structures people work.

It may be useful initially to look briefly at our history. Both social work and counselling have a common ancestry. Brearley (1995) traces the development of both services from the nineteenth century and deals much more comprehensively than this single chapter can do with the links between the two. Both social work and counselling have their roots in the social casework described by such authors as Capen Reynolds (1942), Perlman (1957), Ferard and Hunnybun (1962) and Hollis (1964). Casework's objective was to engage the client in a re-evaluation of the person in their situation (Hollis, 1964). The worker sought to assist the client to a better adaptation to their circumstances and to enhanced coping skills. It drew predominantly on psychodynamic theory and was criticised and eventually superseded in the 1970s because the emphasis on the individual often resulted in the client being pathologised without sufficient critical focus on social and structural factors (Wilson *et al.*, 2011). Social work moved on to be invested with ever increasing legal responsibilities and to develop methods such as those explored in the other chapters of this volume. Counselling developed from a similar background, coupled with the early counselling services of marriage guidance (Jacobs, 1982). Counselling has, however, retained the central emphasis on the individual's adjustment and emotional well-being. In common with social work, counselling has been challenged for its Eurocentric and middle class orientation and has similarly extended, revised and reconsidered many of its practices to include transcultural (d'Ardenne and Mahtani, 2004), feminist (Chaplin, 1999) and narrative approaches (Etherington, 2000) among others.

Because of its shared history it is hardly surprising that the social work and counselling professions share many core skills and values. This historical link however refers to 'counselling approaches' as if we were borrowing these from a profession that has a prior right to them. It may be more helpful to think in terms of a discrete 'social work practice' approach which utilises similar skills but does so as part of our distinctly different objectives and responsibilities. So what precisely do we mean by 'counselling' and what are the difficulties with using it directly as a social work intervention? On the one hand a degree of mystique has gathered around the term which hints at an esoteric body of knowledge and skills set apart for those who practice as 'counsellors'. At the same time, however, we have seen an explosion in 'counselling' covering areas such as careers, debt, even personal 'style' or home decor, much of which clearly does not take the practitioner into intensely fragile areas of the psyche. The counselling literature recognises a distinction between those practitioners who are 'counsellors' and those who provide counselling in the context of a relationship, which is *'primarily focused on other, noncounselling concerns'* (McLeod, 1998: 4). McLeod cites nurses and teachers as examples of this but the definition would be equally applicable to social workers. There are numerous definitions of counselling and a huge volume of literature. What is clear is that counselling is a method of working, which draws on a variety of disciplines, including philosophy as well as psychology (McLeod, 1998) and incorporates a wide range of theories and applications. In 1965, just at the point when the two professions were beginning to diverge, Halmos wrote:

> *. . . all counselling procedures share a method: they are all 'talking cures', semantic exercises, they all attempt treatment through clarification of subjective experiences and meanings.*
>
> (Halmos, 1965: 3)

Within counselling this objective survives largely intact as we see from the British Association for Psychotherapy and Counselling:

> *Counselling and psychotherapy are umbrella terms that cover a range of talking therapies. They are delivered by trained practitioners who work with people over a short or long term to help them bring about effective change or enhance their well-being.*
>
> (BACP, 2010)

Counselling involves communication between two or more people with the sole objective of enabling the client to make progress in terms of growth and change. In most instances this will be change in personally selected directions. It is not usually the counsellor's role to define or impose the objectives, although it should be acknowledged that increasingly counsellors are becoming involved in the work of agencies where there is a clear agenda for social control, such as statutory drug services. Increasing diversity of service provision means that boundaries are more blurred. Counsellors might be constrained by government initiatives such as the 'happiness' counsellors piloted through the NHS (Gould, 2006) and use a particular method to achieve specific outcomes. Equally, social workers may be in private practice or multi-disciplinary teams where they can negotiate their approach to practice. However, the emphasis on non-directive practice suggests possible limitations and conflicts in using counselling as a primary method of intervention for most social workers, since much of our statutory work is about clearly defined issues of management of risks. The situations that bring most people to the attention of social workers today can rarely be resolved by talking alone (Cordon and Preston-Shoot, 1987). If 'counselling' is what is needed then it could be argued that it would be more appropriate to refer the client to a specialist agency such as Cruse or Relate. Clients would be protected from the stigma sometimes attached to social work involvement (Feltham and Dryden, 1993) and it would free up valuable social worker time.

Seden (2005) proposes that counselling is defined by its voluntary nature on the part of the recipient and its purpose of individual and internal sense-making, based on a therapeutic alliance. In contrast she says that social work is based on law and policy that has to respond to constant external change. Social workers have to intervene in social and material environments and do not have freedom of choice about methods or points of intervention.

In statutory social work, even the most carefully negotiated mandates take place in a context of constraint and unequal balance of power, which may call into question the degree of consent that is possible, or the reality of the client's capacity to terminate the counselling or limit its boundaries without at the very least being assessed as 'unmotivated' or 'resistant'. Even when the resource is made available, it remains, in Halmos' phrase, primarily a 'talking cure' which may not be truly accessible to clients with limited cognitive skills or capacity for verbal expression. There are further issues about the appropriateness of counselling, with its essentially Euro-centric origins and values, for clients from all cultural backgrounds (Brearley, 1995). This is a point illustrated very clearly by the review of a clinical counselling service provided to Kosovan refugees in Tasmania which was quickly recognised as inappropriate and replaced by community work provision and flexibly delivered support (Whelan *et al.*, 2002) an example to which we will return.

Finally Payne (1995) draws our attention to the fact that counselling may be inadequate for oppressed groups, who need the broader approach of social work. It is, however, often the case that the benefits of the provision of resources or the effectiveness of interventions to protect will be greatly reduced or even fail completely if Halmos' 'subjective experiences and meanings' are not acknowledged, explored and taken into account.

This has always been recognised. In 1982 the Barclay Report saw 'counselling' as a parallel activity with 'social care planning'; the two functions being 'different but interlocking' (Brearley, 1995). Then came the Griffiths Report and community care legislation. Malcolm Payne says of care planning that it is 'not a management activity . . . It is rather a human interaction' (Payne, 1995: 111) and he offers a tri-partite model in which care management, community social work and counselling are shown as distinct but overlapping processes. Regrettably, the care management function has taken precedence in much statutory practice, emphasising the administrative aspects of managing eligibility and controlling expenditure as key aspects of the social work role. This culture, as Hudson (2009) points out, leaves practitioners ill-equipped to implement the personalisation agenda with success. Furthermore, Lymberry and Postle (2010) argue that the current emphasis on individual choice, self-assessment and brokerage negates a core tenet of social work assessment. What are generally called 'counselling skills' help us to take clients with us, to engage them in the process, to exercise authority without alienating, to challenge and motivate. It is this kind of skilled interpersonal practice that we are suggesting should be seen as fundamentally characterising social work intervention, rather than being an 'add on tool' borrowed from another discipline when needed. Research supports this view (Pilling, 1991). Macdonald and Sheldon identified that 43 per cent of their sample of users of community care services for people with mental health problems cited emotional support and reassurance as the most helpful services provided, as against 32 per cent preferring practical help. The authors note:

> Nearly three quarters of respondents made positive comments about the quality of the working relationship which they enjoyed with staff. In social work the 'medium is

the message' to a greater extent than in other professions. If clients do not trust their would-be helpers they will not confide, and if they do not confide the risk of a crisis due to unresolved pressures is increased.

(Macdonald and Sheldon, 1997: 46)

This is equally true today. Here we have evidence that the judicious use of skills similar to those of counselling enhance the achievement of the clear objectives of modern social work, such as the avoidance of crises which might have repercussions in terms of safeguarding or might result in unnecessary hospital admissions. It is therefore important that we achieve a competent level of understanding and expertise in using these powerful and effective methods. We also need, however, to confront honestly the power that such methods bestow and the inherent responsibility to use them with integrity. We therefore have much of value to learn from the rich vein of counselling literature but we may need to adapt some of its theory to the context of social work practice. This is what we attempt to do in the second half of this chapter.

The worker/client relationship

We will start with the pivotal concept of the use of relationship. Raiff and Shore (1993) tell us that social workers need to pay constant attention to the relationship with the client. It is a view shared by many writers in the social work field (Kadushin, 1990; Lishman, 2009; Payne, 1995; Ruch *et al.*, 2010). This emphasis on relationship dates back to the common roots of social work and counselling referred to above. Two seminal works for the development of both professions were Biestek's *The Casework Relationship* (1957) and Ferard and Hunnybun's *The Caseworker's Use of Relationship* (1962). Writing from about the same time up until 1990, initially in the field of psychotherapy, Carl Rogers produced numerous texts leading to the development of 'person-centred counselling'. This has also been profoundly influential on social work. These early works drew largely on the psychodynamic understanding of what happened in the contacts between client and worker. They saw the relationship as the primary 'tool', using the dynamic between worker and client as indicative of past relationships and unconscious processes as well as a way of enabling constructive changes:

The casework relationship is the dynamic interaction of attitudes and emotions between the caseworker and the client, with the purpose of helping the client achieve a better adjustment between himself and his environment.

(Biestek, 1957: 12)

The relationship between worker and client is still seen as pivotal but the emphasis now is on relationship as an aid to assessment and intervention rather than a primary tool in its own right. Sheldon for instance cites it as the essential 'packaging' for cognitive behavioural methods (Sheldon, 1995). Similarly, in child protection situations, Munro emphasises that, 'conducting an initial assessment requires interviewing skills, in order to elicit relevant information, and reasoning skills to analyse and reach conclusions on the basis of that incomplete and often ambiguous information' (Munro, 2010: 1147). Our understanding of the components of the relationship however still owes much to those early works. Biestek's 'principles' are less quoted now, but Carl Rogers' three essential components of genuineness, unconditional positive regard and empathic understanding, still exercise a profound influence over both professions.

Genuineness

Mearns and Thorne (1988) describe the impact of this as:

> The more the counsellor is able to be him/herself in the relationship without putting up a professional front or a personal façade, the greater will be the chance of the client changing and developing in a positive and constructive manner.
>
> (Mearns and Thorne, 1988: 14)

Is this applicable to social work? Lishman defines genuineness as 'being oneself' (Lishman, 2009) and it is certain that we are ourselves the medium through which interventions are delivered. Our use of self, that is how we are with people, is therefore likely to have a powerful influence on whether or not clients, carers or other professionals respond positively. It is clear, however from both social work and counselling literature, that 'self' is likely to be a product of our own cultural and historical experience that will carry unexamined assumptions and areas of ignorance. Donna Reeve's (2002) examination of the way in which society's disabling relationships are recreated in the counselling room offers an illustration of the risks of uncritical 'use of self'. The BACP ethical framework states that 'practitioners should not allow their professional relationships with clients to be prejudiced by any personal views they may hold about lifestyle, gender, age, disability, race, sexual orientation, beliefs or culture' (2010: 7) but this is much more easily said than done. In order for genuineness to be trustworthy and sensitive then 'self' must be understood as '. . . already implicated in forms of power and powerlessness' (Rossiter, 2007: 32). Practitioners cannot afford to treat self-knowledge as ever complete but rather as a primary focus for study, exploration and reconstruction. 'Being genuine' is something that is created between the practitioner and client through the exchanges (Butler *et al.*, 2007) and is a significant factor in developing the trust essential for meaningful work.

Unconditional positive regard

In the social work literature unconditional positive regard is more often referred to as 'acceptance'. For social workers, as for counsellors, this has to be achieved without any suggestion of condoning behaviour that is damaging to the individual or others. It is not to be confused with tolerance, which comes from a position of superiority, but is more accurately represented in the Indian greeting 'Namaste: the god in me salutes the god in you.'

Acceptance therefore requires a separation of the intrinsic worth of the person as a unique individual, from their behaviour, and conveying this clearly and unambiguously in all forms of communication.

Empathy

Empathy is a key concept in counselling and social work, but one which, because of its subtlety, is difficult to define. Gerard Egan defines it as '*getting in contact with another's world*' (Egan, 1994: 106). This means understanding the *significance* for the other person of their situation: what it means practically, what interpretation *they* put on it and what expectations this leads to, how it meshes or conflicts with their values or their self image, what feelings are triggered, what past events are echoed and old emotions re-awakened. Clearly, this is a tall order. Egan (1994: 106) acknowledges that it may be 'metaphysically impossible' to achieve fully. As Mark Hamer affirms '. . . the worker's role is to learn from the client. People living with the problem have more knowledge of the problem than any expert' (2006: 19). It might be worth pausing here to ask why it is so useful.

Turney refers to the importance of a positive relationship, saying 'If the service user feels valued, understood and secure in their relationship with the social worker, it is more likely that they will feel able to grapple with the distressing and painful parts of their life' (2009: 133–134).

Mearns and Thorne (1988) tell us that receiving empathy builds self-esteem as the client realises that they are 'understandable' and that someone (the counsellor) believes they are sufficiently important to try to understand them. They also suggest that empathy is a powerful influence when working with resistance:

> . . . for it is almost impossible to maintain an alienated position in the face of someone who is showing you profound understanding at a very personal level.
>
> (Mearns and Thorne, 1988: 46)

The same writers draw attention to the process by which empathy exerts its influence. In their view it enables a client to become more aware of feelings, and awareness of feelings is the first step to taking responsibility for them. Understanding is, however, of limited use unless it can be communicated to the client. How might it be possible to know whether we are being successful in empathising? Work undertaken by McCluskey (2005) explores the process of emotional attunement, in which it is clearly possible to distinguish between a dynamic and productive interaction and one which is simply an 'illusion of work' (Shulman, 2011). She illustrates with photographs the change in dynamic connection between helper and helped when the worker's attempts to communicate interest and understanding are close enough for the client to correct or augment. Egan (1994) sees the impact of empathic responses resting in the interviewer's ability to filter out and feed back themes and core messages in the client's communication. Mearns and Thorne call this working on the '*edge of awareness*' (Mearns and Thorne, 1988: 44). But does social work in the current context require such delicacy of technique? The answer lies in the immediacy of the interpersonal task, where the individual social worker still encounters the same confusions, ambivalence, loss of direction and desperation that character-ised similar encounters when social caseworkers first developed such concepts as aids to communication and change. The role has changed and our understanding has developed of the potential for social workers to perpetuate, or to disrupt, oppressive hierarchical relationships. Nonetheless consideration of empathy prompts recognition that constructive relationships between workers and clients do not just happen, they are dependent on both values and skills. In both these respects counselling and social work practice have much in common, but in neither area can concepts be exported whole.

Values

It is important to consider the values that both counselling and social work have in common and the way in which these have been challenged over the past decades. Issues of power have been explored within the counselling relationship as culture, class, gender, disability and sexuality for example have been identified as exclusions. Similarly in social work, it has become more fully understood that cultural and historical perspectives limit psychological, cognitive and even social explanations for human behaviour. Both professions undoubtedly share the basic value of respect for the individual, and major disagreements over this are rarely discernible either in practice or professional literature. Some other counselling values may however need different interpretation or application in the social work field. Social workers have quite different responsibilities from counsellors. This is not to say that counsellors do not sometimes face major ethical dilemmas relating to similar issues (McLeod, 1998), but their statutory obligations are different, their mandates more tightly defined and the values with which they operate quite rightly reflect this. Client self-determination for instance, which is absolutely central to most counselling contracts, may be less easy to apply in social work, where the nature of the professional intervention may be perceived as a very unwelcome intrusion into the client's life. Similarly, the statutory social work agencies do not offer the same level of confidentiality, which private counsellors or even voluntary agencies may provide. There are also major issues for social workers around the value of being 'non-judgemental'. This needs very careful qualifying for social workers in order to differentiate between being non-judgemental as opposed to suspending all capacity to make judgements. Much of our work involves making far-reaching judgements about the conflicting needs of child and parent, victim and perpetrator, carer and dependant or about the risks posed by individuals or their circumstances (Milner and O'Byrne, 2009). Maintaining a non-judgemental stance, however, means that all the individuals concerned are treated with respect and compassion.

Skills for social work practice

Communication skills such as listening, responding, facilitating and challenging are well-articulated in the work of Egan (1994) and Nelson-Jones (2010) in the counselling field and Koprowska (2010), Lishman (2009) and Seden (2005) for social work. This chapter can only touch briefly on these but it will do so by seeking to explore how they translate into an effective social work practice. It is vital that we have the capacity to develop, sometimes very quickly or in very adverse circumstances, the kind of constructive relationships to which we have referred above. There are some key themes for social work that arise from a consideration of counselling and that reflect the relationship-based activity of co-creating meaning for the purpose of improving people's lives in their own terms.

First is the importance of self-knowledge. We must seek to be aware of our own responses, assumptions, limitations and needs (Rossiter, 2007). Even before meeting someone for the first time, we have information about them that can be explored. Using techniques derived from a systemic approach (Kohli and Dutton, 2010) we can ask questions about the referral information such as: How am I responding to this information? What emotions does it trigger in me? What assumptions am I making? What gaps am I filling? What judgements am I making? What does it not tell me about? What does it help me to recognise about myself? These questions support the worker in maintaining a respectful curiosity and maintaining the possibility of multiple explanations.

Second is an understanding of power relations. Psycho-social interventions need to take account of the changing social context and of our growing recognition of the narrow and individualising Eurocentric understanding of the individual. If we are intervening at the level of people's thinking and their experience of their lives, there is substantial potential for that to result in the perpetuation of inequality. People approach social workers with necessary defences and are likely to be, at best, apprehensive about the encounter. This frequently leads to the telling of 'thin' or rehearsed stories that are unlikely to result in significant change. Careful negotiation of an agenda, which acknowledges the client's concerns as a starting point encourages trust in the worker's ability to be helpful. Although derived from work with refugees, Kohli and Dutton's analysis offers valuable insight into the possibilities for work with other groups, particularly where time is limited. They refer to the importance of negotiating a basis for a conversation, which moves quickly from 'thin' to 'thick' stories. Even in a brief meeting we are aiming to '. . . co-create a reflexive experience which can open up new avenues of thinking, description and choice . . .' (Kohli and Dutton, 2010: 94).

Third is the importance of listening and using high quality observation and assessment skills. It is very tempting in pressured work conditions to jump to conclusions too quickly and to foreclose the possibility of a more comprehensive understanding of a situation. We must hold in mind the constructive nature of reality (Fook, 2002; Parton and O'Byrne, 2000) and acknowledge that the worker is not an observer in situations, but is part of its construction. We know that social workers tend to make judgements very quickly and then to process information in a way that confirms their assessment (Taylor and White, 2006). Philosophical orientations such as mindfulness (Hamer, 2006) enable the worker to recognise and maintain awareness of their own impact and even in very pressured situations '. . . to think about speed, and slow down sufficiently so as not to be blurred by the encounter or to appear as a blur' (Kohli and Dutton, 2010).

The quality of an assessment clearly depends on the accuracy of the information obtained. It is vital, for instance, that we can hear what Rogers called *'sensing meanings of which the client is scarcely aware'* (Rogers, 1980: 142) as well as being able to 'hear' with all our senses, not just our ears, and to realise that we can never fully 'know' the lives of others (Ben-Ari and Strier, 2010). We also need to exercise the skills of questioning and exploring so that we can enable clarification of often intensely complex situations. The information social workers need from clients is often extremely personal, emotive, embarrassing and in psychodynamic terms, well defended. If people are to be able to share such information there needs to be a high degree of trust, sense of acceptance and belief that they are understood. Coulshed and Orme (2006) remind us that it is essential that we take account of emotional factors as well as practical ones. This is true even in the apparently most straightforward assessments, which seem to call for only material resources. Without attention to the emotional implications of factors such as deteriorating mobility, isolation or depression, assessment is unlikely to result in a successful outcome.

It is clear that counselling is not applicable in some circumstances where the skills or traditions of verbalising problems may be outside people's experience. Whelan *et al.* powerfully illustrate this in their review of a traditional counselling service for refugees that was replaced by community provision. They created a range of activity spaces in which professionals could 'be there and get to know people' (2002: 17). Such a flexible approach is applicable to residential and day care centres, to activity-based groups and drop-ins. It also highlights the importance of providing a range of ways for people to access social work, beyond the formal 'appointment' system. The use of counselling skills in such situations make the difference between having a chat and undertaking purposeful work.

Two of the characteristics identified by this project included 'well-developed interpersonal skills, including high level communication skills and an ability to quickly establish warm, trusting relationships' and 'an ability to "give of self" while maintaining clear professional goals and boundaries' (*ibid*: 17).

Fourth is the issue of confidentiality and ownership of information. It is common for social work and counselling to be commissioned by someone other than the service user. This means that all information is shared with the organisation. What may feel like a very personal relationship is in fact an interface between agency and user. It is essential therefore that social workers hold this awareness and are not placed in a position of encouraging personal disclosure and then being seen to breach confidence.

Fifth is the importance of counselling skills in supervision. In many statutory employment settings supervision has become a bureaucratic management process in which efficiency of meeting targets is at the centre. Many social workers have been left feeling undervalued and pressured to maintain recording systems at the expense of a critically reflective approach to their work. Counselling emphasises the importance of 'clinical supervision' in which the desired therapeutic alliance is modelled and the practitioner's view of understandings and possibilities extended. Turney (2009) reaffirms the importance of this for practice. It is a theme of the social work review (DFE, 2010) and of the government investigation into child protection services. Skilled practitioners will approach supervision as an opportunity to challenge their own assumptions and recognise blocks to their own listening and accurate assessment.

Conclusion

This chapter has attempted to argue that what are often referred to as 'counselling skills' are as much a part of our inheritance as that of our colleagues who define themselves as counsellors. In particular, social workers need to establish constructive professional relationships with their clients, based on the core components first identified by 'casework', but refined to harmonise with the legal, political and administrative frameworks and restraints under which contemporary agencies function. Workers also need high levels of interpersonal skills, both communication skills and methods of intervention, many of which have been primarily explored and refined within the counselling profession. Although we may often work with people in similar situations, social workers have different responsibilities and objectives to counsellors and there are real difficulties if we allow role confusion to creep in. It is important therefore for social workers to be clear that they are not able to offer 'counselling' in the purest technical sense to their clients, although there will be times when their social work practice will utilise very similar skills and methods, particularly when they are addressing the emotional components of their clients' situations. As identified by Kohli and

Dutton (2010: 86) the cornerstones for trustworthy relationships are '. . . honesty, clarity, reliability, kindness, warmth and precision'.

Finally, it is our hope that by considering social work and counselling as Shakespeare's 'double cherry', that is, distinct professions linked by their common origins, we can avoid giving precedence to either but can acknowledge the differing responsibilities, objectives and expertise of each. Counselling on the whole is probably better at claiming recognition of its knowledge base and skills. It also generally gains a better press, although ironically, many of the practitioners involved in high profile instances of provision of 'counselling', such as in the wake of major disasters, will in fact be social workers (Lavalette and Ioakimidis, 2011). This chapter carries the message that, far from needing to borrow from other professions, social work has its own long and impressive history of uniquely tailored, highly skilled interpersonal interventions, which form a foundation for its complex and multi-faceted practice. It is these fundamental skills which enable the fulfilment of social work's specific roles and responsibilities with some of the most disadvantaged and challenging client groups, and which have application in both 'clinical' and community orientated settings.

References

Ben-Ari, A. and Strier, R. (2010) Rethinking Cultural Competence: What Can We Learn From Levinas? *British Journal of Social Work*, 40, 2155–2167.

Biestek, F.P. (1957) *The Casework Relationship*. London: Unwin Hyman.

Brearley, J. (1995) *Counselling and Social Work*. Buckingham: Open University Press.

British Association for Counselling and Psychotherapy (2010) *Ethical Framework*, http://www.bacp.co.uk/ethical_framework/.

Brown, H.C. (2005) Counselling. In Adams, R., Dominelli, L. and Payne, M. (Eds.) *Social Work: Themes, Issues and Critical Debates*. London: Macmillan.

Butler, A., Ford, D. and Tregaskis, C. (2007) Who Do We Think We Are? Self and Reflexivity in Social Work Practice. *Qualitative Social Work*, 5:3, 281–299.

Capen Reynolds, B. (1942) *Learning and Teaching in the Practice of Social Work*. New York: Rinehart.

Chaplin, J. (1999) *Feminist Counselling in Action*. London: Sage.

Cordon, J. and Preston-Shoot, M. (1987) *Contracts in Social Work*. Aldershot: Gower.

Coulshed, V. and Orme, J. (2006) *Social Work Practice: An Introduction*. London: Macmillan.

d'Ardenne, P. and Mahtani, A. (2004) *Transcultural Counselling in Action*. (2nd edn.) London: Sage.

Department for Education (2010) *Building a Safe and Confident Future One Year on*, https://www.education.gov.uk/publications/standard/publicationDetail/Page1/DFE-00602-2010.

Egan, G. (1994) *The Skilled Helper*. (5th edn.) Pacific Grove, CA: Brooks/Cole.

Etherington, K. (2000) *Narrative Approaches to Working With Adult Male Survivors of Childhood Sexual Abuse: The Clients', The Counsellors', and The Researchers' Stories.* London: Jessica Kingsley.

Feltham, C. and Dryden, W. (1993) *Dictionary of Counselling.* London: Whurr.

Ferard, M. and Hunnybun, N.K. (1962) *The Caseworker's Use of Relationship.* London: Tavistock.

Fook, J. (2002) *Social Work: Critical Theory and Practice.* London: Sage.

Gould (2006) http://www.guardian.co.uk/society/2006/jun/21/mentalhealth.socialcare.

Halmos, P. (1965) *The Faith of the Counsellors.* London: Constable.

Hamer, M. (2006) *The Barefoot Helper, Mindfulness and Creativity in Social Work and the Helping Professions.* Lyme Regis: Russell House Publishing.

Hollis, F. (1964) *Casework: A Psychological Therapy.* New York: Random House.

Hudson, B. (2009) Captives of Bureaucracy. *Community Care*, 9th April, 30–31.

Hugman, R. (2009) But is it Social Work? Some Reflections on Mistaken Identities. *British Journal of Social Work*, 39, 1138–1153.

IFSW (2010) http://www.ifsw.org/f38000378.html.

Jacobs, M. (1982) *Still Small Voice: An Introduction to Pastoral Counselling.* London: SPCK.

Kadushin, A. (1990) *The Social Work Interview: A Guide for Human Service Professionals.* (3rd edn.) New York: Columbia University Press.

Kohli, R. and Dutton, J. (2010) Brief Encounters: Working in Complex Short-term Relationships. In Ruch, G., Turney, D. and Ward, A. (Eds.) (2010) *Relationship-Based Social Work: Getting to the Heart of Practice.* London: Jessica Kingsley.

Koprowska, J. (2010) *Communication and Interpersonal Skills in Social Work.* (2nd Edition) Exeter: Learning Matters.

Lavalette, M. and Ioakimidis, V. (Eds.) (2011) *Social Work in Extremis: Lessons for Social Work Internationally.* London: Policy Press.

Lishman, J. (2009) *Communication in Social Work.* London: Macmillan.

Lymbery, M. and Postle, K. (2010) Social Work in the Context of Adult Social Care in England and the Resultant Implications for Social Work Education. *British Journal of Social Work*, 40:8, 2502–2522.

Macdonald, G. and Sheldon, B. (1997) Community Care Services for the Mentally Ill: Consumers' Views. *International Journal of Social Psychiatry*, 43:1, 35–55.

McLeod, J. (1998) *An Introduction to Counselling.* (2nd edn.) Buckingham: Open University Press.

McLuskey, U. (2005) *To be Met as a Person: The Dynamics of Attachment in Professional Encounters.* London: Karnac.

Mearns, D. and Thorne, B. (1988) *Person-centred Counselling in Action.* London: Sage.

Milner, J. and O'Byrne, P. (2009) *Assessment in Social Work.* London: Macmillan.

Munro, E. (2010) Learning to Reduce Risk in Child Protection. *British Journal of Social Work*, 40: 4, 1135–1151.

Nelson-Jones. R. (2010) *Theory and Practice of Counselling and Therapy.* London: Sage.

Parton, N. and O'Byrne, P. (2000) What do We Mean by 'Constructive Social Work'? *Critical Social Work*, 1:2.

Payne, M. (1995) *Social Work and Community Care.* London: Macmillan.

Perlman, H. (1957) *Social Casework: a Problem Solving Process.* University of Chicago Press, Cambridge University Press.

Pilling, S. (1991) *Rehabilitation and Community Care.* London: Routledge.

Raiff, N. and Shore, B. (1993) *Advanced Case Management: New Strategies for the Nineties.* London: Sage.

Reeve, D. (2002) Oppression Within The Counselling Room. *Counselling and Psycho-therapy Research*, 2: 1, 11–19.

Rogers, C. (1980) *A Way of Being*. Boston: Houghton Mifflin.

Rossiter, A. (2007) Self as Subjectivity: Toward a Use of Self as Respectful Relations of Recognition. In Mandell, D. (Ed.) *Revisiting The Use of Self: Questioning Professional Identities*. Toronto: CSPI.

Ruch, G., Turney, D. and Ward, A. (Eds.) (2010) *Relationship-Based Social Work: Getting to the Heart of Practice*. London: Jessica Kingsley.

Seden, J. (2005) *Counselling Skills in Social Work Practice.* Maidenhead: Open University Press.

Sheldon, B. (1995) *Cognitive-behavioural Therapy: Research, Practice and Philosophy.* London: Routledge.

Sheldon, B. and Macdonald, G. (1999) *Research and Practice in Social Care: Mind the Gap.* CEBSS/Exeter University.

Shulman, L. (2011) *The Skills of Helping Individuals, Families, Groups and Communities.* Itasca: F. E. Publishing.

Taylor, C. and White, S. (2006) Knowledge and Reasoning in Social Work: Educating for Humane Judgement. *British Journal of Social Work*, 36, 937–954.

Turney, D. (2009) *Analysis and Critical Thinking in Assessment.* Dartington Hall Trust and University of Sheffield, Research in Practice.

Whelan, J., Swallow, M., Peschar, P. and Dunne, A. (2002) From Counselling to Community Work: Developing a Framework For Social Work Practice With Displaced Persons. *Australian Social Work*, 55, (1).

Wilson, K., Ruch, G., Lymbery, M. and Cooper, A. (2011) *Social Work: An introduction to Contemporary Practice.* London: Prentice Hall.

Chapter 10

Ecological Systems Theory and Direct Work with Children and Families

Peter Henriques and Graham Tuckley

If we are to intervene effectively in their lives and make the least detrimental decision on their behalf, we must understand children's perceptions of their lived experiences.

(Vera Fahlberg, 1991)

Introduction

There has been a groundswell of interest in systems approaches since the late 1990s that coincided with the advance of New Labour's social policy on children and the family. *The Framework for Children In Need and Their Families Guidance* produced by the Department of Health in 2000 and Eileen Munro's (2010) systematic review of safeguarding practice in Britain have played a significant part in raising its profile. It is therefore likely that systems thinking will continue to exert a strong influence on welfare practice whatever changes in policy are introduced by David Cameron's Coalition government.

This chapter focuses on the re-emergence of ecological systems theory and its associated method and models applied to social work. The benefits of this method with its eclectic qualities will be illustrated by exploring the practice challenges associated with modern adoption practice. Specific emphasis will be given to direct work with children and the management of contact. Although the focus will be on the ecological systems in direct work with children, it needs to be acknowledged from the outset that this approach can be equally applied to a wide range of other practice situations and with different service user groups (Jack and Jack, 2000: 94).

Brief overview of ecological systems theory: life model

There are essentially two perspectives in ecological systems theory, a biological ecological perspective and a sociological perspective. Within social work, the genesis of ecological systems began through the work of Kurt Lewin (1951). Lewin proposed that the behaviour of individuals was determined entirely by the individual's situation. In Lewin's field theory, a 'field' is defined as 'the totality of coexisting factors which are also conceived as mutually interdependent' (Lewin, 1951: 240).

Lewin (1951) suggests that individuals were seen to behave differently according to the way in which tensions between perceptions of the self and of the environment were worked through. The whole psychological field, or 'life space', within which people act has to be viewed in order to understand behaviour. Within this, individuals and groups can be seen in the relationships between parts linked together in a system. Individuals participate in a series of life spaces such as family, work, school etc, and these are constructed under the influence of various force vectors. Lewin (1951: 240) also looked to the power of underlying forces (needs) to determine behaviour and hence expressed 'a preference for psychological as opposed to physical, sociological or physiological descriptions of the field'.

Germain and Gitterman (1980) formulated their own views of ecological theory based upon Lewin's life model for application in social work practice. Germain mapped out an approach to understand human behaviour by recognising inseparable links to environment, identifying interdependent, complementary, and constantly changing factors which contribute to an individual's behaviour (Germain, 1978). In an attempt to articulate this ecological perspective for practice, Germain and Gitterman (1980) joined forces to apply the ecological metaphor to direct social work practice. They viewed the environment as dynamic and complex, comprising a multitude of systems each with their own characteristic structure, level of organisation, and spatial as well as worldly properties. From their perspective, the social environment comprises human beings organised in dyadic relations and social networks, linked to bureaucratic institutions, and other social systems including neighbourhood, community, and society itself. The physical environment comprises those things that make up the natural world and objects. These are the other social constructs that affect human functioning, the objective and physical environments being related in complex ways (1980: 137)

Bronfenbrenner (1979) also used ecological systems theory to explain how a child's environment impacts upon their growth and development. Bronfenbrenner (1979) identified different aspects or levels of a child's environment that influences

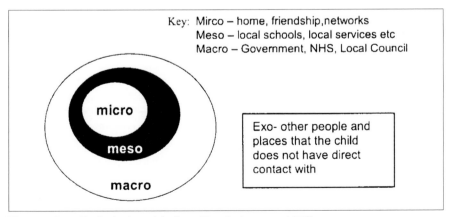

Figure 10.1 Ecological models (from Bronfenbrunner, 1979)

a child's development. These were defined as micro-systems, meso-systems, macro-system and exo-systems.

The micro-systems are those systems which are immediate to the child's environment. Microsystems include any immediate relationships or organisations that the child interacts with, such as birth family members or caregivers, school or day-care providers. How individuals, groups or organisations interact with the child will have a direct effect on the child's growth and development. Consequently, the more positive these relationships, the better the life chances the child will have. In addition, how a child responds to those immediate contacts within their micro-system also reflects on how the child is treated in return.

The meso-system describes how different parts of a child's micro-system work together for the sake of the child. Positive networking between members of the child's micro-system will contribute to the child's overall development. Alternatively, unconstructive connections will impact negatively on growth and development.

The exo-system level includes those other people and places where the child does not interact directly but will have an immediate effect on their well-being, such as a parent's workplace, estranged extended family members, neighbourhood or cultural affiliation etc.

The final level described by Bronfenbrenner (1979) is the macro-system, which is the largest system. This system is totally remote from the child but still influences and impacts on the child's life. The macro-system includes governments, ideological affiliations of adults linked to the child, the economy, social norms and even the global market.

Ecological systems theory in practice

Social workers are trained to apply theories, methods and an array of tools and techniques to help service users, families, groups and communities. To do this and be effective, social workers first have to build meaningful, trusting and professional relationships with the service user and with those whom the service user has links. Giddens (1998) suggests that in today's modern society, relationships have to be 'democratically based'. It is therefore imperative that the relationship between social workers and service users is built on a foundation of respect, trust and reciprocity, sharing skills, knowledge, experiences and resources in order to accomplish satisfactory outcomes.

Today's social workers have to recognise the expertise of others, and the wealth of insight that partners, collaborators and service users bring with them, and must take account of the wishes and feelings of children. Social workers must also recognise that 'service users' are not isolated entities and that each individual will have links to wider family systems, groups and the community. Equally, the service user will also have connections with others that might not be immediately obvious. Each person is connected in a variety of ways to a number of systems which either offer help and support or create difficulties. To function within today's society, we need to recognise that no one lives, works, or socialises in isolation. We cannot cocoon ourselves or live in a 'bubble'.

Understanding how people connect and 'fit' within those systems identified by Bronfenbrenner will help social workers recognise how these connections might directly affect a child's functioning. Furthermore, social workers have to recognise the existence and influence of these systems, how they shape events and mould individuals to develop particular ways of performing. By working with, through and around these systems, social workers can help the service user to become more instrumental in bringing about change to improve their lives. Systems theory in social work does not necessarily see individuals as 'the problem', but recognises that the individual may be symptomatic of a failing or malfunctioning system. Equally, systems theory does not take for granted that an individual is the cause of a system failure, but recognises that an individual can contribute to the malaise of the system or to the system's poor performance.

In order to comprehend how systems theory works, it is important to reiterate the point that an understanding that all parts of a system are in some way inter-connected is critical. Subsequently, what happens in one part of the system will ultimately affect other parts of the system (Coulshed and Orme, 1998: 47). For any system to maintain an equilibrium and steady state, fine tuning, maintenance and adjustment is required. This suggests the system must have the capacity for change to occur and that there is a need for change to occur in order for the system to run smoothly. Davies (1994) in particular emphasises this point when he refers to a 'theory of maintenance'. This theory embraces the view that social workers are the 'maintenance mechanics, oiling the interpersonal wheels' (1994: 1).

Direct work with children

The authors believe that the introduction of the *Framework for the Assessment of Children in Need and their Families* (DoH, 2000) created a window of opportunity to appraise the contribution that ecological systems theory has made to direct work with children and young people. Milner and O'Byrne (2002) suggest that there is a need to move beyond the general framework introduced by Pincus and Minahan (1973) and embrace their 'map of the world' concept. They recommend this as the starting point to obtain 'one's bearings' and work out who is doing what, for whom and for what purpose.

Payne (2005: 154) takes this view a stage further by arguing that we need to understand the complexity of interdependence and value the diversity of human relationships. When considering adoption practice and more specifically the assessment of contact, the relevant basic ecological ideas for social work are clearly apparent.

According to Payne (2005: 154) these are:

- Integration and connectedness.
- The importance of becoming rather than only what exists now.
- Maintaining diversity.

He further argues that social work needs to focus on reducing human and ecological stress in particular by focusing on grief work and loss.

Teater (2010: 35) echoes the views of Payne, while using terms such as *interconnection* and *interdependence* and emphasising the importance of understanding the level of fit for a person with their environment. Where each individual has a positive level of fit this will create a sense of adaptiveness. The natural progression from this symmetry will be a reduction in levels of stress and the promotion of positive growth and development of the individual.

Teater (2010) acknowledges that interventions, particularly through use of the life model, endeavour to explore the life stressors associated with difficult transitions across the life course. The authors would like to build on Germain and Gitterman's life model to illustrate this point further. This is because it is particularly relevant to direct work with children in the context of adoption practice.

Bingley-Miller and Bentovim (2007: 30) are two writers who have endeavoured to make a direct link between the Framework and the assessment of adoption support needs. They argue that the use of an evidence-based approach is essential in ensuring assessments are based on clear and systematic ways of collecting and analysing information. They go on to state that using assessment tools which are grounded in good practice and empirically validated help provide results which can be evidenced. By this they mean that the evidence on which professional judgements are based can be clearly communicated. The authors endorse this view and believe genograms and ecomaps epitomise the credence to which Bingley-Miller and Bentovim refer. They also represent standardised tools that allow for comparison across different contexts. This is particularly pertinent in adoption when comparing the child's needs in their birth family, when with substitute carers, their likely needs when joining an adoptive family and needs once in placement (Bingley-Miller and Bentovim, 2007: 30). These stages all represent significant transitions which need to be captured and understood.

The strength of genograms and ecomaps are also acknowledged by Seddon (2010). He argues that genograms and ecomaps are tools for analysing the person and their situation holistically, linking individual and environmental factors such as family, community, hospitals or school. Dynamic interactions can be observed between the constituent parts, with some relationships in the system clearly more crucial than others.

Butler and Roberts (2000) champion the use of genograms because they help fix and order our experiences by reference to patterns of relationships through time. At its simplest, a genogram is little more than an annotated family tree. The annotations can include major family events, occupations, places of residence and even patterns of contact. The genogram uses basic symbols: a square

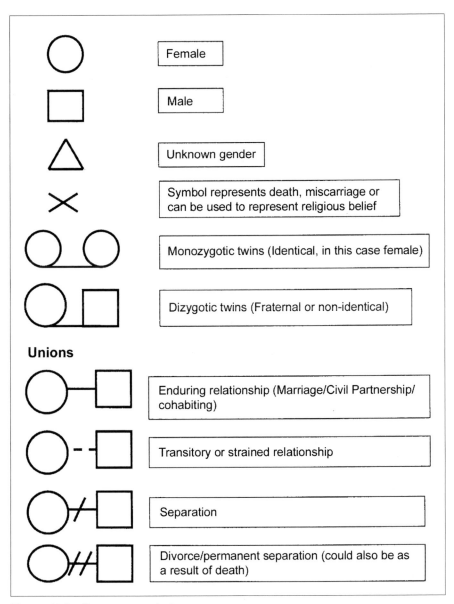

Figure 10.2 Genogram symbols

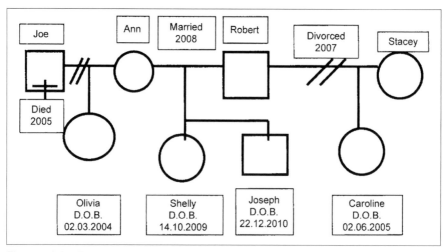

Figure 10.3 Example of family and relational connections

represents male, a circle represents a female, and a triangle represents circumstances where the sex is unknown (e.g. an unborn child or distant relative) and a cross drawn through on of the figures represents death. The strength of relationships between individuals is shown by lines: enduring relationships by a firm line and a transitory relationship by a broken one. These lines can be crossed through to reflect separation (single) or divorce (twice). When drawing the genograms, the children of a particular couple are usually entered according to age, starting with the oldest on the left. It can be useful to draw a dotted line around all those living in the same household. The following example illustrates the basic form of a genogram covering three generations (Butler and Roberts, 2000: 164).

At its best the genogram can present very complex family relationships in a concise and accessible form. It can highlight themes and patterns that are echoed across the generations and it can serve to map key relationships and patterns of communication

Coulshed and Orme (1998: 173) also recognise the value of genograms. In their view genograms are tools that can assist in understanding family dynamics and are often used in the assessment of adoptive and foster families. The additional value of genograms is that they can provide a useful talking-point for families while they are helping the worker to complete them, and begin to uncover unwritten rules, myths, secrets and taboos. This is one of the many strengths of this tool the authors wish to reinforce.

Ecomaps

While the family is one important context in which to establish relationships it does not always provide a sufficient picture. As previously mentioned, individuals have relationships with individuals and groups around them and their particular household. A universally acclaimed way of representing the various affiliations and the nature of a family or individual relationships to the wide community is the ecomap.

Ecomaps can be drawn of families or individuals but in either case the key person is represented by a circle in the middle of the page. Around this, some at distances intended to represent the proximity of the relationship, other circles are drawn to represent important connections, either to other members of the family and particular individuals, or to groups. As with the genogram, the lines used to join the various circles can also carry additional information: a solid line can represent a strong relationship, a dotted line a weak one and a hatched line a stressful one. Arrow heads can be added at either or both ends of the line to demonstrate the flow of information, interest or resources between parties.

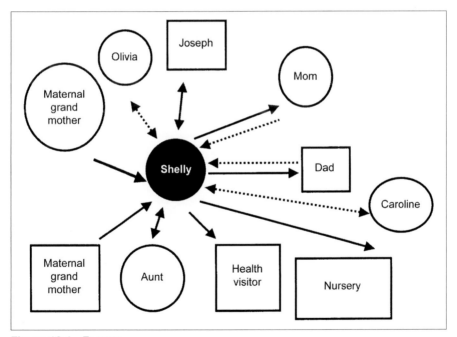

Figure 10.4 Ecomap

Reasons for undertaking direct work with children

Before examining the benefits of applying ecological systems approaches to work with children, it is necessary to establish the context for why this work is important in:

- Preparing them for new relationships.
- Gaining an understanding of the child's perception of their life.
- Explaining plans for the future.
- Addressing current areas of concern.
- Enhancing attachments to current family/carers.
- Facilitating identity formation – understanding of self.
- Re-interpretation of early life events.
- Focusing on life long issues.
- Accurately constructing the child's placement history.
- Identifying attachment figures in the child's life.
- Establishing which individuals are most significant to the child.

Whilst we have presented each of these techniques as a useful means of sorting existing information, it should be clear how they might be used in direct work, either to elicit further information on the basis of the gaps that show up in available data or to convey or interpret information that is not shared or understood by members of the family or individuals with whom the practitioner may be working.

Webb's (2006) conceptualisation of risk is highly relevant when critically exploring the value of ecological tools with children. He argues that story telling is just as important as the factual information obtained. Risk claims are not simply propositions, but are also moves in a narrative that attempts to develop an argument for or against a particular decision.

This observation by Webb (2006) is clearly apparent in adoption practice, especially when making a case for or against ongoing contact. A contemporary example of this is the issue of allowing the exchange of photographs of children placed for adoption with their birth parent as part of letterbox arrangements. As a consequence of a relatively small number of cases where birth parents have misused photographs by placing them on social networking sites like Facebook, some social workers and adoption agencies have over-reacted. The furore surrounding it represents a significant ideological shift in thinking about letterbox contact. The strength of feeling has been such that some adoption agencies have imposed a blanket ban on the exchange of photographs. The justification for this action is based on the perceived risk to stability of the adoptive placement where this is considered too great (Fursland, 2010). This perception is not fully supported by practice evidence given the huge number of successful indirect contact arrangements (including the exchange of photographs) that take place each year nationally.

Using genograms and ecomaps when managing adoption and contact

The Adoption and Children Act 2002 (DoH, 2002) establishes a framework for considering arrangements for contact. There is no longer a presumption in favour of contact with adoption. The Act does however introduce provisions which oblige the court to consider arrangements for contact (Brammer, 2007: 342). Planning for contact and adoption routinely presents ethical challenges for the practitioner. The authors believe this dilemma is compounded by requirements of the Act, because contact must be considered as an aspect of subsection (f) in the Welfare Checklist. Practitioners are therefore required to give weight to the relationship which the child has with birth relatives, the likelihood of the relationship continuing and the value to the child of it doing so. In addition, the wishes and feelings of any of the child's relatives or any such person, regarding the child should also be taken into account.

Bingley-Miller and Bentovim (2007) state that in the context of adoption the importance of the child's experience in their birth family, the heritage and sense of identity they bring with them to adoption and the meaning and impact of any continuing contact should be considered. Conceptually, practitioners need to bear in mind the relationship between the two families for the child in order to anticipate some of the challenges (and rewards) the adoptive family may encounter.

Argent (2003: 282) adds further weight to the argument by highlighting that the assessment of the family functioning, relationships and children's needs is critical to making effective plans for children and to providing good quality information for prospective adopters. She highlights a commonly held concern that child development and attachment are not well understood by workers. This knowledge deficit has led to accusations that such assessments may be flawed. The authors believe that this is the very reason why genograms and ecomaps have much to offer.

Bingley-Miller and Bentovim (2007) provide a welcome reminder that the assessment of need for support services should take into account that the adopted child is a member of the adoptive family and has the heritage of being born into their birth family. The past and current involvement of members of the birth family in the child's life and their impact on the child has to be incorporated into the assessment of needs for Adoption Support Services. The authors would give extra emphasis to this point by highlighting how critical this is when arranging and managing post adoption contact.

McGoldrick, Gerson and Petry (2008: 153) concur with this view and make a strong case for genograms being part of the practitioner's toolbox. For them one of the most powerful aspects of genograms is the way in which they can steer the practitioner to the possibilities of complex kinship relationships, which continue throughout life to be sources of connection and life support. It is not just our shared history that matters, but also current connections that strengthen and which can enrich the future.

McGoldrick *et al.* (2008: 154) fully embrace the richness and breadth of information that genograms can generate. For these authors whether relationships have been good or bad, beneficial or injurious, they are not to be dismissed, and most of the time they are not all positive or negative, but rather some of each. They go on to surmise that organising family data on genograms has enabled people to put many fragments of their lives back together in a meaningful way. Furthermore they believe that constructing a genogram can counter the tendency to oversimplify the 'cut off point' by making clear the enormity of the losses, as one scans the numerous people involved. For them this is one more illustration of the importance of creating genograms and ecomaps – to bear witness to the truth and complexity of people's lives, no matter how traumatic their experiences have been (*ibid*, 2008: 155). This is particularly pertinent to adoption practice and specifically the challenge of managing contact.

Bingley-Miller and Bentovim (2007) and McGoldrick *et al.* (2008) make a direct link between ecological systems tools i.e. genograms and adoption. McGoldrick *et al.* (2008: 184) however, stress the importance of the relational patterns and triangles that may be evident. They assert that families with adopted children are like remarried families in that there are two families involved: the caretaking family and the biological family. This is true whether the biological parents are known or not, because people triangulate a memory or idea as well as actual people.

The emerging patterns from a genogram map often amplify the child's perception of their situation. According to McGoldrick *et al.* (2008) an adoptive child may fantasise about their biological parents that they would be more loving, generous and so on. Evidence is emerging from practice experience that this

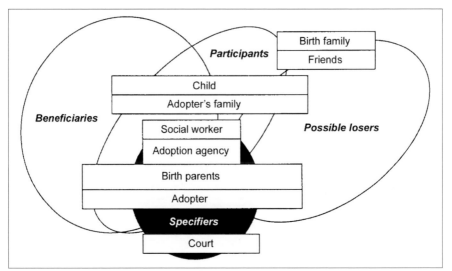

Figure 10.5 Players in adoption, customer roles and connections (Adapted from Martin *et al.*, 2010: 97)

distorted perception of birth parents can be apparent throughout childhood. Furthermore, if there are birth children in the adoptive family as well, triangles between adopted and biological children are common.

The rich potential for using genograms is well illustrated by McGoldrick and his co-authors. The critical question however is how this helps the practitioner attempting to understand and manage post adoption contact arrangements. Garrett (2003) Argent (2003) Vincent and Graham (2002) and Lowe *et al.* (1999) all stress the importance of setting a context for this work. They argue that some critical questions need to be answered by the emerging data and it is on this basis that child-focused contact plans should be determined.

Commentators have mentioned earlier in this chapter that the management of adoption and contact needs to be informed by sound theoretical knowledge. This is particularly relevant when considering the added dimension of sibling contact. Garrett (2003: 141) argues that sibling contact is likely to be sustainable between siblings placed in different adoptive homes when adopters are compatible in terms of class, values and aspirations. Wide differences and tensions are likely to drive a wedge between siblings.

Genograms and ecomaps have the potential to reveal these tensions and allow the practitioners to take remedial action. The tools can also help with judgements about the timing or degree of contact while taking account of the child's need to attach to a new family and the adopter's need to claim the child. By anticipating the emotional reactions conveyed in the maps, the practitioner is better placed to manage the tensions associated with contact. This also enables the child to be given sufficient time to enhance feelings of security with the adoptive placement (Garrett, 2003: 141).

Conclusion

The interactive qualities of genograms and ecomaps make them ideal tools for undertaking direct work with children. They can be used to engage children and give them a voice to articulate their perception of their relationships. They can dispel the misunderstandings surrounding family ties and bring clarity to the relationships children and young people consider meaningful and worthy of sustaining beyond adoption.

This chapter illustrates there is compelling evidence that ecological systems tools can be successfully used in direct work with children when assessing arrangements for adoption. The evidence supporting decision-making must be substantial and refutable. As we have seen, any judgement that a relationship is not sustainable after adoption has to be weighed against the loss that the child will experience. This is why the genograms of adoptive families and genograms of children provide valuable tools for making predictions about gains and losses following the adoption. Adoption by its very nature involves compromises and risks.

Managing any form of contact inherently involves compromises and the associated risks need to be reduced. Openness is the key and even where children are unable to voice their concerns or were placed as babies, communicative openness helps keep their story alive and ensures its construction remains balanced and proportionate. The why, who, what and how take on a transparency because they are openly discussed.

The argument being made here is that ecological systems theory allied to the use of genograms and ecomaps offer a window for social workers and other allied professionals to understand the integral and complex dynamics of family forms. The patterns and connections highlighted by the application of these tools provide valuable insights into family functioning at different stages in the life course.

The authors believe practitioners need to rediscover the art of undertaking direct work with children. They need to utilise tools that give children a voice, provide a context for their life histories and promote a sense of belonging. The use of genograms and ecomaps strongly promoted in this chapter offers immense potential and to a large extent unrealised benefits to both social workers and users. This is not to suggest that these tools offer utopian solutions to complex family structures. This point is endorsed by Rose (2002) who highlights that the lack of consensus governing what constitutes evidence let alone how it should be measured or judged cannot be ignored.

She goes on to argue that it is easy to be seduced by the idea that there is a clear body of evidence contributing to practice to the point that this becomes the holy grail. The authors are equally mindful of this and it is with tempered enthusiasm they articulate the proportionate benefits of using genograms and ecomaps, whilst acknowledging their limitations.

What needs to be recognised is that these tools offer practitioners a window to explore the child's world as the child perceives it. The Facebook debate coupled with the emerging practice wisdom around Post Box exchanges has highlighted for the authors some fundamental gaps in core knowledge and response strategies for managing uncertainty.

Adoption is by its very nature planning for the unknown and unpredictable. It is a journey of hope and discovery. What we learn is rooted in the fabric of the life course members of the adoption triad experience. Using an ecological systems approach is one way in which practitioners can start to explore the interconnectedness of adoptive and birth families. This will enable the development of contact plans that reflect and promote the most meaningful attachments for children and significant figures in their lives.

References

Argent, H. (Ed.) (2003) *Models of Adoption Support: What Works and What Doesn't.* London: BAAF.

Bingley-Miller, L. and Bentovim, A. (2007) *Assessing the Support Needs of Adopted Children and Their Families*. London: Routledge.

Brammer, A. (2007) *Social Work Law*. 2nd edn. Harlow: Pearson Education Limited.

Bronfenbrenner, U. (1979) *The Ecology of Human Development: Experiments by Nature and Design*. Cambridge, MA: Harvard University Press.

Butler, I. and Roberts, G. (2000) *Social Work with Children and Families*. London: Jessica Kingsley.

Coulshed, V. and Orme, J. (1998) *Social Work Practice: An Introduction*. 3rd edn. Basingstoke: Macmillan.

Davies, M. (1994) *The Essential Social Worker: A Guide to Positive Practice*. 3rd edn. Aldershot: Arena.

Department of Health (2000) *The Framework for Children and Families.* London: HMSO.

DoH (2002) *The Adoption and Children Act 2002*. London: HMSO.

Fahlberg, V. (1991) *A Child's Journey through Placement*. Indianapolis: Perspectives Press.

Fursland, E. (2010) *Facing up to Facebook: A Survival Guide For Adoptive Families*. London: BAAF.

Garrett, P.M. (2003) *Remaking Social Work with Children and Families.* London: BAAF.

Germain, C. (1978) *Social Work Practice: People and Environment*. New York: Columbia University Press.

Germain, C. and Gitterman, A. (1980) *The Life Model of Social Work Practice*. New York: Columbia University.

Giddens, A. (1998) *The Third Way: The Renewal of Social Democracy.* Polity Press.

Jack, G. and Jack, D. (2000) Ecological Social Work: The Application of a Systems Model of Development in Context. In Stepney, P. and Ford, D. (Eds.) *Social Work Models, Methods and Theories.* Lyme Regis: Russell House Publishing.

Lewin, K. (1951) *Field Theory in Social Science: Selected Theoretical Papers.* D. Cartwright (Ed.). New York: Harper & Row.

Lowe, N. (1999) *Supporting Adoption: Reframing the Approach*. London: BAAF.

Martin, V., Charlesworth, J. and Henderson, E. (2010). *Managing in Health and Social Care*. 2nd edn. Abingdon: Routledge.

McGoldrick, M., Gerson, R. and Petry, S. (2008) *Genograms: Assessment and Intervention*. 3rd edn. London: W.W. Norton.

Milner, J. and O'Byrne, P. (2002) *Assessment in Social Work.* Basingstoke: Palgrave.

Munro, E. (2010) *Review of Child Protection: Better Frontline Services to Protect Children*. London: HMSO.

Payne, M. (2005) *Modern Social Work Theory.* Basingstoke: Macmillan, Palgrave.

Pincus, A. and Minahan, A. (1973) *Social Work Practice: Model and Method.* Ithaca, Il: Peacock Publications.

Rose, W. (2002) Two Steps Forward, One Step Back: Issues in Policy and Practice. In Ward, H. and Rose, R. (Eds.) *Approaches to Needs Assessments in Children's Services*. London: Jessica Kingsley.

Seddon, J. (2010) *Systems Thinking: From Heresy to Practice: Public and Private Sector Studies.* Basingstoke: Palgrave Macmillan.

Teater, B. (2010) *An Introduction to Applying Social Work Theories and Methods.* Maidenhead: Open University Press.

Vincent, A. and Graham, A. (2002) Through Letterbox: Indirect Contact Arrangements. In Argent, H. (Ed.) *Staying Connected: Managing Contact Arrangements in Adoption.* London: BAAF.

Webb, S.A. (2006) *Social Work in a Risk Society: Social and Political Perspectives.* Basingstoke: Palgrave Macmillan.

Chapter 11

Community Social Work

Paul Stepney and Keith Popple

The development of community social work has been littered with high hopes, modest achievements and some messy failures.

(David Sawdon, 1986)

Introduction

In this chapter a rigorous attempt will be made to set out the theoretical knowledge base, methods and models of community social work, acknowledging that the way theory informs practice is necessarily contested. The backdrop to this chapter emanates from our concern to address the issues outlined in Chapter 1 regarding the 'Big Society' debate and the move by the Tory led government towards localised and decentralised public service provision (Cameron, 2009). The key themes, issues and dilemmas facing the practitioner will be analysed in the context of developing collaborative working partnerships with other professionals, local service users and community members.

There is a certain ambiguity about the current identity and status of community social work. This in part reflects a paradox concerning limitations in the predictive capacity of social work to resolve many of the problems it identifies in the community, in its theory and practice (Hugman, 2005), at a time when methods of community intervention are back in fashion. Community social work has undergone a transformation from the pioneer days of small patch teams being set up by local authorities in the 1980s (Cooper, 1983) alongside preventive projects in the voluntary sector (Holman, 1981), to become part of a process of social inclusion and neighbourhood renewal (Popple, 2006). However, underlying such development is a tension about the changing relationship between the state and its citizens. In particular, whether the modernised welfare state can promote change at the local level in favour of marginalised groups, and develop preventive policies for collaboration and inclusion whilst resisting pressure for more enforcement and control (Stepney, 2006).

This tension points to a paradox at the heart of community social work. On the one hand it has sought to foster a sense of social responsibility reflected in its professional culture and commitment to social justice – such as, setting up new services and promoting initiatives for inclusion and change. On the other, it is working at the front line in local agencies where ultimately opportunities for meeting such aims may be limited and highly proscribed. It follows that problems of inadequate resources and support in the community, poor infrastructure services, fragmentation of community networks and so on, may all come within a worker's remit but remain frustratingly beyond their capacity to solve. This contradiction has traditionally been resolved by stressing the innovatory nature of the work, its emphasis on prevention and commitment to empowerment through the mobilisation of community resources. However, another path to resolving this dilemma is revealed by evidence that in the last 25 years or so community based approaches have come of age and become a respected activity moving 'from outside to inside the citadel' (Popple, 2000: 113). This raises a fresh dilemma associated with social legitimation and the incorporation of community social work's more radical agenda for change, suggesting that development has been largely conditional and dependent upon the politics of the state (Popple, 2006).

There has certainly been a reawakening of interest in the development of community based interventions, especially for health and social care professionals (Mizrahi, 2001). This is reflected in proposals to enhance partnership working and develop more sustainable communities. Collaboration with health professionals and partnership work with staff in voluntary agencies and a range of community members increasingly shape professional agendas (Rummery and Glendinning, 1997). Nonetheless, as referred to in chapter one, practitioners must now practice in a policy paradox and balance measures for prevention with procedures for risk assessment, protection and control (Jordan, 2004). As policy has become more prescriptive and target driven, reflecting managerial and marketised imperatives, there is an increasing need to find creative solutions and establish new and more inclusive partnerships with a diverse range of community members (Heenan, 2004). The practitioners' dilemma is that the creative potential of the latter may be undermined by an over-emphasis on the former, with practice becoming increasingly shaped by efforts to meet government targets.

One of the essential appeals of community social work is that it has the potential to match the aspirations of those in the community, who want to be empowered and participate in local decision making, with those in government seeking ameliorative reform. Although there is clearly some common ground here, the former is ultimately concerned with emancipatory change, whilst the latter draws on the more conservative tradition of restoring or rebuilding community. The result perhaps inevitably is often disappointment on both sides and hence the case for community social work needs to be made.

The case for community social work

Community social work in our view is a valuable method of intervention which has been sidelined in the new social work order where managerialism, marketisation and individual accountability has been in the ascendency. Community social work is at the other end of the spectrum from individualised social work delivery, as it operates close to neighbourhoods and uses methods of groupwork and utilises informal social networks. However, this context still provides scope for social workers to promote inclusion by moving beyond the modernising rhetoric and developing:

- the preventive potential of public services (Hadley and Leidy, 1996);
- work in collaborative partnership with health professionals and other public sector staff, voluntary agency workers and community members;
- the encouragement of initiatives to support and enhance informal community development and to work alongside a range of community members.

However, in practice this may prove quite difficult unless practitioners understand the nature of this wider policy paradox and are able to exploit opportunities whilst simultaneously managing the constraints now imposed on all welfare agencies. This will mean practitioners orientating themselves more clearly in the direction of community initiatives, so that they become pro-active about community development and resist the tendency to reproduce regimented, residualised and reactive services (Heenan, 2004).

Collaboration has increasingly played an important role both in policy making as well as practice. The move towards greater collaborative working can be situated within a much longer policy shift associated with de-institutionalisation and de-segregation (Payne, 1995). The change from institutional to community-based care (Barr et al., 1999; Sibbald, 2000) meant that the demarcations and hierarchical relations between professions were neither sustainable not appropriate. New more collaborative ways of working that crossed professional boundaries had to be created, in order to allow a more flexible approach to care delivery in the community (Malin et al., 2002). Some commentators have referred to the task of collaborative working as analoguous to building social capital and contributing to the stock of mutual understanding and values that help bind the social fabric of a community together (Putnam, 2000). However, such communitarian ideas now prominent in notions of the 'Big Society' remain contested and do not adequately acknowledge the structural dimension of community problems. As part of the task of setting out the theoretical knowledge base and methods underpinning contemporary practice, it is important to examine the road taken by social work. In the early 1980s an attempt was made to move social work practice decisively in the direction of community based practice, to produce a more integrative and inclusive approach, and this will be the focus of the next section.

The development of community social work – seeking the less travelled road?

Although community based interventions can be traced back to the nineteenth century settlement movement, community social work as it emerged following the publication of the 1982 Barclay Report revealed a number of key features that were highly contested. The Report recommended that community social work should become a central feature of social services provision and social workers should seek to integrate formal services with informal networks of support. However, subsequent research quickly exposed a serious weakness in the analysis informing this central recommendation, in that those in greatest need frequently had inadequate or non-existent informal networks of support (Abrams *et al.*, 1989; Oakley and Rajan, 1991) or in the current vogue, low levels of social capital (Putnam, 2000). Thus, a compelling case for implementation was undermined by inadequate research evidence. This was quickly seized upon by opponents who saw community social work as misguided, naive and romantic, and ultimately trying to swim against the rising tide of social change (Pinker, 1982).

In seeking a definition of community social work, comparisons are sometimes made with community work and community development, as both appear to share common theoretical assumptions, methods and core skills. However, it is important to acknowledge a fundamental difference in orientation. Community work and community development are concerned with tackling injustice and inequality by organising people and promoting policy change at the local level, all of which is likely to find expression in collective action (Popple, 1995). On the other hand, community social work is concerned with developing more accessible and effective local services (Smale *et al.*, 1988) and attempts to find alternative ways of meeting the needs of individual service users. Both approaches, of course, seek to build on indigenous skills and utilise a range of local resources rather than import them from outside the community (see also Mayo, 1998).

The Barclay Committee recognised that the vast majority of care in the UK , then as now, is provided informally and much of this work, about 65–70 per cent of it according to recent survey data (OPCS, 2002), is provided by women in their role as informal carers. It is difficult to determine how much this saves the state. In the case of frail older people in the Gateshead care scheme, research has estimated that the average cost per case incurred by social services, the NHS and society as a whole was about £8,800 per year (calculated at 1981 prices, so this figure will be considerably higher now), of which something like £5,000 represented the costs borne by informal carers, resources consumed by the older person themselves and included a housing allowance (Challis *et al.*, 1991). More recently, the charity Carers UK (2011) has estimated that across the UK, carers save the State £87 billion annually and that without them, health and social service spending would double. Consequently, the potential for community social work to reinforce a discourse of care informed by traditional gender roles and a cost saving imperative has been a continuing point of concern (Twigg, 1998). In other words a patriarchal discourse has shaped not only models of care but frequently forms of support and assumptions about who should bare the cost as well.

The Barclay Committee advocated new forms of collaborative partnerships between formal service providers and community members in the provision of care, but surprisingly underestimated the need for basic community development (York, 1984). As noted above, without attention to such detail it would prove impossible to distinguish between those communities where a community social work approach might work, by building upon existing networks, and those more fragmented areas where this would be much more difficult to achieve because no such networks existed. Predictably, there is often an urgent need for community social work in neighbourhoods like the latter. However, these ideas have always been contested. At the time when the report was being written the Committee was fraught with tensions between Robert Pinker (Professor of Social Work at the LSE and a traditionalist), who was very sceptical and dismissive of community based interventions, and Roger Hadley (Professor of Social Policy from Lancaster University and a more radical thinker committed to community action), who argued that the report didn't go far enough in terms of devolving responsibility and power (Barclay Committee, 1982).

As Hadley, Holman and others have noted, community social work as it developed during the 1980s was a loose knit collection of different interest groups that took a variety of forms. However, community based approaches have a number of common organisational features; for example, a stress on working with people to develop their informal networks; emphasis on early intervention; a concern with preventive action; the desire to utilise and enhance local resources; and ultimately the empowerment of community members for the common good (Hadley *et al.*, 1987; Smale *et al.*, 1988; Holman, 1993).

During the 1980s the state began to experiment with community based projects including decentralising services into small 'patch' teams, developing more integrative services and promoting a degree of community (and user) participation. One way of implementing this approach was to adopt a patch system of locally based staff serving relatively small populations of say 12–15,000 people. Various patch models emerged in such places as Normanton in West Yorkshire, East Sussex, Islington and Humberside (Cooper, 1983; Beresford and Croft, 1986; Smale *et al.*, 1988). The staff in a patch team were likely to include two or three professional social workers, plus community care workers, occupational therapists as well as local people employed on a paid and unpaid basis, as carers, street wardens, home helps and so on.

Despite evidence of effectiveness (see later), by the early 1990s staff began to experience the same forces of fragmentation and exclusion that had been affecting the communities in which they worked. According to Hadley and Leidy (1996: 825) this was a consequence of 'the conjunction of central government policies which combined to reduce local authority autonomy, cap spending, prescribe essential separate services for children and other users and introduce market mechanisms into social care'.

Holman (1993) suggests three reasons for the marginalisation of community social work from mainstream practice:

- first, the media focus on child abuse post-Cleveland (the inquiry controversially brought the issue of child sex abuse and problems of diagnosis it into the public eye (see Jack and Stepney, 1995) and persuaded social services departments to concentrate resources on statutory interventions;
- second, the belief that community social work would undermine efforts to improve the status of the profession;
- third, the growth of managerialism which promoted a more centralised and marketised approach.

It is significant to note that during the latter part of the 1990s and the early part of the 21st Century, the debate about community was also influenced by two further developments. The movement for enhancing citizenship rights and promoting user involvement on the one hand, and the development of systems of care management, with the social worker redesignated as a care manager on the other. Whilst in theory these two developments were mutually reinforcing and consistent with producing a needs led service, in practice they have been fraught with contradictions. This is principally because the model of care management developed by local authority social service departments in the UK contained an inbuilt tension between empowerment and cost containment. This model of care management was influenced by the North American form of case management. To understand the situation community social work found itself in, we need to develop a more extensive theoretical framework, and this is the focus of the next section.

A theoretical framework for community social work

At one level community social work might be said to be informed by a broad range of theoretical approaches associated with systems theory, community networking and theories of empowerment. Community social work does not owe alliegence to any one theoretical model but rather uses theory in an integrative and somewhat eclectic way. Community social work is not the only method that uses theory in this way, and as Payne (2005) notes, similar views have been advanced about task-centred practice. However, it is worth looking at the theoretical elements in a little more depth.

Systems theory appears to have wide applicability to practice and an ecological approach seems especially relevant to working with different groups in the community. Unlike earlier unitary versions of systems theory (Pincus and Minahan, 1973), eco-social work 'incorporates analysis of structural causes of disadvantage and includes full consideration of wider support networks beyond the nuclear family' (Jack and Jack, 2000: 93). An eco-systems approach encourages the practitioner to recognise that problems arise out of 'a poor fit between a person's environment and her/his needs, capacities, rights and aspirations' (Germain and Gitterman, 1996). Community based practitioners will seek to focus on transactions within and across systems and seek more sustainable rather than 'quick fix' solutions (Henriques, 2005). In practice this means working holistically with service users recognising that change in one part of a system will influence activity in another – for example, strengthening the support network is likely to have a positive impact on a user's home situation or micro system. If as Henriques (2005: 5) notes 'individuals and their environment can never be understood separately', then the application of an eco-systems model leads logically towards the theory of networking.

A network may be seen as a 'system or pattern of links between points which have particular meanings for those involved' (Seed, 1990, cited in Payne, 2005: 156). It is often helpful to identify a service user's network in the community and links with various agencies as a basis for assessing the right blend of formal and informal support. Social workers may be required to engage with networks in one of three ways: 'identify them, consult with them and, cynics might say, they will have to create them' (Coulshed and Orme, 2006: 276). Smale argues that it is the quality of the relationship between people in a network that is important and it is the processes the worker engages in which determine the objectives of community social work (Smale *et al.*, 1988).

Community empowerment is a strong element in community social work, and as Dominelli (2000: 125) notes it has become a 'trendy catchword that has aquired resonance across the political spectrum . . . making it an intellectually messy concept'. It follows that empowerment is a contested term concerned at one level with societal transformation (Rees, 1991) and 'changing the relationship between rich and poor' (Berner and Phillips, 2005: 26), whilst at another level it is concerned with the psychology of liberation and personal change (Riger, 1993). As a multi-level construct it may be concerned with individual development, group processes and organisational change (Forrest, 1999). However, whilst personal change may be a by-product of wider collective political action (Dominelli, 2000), community social work tends to work through individuals and groups for the wider benefit of the community. But empowerment theory offers us a broader context for practice and raises questions about social justice, diversity and equality that must also be addressed.

At the societal level, theory has the potential for providing a framework which connects personal experience with empowerment and 'collective action for a more just, equal and sustainable world' (Ledwith, 2005: 61). It must therefore offer a paradigm for practice that addresses issues of justice, difference and change. The ideas of Freire (1972) and Gramsci (1986) are relevant here and helpful for constructing such a paradigm as they offer a 'critical way forward' (Popple, 1995: 102). Freire (1972) suggests that large numbers of people are effectively disenfranchised by the dominant ideology and divisive social relationships that exploit them, a theme that connects with Gramsci's (1986) notion of hegemony and the notion of power that permeate all relationships and reality to achieve consent.

Community social work generates responses to local problems and uses Freirean-Gramscian dialogical methods of empowerment, in partnership with service users and community members (Ledwith, 2001). Although hitherto it has tended to work at the self help/service reform end of the continuum using a range of intervention methods.

Methods of intervention in community social work

Drawing on our practice experience and the wider literature, two methods will be examined – eco-social models (Matthies *et al.*, 2000) and community social work process models (Stepney and Evans, 2000). It will be found that there are points of overlap between both approaches, as each are concerned with developing a more holistic, integrated and empowering model of practice. When these are taken together they provide elements of what might be termed critical practice, and this will be taken up in Chapter 15.

Eco-social models: towards eco-criticality

Whilst ecological systems theory situates individuals in their community and sees them as interdependent with each other in a reciprocal relationship with wider environmental systems, eco-social models are much more political and highlight how ecological ideas have transformative potential (Payne, 2005). In short, ecological ideas and the systems which support them must be placed in a wider policy context concerned with social exclusion if change for marginalised groups is to be realised (Matthies *et al.*, 2000). This enables the environmental impact of ecological policy initiatives to be assessed including the influence on different social groups – for example, eco-feminism would assess the environmental impact on women and how social systems may proscribe certain roles in the community that are inherently oppressive.

The issue of sustainability has been addressed by a number of writers (Payne, 2005; Coates, 2003) where our relationship with the environment may become more tenuous and disconnected in an age of globalisation. Eco-social models seek to combine diversity with social responsibility not just for the local environment but for the future of the planet. In other words this is where social capital building, community action and Green politics potentially collide in an attempt to develop more sustainable communities. Lifestyles, jobs, relationships, housing, health and community well-being are all brought into the equation, and social work practice must rise to the challenge of relating such environmental concerns to the situation that clients and poor people generally find themselves in. In the past the green agenda has tended to be the preserve of the middle classes, who could afford to promote and display sustainable lifestyle choices, but eco-social models help to highlight its relevance for marginalised groups.

In an important contribution to both comparative research and practice knowledge, Matthies *et al.* (2000) develop an eco-social approach for tackling exclusion based upon research in three European cities – Jyväskylä (Finland), Magdeburg (Germany) and Leicester (England). The research had three broad aims:

- To develop practice methods that enable citizens to improve their environment through community participation;
- To provide social impact assessments drawing on social work knowledge to influence planning and political decision making around issues of sustainability;
- To incorporate an eco-social approach to the problem of exclusion in different European contexts and thereby contribute to the theoretical knowledge base of social work.

(adapted from Matthies *et al.*, 2000: 44)

Although the research designs and strategies in each city were different, involving elements of locality development, social planning and social action, the level of collaboration encouraged 'the development of a new European model against social exclusion' (Matthies *et al.*, 2000: 44) based upon social work practices in each locality. The model draws on the policies of the Green movement in Germany designed to achieve ecological sustainability, environmental sociology from Finland and the social action tradition from the UK. This produces an eco-social model of social work that may be characterised as:

- Holistic in its analysis of the living environment and the local/global connections.
- Practical in involving people in decision making about local policy and planning.
- Theoretical in incorporating sustainability in its conception of social work practice.
- Developmental in understanding exclusion as a multi-dimensional problem relating to segregation from a range of systems, relationships and environments.
- Respectful of the position of marginalised people and community members including a commitment to empowerment through social action.

What the research teams found was that instead of producing one clear cut and universal European eco-social model applicable to any context, a number of approaches emerged with a mixture of common elements (set out above) and unique local features. So the model by definition must be flexible and adaptable without compromising its core values and commitment towards producing a fairer and more sustainable environment.

The application of an eco-social model to practice can be illustrated in relation to work with young people (Sanders and Munford, 2005); children (Henriques, 2005, Jack, 1997); children with disabilities (Jack and Jack, 2000) and older people (Stepney and Evans, 2000). The use of eco-maps and social network maps allied to a sensitivity for community development offers a valuable set of resources for working with each group and understanding the nature of the social landscape. As Sanders and Munford (2005: 201) note, 'being able to describe all the different dimensions of relationships gave us a rich understanding of the complex and sometimes delicate balancing young people needed to engage in as they positioned themselves in their relational landscapes'. Such insights can be supplemented with life story work, use of toys, books and pictures in direct work with children (Henriques, 2005), cultural and historical artefacts in reminiscence work with older persons, as well as more traditional methods involving interviewing.

Practice Focus 1 – Direct work with children (can be adapted for reminiscence work with older people focussing on a period, such as the 1930s, or when participants were 18)

Recall the family home you lived in as a child when you were eight years old. Draw a floor plan of the living room and what you remember about the key features of the room. What do you remember about your family and the character of the people you lived with, also your best friends. Do you remember your favourite TV/radio shows, books, music and the sporting or film stars of the day?

What do you recall about the local community in which you grew up and the people who lived in it? Draw an eco-map of the local community and what you remember about its most important features.

Community social work process models

The following model draws on the work of Vickery (1983), Smale *et al.* (1988), Sawdon (1986), Mayo (1998) and can be applied to virtually any community setting. The main circle in the diagram shows the community social work (CSW) process and some of the activities which might spring from it.

There are six phases to the model which to some extent overlap and may not follow in precise sequential order – for example, phase 6, the research to evaluate effectiveness would clearly need to be set up at the outset. The six phases are:

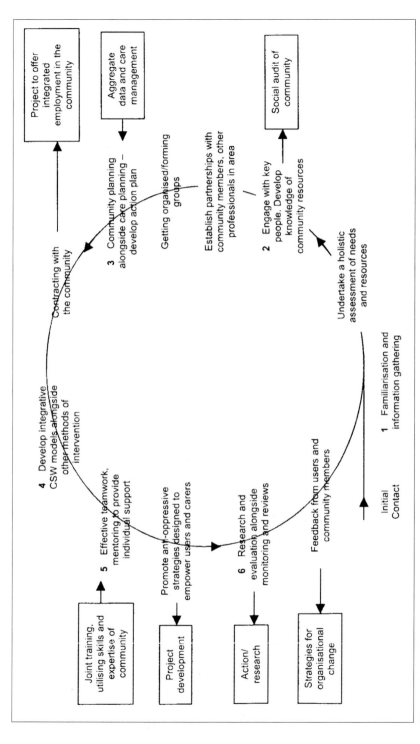

Figure 11.1 A six phase model of the community social work process (Stepney and Evans, 2000: 113)

1. Familiarisation and information gathering
2. Engagement and assessment
3. Organisation, planning and partnerships
4. Intervention in collaboration with community members
5. Mobilising team resources for empowerment (users and staff)
6. Research and evaluation

The practitioner will need to adapt the model to particular situations, noting that at each stage in the process there are additional opportunities or requirements depicted by the seven rectangles, which open up new possibilities for constructive action – for example, after phase 2, it may be useful to carry out a social audit of the wider community to map out the full range of needs and resources; after phase 3, opportunities for contracting could involve setting up a project to provide employment for local people (Stepney and Davis, 2004); during phase 5, training strategies might include planning joint sessions with user groups and other community members.

Practice Focus 2 – The case of Mr Beasley alongside Peggy and Ruth Lyle

Mr Beasley is a man in his 50s with mental health problems who suffers from depression with memory loss due to earlier alcohol abuse. He stopped working about two years ago after the death of his wife, and now attends a horticultural project run by a local ASW one day per week. He lives alone in a high rise flat in an area of town which suffers from environmental decay, with boarded up houses, a derelict factory and few shops and infrastructure services.

Apart from attending the project Mr Beasley hardly goes out as he fears that he might be mugged after reading that the neighbourhood has the highest crime rate in the town. He is quite isolated and hardly knows any of his neighbours. The other neighbours in the block of flats include Peggy and Ruth Lyle who are disabled and also quite isolated (See Stepney and Evans, 2000, p 107 for further details of this case) as well as a number of refugee families offered short term emergency accommodation by the council. A housing association has recently taken over management of the flats and would like to upgrade them. The council has plans to regenerate the area and some limited funds are available to support community activity.

How might a community social work/eco-social approach be used to good effect here?

What kind of model would you use and which local people would you seek to involve?

Do you think it would be appropriate to treat the case of Peggy and Ruth separately from Mr Beasley or could they be tackled using a combined strategy? If the latter, how might this work in practice?

Research evidence concerning the effectiveness of community social work

A review of the literature by Ohmer and Korr (2006) found that there were 269 journal articles published between 1985 and 2001 that focussed on community based practice. The vast majority were from the US literature and many employed qualitative designs including a rich array of case studies and ethnographic accounts. A quantitative methodology was adopted by 20 studies and only 9 used an experimental design to evaluate the effectiveness of community practice interventions which were invariably found to be 'complex with multiple locations, goals and activities that makes them difficult to evaluate' (Coulton, 2004, cited in Ohmer and Korr, 2006: 143).

In a majority of the US studies a consensus emerged indicating that community based practice interventions were more effective 'on the psycho-social aspects of communities, especially influencing citizen participation . . . and its effect on participants in terms of increasing self awareness and self esteem' (Ohmer and Korr, 2006: 142). The impact on the physical and economic environment was found to be mixed, with some studies reporting improvements whilst many did not. These findings are by and large supported by UK research (Popple, 2013).

In the UK, although community social work appears well suited to operating in conditions of uncertainty and conflict, it has proved quite difficult to provide robust empirical evidence of effectiveness. Many initiatives were by definition small scale and localised. For example, research in Yorkshire by Hadley and McGrath (1984) suggested that if community social work initiatives were properly resourced then the long term outcomes could be impressive. The Normanton patch team was investigated and compared with a traditional social work fieldwork team in nearby Featherstone. It was found that crisis work, including the use of emergency protection orders, were similar in both teams in year one, but reduced significantly during the second and third years of the Normanton project. In Normanton 40 per cent of clients officially referred were known to the team as opposed to only three per cent in Featherstone (Hadley and McGrath, 1984). It emerged that working with older people, using local residents as street wardens or homehelps, resulted in a lower proportion entering residential care; as well as leading to increased satisfaction with the services and improved life expectancy – findings which importantly correspond with influential research carried out in Kent during the same period by Challis and Davies (Davies and Challis, 1986).

According to Holman (1993) partnerships based on availability, local knowledge and joint action are the essence of community social work. Social workers need to find ways of developing more effective partnerships between statutory service providers, voluntary agencies and informal carers (Holman, 1993). Research by the Children's Society, based upon its work in different child care projects and family centres also demonstrate that this approach can be preventive – preventing crisis through strengthening communities – as well as cost effective in terms of reducing the number of official referrals and statutory interventions (cited in Holman, 1995). Further, research by the Department of Health (1995) suggested that families without adequate community support were being drawn into the child protection system (Gill, 1996). It is also known that economic and environmental deprivation act as 'powerful stress factors which . . . make it more difficult to be an effective parent' (Utting *et al.*, 1993 cited in Southwell, 1994). There is also evidence that families referred to family centres by social workers as a child protection strategy have similar problems to other families from the same community and therefore should have access to the same facilities (Southwell, 1994). Moreover, there is evidence that variations in rates of child mistreatment are associated with the strength of social support networks and general poverty levels in many European welfare states (Gilbert, Parton and Skivenes, 2011; Garbarino and Kostelny, 1992, cited in Jack, 1997).

Research has consistently demonstrated the innovatory role that universities can play in supporting community initiatives. Barron and Taylor (2010) report on the experience of promoting community development practice learning as part of social work student placements in Northern Ireland. They argue that social workers need to have the knowledge and skills to participate in community development initiatives and that student placements represent an effective way of facilitating this. More generally the investment of university resources can help to build and sustain a range of university-community partnerships, which in turn may bring other 'knowledge transfer benefits' and increase opportunities for funding community projects (Begum *et al.*, 2010).

Research evidence is an increasing requirement of government funding against a backdrop of effectiveness research provided by the movement for evidence-based practice (Sheldon and Macdonald, 1999). As we have noted, effectiveness research in community settings has tended to adopt qualitative methodologies utilising soft outcome measures, such as changes in the attitude of participants, strength of informal networks etc., rather than hard outcome measures to do with jobs, skills and qualifications that can be more easily quantified. Paradoxically, as Ohmer and Korr (2006: 142) note, it 'may be easier for community practice interventions to positively effect citizen participation and its effects on participants, than it is to improve complex social and economic problems in poor communities'. This view is supported by Barr (1997) who suggests that there are few instances where community social work has solved the problems of disadvantaged communities, but many examples of increasing the self-confidence, self-respect and skills of local people. However, passing over the problems inherent in using mixed methodologies, evidence of the impact of citizen participation, although not easy to measure, may be supported by other data relating to referral trends and numbers using particular services. Further, community social work is not generally suited to experimental methods of evaluation such as randomised controlled trials both for ethical and practical reasons. What is critical is that, as noted in each intervention method outlined above, a research or evaluation component should be integrated into practice from the outset. The challenge is to use the models in ways that can address structural problems alongside enhancing the knowledge and skills of community members.

Conclusion

It is at this point, on the basis of a different social ethic, that one becomes awkward.
(Raymond Williams, 1963)

In this chapter we have explored the current identity and status of community social work. Encouragingly, since the mid 1990s there has been a reawakening of interest in the method, as well as partnership working and notions of ecologically sound community empowerment in Britain, Europe, Australia and the USA. This connects with notions of the 'Big Society' which were discussed in more detail in Chapter 1, in terms of promoting localisation and relationships based upon mutual association. A more critical view would suggest that this is a response to the limitations of market led, centralised services as well as a general disenchantment with new managerial methods.

In this chapter we have argued that community social work now operates in something of a policy paradox: competing for priority on professional agendas that are increasingly shaped by a centrally driven emphasis on risk assessment, protection and control of resources. Whilst collaboration with community members to achieve inclusion through the development of locally run services has received official sanction, this is unlikely to satisfy those who call for the genuine empowerment of marginalised groups. The tension between these two visions or paradigms of change has parallels with an earlier debate – between those who saw community participation as an inherently ineffectual response to the problems of poverty and disadvantage, and those who saw it as a valuable contribution in its own right (Piven and Cloward, 1972). Professionals who embrace partnership working may work on the inside to promote change and try to counteract the trend towards 'de-professionalisation, downsizing and privatisation' (Mizrahi, 2001).

Community social work continues to develop, albeit in the shadow of the market economy, and Bob Holman (2000) reports on the continuing relevance of this approach in Glasgow. Hadley and Leidy refer to community based experiments in Pennsylvania State, USA (Hadley and Leidy, 1996) while Banks and Wideman (1996) describe macro social work in Ontario, Canada. Further, Mizrahi (2001: 183) reports on 'practitioners struggling to find creative ways to create community driven, client centred stuctures and infuse business orientated, social entrepreneur roles with socially compassionate and socially just agendas'. This reminds us of both the wider context and the professional challenge. Community social work uses theory in an integrative and eclectic way and has developed a range of models – with two approaches to practice explored in this chapter. The effectiveness of community social work has been demonstrated by a strong literature informed by largely qualitative research (Ohmer and Korr, 2006). This suggests that locality based practice increases levels of participation, whilst improving the self confidence and self esteem of community members. The impact on the physical and economic environment has been less clear cut both in the US and UK.

In Europe, community based social work as part of efforts to regenerate communities in ecologically sound ways remains popular and importantly, supported by municipal agencies (Matthies *et al.*, 2000). Community social work can promote the notion of a diverse and critical community, opening up possibilities for the inclusion of marginalised groups as part of a wider struggle against oppression and exclusion. For this to happen social workers must be prepared to travel where influential figures may fear to tread – into the cold and troubled side of the community – and grapple with a complex array of messy problems and everyday realities. In undertaking such work, critical thinking in the Freirean-Gramscian tradition, the ability to reconnect theory with practice and a commitment to justice may be more important than reliance on any specific technical skills.

Acknowledgement

This chapter includes updated and revised material first published by the authors in Stepney, P. and Popple, K. (2008) *Social Work and the Community*, Palgrave Macmillan. It is included with kind permission of the publisher.

References

Abrams, P., Abrams, S., Humphrey, R. and Snaith, R. (1989) *Neighbourhood Care and Social Policy.* London: HMSO.

Banks, C. and Wideman, G. (1996) The Company of Neighbours: Building Social Support Through The Use of Ethnography. *International Social Work*, 39: 317–328.

Barclay Committee (1982) *Social Workers: Their Role and Tasks.* London: Bedford Square Press.

Barr, A. (1997) Reflections on the Enigma of Community Empowerment. *Scottish Journal of Community Work and Development*, 2, 47–59.

Barr, H., Hammick, M., Koppel, I. and Reeves, S. (1999) Evaluating Interprofessional Education: Two Systematic Reviews For Health and Social Care. *British Educational Research Journal*, 25(4) 533–543.

Barron, C. and Taylor, B. (2010) The Right Tools for the Right Job: Social Work Students Learning Community Development. *Social Work Education*, 29(4) 372–385.

Begum, A., Berger, L., Otto-Salaj, L. and Rose, S. (2010) Developing Effective Social Work University-Community Research Collaborations. *Social Work*, 55(1) 54–63.

Beresford, P. and Croft, S. (1986) *Whose Welfare? Private Care or Public Services.* Brighton: Lewis Cohen Centre for Urban Studies.

Berner, E. and Phillips, B. (2005) Left to Their Own Devices? Community Self-Help Between Alternative Development and Neo-Liberalism. *Community Development Journal*, 40(1) 17–29.

Cameron, D. (2009) *The Big Society.* Hugo Young Memorial Lecture, London: 29 November.

Carers UK (2011) *Sick, Tired and Caring: The Impact of Unpaid Caring on Health and Long Term Conditions*, 25 January 2011, available at www.carerscotland.org

Challis, D., Darton, R., Johnson, L., Stone, M. and Traske, K. (1991) An Evaluation of an Alternative to Long-Stay Hospital Care For Frail Elderly Patients, Part II: Costs and Effectiveness. *Age and Ageing*, 20, 245–254.

Coates, J. (2003) *Ecology and Social Work: Towards a New Paradigm.* Halifax NS: Fernwood.

Cooper, M. (1983) Community Social Work. In Jordan, B. and Parton, N. (Eds.) *The Political Dimensions of Social Work.* Blackwell.

Coulshed, V. and Orme, J. (2006) *Social Work Practice: An Introduction.* 4th edn. especially ch.10, Basingstoke: Macmillan.

Coulton, C. (2004) The Place of Community in Social Work Practice Research: Conceptual and Methodological Developments. paper presented at Aaron Rosen Lecture, Society for Social Work Research, New Orleans, January.

Davies, B. and Challis, D. (1986) *Matching Resources to Needs in Community Care: An Evaluated Demonstration of a Long Term Care Model.* Aldershot: Gower.

Department of Health (1995) *Child Protection: Messages from Research.* London: HMSO.

Dominelli, L. (2000) Empowerment: Help or Hindrance in Professional Relationships. In Stepney, P. and Ford, D. (Eds.) *Social Work Models, Methods and Theories: A Framework for Practice.* Lyme Regis: Russell House Publishing.

Forrest, D. (1999) Education and Empowerment: Towards Untested Feasibility. *Community Development Journal*, 34(2) 93–107.

Freire, P. (1972) *Pedagogy of the Oppressed.* Harmondsworth: Penguin.

Garbarino, J. and Kostelny, K. (1992) Child Maltreatment as a Community Problem. *Child abuse and Neglect*, 16, 455–464.

Germain, C.B. and Gitterman, A. (1996) *The Life Model of Social Work Practice: Advances in Theory and Practice.* 2nd edn. New York: Columbia University Press.

Gilbert, N., Parton, N. and Skivenes, M. (Eds.) (2011) *Child Protection Systems: International Trends and Orientations.* New York: Oxford University Press.

Gill, O. (1996) Child Protection and Neighbourhood Work: Dilemmas For Practice. *Practice*, 8(2) 45–52.

Gramsci, A. (1986) (edited and translated by Hoare, Q. and Smith, G.) *Selections from Prison Notebooks.* London: Lawrence and Wishart.

Hadley, R. and Leidy, B. (1996) Community Social Work in a Market Environment: A British-American Exchange of Technologies and Experience. *British Journal of Social Work*, 26(6) 823–842.

Hadley, R. and McGrath, M. (1984) *When Social Services are Local: The Normanton Experience.* Allan & Unwin.

Hadley, R., Cooper, M., Dale, P. and Stacey, G. (1987) *A Community Social Workers Handbook*. London: Tavistock.

Heenan, D. (2004) Learning Lessons from the Past or Re-visiting Old Mistakes: Social Work and Community Development in Northern Ireland. *British Journal of Social Work*, 34, 793–809.

Henriques, P. (2005) General Systems Theory and Eco-Systems. Lecture to BA social work students, University of Wolverhampton, November.

Holman, B. (1981) *Kids at the Door.* Oxford: Blackwell.

Holman, B. (1993) Pulling Together. *The Guardian*, 20.01.93.

Holman, B. (1995) *Putting Families First.* Basingstoke: MacMillan.

Holman, B. (2000) *Kids at the Door Revisited.* Lyme Regis: Russell House Publishing.

Hugman, R. (2005) Looking Back: The View from Here. *British Journal of Social Work*, 35, 609–620.

Jack, G. (1997) An Ecological Approach to Social Work with Children and Families. *Child and Family Social Work*, 2(2) 109–120.

Jack, G. and Jack, D. (2000) Ecological Social Work: The Application of a Systems Model of Development in Context. In Stepney, P. and Ford, D. (Eds.) *Social Work Models, Methods and Theories: A Framework for Practice.* Lyme Regis: Russell House Publishing.

Jack, G. and Stepney, P. (1995) The Children Act: Protection or Persecution? Family Support and Child Protection in the 1990s. *Critical Social Policy*, 15(1) 43, 26–39.

Jordan, B. (2004) Emancipatory Social Work? Opportunity or oxymoron. *British Journal of Social Work*, 34(1) 5–19.

Ledwith, M. (2001) Community Work as Critical Pedagogy: Re-envisioning Freire and Gramsci. *Community Development Journal*, 36(3) 171–182.

Ledwith, M. (2005) *Community Development: A Critical Approach*. Bristol: Policy Press.

Malin, N., Wilmot, S. and Manthorpe, J. (2002) *Key Concepts and Debates in Health and Social Policy.* Buckingham: Open University Press.

Matthies, A-L., Turunen, P., Albers, S., Boeck, T. and Närhi, K. (2000) An Eco-Social Approach to Tackling Social Exclusion in European Cities: A New Comparative Research Project in Progress. *European Journal of Social Work*, 3(1) 43–52.

Mayo, M. (1998) Community Work. In Adams, Dominelli and Payne, *Social Work: Themes, Issues and Critical Debates.* Basingstoke: MacMillan.

Mizrahi, T. (2001) The Status of Community Organising in 2001: Community Practice Context, Complexities, Contradictions and Contributions. *Research on Social Work Practice*, 11(2) 176–189.

Oakley, A. and Rajan, L. (1991) Social Class and Social Support: The Same or Different? *Sociology*, 25(1) 31–59.

Ohmer, M. and Korr, W. (2006) The Effectiveness of Community Practice Interventions: A Review of the Literature. *Research on Social Work Practice*, 16(2) 132–145.

Office of Population Sensus Surveys (2002) *General Household Survey: Carers in 2000.* London: Government Statistical Service.

Payne, M. (1995) *Social Work and Community Care.* Basingstoke: Macmillan.

Payne, M. (2005) *Modern Social Work Theory.* 3rd edn. Basingstoke: Palgrave.

Pinker, R. (1982) An Alternative View. *Social Work Today – The Barclay Report*, 13(33) 23.

Pincus, A. and Minahan, A. (1973) *Social Work Practice: Model and Method.* Itasca, IL: Peacock.

Piven, F. and Cloward, R. (1972) *Regulating the Poor.* London: Tavistock.

Popple, K. (1995) *Analysing Community Work: Its Theory and Practice.* OU Press.

Popple, K. (2013) *Analysing Community Work: Its Theory and Practice*, 2nd edn. Maidenhead: Open University Press (forthcoming).

Popple, K. (2000) Critical Commentary: Community Work. *British Journal of Social Work*, 30, 109–114.

Popple, K. (2006) Critical Commentary: Community Development in the 21st Century: A Case of Conditional Development. *British Journal of Social Work*, 36, 333–340.

Putnam, R. (2000) *Bowling Alone: The Collapse and Revival of American Community.* New York: Simon and Schuster.

Rees, S. (1991) *Achieving Power: Policy and Practice in Social Welfare.* London: Allen and Unwin.

Riger, S. (1993) What's Wrong with Empowerment? *American Journal of Psychology*, 21(3) 279–292.

Rummery, K. and Glendinning, C. (1997) *Working Together: Primary Care Involvement in Commissioning Social Care Services, Debates in Primary Care.* University of Manchester.

Sanders, J. and Munford, R. (2005) Activity and Reflection: Research and Change with Diverse Groups of Young People. *Qualitative Social Work*, 4(2) 197–209.

Sawdon, D. (1986) *Making Connections in Practice Teaching.* Heinneman, NISW.

Seed, P. (1990) *Introducing Network Analysis in Social Work.* London: Jessica Kingsley.

Sheldon, B. and Macdonald, G. (1999) *Research and Practice in Social Care: Mind the Gap.* Centre for Evidence Social Services, University of Exeter.

Sibbald, B. (2000). Inter-disciplinary Working in British Primary Care Teams: A Threat to The Cost-Effectiveness of Care? *Critical Public Health*, 10(4) 439–451.

Smale, G. *et al.* (1988) *Community Social Work: A Paradigm for Change.* NISW.

Southwell, P. (1994) The Integrated Family Centre. *Practice*, 7(1) 45–54.

Stepney, P. (2006) Mission impossible? Critical Practice in Social Work. *British Journal of Social Work*, 36(8) 1289–1307.

Stepney, P. and Davis, P. (2004) Social Inclusion, Mental Health and The Green Agenda. *American Journal of Social Work in Health Care*, 39(3/4) 387–409.

Stepney, P. and Evans, D. (2000) Community Social Work: Towards an Integrative Model of Practice. In Stepney, P. and Ford, D. (Eds.) *Social Work Models, Methods and Theories: A Framework for Practice.* Lyme Regis: Russell House Publishing.

Twigg, J. (1998) Informal Care of Older People. In Bernard, M. and Phillips, J. (Eds.) *The Social Policy of Old Age.* London: Centre for Policy on Ageing (CPA).

Utting, D., Bright, J. and Henricson, C. (1993) *Crime and the Family.* London: Family Policy Studies Centre.

Vickery, A. (1983) *Organising a Patch System.* London: NISW.

Williams, R. (1963) *Culture and Society 1780–1950.* Harmondsworth: Penguin.

York, A. (1984) Towards a Conceptual Model of Community Social Work. *British Journal of Social Work*, 14(1) 241–255.

Chapter 12

Existentialist Practice

Neil Thompson

Introduction

Although existentialist philosophy has had a significant impact on both social thought in general and particular individual disciplines such as counselling (see, for example, van Deurzen and Arnold-Baker, 2005), its influence in social work has never been of major proportions (Thompson, 1992a; 2011a). None the less, a case can clearly be made for its relevance and value as a body of knowledge and a theoretical framework which can cast light on many aspects of social work, particularly its dilemmas, insecurities and uncertainties. In particular, what existentialism can be seen to offer is a framework of understanding which chimes well with the social worker's experience of practice as complex and uncertain, with an absence of clear-cut or guaranteed solutions. This chapter, then, seeks to map out some of the key concepts and issues arising from an existentialist approach and to consider their implications for practice.

The first part of the chapter provides a brief overview of the main tenets of existentialism as a social philosophy by commenting on some of the key concepts and providing examples of their applicability to practice situations. The second part explores and summarises the implications of eight 'Principles for practice' first introduced in Thompson (1992a).

These are not presented as simple formulas or recipes to be followed uncritically. Rather, they are intended as an introduction to the complexities of existentialist thought as an underpinning foundation for practice. What is presented therefore needs to be seen in the context of reflective practice: a set of ideas to be drawn upon critically and reflectively as part of the continuing challenge of integrating theory and practice, as opposed to a set of ready-made technical solutions (Thompson and Thompson, 2008). Indeed, it is a principle of existentialism that there can be no pre-defined answers – human existence is characterised as a continuous struggle to maintain a coherent thread of meaning in a confused and confusing stream of events and developments. In this way, existentialism resonates well with the emerging emphasis on spirituality in social work (Holloway and Moss, 2010).

Social work operates at the intersection of the personal and the social, and where issues of loss, pain, distress, crisis, deprivation, discrimination and social inequality are to the fore. But much the same can also be said of existentialism:

- It addresses the meeting point between the individual (the subjective level) and his or her sociopolitical context (the objective level).

- Experiences of crisis, loss, pain and distress are recognised as major features of existential subjectivity (the individual).
- Similarly, deprivation, discrimination and social inequality feature strongly as important elements of the objective world (the sociopolitical context).

In similar fashion, Mahon (1997: 8) describes existentialism as 'a kind of philosophy which is preoccupied with the most salient and poignant features of human existence, such as death, love, responsibility and despair' – see also Tomer et al., 2008).

Social work is a professional activity which seeks to respond to social problems through a personalised approach (Thompson, 2009). As such, it wrestles with a wide range of complex and demanding issues, many of which are beyond resolution, and few of which fit neatly into formula solutions. Indeed, Schön's (1983) critique of 'technical rationality' is very relevant here, as it is clear that the type and range of problems encountered in social work do not lend themselves to relatively straightforward technical solutions. Rather, they tend to be, as Schön would put it, 'messy' – characterised by complexity, uncertainty, ambiguity, conflicting perspectives, and constantly subject to change. What is needed, then, is not a theoretical framework that seeks to provide a neat set of technical-type solutions, but rather one that helps to equip practitioners for the very messy reality of human existence which befalls them.

Existentialism does not offer direct solutions, but does provide a basis from which we can develop a critically reflective practice, in the full recognition that there are no easy answers (and just as importantly, that answers which appear easy are very likely to be dangerous oversimplifications). Existentialism recognises that being unable to come up with neat, simple solutions is not a sign of weakness or failure on the worker's part, but rather an indication of the bewilderingly complex uncertainties of human existence in general and, in particular, the existential challenges that social work's clientele faces.

There is therefore great potential for drawing on existentialist concepts and themes in seeking to guide and make sense of social work practice (Thompson, 2011a).

What is existentialism?

Existentialism is a complex philosophy with a long history (see Macquarrie, 1973). Consequently, it is a very difficult task to explain it briefly. What follows is therefore a very basic and limited account and should be used as a gateway to other literature on the subject, rather than regarded as a sufficient introduction in its own right.

Perhaps the most fundamental and far-reaching element of existentialism is its emphasis on human freedom and the 'fluid' nature of the self. Sartre's view was that we are 'what we make of what is made of us'. The 'what is made of us' part refers to the influence of the context in which we operate: social, political, economic, interpersonal and organisational factors that have a bearing on how we act and how we perceive ourselves. The 'what we make' part refers to our own role in responding to (and, in part, shaping) these wider factors.

Such a view of the self is:

1. *Dialectical* It is based on a dynamic, interactive view of the self in which change and movement are basic characteristics.
2. *Non-essentialist* It does not see individual personality as fixed or immutable (an 'essence'). Rather, it presents selfhood as a process in which we both influence and are influenced by the external circumstances in which we find ourselves.

The existentialist model of the self is therefore one based on the key concept of the dialectic of subjectivity and objectivity (Thompson, 1998a) – a theme to be developed below.

Another important concept is that of 'contingency', the idea that life is characterised by change, uncertainty and insecurity. Where we have a degree of stability and continuity, this can be attributed to the series of choices and actions that have contributed to establishing and maintaining such stability – continuity, where it exists, is the result of our actions, rather than simply a 'natural' state. Continuity is *constructed* in and by our actions, rather than a 'natural' state of affairs.

This relates closely to the concept of 'ontological security', the sense of 'rootedness' each of us seeks to maintain to hold together the various strands of our experience and retain a coherent identity in the face of contingency and change:

> Ontological security refers to the individual's ability to maintain a coherent thread of meaning and a relatively stable sense of self over time and across a range of situations. It is a sense of being a person in one's own right and feeling comfortable with oneself and one's current circumstances. It is through ontological security that we maintain a sense of self or identity.
>
> (Thompson, 1998b: 169–170)

We seek to maintain a degree of ontological security by adjusting and responding to the changes in our lives that we constantly encounter.

The existentialist emphasis on contingency and flux fits well with the contemporary emphasis on the significance of risk in social work and the dangers of adopting too defensive a perspective, or an oversimplified approach to a very complex matter (Denney, 2005; Webb, 2006).

A further important 'ingredient' of existentialism is that of phenomenology, a term which refers to the study of perception, and is therefore concerned with how we make sense of our experience, how we construct meaning:

Phenomenology is concerned with 'phenomena' which, taken literally, means 'appearances'. Phenomenologists stress the importance of perception and the relationship between appearance and reality. Frameworks of perception, how meaning arises, how time is construed, the role of ideology are all significant areas for phenomenological analysis.

(Thompson, 1992a: 38–39)

This again indicates that there are strong links to be drawn between existentialism and spirituality (Thompson, 2007a).

Our subjective perceptions of the world play an important part in shaping our behaviour, attitudes and responses: how we live our lives will, of course, owe much to how we perceive, and make sense of, the world, and to the worldview we adopt (Moss, 2005). Phenomenology is therefore a theoretical approach which has much to say about social reality. It is an approach which seeks to cast light on everyday experience by exploring and emphasising the significance of the subjective dimension of our lives – the role of interpretation and meaning construction.

However, this is not to say that phenomenology ignores the objective dimension of human experience, the external social world. Indeed, a central theme of existentialism is that of the dialectic of subjectivity and objectivity – the dynamic interplay of the subjective dimension (the individual's perceptions and the meanings attached to these) and the objective dimension (the wider social world, the context in which the individual exists). My actions (or 'agency') play a part (albeit a small part in the overall scheme of things) in shaping the wider social field (the objective dimension) and, in turn, the objective dimension plays a part in shaping my subjective experience by influencing and constraining my actions in various ways.

One important distinction to draw is that between choice and choices. Choice (that is, the ability/necessity to choose) is seen, in existentialist terms, as *absolute*, while the range of choices or options available at any give time is constrained and structured by wider social factors, such as class, race and gender – and is therefore *relative* (that is, relative to our position in the social structure and the differences in life chances we will experience as a result of this). While the range of options available to a given individual will owe much to his or her social location, the necessity to choose will remain absolute, in the sense that we cannot choose not to choose (for example, avoiding making a decision is in itself a form of choice). As Billington (1990: 102) puts it: 'Even leaving things in the 'pending' tray until it is too late for any meaningful decision to be made is a decision'.

A central feature of existentialist philosophy is the concept of 'bad faith'. This refers to the tendency to deny human freedom, to think and act as if other factors were responsible for our actions (genetic, environmental or other forms of determinism), thus seeking to minimise the role of choice and decision-making. Bad faith is therefore a form of self-disempowerment. Consequently, we can recognise that one of the implications of existentialist philosophy is the need to avoid and undermine bad faith – to promote *authenticity*. An authentic existence is one in which choice, responsibility and freedom are taken seriously and efforts are made to follow through the implications of such freedom, rather than seek to deny, distort or minimise it. As we shall see below, the aim of existentialist social work can be defined as supporting clients in developing and sustaining authenticity – moving away from the self-defeating and limiting tendencies of bad faith.

Existentialism is a *dynamic* philosophy. That is, it is concerned with change and movement. This is exemplified in the use of what, based on the work of Sartre (1982), I will refer to as the 'progressive-regressive method' (see also Sartre, 1963). This refers to an understanding of human existence in which our present is influenced by both future plans/intentions/aspirations (progressive) and past learning and experience (regressive) and the interaction between the two. That is, my future plans will have been influenced by my past experiences, but I will also 'reconstruct' my past in line with my future expectations. This is not to say that I will distort my own biography to fit in with future plans, but rather that the significance I attach to past experiences will depend in part on my future intentions. For example, which aspects of my past life I draw upon in the present will depend largely on where I am hoping to go in the future, as in a job application where I would emphasise the aspects of my past which are relevant to, and supportive of, that application.

The progressive-regressive method is therefore an analytical tool for understanding the present circumstances by reference to the combined influences of the past and our proposed future:

> *Human existence can be characterised as a process in which the present moment represents a focal point between the outcomes of past actions and the influence of future intentions. This 'progressive-regressive' conceptualisation can be used as an analytical framework to guide assessment and subsequent interventions.*
>
> (Thompson, 1998a: 704)

It should be apparent from this brief overview that existentialism is a complex philosophy, but it is to be hoped that it is also apparent that it is an approach to understanding social reality that offers much by way of themes and concepts which can cast considerable light on the intricacies of practice, with all their subtleties, multiple layers and interconnections.

Principles for practice

Existentialism is not only a complex philosophy but also an evolving one. We should therefore be wary of coming up with simple and definitive prescriptions for practice. What follows, then, should be seen as guidelines to feed into an informed reflective practice rather than a set of 'rules' to be applied mechanistically and uncritically.

1. Freedom and responsibility are basic building blocks of human experience

Our lives are characterised by the constant pressure to make decisions and to live by their consequences. The responsibility to choose is one that we face each day, to make choices within what Sartre (1958) calls the 'structured field of possibilities'. In this context, the broad role of the social worker can be seen to be twofold. First, there is a part to play in helping people recognise those areas of their lives in which they have a degree of control, especially where this capacity for choice and control may be masked by bad faith to the extent that the individual, family or group concerned may not even be aware that they have choice. Second, there is likely to be a role in seeking to influence the range of options available, for example through access to resources, advocacy or the use of influencing skills generally.

This principle requires practitioners to recognise that clients are not simply passive recipients of services, but active agents who play a central role in determining the course of their lives. The ability to make choices and the range of choices available are therefore key factors to take into consideration.

Consequently, assessment and subsequent interventions should take account of both the subjective and objective dimensions. In order to do justice to the complexity of human existence and the reality of clients' circumstances, it is necessary to look at (i) the *subjective* element – how the situation is experienced by those involved, the significance they attach to it; and (ii) the *objective* element – the range of broader factors that have a bearing on the current situation. This helps to avoid two pitfalls: the dangers of, on the one hand, addressing broader issues without taking account of the uniqueness of the situation for the individual concerned and, on the other, focusing exclusively on the personal elements without recognising the significant role of cultural and structural factors. Effective social work practice needs to address *both* dimensions.

2. Freedom is both liberation and heavy burden

The necessity to choose gives us tremendous potential for changing aspects of our situation, for taking as much control of our circumstances as the objective constraints of the social world will permit – it is the basis of personal liberation and empowerment. However, this freedom is also a heavy burden to bear, in the sense that it brings responsibility for our actions and their consequences. The social work task can therefore be seen to include efforts to convert negative aspects of the experience of freedom (anxiety, fear, insecurity and so on) into positive ones (confidence, self-esteem, self-control and so on). In some ways, this reflects traditional approaches to the psychology of human development which lay stress on the need to boost confidence and self-esteem. However, what we are proposing here goes beyond this, in so far as it recognises anxiety and related factors as basic elements of human existence, rather than as signs of individual weakness or inadequacy. They are *ontological* matters, rather than purely psychological.

Indeed, in terms of ontology, many of the problems social work clients encounter can be related to the existential challenges they face. As we move through life, we face a series of challenges, some of which act as turning points or 'crises' which can have a significant bearing on our subsequent attitudes and actions and the meanings we attach to the life events we encounter (Thompson, 2011b). In order to respond appropriately to the situations which arise in practice, it is necessary to establish the existential basis by relating the circumstances to specific challenges and/or crisis points. For example, work with older people needs to take account of the particular challenges that arise in later life, such as retaining a sense of identity and self-esteem in an ageist society (S. Thompson, 2005).

3. Authenticity is the key to liberation while its opposite, bad faith, is the common (unsuccessful) strategy for coping with the burden

While the tendency to deny human freedom (bad faith) is relatively common, an authentic existence – that is, one based on an acceptance and recognition of freedom and responsibility – is what is required to deal with the challenge of the responsibility our freedom brings. While attempts to boost confidence and self-esteem may well at times be invaluable in helping people cope with the burden of freedom, a wider commitment to promoting authenticity is called for. That is, what is needed is a form of empowerment based on seeking to replace bad faith with authenticity. This is not necessarily a straightforward or short-term task, but social work can contribute positively to this process, rather than run the risk of reinforcing bad faith and its destructive effects in limiting opportunities for growth, development and active problem solving. This calls for more than encouraging or supportive words and actions – it requires a concerted effort to explore the presenting situation for opportunities to assist clients in gaining greater control over their lives and a sensitivity to those factors that stand in the way of authenticity.

Henry (1997: 158) comments that: 'Kierkegaard's concept of dread concerns the anxiety that paralyzes the human self as it senses its aloneness in the face of the cosmic dance of life'. Part of the social work task, then, is to help tackle that sense of dread or anguish and thus support people in taking responsibility for making progress towards their goals. This can be seen as an important part of empowerment.

In addition, of course, we need to recognise that we cannot promote authenticity in others unless we take seriously the challenge of our own authenticity. There is little point in seeking to support others in empowering themselves if practitioners disempower themselves through their own bad faith. Social work is a skilled activity that requires a degree of sensitivity and self-awareness. It is therefore important that we should not place barriers to our own development of skill, sensitivity and awareness by denying our own freedom and responsibility. This is not to say that we should attempt to put our own house completely in order before we are able to try and support others. This would be unrealistic, as it has to be recognised that the development of authenticity is a long-term project and not simply a one-off decision. The notion of 'continuous professional development' is an important one in terms of the development of knowledge, skills and values in general, but it can also be seen as significant in terms of continuing to learn about ourselves. Indeed, this is fully consistent with the existentialist view of the person as a process of growth and development, rather than a fixed entity or 'essence'.

4. Despite freedom, existence is characteristically experienced as powerlessness and helplessness

The terms, 'freedom' and 'liberation' can be misleading, in so far as they mask the strong sense of powerlessness that is so often characteristic of human existence. Feeling powerless and *being* powerless are, of course, not the same thing. The task, therefore, is to attempt to overcome feelings of powerlessness by supporting people in establishing control gradually and steadily as part of a process of empowerment. Bad faith, as a form of self-disempowerment and thus a source of feelings of powerlessness, must therefore be challenged. Although bad faith can clearly be seen as a barrier to progress, it is none the less evident in so many people's day-to-day lives. To leave bad faith unchallenged is therefore a serious mistake, in so far as this is likely to undermine any attempts to implement a positive plan of intervention. This is not to say that the social worker can or should make major changes to clients' self-perception or expect radical transformations in how they conduct their lives. However, it none the less has to be recognised that to fail to address bad faith is to collude with it and therefore to reduce the chances of success as far as any programme of intervention is concerned. Skills in gently and constructively challenging bad faith and supporting people in the development of a more authentic approach to their lives should therefore be at a premium.

5. Existentialism proposes a shared subjective journey – a partnership in helping

The important role of perception and meaning indicates the uniqueness of each individual, that each of us is ultimately alone in the world. It is therefore a fundamental principle of existentialism that we need to work together, to build alliances in tackling the range of existential challenges we face in our lives. This partnership approach operates at two separate but inter-related levels. First, it is important to work collaboratively with *clients*, to move away from a model in which it is assumed that the worker is the 'expert' who has the 'answers'. Involving clients directly in the social work process is a fundamental element of empowering forms of practice. Second, partnership needs to involve other *professionals*, to develop a shared perspective so that resources for change and development can be harnessed from a wide range of sources.

6. The dynamic tension between authority/control/statutory duties on the one hand and creative, non-directive work on the other is one to be recognised. It is a conflict that has to be managed in our everyday work rather than resolved once and for all

Mahon (1997: 7) makes the point that: 'the human world is a human construction which continually demands reconstruction, and in thus reconstructing the world I inescapably side with some human beings against others'. That is to say, conflict is an inevitable feature of human experience. It would therefore be naive in the extreme to assume that issues of control will not arise. In order to protect some people it is necessary to control others (as in child protection, for example). As representatives of the state or other formal organisations, social workers are inevitably involved in the use of authority. However, this is not an inevitable barrier to empowerment, provided that such power is not abused or misused. Indeed, the power of the worker can often be an important factor in creating situations in which empowerment becomes a possibility (see Thompson, 2007b; 2011a). Power and control should be used appropriately and constructively, rather than naively wished away.

Existentialism recognises that power is an ever present feature of human interaction, and would therefore take account of power imbalances and the potential for the deliberate abuse or unwitting misuse of such power. The task, then, is not for the social worker to use his or her power to coerce or cajole clients into following a particular course of action, but rather to use such power constructively in identifying and working towards agreed goals as part of a process of partnership. Where it is not possible to agree goals (as a result of a statutory duty being in conflict with a client's wishes, for example), the use of power should be clear and explicit so that there is no confusion or underhandedness, which in themselves could constitute a misuse of power. However, to ignore, deny or trivialise the power dimension of human interactions is to run the risk of dangerous practice, possibly doing more harm than good by failing to recognise the significance of power and control in a social work context.

7. Existence is movement. There is no 'natural' stability as our life-plans are constantly being reconstructed and so development, disintegration or stability are perpetual possibilities – contingency is everpresent

While clients may at times be understandably resistant to change or defeatist about the possibility of positive change, the fact remains that existing stability in a given situation is reinforced by people's actions and attitudes and can therefore be undermined if that is what is required to make progress towards agreed goals. It is therefore important for social workers to be realistic about the possibilities for change, being neither unduly defeatist about the potential for change nor setting people up to fail by failing to take adequate account of the barriers to change. Assessing the potential for change therefore needs to take account of both the subjective dimension (the factors that are within the individual's control) and the objective dimension (the range of factors, some of which may facilitate change, while others may act as a barrier). An 'essentialist' view which regards people as being unable to change can be a significant obstacle to progress by ruling out important possibilities for moving forward (another example of bad faith).

An important implication of contingency as a basic feature of human existence is that meaning has to be recognised as a key issue in making sense of, and responding to the uncertain 'shifting sands' of life in general and the situations encountered in practice in particular. In seeking to develop an adequate understanding of each practice situation, attention therefore needs to be given to the specific meanings attached to events or circumstances. For example, as Bevan comments in relation to social work in a palliative care context:

> A person who is dying may question the meaning and purpose of their own lives and those close to them. Their own personal systems of meaning may be questioned at this time. This may or may not involve formal or informal religious beliefs. It seems that what we are exploring here is the freedom for those who are dying to seek peace.
>
> (Bevan, 1998: 28)

This passage illustrates the importance of appreciating, and respecting, systems of meaning which will change and adapt to new situations, rather than simply seeking to impose our own interpretation of events.

8. Existential freedom – the process of self-creation – is a prerequisite to political liberty. To deny the former is to foreclose the latter and thus render an authentic social work impossible

If we rely on deterministic notions which deny freedom and responsibility, we create artificial barriers to progress at a sociopolitical level. That is, if we regard individuals not as self-creating processes who exercise choice and agency, but rather as pawns pushed here and there by forces beyond their control, then we rule out the possibility of changing or influencing the broader circumstances which are often a significant source of pressure and difficulties (poverty, deprivation, discrimination and so on). Recognising that we have a degree of control over our actions (and responsibility for their consequences) enables us to work towards a collective approach to social problems. The recognition of such freedom at a personal level is not a denial of the importance of wider cultural and structural factors, but rather an acknowledgement that the three levels (personal, cultural and structural) are intertwined and interdependent.

As Birt comments:

> There can be no liberation of consciousness separate from the total struggle for social liberation, just as there can be no social liberation without a liberating consciousness. There can be no radical transformation of identity without an entire struggle to radically transform the social order. And no radical transformation of the social structure is possible (nor would it have a purpose) without the transformation of identity – the self-creation of a new kind of human being. It is this self-creation and renewal that is the aim of all effort.

(Birt, 1997: 211)

Social work, by helping clients realise their potential as free individuals thereby contributes to the broader emancipatory project of social transformation towards a greater degree of social justice.

Conclusion

An authentic social work practice cannot dodge the difficult issues of human existence and experience – crisis, loss, grief, pain, suffering, fear, frustration, uncertainty, alienation, deprivation, discrimination and oppression. What is needed, then, is a theoretical base which similarly does not shirk such difficult issues, and which, in fact, places such concerns at centre stage. Clearly, existentialist philosophy is one such theoretical framework. As the name implies, it begins with human existence. It takes the fact that we exist (ontology) as its basic starting point and then seeks to make sense of that existence, to see how meaning operates as a central feature (phenomenology). It then seeks to draw out the implications of all this for our day-to-day lives as we wrestle with the ambiguities, uncertainties, contradictions and paradoxes that confront us in the course of maintaining a coherent thread of meaning and rising to the existential challenges.

Social work is a complex and demanding endeavour. It is therefore understandable that some practitioners should seek simple, straightforward answers to complex problems. However, existentialism recognises the subtle intricacies of human existence in general and problem-solving activities such as social work in particular and therefore alerts us to the dangers of oversimplification. Two such dangers are reductionism and essentialism (Sibeon, 2004). The former refers to the tendency to reduce a complex, multi-level phenomenon to a single level or explanation. For example, the view that 'all social workers are racist' fails to take account of the different levels of discrimination and oppression and thereby reduces a personal, cultural and structural issue to simply a personal one. The latter refers to the tendency to regard phenomena which are fluid and open to change as if they were fixed and immutable. For example, aspects of an individual's identity may be seen as beyond change, thus failing to recognise that identity is not a fixed entity and is influenced by a wide range of social and psychological processes – and is therefore partly within the control of the individual. Existentialism cannot be a simple philosophy offering simple solutions, because it seeks to make sense of the immensely complicated and intricate nature of human existence – it is therefore clearly antithetical to such dangerous processes as reductionism and essentialism which fail to appreciate the enormously complex nature of social reality.

However, although existentialism cannot offer simple answers, what it can offer us is a number of important themes and concepts which can be extremely useful in looking for ways forward in getting to grips with the challenges that face us in social work as we deal with not only the complexities of human experience in general, but also those particular situations which reflect the extremes of life, where pain, suffering, deprivation and oppression are to the fore. The demanding territory of social work practice is also very much the theoretical territory of existentialism, with its focus on those aspects of life which can challenge our ontological security. Such ontological security is necessary to nourish and sustain the sense of identity and rootedness which enables us to respond to the existential challenges that we all face at certain times in our lives, but which many people face far more frequently, and perhaps more intensely, as a result of their social location and of the effects of discrimination and oppression in a society characterised by structural inequalities and by the cultural discourses that help to sustain them:

> *Existentialism is a practical philosophy. It seeks not only to understand the world but also to change it. It is this practical focus, together with its emphasis on the inherent suffering, unpredictability and risk of human existence, which makes it a useful basis for taking forward our thinking . . . Existentialism is a philosophy of empowerment. It recognises the fundamental freedom of human existence but also takes cognisance of the internal or subjective self-made barriers of bad faith and the external or objective constraints of social divisions and the attendant inequalities and oppressions of sexism, racism and so on. Existentialism offers a way forward in the perpetual struggle to maintain an authentic existence which avoids the indulgences and false salvation of bad faith, and which challenges and undermines the oppressions which seek to constrain or destroy our freedom.*
>
> (Thompson, 1992b: 36–37)

Existentialist practice, then, is not a form of practice based on easy answers or stock responses, but rather an approach which recognises the complex demands of human existence and seeks to wrestle with them in an informed way – informed by our understanding of the nature of human reality as discussed, described and debated in the wealth of existentialist literature we have at our disposal.

References

Bevan, D. (1998) Death, Dying and Inequality. *Care: The Journal of Practice and Development*, 7(1) 27–38.

Billington, R. (1990) *East of Existentialism: The Tao of the West.* London: Unwin Hyman.

Birt, R. (1997) Existence, Identity and Liberation. In Gordon (1997).

Denney, D. (2005) *Risk and Society*. London: Sage.

Gordon, L.R. (Ed.) (1997) *Existence in Black: An Anthology of Black Existential Philosophy.* London: Routledge.

Henry, P. (1997) Rastafarianism and the Reality of Dread. In Gordon (1997).

Holloway, M. and Moss, B. (2010) *Spirituality and Social Work.* Basingstoke: Palgrave Macmillan.

Lesnik, B. (Ed.) (1998) *Countering Discrimination in Social Work.* Aldershot: Arena.

Macquarrie, J. (1973) *Existentialism.* Harmondsworth: Penguin.

Mahon, J. (1997) *Existentialism, Feminism and Simone de Beauvoir.* London: Macmillan.

Moss, B. (2005) *Religion and Spirituality.* Lyme Regis: Russell House Publishing.

Sartre, J-P. (1958) *Being and Nothingness.* London: Methuen.

Sartre, J-P. (1963) *Search for a Method.* New York: Vintage.

Sartre, J-P. (1982) *Critique of Dialectical Reason.* London: Verso.

Schön, D.A. (1983) *The Reflective Practitioner: How Professionals Think in Action.* London: Temple Smith.

Sibeon, R. (2004) *Rethinking Social Theory.* London: Sage.

Thompson, N. (1992a) *Existentialism and Social Work.* Aldershot: Avebury.

Thompson, N. (1992b) *Child Abuse: The Existential Dimension.* Norwich: University of East Anglia Social Work Monographs.

Thompson, N. (1998a) The Ontology of Ageing. *British Journal of Social Work*, 28(5) 697–707.

Thompson, N. (1998b) Towards a Theory of Emancipatory Practice. In Lesnik (1998).

Thompson, N. (2007a) *Power and Empowerment.* Basingtsoke: Palgrave Macmillan.

Thompson, N. (2007b) Spirituality: An Existentialist Perspective. *Illness, Crisis & Loss* 15(2).

Thompson, N. (2009) *Understanding Social Work.* 3rd edn, Basingstoke: Palgrave Macmillan.

Thompson, N. (2011a) *Promoting Equality: Working with Difference and Diversity.* 3rd edn, Basingstoke: Palgrave Macmillan.

Thompson, N. (2011b) *Crisis Intervention.* 2nd edn, Lyme Regis: Russell House Publishing.

Thompson, S. (2005) *Age Discrimination*. Lyme Regis: Russell House Publishing.

Thompson, S. and Thompson, N. (2008) *The Critically Reflective Practitioner.* Basingstoke: Palgrave Macmillan.

Tomer, A., Eliason, G.T. and Wong, P.T.P. (Eds.) (2008) *Existential and Spiritual Issues in Death Attitudes.* New York: Lawrence Erlbaum Associates.

van Deurzen, E. and Arnold-Baker, C. (Eds.) (2005) *Existential Perspectives on Human Issues: A Handbook for Therapeutic Practice.* Basingstoke: Palgrave Macmillan.

Webb, S.A. (2006) *Social Work in a Risk Society: Social and Political Perspectives.* Basingstoke: Palgrave Macmillan.

Chapter 13

Empowerment: Help or Hindrance in Professional Relationships?

Lena Dominelli

Empowerment is a trendy catchword that resonates across the political spectrum, regardless of adherents espousing traditional or progressive philosophies. The concept's potential to have meaning for all shades of political opinion makes it intellectually messy. This can frustrate attempts to critically examine its usefulness in professional social work relationships. In this chapter, I consider empowerment in professional caring relations for its capacity to describe practitioners' attempts to share power with those they claim to serve – 'clients'.[1] I conclude that empowerment is necessary but contradictory and insufficient in realising emancipatory social work. I embark on this exercise because I think that power relations between professionals and 'clients' are central to the kind of helping relationship that can be developed between them. Understanding these dynamics identifies the conditions under which 'clients' can engage in processes that assert responsibility for and control over their own affairs. Empowerment is also a key ingredient in their ability to hold professionals accountable for their actions and demand services that are user-led. Through this exploration, I seek to explain why empowerment is acceptable to both rightwing politicians promoting discourses of choice and market solutions to the delivery of welfare services and those supporting social justice for marginalised or socially excluded groups.

Empowerment: what is it?

Empowerment is difficult to define. It was popular in discourses around community action in the late 1960s and 1970s, but the New Right appropriated it for its own radical agenda during the 1980s. Now it is fashionable in the corporate world. Definitions utilised by community activists convey ideas of a transfer of power across social categories; those of rightwing politicians emphasise individual control over their situations; and corporate entrepreneurs assert choice in the market place. The last two portray individualised views of empowerment and focus on interpersonal relations, or what an individual can do when interacting with others. Community activists concentrate on transformational changes at the structural or societal levels. Those engaging with either

---

[1] I have placed 'client' in quotes to indicate that it is a problematic concept.

conceptualisation of empowerment criticise their opponents for ignoring the points they have raised.

Stuart Rees (1991) has advocated strongly for using empowerment to promote structural change. Individuals are empowered in the process of achieving that objective. Wallerstein and Bernstein (1994: 142) focus on structural empowerment by defining it as a:

> ... social-action process that promotes participation of people, organisations and communities towards the goal of individual and community control, political efficacy, improved quality of community life and social justice.

Dominelli's (1997) typology of empowerment differentiates between its empowering and disempowering dimensions. It contains:

- *Tokenistic or fashionable* empowerment as a superficial form that seems to empower individuals when it does not, e.g. using cosmetics to beautify the body.
- *Bureaucratic or routinised* empowerment that focuses on procedural empowerment, e.g. Citizens' Charters.
- *Commodified or consumerist* empowerment that is about exercising choice in the marketplace.
- *Interpersonal* empowerment that assumes that personal interactions can change all aspects of oppression.
- *Structural* empowerment that focuses only on social structures and ignores individuals.
- *Emancipatory or transformational* empowerment that is a holistic form that empowers at both personal and structural levels.

Understanding this typology assists in identifying how structural approaches can exclude individual empowerment either at the personal level or through a collective process. If it occurs, individual empowerment can be a by-product of collective processes rather than a direct objective. Those concerned with individual psychological development assert that empowerment is the process of facilitating personal change by enabling individuals to assume control of their activities (Riger, 1993). Insights into structural change can be enhanced through the typology. Individualising views of empowerment fostered through managerialist pronouncements have introduced complaints procedures and other bureaucratic forms of control over professional behaviour. Dominelli (1996; 1997) has critiqued managerialist approaches for ignoring process issues and focusing on bureaucratised forms of empowerment because these fail to address systemic inequalities and structural sources of individual disempowerment. Dominelli (1997) also argues that managerialist approaches lock individuals into tokenistic empowerment because control over the creation and design of services rests with management. In saying this, I do not endorse arguments legitimating professionals' capacity to act as autonomous beings who are unaccountable to 'clients' as Lloyd (1998) claims. Rather, it suggests that professionals exercising critical judgement and discretion are more likely to allow for the possibility that when people's circumstances do not reflect normative behaviour their needs can be met because 'clients' have opportunities to engage in real dialogue with practitioners and have their views heard. Professionals in these situations, aware of the danger of exercising discretion in discriminatory ways, can avoid doing this by utilising empowerment at *both* personal and structural levels.

Concentrating on collective empowerment amongst 'black' people,[2] Solomon (1976) argues eloquently that individuals must become involved in empowering their communities to bridge the gap between the two polarised positions of either structural or personal change. To reach this goal, Solomon suggests that community groups begin the process by redefining issues to be addressed in terms of what they want to achieve. By participating in collective action, people who have been marginalised individually and collectively become empowered because they begin to assert their own definitions of what is to be done and challenge their being cast as pathological individuals and communities. Consequently, Solomon (1976) challenges commonly accepted definitions of socially excluded groups by constructing their 'difference' or deviation from the dominant norms as a source of strength and not of powerlessness. Empowerment in these situations becomes a matter of process and outcomes. Professionals may become involved in organisational processes as facilitators of an agenda set by the community groups.

Power relations and who has the power to define them in particular ways are crucial to issues of empowerment. Power is itself a disputed concept (Lukes, 1974; French, 1985; Clegg, 1989; Riger, 1993). Power has been conceptualised in three different ways as *power over*, *power to*, and *power of*. *Power over* involves relations of domination. Analysts like Talcott Parsons have presented *power over* as a 'zero-sum' entity, i.e. a force that is imposed upon others or something that people *do to* other people (Parsons and Bales, 1955). It can be exercised to impact on individuals and groups in either deleterious or disadvantageous ways. In many respects, this definition has gained commonsense currency. People assume that power is finite. It can only be taken away from those that have it through conflict of some kind. Although power involves action, *power over* is characterised by a certain fixedness which disables those at the receiving end of ministrations by more powerful others and renders individuals passive against its onslaught. The application of *power over* others is usually experienced as disempowering by those at the bottom of a hierarchy of dominance.

---

[2] I have placed quotes around the terms 'black' and 'white' to demonstrate that these categories are not unitary and homogeneous.

Relations of domination that rely on the exercise of *power over* others are usually portrayed in dichotomous terms that sit in binary opposition to each other. Individuals either have power or they do not. If one individual has *power over*, others can take it away and disempower them in turn. Thus, people talk about taking control over one's life to counter this state of affairs. Those at the receiving end of such power relations are usually deemed passive victims who can do little about their situations. Passivity and lack of vision depicting alternative positions limit people's potential to see the possibilities for changing their environment. Discourses centring on *power over* others tend to focus on individual skills and cast those lacking power as inadequate or pathological. Moreover, by interacting with more powerful others, individuals internalise dominant definitions of their positions and become less convinced of their capacity to resist status quo arrangements or question the relations within which they are located. Another set of theorists, particularly feminist ones, have questioned this 'zero-sum' view of power, postulating it as a complex force which emanates from many sources and which can be created and re-created through social interactions (French, 1985).

Power is considered multi-faceted and involves people negotiating with each other to create and recreate power through social relationships. Power can be both a positive and a negative source of energy and can be used creatively. Other people's powers can be diffused and their impact upon one's life limited. Thus, the issue is not simply a question of taking power away from someone else. Power can be shared and new forms of power can arise. People engage in power relations by exercising agency either individually or collectively. There is no passive victim of other people's actions, although endeavours to assert agency may or may not be successful. Moreover, there is nothing predetermined about the outcome of their negotiations with others (Dominelli and Gollins, 1997). Powerful people are not totally powerful and powerless people are not without power (Dominelli, 1986). Neither the powerful nor the powerless are locked into positions from which they cannot move to advance or retreat. They can also stand still. Their negotiations do not necessarily occur in a linear fashion. And, they take place in the routines of everyday life.

Individuals' structural positioning is important in setting the scene for a negotiated encounter with others. This is particularly significant in accessing and developing support networks. These networks are forms of social capital that can ease one's way in life, for they assist in identifying the resources that are available, and enhance morale (Craig and Mayo, 1995). In negotiations involving power dynamics, the outcome can go either way, depending on the situational circumstances and resources brought by the interacting parties. Since power in a negotiation can go either way, nothing is predetermined, although experience and statistics can demonstrate the probability that if an individual is poor and 'black', they will have less access to opportunities, resources and networks than if they were 'white'.[2] This reality reduces 'black' people's capacity to assert their power as individuals effectively. But this dimension can be challenged more forcefully through collective action. Personal relationships matter in *power over* situations because they can mitigate the dominant group's potential to undermine or humiliate those who have been subordinated. Overcoming adverse conditions can be crucial to an individual's chances of survival. For example, individuals abducted in hostage-taking incidents are more likely to be treated with less hostility or be released if they successfully get their captors to see them as persons with whom they can relate even when the immediate balance of power overwhelmingly favours the hostage-taker. By engaging in a personal relationship, the *power over* relation can be diffused somewhat.

Relational dynamics reveal that empowerment and disempowerment feature simultaneously in any given situation. The rethinking of power relations suggests that power involves doing something about one's situation. This is reflected in the remaining two considerations of power. The first, *power to*, entails resistance to subordination and oppression and implies that individuals come together to collectively express their ability to take action in terms they set. This conceptualisation of power is dynamic and allows oppressed people to reject in myriad ways the position in which they find themselves and is deemed empowering. The exercise of *power to* do something with others can easily shift into the dynamics of *power over* others. The second, *power of*, occurs as a result of individuals coming together as a united (not unified or homogeneous) group to form collective organisations capable of challenging oppression, especially the imposition of *power over* them. Dominelli (1986) refers to the 'power of the powerless' in analysing a marginalised group of women's ability to organise themselves to challenge sexist social relations. Groups who create *power of* relationships for themselves experience the exercise of power as empowering because they are able to construct their own agenda for action.

Useful as these notions are in understanding power, they are problematic insofar as they fail to take on board the full complexities of power. These include the relevance of the three forms of power considered above and their interaction with each other in specific incidents. A detailed analysis of any situation will reveal that power – *power over*, *power to* and *power of* – will be present simultaneously. Unpacking the concept is further complicated by the perception of power as an entity that operates within a dichotomous world. This is particularly pertinent in envisaging power relations as *power over*, the element that sits uneasily at the foreground of many people's understandings of power. Consequently, in *power over* social relations, issues of oppression are considered in binary terms. A situation which is described as either 'this' or 'that', presents an instance of the 'us – them' mentality. According to this version of power, people either have it or they do not. It is like having a good that can be traded or taken away. Therefore, an individual or group is either oppressed because they lack power or liberated because they have it. In these characterisations of power, liberation is simply a question of reversing existing zero-sum configurations of social relations. In Marxist world-views, for example, the power of the bourgeoisie was to be challenged and replaced by the power of the proletariat. Professional discourses of 'zero-sum' versions of power position empowerment as a bureaucratised halfway house between being powerful and powerless.

Having control over one's affairs is not the same as feeling empowered within them. In professional bureaucratic responses, empowerment objectives can be thwarted by a concern with the mechanics of empowerment at the expense of process and outcome – the *how* and *who* of social relations. A disillusioned Oliver (1990) writes that the most that professionals can achieve is to not disempower their 'clients'. Although couched in terms of *power over*, empowerment for Oliver (1990) is something that an individual can only do for themselves within the context of collective action around their particular conditions. Those committed to power sharing forms of empowering social interactions have sought to meet in this halfway house to ensure that the acquisition of skills, allocation of roles or tasks and participation in decision making involve all members of a group (Belenky *et al.*, 1997). Through these, there is an attempt to validate experiential ways of knowing, not just empirical evidence. There is a reliance on mechanisms that share power, e.g. rotating formal positions to ensure that each person can learn different tasks and obtain the skills and knowledge that accompany these. Everyone participates in expressions of grief over collective failures and joy over group successes. Empowerment in these conditions can impact on both personal and structural levels, as have, for example, feminists organising in political parties.

Successes in this arena have not transformed social relations in emancipatory ways for women (see Dominelli and Jonsdottir, 1989). Further obstacles in unpacking power dynamics relate to the organisation of social relations in ways that maintain divisions between the public and private spheres. The setting of this boundary is especially significant in the exercise of *power over* others. Public matters can be relegated to the private domain through discourses or other forms of action if accountability lapses. Similarly, raising concerns usually located in the domestic arena in the public one pushes issues of accountability and responsibility to the forefront of the public agenda. This was a tactic employed by feminists to raise public recognition of domestic violence and child sexual abuse within family settings at a time when denial about their existence was rampant (Rush, 1980; Kelly, 1988; Dominelli, 1989; Basu, 1995). In the process of meeting this objective, women involved in such consciousness-raising activities began to feel confident in their abilities to set their own agendas and felt empowered as a result (Ruzek, 1986; Basu, 1995).

The public-private divide also became important in creating a welfare marketplace. By defining care as a private responsibility, commercial providers are encouraged to develop facilities that provide caring services. And, they begin to charge for these to assure the provider of a profit margin. Moreover, by transforming human interactions into commodity relations, social relationships become privatised, that is, a matter between individuals who are 'free' to negotiate a contract with each other. In this context, structural limitations, like the large numbers of people who are too poor to participate in 'free' choices about their needs do not even get into the picture, let alone penetrate market space to engage in the ongoing discourses in their own voices.

In globalised contexts, commodifying social relations tend to reproduce *power over* relations as managerial and corporatist voices dominate at the expense of those of professionals and 'clients'. Empowerment, defined as the ability to choose options within a range of available possibilities is problematic for those seeking equality because it assumes that individuals can enter the commodity relationship on an equal basis, that is, each has the same access to information and resources and that provisions on offer are acceptable. This is not the reality for a majority of the world's population, as the latest United Nations' report on human social development indicates (UN, 2011). Three billion of the earth's inhabitants live on US $2 or less per day, hardly enough for a cup of coffee in the global market place. Real choice can be exercised only by the privileged few. Corporate capacity to conduct empowerment discourses by presuming equality rather than demonstrating its presence in commodity relations makes the concept attractive to right wing ideologues, policy makers and entrepreneurs.

The problems highlighted above raise concerns about the conceptualisation of empowerment as a negotiating position that lies in the middle of a continuum with oppression at one end and liberation at the other. If its potential for action derives from this location, then empowerment becomes a way of mediating power relations within tightly circumscribed constraints over which the individual as individual can have only limited leverage. Under these restraints, altering a situation relates to individuals' structural position, not personal volition. This limitation poses the question of the importance of collective endeavours in ensuring individual empowerment and success in a person's ability to exert control over his or her affairs. As part of the situational context, structural constraints also create major hurdles that have to be overcome by professionals who seek to work in empowering ways with 'clients'. This point emphasises another key difficulty in conceptualising power and empowerment as an individual or personal activity, that is, the decontextualisation of the person from their social context.

Recognising the significance of situational contexts in an individual's capacity to assert control over their activities is missing from professional interventions (Thorpe, 1993). Social workers frequently act as if the context in which poor people suffering from structural inequalities exist is absent and treat them as if all individuals are the same when they are not. This is particularly evident when practitioners respond to people facing structural inequalities as if their life chances mirror those of the dominant group. This happens, for example, when they treat 'black' people as if they were 'white' (Dominelli, 1988, 2002a; Ahmad, 1990) or women as if they were men (Hanmer and Statham, 1988; Dominelli and McLeod, 1989; Dominelli, 2002b). Endorsed in the professional ideology of 'universalism', this stance ignores diversity and creates a totalising unity that negates the actual living conditions which individuals and groups experience. Ignoring the conditions within which individuals are embedded results in a failure to acknowledge the boundaries that constrain the individual as an individual who can take action to empower themselves. A similar problem is endured by marginalised groups who also encounter these limitations in their capacities for resistance in their lived experience on a daily basis.

A decontextualised view of power also neglects to take account of the commodified social relations which are occurring simultaneously within the welfare market-place. Consequently, qualitative issues once deemed outside commodity relations have been quantified and subjected to measurement, thereby enhancing bureaucratic forms of power which are usually controlled by agency managers and the professionals they employ. Bureaucracies are sites of entrenched forms of power which individuals have difficulty in challenging effectively when operating within the terms that those running them establish. Furthermore, in the welfare market-place, professionals in bureaucratic settings interact with their 'clients' as individual consumers who are receiving a commodity for which they can expect to pay instead of a service delivered free of charge. Engaging with 'clients' within commodity relationships requires different responses from professionals than those involved in forming professional relationships rooted in interpersonal relations. While commodity relations can empower individuals who have the capacity to exercise choice to avail themselves of services geared to their needs, the majority of 'clients' are not in a position to do so because their situational context is one of structural inequalities embedded in poverty and marginalisation. Money determines the extent to which individuals can become purchasers in the service market place, despite their having being constructed as powerful, atomised consumers by entrepreneurs in discourses of market-place welfare.

Commodity relations have de-professionalised the profession by reducing complex professional tasks to simplified constituent parts (Dominelli and Hoogvelt, 1997). This development has fed the proletarianisation of once autonomous professionals who previously exercised a considerable degree of control over their labour process. And it has opened the door to employing less qualified individuals in caring situations then demanding more professional expertise than ever because 'clients' being referred to welfare agencies have increasingly complex needs (Teeple, 1995). Many welfare state activities have become subject to managerialist imperative and procedural forms of control (Culpitt, 1992; Teeple, 1995). These have made it difficult for those working within the welfare bureaucracies or seeking to access services, to challenge them. Neither do they make it easy to hold professionals accountable for their interventions or failing to engage with clients' concerns. The Taylorisation of social work that accompanied market relations in the welfare arena (Dominelli and Hoogvelt, 1997) has had devastating consequences for both professionals and 'clients'. For professionals, it has meant the loss of individual control over how they work. For 'clients', it has resulted in their having little real say in creating services or developing criteria for accessing them.

'Clients' have made gains in holding professionals accountable. The personalisation agenda has enabled 'clients' to choose which services they will purchase through individual budgets without altering the general reality of disempowerment in the market-place because choice remains limited to existing provisions and 'clients' are positioned as consumers of limited means. And 'clients' become employers of personal assistants and unpaid tax collectors. In other words, an employer-employee relationship is set up regardless of the view of the person requiring the services. Service users are required to employ individuals themselves directly, thereby engaging in a recruitment and selection process, and the other obligations of being an employer including paying their employee's superannuation, national insurance and taxes by deducting these at source from the personal assistant's salary. Moreover, they may not be skilled enough to do this work, and they do not get paid for doing it. Thus, any assistance they need to complete the government's forms requires them to employ experts such as accountants or tax collectors. This sum will have to come out of their benefit.

Politicians, corporate entrepreneurs and wealthy users gained most from the reorganisation of welfare relations. Politicians controlling the state apparatus have gained by successfully shedding the state's responsibilities for ensuring the welfare of citizens. Entrepreneurs are advantaged because a new source of getting rich opens up when they land lucrative (mainly state) contracts that yield substantial profits for services provided to targeted individuals, their customers. Wealthy users gain because their choices enlarge quantitatively and qualitatively. And, they no longer receive services alongside less affluent 'clients' or have to experience discomfort when doing so.

The bureaucratisation of consumer power in the welfare sphere and managerialist control over professionals through performance related pay, competence-based definitions of caring tasks and workplace-based training have meant a loss of control over the conditions in which both professionals and 'clients' conduct key areas of their lives (Dominelli, 1996). To effectively challenge commodity relations in the welfare arena, change needs to occur at both individual or personal level and structural level. Change has to take place in the 'client's' behaviour, the professional's repertoire of skills, the organisation of welfare services, and society's cultural and value systems so that the entire basis on which social relations are organised and conducted can be altered. Only then can the scene be set for empowerment, as liberation, to take place.

Accusations of reification, essentialism or reductionism in debates over empowerment (see Lloyd, 1998) ignore the social construction of particular social categories at specific points in time by particular groups or individuals. It's not that these categories are totalising and immutable, for an examination of their composition reveals that they are simultaneously unifying and diverse. They may be described otherwise by those setting the terms within which discourses are conducted. Treating them *as if* the category were homogeneous could enable *power over* relations to be reproduced. To create discourses that transcend such power relations, language has to go beyond using simplified symbols to describe complex realities. A symbol is both a signifier and representational of people's actions, behaviours, thoughts and meanings, each of which is only partially conveyed through language. What lies 'hidden' behind symbols is as important as the *partial* reality conveyed, for this includes power relations which are also operative within a given interaction whether an individual is actively conscious of them or not.

For these reasons, empowerment theories should steer shy of theoretical frameworks that totalise social categories and examine the diversity that exists within the unity of a category that contradicts totalising discourses. Finding commonalities with their diversities would acknowledge unity as a symbolic representation for particular purposes only. Their diversities would remain. Such considerations matter when taking action. Activists are mindful of not treating any category as 'all the same'. For example, targeting women in struggles to end domestic violence is useful if the focus on women recognises differentiated experiences of domestic violence amongst women even though it affects all women. A useful framework does not consider such categories as a simple set of homogeneous groups.

Research can highlight both similarities and differences to be addressed. Research can reveal how it may be convenient for those doing the defining to treat women as a homogeneous group for particular purposes or because they have not thought out the implications of their categorisations. This occurred in the early days of the feminist movement when white middle-class American feminist writers treated women across the globe as if they occupied the same privileged position as they (see Friedan, 1974). It was also evident when 'sisterhood' was declared 'universal' (Morgan, 1971) with little appreciation that the slogan denied the actual experiences of being a woman for the majority of women in the global context (Mohanty, 1995; Basu, 1995). Honi Fern Haber (1994) utilises the concept of the 'individual in the community' to move away from a totalising universalism and related concepts linked to dichotomous thinking which privileges powerful people. Instead, she examines bonds of solidarity that recognise the uniquenesses symbolised by 'difference' as well as the unities within and amongst them. These can be developed to both empower and disempower individuals or groups. The main message that can be derived from her analysis is that any connection with others *must be created and not assumed*.

Those creating spaces of empowerment acknowledge the legitimacy of individual and group identity boundaries and valorise strengths embodied within them at all levels. Empowering professionals desist from thinking about 'difference' as a 'deficit' and a pathology that must be eradicated (Dominelli, 1997, 1998). The acknowledgement of 'difference' places identity at the forefront of self-expression and the development of empowering power relations. The politics of identity can provide common objectives which will feed the webs of connection which can transcend 'difference' without obliterating it (Haraway, 1988). Unity of this kind differs from the assimilationist form advocated by those running the nation-state during their nation-building ventures and those subsequently replicated through the welfare state (Lorenz, 1994). These have denied 'difference' and based access to entitlements on exclusionary definitions of citizenship that reduced the rights of women and 'black' people to receive its benefits (Lister, 1997). Under assimilationist discourses of universalism, 'difference' was suppressed, but did not disappear. The resurgence of claims for 'national' identity in the UK and elsewhere exemplifies this. The tensions of diversity to not obliterate unity and vice-versa do not cease through assimilationism. These factors are replicated in discourses over 'independence lite' in Scotland and the formation of a European identity that encloses 27 different nations and growing.

Professionalism and empowerment

Are professionals promoting empowerment to be mistrusted as Oliver (1990) suggests or is it possible to transform professionalism so that power sharing with 'clients' becomes the norm as Dominelli and Jonsdottir (1989) imply? Clearly, as countless groups and the 'new' social movements have demonstrated, unlimited professional power, or the exercise of professional *power over* others is unacceptable to people demanding social justice. Social justice, Flax (1990) suggests, is a bridging concept which is rooted in the recognition of 'difference' and enables individuals to organise around identity issues experienced at both individual and collective levels. Empowerment which aims to realise social justice has to address 'difference' in terms that will valorise its existence and value the strengths which arise from its recognition as a positive factor in people's lives. Professionals contribute to this objective by appreciating and valuing 'difference' and relating to individuals in culturally appropriate social contexts. Culture is defined more widely than ethnic culture to encompass all life practices. Everyone has a culture that is fluid, changing, adaptive and stable by providing continuity within discontinuities (Dominelli, 2009).

This attitude will help practitioners utilise their experience in ways that contribute towards the well-being of their 'clients'. People want to work with experts who are accountable to them and can be held responsible for their behaviour (Oliver, 1990). Moreover, as feminists and disability movements have indicated, professionals should reconsider their definition of professionalism and turn it into one which is about placing expertise in the hands of users. Thus, it is about professionals *servicing* 'clients'' needs rather than providing them with a service as a commodity. 'Clients' are quite capable of providing their own services – those that they design and run, once they have access to the necessary resources. A professional can become a resource like the other resources that 'clients' have at their disposal to enhance their well-being. This stance can raise a number of awkward questions for practitioners, e.g., are 'clients' always correct in identifying their own needs? Aside from queries to determine who is the 'client', particularly in complex situations where there may be more than one, should professionals simply go along with the needs identified by 'clients'? Whilst an affirmative reply may often be unproblematic, what happens if a social worker is working with a young male sex offender who identifies his need as having access to children against whom he commits sexual assaults? Or the man who believes he is 'right' to constantly beat his wife when he feels aggrieved? Both these behaviours would be deemed unacceptable by most professionals and their stance would be endorsed by their code of ethics. In less clear-cut cases like indirect discrimination occasioned by employment policies requiring qualifications which are normally accessed primarily by 'white' men, the outcome of underrepresentation of 'black' men and all women is less likely to be noticed and condemned.

Moreover, as numerous inquiries into the abuse of children in residential care have demonstrated, 'clients' cannot assume that professionals will not abuse their *power over* them (see Haig-Brown, 1988; Kahan, 1989; Pringle, 1992). How can professionals demonstrate their trustworthiness to 'clients'? What kinds of relationships and controls are necessary to reduce the potential of their *power over* others to harm them? Obviously, compliance to a code of ethics, training and managerial controls can secure professionals' compliance with this objective. Empowering 'clients' to assert their voices and interests in their affairs becomes a powerful means for holding professionals accountable for their behaviour. How 'client' control and empowerment can best be achieved remains highly controversial. Another tricky issue for professionals to address is that of relativism, the idea that one position is as valid as another. While laudable in ensuring that one world view does not dominate others in professional encounters, relativism can lead to unhelpful uncertainty and indecision if applied indiscriminately to every situation – a condition that I would argue is more a solipsism in which anything goes, than relativism.

In a post-modern world, ambiguity in practice is promoted as a positive skill (Parton, 1998). Ambiguity results from social workers acting as intermediaries between the state and civil society. Ambiguity and uncertainty in daily discourses are taken to mean holding more than one position simultaneously. Operationalised in practice contexts that disregard the situation that a 'client' is in can cause indecision that may be costly for vulnerable individuals. For example, how can social workers imbued with a belief that 'truth' is relative deal with unacceptable behaviour amongst more powerful others whether this is men, sex offenders, or any other 'client' group abusing a less powerful one? On one level, social workers have always dealt with ambiguity and uncertainty as part of their daily routines. But at the end of the day, they have had to take action, to make decisions on which the livelihood and safety of others have depended. This requires some appeal to universal principles such as the valuing of human life and others contained within a code of professional ethics and the United Nations Declaration of Human Rights.

While mistakes have been made, practitioners have based decisions on their assessment of an individual's situation without always taking account of their social context, but operating within a legal framework accompanied by a professional code of ethics and their own value system. Within this value system, valuing the lives of vulnerable people has been a crucial element that has transcended relativistic positioning. If the importance of going beyond a relativist position is not recognised and maintained for whatever reason, the lives of vulnerable individuals may be placed in jeopardy and social workers may not be able adequately to carry out their support and monitoring roles. At such points, social workers fail 'clients'. This has happened to children on 'at risk' registers whose family members have gone on to murder them because social workers have failed to insist on their statutory obligations to investigate private relationships and give priority to children's interests when these conflict with those of their carers. In the case of Victoria Climbié, one 'black' culture was assumed the same as another. However, the difficulties in such cases are complex and social workers can become overwhelmed by their own needs for clarity over what they observe as conflicting goals and a situational context which they experience as disempowering (see Blom-Cooper, 1986). Social workers engage with both universal and relative values in the professional judgments they make. Their actions must not occur within assumptions about the superiority of workers' own views. That they do so is a failing which occurs far too often when they are working with diversity and difference (see Dominelli, 1988, 2008; Hanmer and Statham, 1988; Dominelli and McLeod, 1989; Ahmad, 1990). It also happens when they distance themselves from 'clients' because they label them as 'other' and deem them pathological, inadequate and inferior.

Practitioners working within an empowerment framework engage with 'clients' rather than distancing themselves by casting 'clients' as 'other'. Respecting the person and treating them with dignity does not mean condoning their behaviour. Instead of confronting unacceptable behaviour through dialogue they can focus on how abuse attacks the dignity of vulnerable people and follow through with action that increases understanding of the damage done to those perpetuating the abuse and those at its receiving end and insist on a cessation of inappropriate behaviours. A value system based on universal human rights can help negotiate this task. Furthermore, empathy has to be achieved whilst holding ambiguity and then dealing with it by taking *specific action in a specific situation*. Empathy is a key dimension in social work relationships (Egan, 1990). Empathy can only result if social workers can put on another person's shoes while retaining their capacity for independent judgment according to universal principles embedded in the realisation of human rights that acknowledge 'difference' within group and individual allegiances and experiences. A universalism that addresses 'differences' and is rooted in universal human rights provides social workers with a concept that goes beyond the self and the sectarian politics sometimes associated with identity politics.[3] This can only be relevant to their work as practitioners if they can recognise that universalism calls upon other values as prerequisites in the process of its realisation. These include solidarity, mutuality and interdependence.

Each of these values is implicated in the creation of webs of support which enable empowerment to occur more readily under the control of those whom professionals seek to serve. These values cannot be considered in dichotomous terms that pit the interests of one part of the community against those of another. It recognises that there are a number of interdependent considerations that must be deemed together as part of the whole picture. For example, empowering a sex offender requires that his offending behaviour, i.e. the sexual (and other forms of) abuse of others is terminated. Doing so takes on board the fact of the male sex offender being a 'client' who needs a different set of supports and resources than those required by victim-survivors to enable him to stop abusing people. In terms of interdependence, the safety of sexually abused children depends on ensuring that sex offenders' need for rehabilitation is met by their learning new, non-exploitative ways of relating to children and less powerful others. The punishment given for committing crimes against a child becomes an opportunity for introducing behavioural change at the personal level rather than considering it solely a matter of incarceration as punishment for offenders and protection of victims.

Getting to the stage of redefining the problems to be addressed requires: personal change on the part of the offender; structural change at the institutional

---

[3] I am aware of the critique of universal human rights as a Western concept because it individualises rights. Rights are both individual and collective. However, it can be helpful to focus on individual rights to assist oppressed collectivities in defending their rights. Women in industrialising countries have used individualised universal human rights to challenge collective collusion with the violation of their rights. For example, Bangladeshi women organised a Coalition Against Trafficking of Women of Bangladesh to halt the sale of women into forced prostitution (*Vancouver Sun*, 1999).

level so that this response can become commonplace; and change at the cultural level so that sex offenders are considered people who also need help, even if it is offered by a different practitioner than the one who is working directly with the child and/or the non-abusing parent, usually the mother. Reciprocity occurs when the sex offender assumes responsibility for his behaviour and acknowledges its damaging impact on others; while society, via the professional acting on its behalf in working with him, facilitates his access to rehabilitative resources. Solidarity is expressed through a joint commitment to ensuring the safety and well-being of all. Acting within the principles of universalism which acknowledge the specificity of context, can be risky and tricky.

Even in the illustrations covered above, 'success' cannot be guaranteed. Consequently, to empower themselves in complex interventions, professionals have to come clean about their ambiguity and uncertainties. They do not always know the 'right' answer. They do not always live up to their own expectations when it comes to providing 'client'-centred services which respond to the unique needs of individuals. They do not always have the resources necessary to work with 'clients' in accordance with mutually agreed plans of action. The following case study (in which all the characters have fictitious names) explores some of the ambiguities and uncertainties which complicate practice aiming to empower 'clients' so that it becomes contradictory and paradoxical (Lupton and Nixon, 1999), or even disempowering in a number of crucial respects:

Case study: the Goodson family

Clark Goodson was a 30-year-old white man living with his wife Selma, a 28-year-old white woman, and two children, Christine, aged three and Sally aged two. Clark was an unemployed miner who had been unable to get a job for over five years. Selma had become the family breadwinner by working at four part-time jobs as a cleaner. As one of the working poor, their income was supplemented by Family Credit. Yet, it was difficult to make ends meet. Selma often went without food although Clark was allowed the odd drink at the pub with his mates for old times' sake. Secretly, Selma was glad of this weekly ritual for it got Clark out of the house and gave her a few hours of peace with only squabbling children to worry about.

Selma was constantly tired and on edge. Her relationship with Clark was getting increasingly strained. She didn't feel he tried to find work hard enough. He complained bitterly that as a young man, he had been 'thrown on the scrapheap'. The crunch came one evening when Selma's old car which had been getting her to and from her various jobs broke down irreparably. Now carless, she didn't manage to get home until nearly midnight. Clark was furious when she returned. He had missed his pub night and the children had been impossible to get to bed. Indeed, they were still fussing about, though in their pyjamas. He started blaming Selma for all that had gone wrong with his evening. This proved too much for Selma and before long the worst row the two had ever had erupted. It also got ugly. Clark started to hit Selma, punching her in the face and chest. The children who were witnesses to his violence started screaming.

Christine ran to her mother just as Clark was punching her and one of his blows landed on Christine's skull. Christine fell over and bumped into a chair, hitting it with the side of her head, and slumped to the floor. Meanwhile, the neighbours who had heard all the screaming, shouting and other noises had called the police. Selma phoned for an ambulance. Both arrived at the same time. Christine was rushed off to hospital where the examining doctor diagnosed several other signs of earlier bruising and violence – a fractured rib and arm that had healed. Eventually, Clark admitted that he had hit her several months earlier when Selma had been asked to work late on his pub night.

Selma felt disgusted with him, mortified by his behaviour coming to light in these circumstances and guilty for having to go out to work instead of staying home to look after the children. And, she also felt angry that Clark had placed them in this position because he had been either unable or unwilling to land a job. The family was referred to social services for an investigation as a case of non-accidental injury (NAI). The social worker who visited the family at home was a young newly qualified childless 22-year-old 'black' woman of African descent called Angela.

Though feeling sickened by letting his temper get the better of him and subjecting his family to what he thought would be a demeaning experience, Clark was in a belligerent mood. He kept telling himself he loved his family and was not going to let any young 'whipper-snapper' tell him how to lead his life. 'NAI, indeed!' he expostulated. If they really wanted to help him, why couldn't someone just give him a job? He didn't need anything else. He'd had no problems when he was bringing home a good wage. Although the children had not been born at that point, he and Selma had had a great relationship and he was sure they would again if only he could bring in the money and hold his head high once more.

The social worker sensed Clark's hostility the moment he opened the door. She couldn't decide whether it was because he was anxious about what might happen; did not want a 'black' worker; lacked confidence in her ability to handle the situation adequately because she was relatively inexperienced; or had other reasons. However, she smiled at him and tried to put him at ease. Then she asked if she could go inside and meet the rest of the family. He reluctantly let her in. Selma's reaction to Angela was guarded. During the interview, she said little. Clark took on the role of responding for them both. Angela worked in as facilitative a manner as she could and tried to create the space that Selma and Clark needed to give their own views about what should be done to help them with their problems. She also made it clear to the two parents that her main concern was the welfare of the two children. She was looking for assurance that the children were not at risk of further acts of violence being perpetrated against either of them.

The more Angela spoke to the couple, the more she realised that their problems were many and complex. She also realised that focusing simply on protecting the children from further harm was not going to work. The family was in need of a wider range of support services than she could offer within the remit of an NAI investigation. Moreover, she didn't know how she could ensure that the children would be safe as long as the stresses and strains on the family continued as they were. Money was in short supply, but whilst Angela could make a one-off payment to safeguard the children's interests, she could not take on the commitment of supplementing Selma's meagre wages for an indefinite period.

Moreover, Selma needed rest. Selma and Clark required marital counselling. And Clark was in desperate need of a job. Meeting most of these requirements was not the responsibility of the social services department.[4] Responses to appeals to other agencies for additional resources were limited. Many charities were already overwhelmed by requests for assistance that they could not fulfil. Angela felt confounded by the situation that confronted her. Here she was intervening in the lives of people that she could scarcely help. She could place their children on the 'at risk' register or get them looked after by foster parents if she felt maintaining their safety warranted it, but she could offer little in the form of direct support to the family. At best, this could be attendance at a Family Centre a few days a week, a playgroup space and a volunteer to help out around the house. No option was ideal.

At the case conference subsequently held to discuss the family, Angela reported her findings and misgivings. Her colleagues shared her sense of frustration, but as the chair of the case conference said, they had to operate within the legal remit and resourcing that they had available. Those attending concluded that the children would be placed on the 'at risk' register for a period so that the situation could be monitored. Meanwhile, the family would also be given the support services that Angela had identified. Although the outcome was as she had predicted, Angela's disappointment as she left the meeting was enormous. She dreaded having to tell Selma and Clark who chose not to attend the case conference, the result. She knew they would also feel disappointed, angry and perhaps betrayed. Betrayed by a system and people who had heard their calls for help but were unable to provide the support which would enable them to rise out of the low income

---

[4] Social services departments have been restructured since this case study was compiled, but I have left it as it was because the issues discussed transcend these specific arrangements.

trap into which they had fallen and restore Clark's sense of purpose and self-esteem.

Meanwhile, Selma had no alternative but to continue juggling the demands of home with those of work to try and salvage some shreds of dignity for herself and her family. She told Angela she felt betrayed by her intervention and that providing her with some relief in the care of the children was like putting a tiny plaster on a very large running sore.

In reflecting upon the Goodsons' predicament, we see that Angela was able to respond in an empowering manner through the process of her interventions by listening to the couple's definition of the problems they faced and even agreeing with their assessment of the situation. But this was only possible at the interpersonal level. She had no impact on the structural inequalities that pervaded the Goodsons' lives. Although the Goodsons had been able to express their own views and exercise agency in these circumstances, the situational context was one that proved impervious to their wishes. Thus, processual empowerment can result in a disempowering outcome.

The children's empowerment scarcely enters the scene, despite the focus of attention being upon their welfare. The adults are expected to cater to their needs by acting altruistically and in their best interests without necessarily involving them in any of the decision making processes. From the children's perspective, this can lead to patronising practice (Thorpe, 1993). In short, the empowerment of the Goodsons was only achieved to a limited extent. Throughout this work, Angela felt disempowered as a professional by structural inequalities, personal prejudices and institutional failings. There were few opportunities for her to explore her ambiguities and uncertainties with others. She knew that her supervisor would listen to her sympathetically but would be unable to address them. Her needs as a young, 'black' practitioner were poorly acknowledged and not acted upon. Working with Angela to empower her as a professional was not considered. The message of the failure of empowerment in professional helping relationships to liberate people from the daily grind of their life condition has been reinforced in this scenario. Angela felt she had tried to assist the Goodsons and done the best she could within the constraints evident in the situation without responding to other important matters. Empowerment focussing on interpersonal empowerment both helps by identifying issues and treating persons with respect and hinders by not addressing resource shortages and structural reform.

Issues of identity figure prominently in the case scenario, particularly around class, gender, age and 'race', even though they are largely neglected. For example, the gendered roles within the family were critical to its inability to meet the needs of its members. Clark's views on masculinity and Selma's on femininity were not enabling them to be responsive to their altered circumstances. If they had been helped to become more flexible in their gender expectations of each other and value both men and women who undertake domestic work and share it more equitably between them, some of the stresses and strains of their daily lives would have been diminished. Clark might have even been enabled to adopt a new role that gave him status and promoted his well-being. However, changing their lives in this respect would not have dealt with the fundamental problems of poverty, which also debilitated their development as a family whether as individuals or a unit. This case is a good illustration of the importance of change taking place at the micro-, meso- and macro-levels. Transforming the situational context that shapes the living conditions of the Goodson family is only possible when both personal and structural change occur together. Providing 'clients' with a breathing space that is affirmed by listening to their opinions is *not* good enough. Structural change involving society's unequal social relations, work-family life balance, resource allocation, organisations, legislation, policies and practice would transform the Goodson's predicament.

Conclusions

Empowerment does not exist as a purely ideological phenomenon. It occupies contested terrain that impacts upon personal and structural issues to be addressed in securing the transformational changes necessary for human well-being. These forces lead to its realisation as imperfect practice that can disempower or empower individuals and groups. The final outcome depends on whether practitioners and 'clients' who negotiate with privileged others during their daily routines and interactions can bring their agendas as equal concerns to the proceedings. Any altruism that may provide grounds for optimistic interpretations of professional capacities and commitments to empower those at the bottom of social hierarchies carries little purchase in the market economy. As the Goodson case demonstrates, hard-nosed decisions are taken on the basis of resources available to practitioners and not what people actually need or define as wanting. Mark, a First Nations Mohawk in Canada questions the appropriateness of commodity relations in caring relationships and issues a challenge to all professionals who believe in empowering 'clients' in the following terms:

> The alcohol and drug abuse centres, everything that they do revolves around money. It don't revolve around compassion. They don't want to see alcohol and drug abuse end because the people that run those things are out of a job then. They're gettin' paid and that's wrong. I don't think there should be any payment have (sic) to be made for helpin' a brother or sister get away from alcohol or drugs. I think the payment is just seein' that they don't do it anymore. That's payment enough.
>
> (Maracle, 1993: 184)

Mark has rejected paid professionalism as a phenomenon that commits a disservice to people. Although he is referring to a specific context of the oppression of aboriginal First Nations peoples in Canada, he is raising points that are of concern to all professionals. Who should provide welfare services that are non-exploitative and do not appropriate the energies of 'clients' for their own ends? Should professionals assist in their creation? If the answer is affirmative, how can this task empower both 'clients' and professionals? Who will pay for the necessary services? What will the profession's responses to Mark's questions be? Is the problem having paid caring professionals or asking them to administer an unworkable system? Or both? For as Selma's predicament in the case study above makes clear, without transformative changes at both personal and structural levels, empowerment in existing helping environments can be experienced as more hindrance than help. Transformative social changes can address Mark's point about accessing services without having to pay for them at the point of need if universality of provision, rather than user payment systems is enacted.

It is unfashionable to propose such a solution in the current historical conjuncture. Professionals have to insist that their experiences suggest that solving social problems through the market place is no solution for some people, the majority of whom are in poverty. Also, unless women are to be exploited indefinitely as unpaid care workers in the name of 'community support', a way has to be found for paying for the services women give. It is irresponsible to argue that the state has no responsibility for picking up the tab. In societies that have the gross inequalities of wealth that exist in the world today, the state has a major role to play in ensuring that those who have considerable resources contribute to those that do not. Redistribution of this nature signifies recognition of the interdependence of individuals. It symbolises solidarity with others and involves reciprocity. People who are empowered can contribute more fully to society and increase the well-being of all those who live within it. The empowerment of the individual rests on the empowerment of and by the whole collective. It is time professionals put their efforts into the mutual empowerment of all.

References

Ahmad, B. (1990) *Black Perspectives in Social Work*. Ventura Press.

Basu, A. (Ed.) (1995) *The Challenge of Local Feminisms: Women's Movements in Global Perspective.* Boulder: Westview Press.

Belenky, M.F., Clinchy, B.M., Goldberger, N.R. and Tambe, J.M. (1997) *Women's Ways of Knowing.* 2nd edn. New York: Basic Books.

Blom-Cooper, L. (1986) *A Child in Trust: The Report of the Panel of Enquiry into the Death of Jasmine Beckford.* London: London Borough of Brent.

Clegg, R.S. (1989) *Frameworks of Power.* London: Sage.

Craig, G. and Mayo, M. (Eds.) (1995) *Community Empowerment: A Reader in Participation and Development.* London: Zed Press.

Culpitt, I. (1992) *Welfare and Citizenship: Beyond the Crisis of the Welfare State?* London: Sage.

Dominelli, L. (1986) Power and the Powerless: Prostitution and the Enforcement of Submissive Femininity. *Sociological Review*, Spring: 65–92.

Dominelli, L. (1988) *Anti-racist Social Work.* London: Macmillan.

Dominelli, L. (1989) Betrayal of Trust: A Feminist Analysis of Power Relationships in Incest Abuse. *British Journal of Social Work*, 19(4) Summer: 291–307.

Dominelli, L. (1996) Deprofessionalising Social Work: Equal Opportunities, Competences and Postmodernism. *British Journal of Social Work*, 26(2): 153–175.

Dominelli, L. (1997) *Sociology for Social Work.* London: Macmillan.

Dominelli, L. (1998) Anti-oppressive Practice in Context. In Adams, R., Dominelli, L. and Payne, M. (Eds.) *Social Work: Themes, Issues and Critical Debates.* Basingstoke: Macmillan.

Dominelli, L. (2002a) *Anti Oppressive Social Work Theory and Practice.* Basingstoke: Palgrave Macmillan.

Dominelli, L. (2002b) *Feminist Social Work Theory and Practice.* Basingstoke: Palgrave.

Dominelli, L. (2008) *Anti-Racist Social Work.* Basingstoke: Palgrave.

Dominelli, L. (2009) *Introducing Social Work.* Cambridge: Polity.

Dominelli, L. and Gollins, T. (1997) Men, Power and Caring Relationships. *Sociological Review*, 45(3) August: 396–415.

Dominelli, L. and Hoogvelt, A. (1997) Globalization and the Technocratization of Social Work. *Critical Social Policy*, 47(2) April: 45–62.

Dominelli, L. and Jonsdottir, G. (1989) Feminist Political Organisation: Some Reflections on the Experiences of Kwenna Frambothid in Iceland. *Feminist Review*, 30 Autumn: 36–60.

Dominelli, L. and McLeod, E. (1989) *Feminist Social Work.* London: Macmillan.

Egan, G. (1990) *The Skilled Helper.* 4th edn. Pacific Grove, CA: Brooks/Cole.

Flax, J. (1990) *Thinking Fragments: Psychoanalysis, Feminism and Postmodernism in the Contemporary West.* Berkeley: University of California Press.

French, M. (1985) *The Power of Women.* Harmondsworth: Penguin.

Friedan, B. (1974) *The Feminine Mystique.* New York: Dell.

Haber, H.F. (1994) *Beyond Postmodern Politics: Lyotard, Rorty and Foucault.* London: Routledge.

Haig-Brown, C. (1988) *Resistance and Renewal: Surviving the Indian Residential School.* Vancouver: Tillacum Library/Arsenal Pulp Press.

Hanmer, J. and Statham, D. (1988) *Women and Social Work: Woman-Centred Practice.* London: Macmillan.

Haraway, D. (1988) Situated Knowledges: The Science Question in Feminism and the Privilege of Partial Perspective. *Feminist Studies*, 14(3): 575–599.

Kahan, B (Ed.) (1989) *Child Care Research, Policy and Practice.* London: Hodder and Stoughton.

Kelly, L. (1988) *Surviving Sexual Violence.* Cambridge: Polity Press.

Lister, R. (1997) *Citizenship: Feminist Perspectives*. Basingstoke: Macmillan.

Lloyd, L. (1998) The Post- and the Anti-: Analysing Change and Changing Analyses in Social Work. *British Journal of Social Work*, 28(5) October: 709–727.

Lorenz, W. (1994) *Social Work in a Changing Europe.* London: Routledge.

Lukes, S. (1974) *Power: A Radical View.* London: Macmillan.

Lupton, C., and Nixon, P. (1999) *Empowering Practice? A Critical Appraisal of the Family Group Conference Approach.* Bristol: Policy Press.

Maracle, B. (1993) *Crazywater: Native Voices on Addiction and Recovery.* Toronto: Penguin.

Mohanty, C.T. (1995) Under Western Eyes: Feminist Scholarship and Colonial Discourse. In Mohanty, C.T., Russo, A. and Torres, L. (Eds.) *Third World Women and the Politics of Feminism.* Bloomington: Indiana University Press.

Morgan, R. (1971) *Sisterhood is Powerful.* New York: Vintage Books.

Oliver, M. (1990) *The Politics of Disablement.* Basingstoke: Macmillan.

Parsons, T. and Bales, R.T. (1955) *Family, Socialization and Interaction Process.* New York: The Free Press.

Parton, N. (1998) Risk, Advanced Liberalism and Child Welfare: The Need to Rediscover Ambiguity and Uncertainty. *British Journal of Social Work*, 28(1) February: 5–28.

Pringle, K. (1992) Child Sexual Abuse Perpetrated by Welfare Professionals and the Problem of Men. *Critical Social Policy*, 12(3): 4–19.

Rees, S. (1991) *Achieving Power: Policy and Practice in Social Welfare.* London: Allen and Unwin.

Riger, S. (1993) What's Wrong with Empowerment? *American Journal of Psychology*, 21(3): 279–292.

Rush, F. (1980) *The Best Kept Secret: The Sexual Abuse of Children.* New York: McGraw-Hill.

Ruzek, S.B. (1986) Feminist Visions of Health: An International Perspective. In Mitchell, J. and Oakley, A. (Eds.) *What is Feminism?* Oxford: Basil Blackwell.

Solomon, B. (1976) *Black Empowerment: Social Work in Oppressed Communities.* New York: Columbia University Press.

Teeple, G. (1995) *Globalization and the Decline of Social Reform.* Toronto: Garamond Press.

Thorpe, R. (1993) Empowerment Groupwork with Parents of Children in Care. In Mason, J. (Ed.) *Child Welfare Policy: Critical Australian Perspectives.* Sydney: Hale and Ironmonger.

United Nations (2011) *The 2011 Report on Human Social Development.* New York: United Nations.

Vancouver Sun (1999) Women Target Sexual Trafficking. *Vancouver Sun*, January 26th: A7.

Wallerstein, N. and Bernstein, E. (1994) Introduction to Community Empowerment, Participatory Education and Health. *Health Education Quarterly*, 21(2): 141–8.

Chapter 14

Groupwork Theory and Practice

Pamela Trevithick

Introduction

This chapter looks at groupwork theory and practice within social work. A particular emphasis is placed on groups that are purposely or artificially *formed* and led by practitioners, as opposed to self-help groups or those that are classified as *natural* groups, such as family groups. In so many ways, groups are part of everyday life. The family is a group and the teams we work in also constitute a group. In addition, the features that are evident in networks, communities, organisations and the structure of society as a whole can be seen to represent some of the same processes and dynamics that commonly occur in groups. What has happened in social work in recent years is that the knowledge and skills that are needed to understand and to work with groups effectively are increasingly becoming lost. In order to address this situation, the following provides a practice guide and an account of key areas of groupwork theory and practice. It draws on my experience as a groupwork practitioner over many years where I worked primarily with disadvantaged sectors of the population. This chapter begins with an account of the importance of groupwork and the relationships we build. It looks at the different theories used to analyse group dynamics and processes before focusing on a number of practical issues to consider when setting up a group, such as what leadership style to adopt, and how to evaluate the effectiveness of the work undertaken.

Groupwork and social work

When referring to groupwork, I am describing a practice method where three or more individuals meet together in order to address some common need, desired objective or agreed purpose. Social work has had a long involvement in groupwork but over the past few years, groupwork has become increasingly marginalised due, in part, to the changing role of social work within health and social welfare settings. In the past, social workers' particular contribution centred on illuminating the part played by social or systemic factors in relation to a particular problem area. This work involved the ability to analyse, contextualise and work with factors located outside the clinical setting or beyond the remit of one-to-one work. It involved broadening bio-medical perspectives which are tending to dominate more and more in multi-disciplinary and inter-agency work settings.

I would argue that one reason why a sound knowledge of groupwork theory and practice is not being promoted on professional training courses – both within and outside social work – is because the personal and social dilemmas that people face are increasingly being individualised and personalised. It means that problems are tending to be conceptualised in terms of 'personal troubles' and not as 'public issues' (Mills, 1959: 130). Yet it is not possible to understand human beings and the complexities of human experience solely from an individual or surface perspective because people are social beings who grow up and live in social systems – in families, neighbourhoods, communities, and within a culture and society of which they are a member. This surface approach (Howe, 1996) to the complex yet rich nature of human experience presents three major threats. First, it locates problems or difficulties solely in terms of the individual, as if other factors that are located outside the individual – over which they may have little influence – have no importance or relevance. Second, individualisation obscures from view the possibility of seeing the overall picture, particularly the structural and political features that give rise to certain problems and the extent to which these same problems impact on people's lives and sense of well-being in similar ways. Third, the individualisation of problems tends to lead to the individualisation of solutions. This often denies the opportunity for people to identify what they have in common.

In relation to direct practice, the individualisation of problems and solutions can best be seen in the shift toward one-to-one work and away from groupwork. For some practitioners, this change has resulted in the loss of groupwork skills through lack of practice. In most practice settings, managers and other senior staff are not thinking about groupwork as an option and instead, what we have tended to see is the introduction of more *package* or *programme-based* behavioural methods, such as those that fall under the headings *Anger Management*, *Managing Difficult Behaviour Groups*, or groups on *Parenting Skills*. Whilst these programme-based approaches can be beneficial for some people, they do not require practitioners to be familiar with group-work theory because the importance of understanding people – and their unique situation – is not a central feature. Instead for programme-based approaches the 'central organising principal of this orientation is that behaviour, emotions, and cognitions are learned and therefore can be changed by new learning' (Malekoff, 2009: 253). It means that providing information and re-hearsing and learning new ways to behave or to react dominate with little, if any, emphasis placed on group dynamics and group processes. As such, the learning that group members gain through relating to and interacting with one another, and the important sense of connection and commonality that groups can inspire, is largely lost.

Groupwork theory and practice

For groupwork to provide an appropriate and helpful experience in ways that are effective, it needs to be grounded in a sound knowledge and skills base (Trevithick, 2012). In this task, it is essential to understand the importance of human relationships.

Human relationships and the capacity to relate

Human relationships straddle all areas of social work. I have categorised the problems that are regularly encountered in terms of problems in relation to the *self*, *others* and to *society* at large (SOS) (Trevithick, 2003; 2012). This conceptualisation looks at how people relate to themselves, such as their sense of worth, self-esteem and self-image; how they relate to others including the quality of the relationships they have formed with partners, family members, friends, neighbours, casual acquaintances and professionals. Finally, how people relate to society at large looks at people's relationships with the resources that may be available within their immediate and extended environment, particularly the social inclusion and social exclusion and the extent to which, for example, poverty may be effectively excluding the opportunity to participate in the life of a community or social structures. This perspective emphasises the fact that many of the personal problems regularly encountered in social work could be summarised in terms of a breakdown in people's ability to sustain beneficial, constructive and nurturing relationships. These difficulties, if entrenched or enduring, tend to reflect the impact of negative childhood experiences on the development of the personality – a point noted by Howe:

> The poorer the quality of people's relationship history and social environment, the less robust will be their psychological make-up and ability to deal with other people, social situations and emotional demands.
>
> (Howe, 1998: 175)

This comment emphasises the importance of the social environment in which people live and work – an emphasis that is central to a psychosocial and systemic perspective. It reminds us that social work is located at the interface between the individual and the social, between the individual and his/her environment and that the impact of social, cultural and environmental issues, both positive and negative, need to be seen alongside the understanding given to early childhood development and attachment histories (Bowlby, 1979). In addition to providing an insight on past and current experiences, the relationships that are built between social workers and service users can act as a central catalyst for change – a context where people can learn about themselves and what they need from others in order to move on and move forward. In groupwork, the relationship created between groupworkers and participants is of central importance but an even more important resource and source of support can be the relationships that are established among the group members.

Social and structural factors: groupwork in 'tough' environments

However, it would be a mistake to conceptualise the problems that people face solely in terms of the quality of their relationships. There are social and structural factors that impact on people's lives that give rise to certain types of problems – problems that are rooted in social, health and income inequalities. The extent and impact of poverty in the UK is an example and a problem that directly relates to government policy and to the way that UK society is organised and stratified (Dorling, 2010; Marmot, 2010; Wilkinson and Pickett, 2009). For example, 13.4 million people in the UK (22 per cent) in 2009 were designated as income poor (that is, their income was located at under 60 per cent of the median figure after income tax, council tax and housing costs have been deducted). This is over a fifth of the population – and the highest level since 2000 (Joseph Rowntree Foundation, 2009: 17). I would argue that social workers need to focus more on addressing the impact of poverty and groupwork can be invaluable in this regard. For example, I once set up a group called *Money Matters.* Its purpose was to attempt to find new and different ways to help people to make ends meet, such as applying to charities, running jumble sales, and also to provide an opportunity for people to come together and to share their feelings about poverty and its impact. Two initiatives that emerged involved a group of boys setting up a car washing service and a group of women running a small household cleaning service but the emotional benefits of attending this group were equally striking.

When attempting to run groups in communities that are deprived, neglected and broken-down, it is important to take account of the fact that the energy, enthusiasm and commitment needed may be largely absent. This situation calls for us to carry the sense of hope and possibility that people have lost and for us to be highly creative in the kind of groups that we set up. For example, I once set up a group for homeless, rootless young women who worked the streets 'selling sex' in order to pay for their 'drug habit'. In an attempt to reach this deprived group of young women, the group we set up was modelled on a 'beauty parlour', offering hairdressing, manicure and pedicure, a clothes shop, facial massage and make-up sessions. We were largely unsuccessful in our efforts because too many factors worked against this group becoming established but we learned a great deal about the lives of the women we met. In particular, we learned how to ask good questions and how to use our capacity for empathy as a starting point from which 'to enter imaginatively and yet accurately into the thoughts and feelings and hopes and fears of another person' (Winnicott, 1986: 117).

In a different example, I and other group workers once ran a group for women who were the victims of domestic violence and abuse. This group ran for ten weeks and the only intervention we used during this period was the following question:

'Are you living the life you want to live and if not, why not?'

This intervention highlighted the extent to which external, as well as internal, factors were inhibiting the opportunity for the women in this group to take charge of their lives and to move forward. The poignant and heart-breaking experiences that they shared with one another helped to rectify the misconception that events were 'their fault' and provided an opportunity for women to support one another. This work highlighted the absence of adequate support from relevant agencies, which meant that as groupworkers we felt it appropriate to work outside the group in order to locate resources and address provision failures. The groupwork skills related to this work mainly involved the ability to observe, listen, and adapt the groupwork approach in ways that could contain the women's anxieties and communicate a sense of hope and possibility.

The therapeutic benefits of groups: Yalom's 12 'therapeutic factors'

The important interactions and sense of connection that can take place in groups are indicated in Yalom's influential research-based account of 12 'therapeutic factors'. These are:

1. *Altruism* – the positive emotions that come from helping or giving to others.
2. *Group cohesiveness* – a shared sense of connection, belonging, acceptance, approval and commitment.
3. *Universality* – that others share similar problems and that others know what it's like.
4. *Interpersonal learning – input* – how a person comes across to other people in the group, and the learning this involves for the individual in question.
5. *Interpersonal learning – output* – learning how to deal with difficulties that arise in relation to group members.
6. *Guidance* – the importance of providing advice or offering guidance.
7. *Catharsis* – the expression of emotions in ways that bring about a sense of 'relief' from the anxieties and fears that previously surrounded these emotions, memories or events.
8. *Identification* – experimenting with new ways of behaving based on observing and imitating other people's behaviour and their response to certain situations.
9. *Family re-enactment* – the opportunity to 'relive' family patterns that present themselves in the group and the 'hang-ups' being carried from experiences with parents, brothers, sisters, relatives, or other important people.
10. *Self-understanding* – discovering and accepting new areas of self-understanding.

11. *Instillation of hope* – a belief that change or recovery is possible and that others have made these changes.
12. *Existential factors* – coming to terms with the fact that life is often unfair; that pain is a part of life; that we are ultimately alone; that we must bear ultimate responsibility for our actions.

(Adapted from Yalom and Leszcz, 2005: 82–86)

These categories and rankings are based on Yalom's work in therapeutically-based groups. Nevertheless, they are relevant to other forms of groupwork but with differences depending on the type of group being run, the characteristics of the group members, the orientation of the group leaders, and other contextual factors. Of particular importance is the safe and supportive atmosphere provided by the group leaders irrespective of their theoretical orientation or practice approach (Tosone, 2009). In my experience, one of the most important benefits offered by groupwork in a social work context is the sense of relief that participants gain from sharing their experiences and from knowing that they are 'not alone'. It can be a realisation that leads to greater group cohesion but can also lead to the group taking action to address shared concerns.

Although groupwork can have many advantages, it is not appropriate for all people or when addressing certain problems where one-to-one work may be more appropriate. Also, it is worth remembering that for some people joining a group can be an intimidating or anxiety-provoking experience. What may be revived is the memory of difficult group experiences, the most common being people's experience of their family or at school. That family experiences are revived is understandable because a group can resemble the family in a number of important ways that include:

- The presence of authoritarian parental figures embodied in the group leaders.
- The sibling rivalry among members, particularly when competing for 'parental' approval.
- The exposure of personal feelings and revelations that are similar to those that might be shared among family members.
- The strong emotions aroused that echo family dynamics.

The fears articulated in relation to school experiences often involve the painful events that accompany the intense rivalry and excluding behaviour that can be a feature of peer group behaviour. Other concerns may be focused on the authoritarian behaviour of teachers, sometimes compounded by the repressive behaviour of parents. When working with children and young people, it is essential to discuss these concerns in some detail before setting up a group in order to ensure that a clear line and distinction is drawn between school groups and the groupwork on offer. This same boundary may need to be drawn for adults who link the idea of being in a group to painful experiences at school, in the family or the workplace or to any other distressing memory.

Work in teams

Teams can be defined in terms of groups of people who come together to co-operate and collaborate in order to carry out a joint task or specific undertaking. In many ways, the dynamic of a team can resemble that of any group but the organisation's culture is likely to be highly influential. This culture may be evident in relation to:

1. The extent to which collaborative team work and co-operation are a feature and differences and conflicts are addressed and resolved.
2. The extent to which team members participate in decision-making in ways that influence policy and practice.
3. The effectiveness of communication within the team and communication systems within the organisation.
4. The extent to which initiatives are encouraged and different attributes acknowledged and valued.
5. The extent to which the leadership of the team reinforces a commitment among team members to the task and to one another.

Belbin's Team Roles

Belbin's account of nine team roles describes the strengths and weaknesses of the various roles that different team members are likely to take up. These are summarised as follows:

1. Plant
Strengths: creative, imaginative, unorthodox. Solves difficult problems.
Allowable weaknesses: ignores details. Too preoccupied to communicate effectively.

2. Resource investigator
Strengths: extrovert, enthusiastic, communicative. Explores opportunities. Develops contacts.
Allowable weaknesses: over optimistic. Loses interest once initial enthusiasm has passed.

3. Coordinator
Strengths: mature, confident, a good chairperson. Clarifies goals, promotes decision-making, delegates well.
Allowable weaknesses: can be seen as manipulative. Delegates personal work.

4. Shaper
Strengths: challenging, dynamic, thrives on pressure. Has the drive and courage to overcome obstacles.
Allowable weaknesses: can provoke others. Hurts people's feelings.

5. Monitor evaluator
Strengths: sober, strategic and discerning. Sees all options. Judges accurately.
Allowable weaknesses: lacks drive and ability to inspire others. Overly critical.

6. Teamworker
Strengths: co-operative, mild, perceptive and diplomatic. Listens, builds, averts friction, calms the waters.
Allowable weaknesses: indecisive in crunch situations. Can be easily influenced.

7. Implementer
Strengths: disciplined, reliable, conservative and efficient. Turns ideas into practical actions.
Allowable weaknesses: somewhat inflexible. Slow to respond to new possibilities.

8. Completer
Strengths: painstaking, conscientious, anxious. Searches out errors and omissions. Delivers on time.
Allowable weaknesses: inclined to worry unduly. Reluctant to delegate. Can be a nit-picker.

9. Specialist
Strengths: single-minded, self-starting, dedicated. Provides knowledge and skills in rare supply.
Allowable weaknesses: contributes on only a narrow front. Dwells on technicalities. Overlooks the 'big picture'.

(Belbin, 1993: 22)

It is important to note that these roles within the team are often not fixed but likely to change over time and one team member can demonstrate a strong orientation toward several roles. Also, this conceptualisation describes behaviour and not team members' personalities. Its advantage is that it can be used to initiate team discussions on different members' contributions, and in particular highlight the aware and unaware take up of roles and the part played by the dynamic of the group.

Group dynamics, processes and developments

The extent to which a focus is maintained on the processes and dynamics of a group will largely depend on the nature, composition and purpose for which the group was formed. One way to see the constant motion and dynamic of a group is as a snapshot at a particular point in time:

Group dynamics is concerned with different ways of looking at groups, that is, ways in which a static analysis of a group can be made. A group in action is rather like a film, that is, the relationships, the action, the positions of members are constantly changing within definite limits. The group is a 'dynamic' activity.

(Douglas, 1976: 12)

An important feature is the quality of interaction between group members and how the group is shaped and develops over time. My own preference is to think of the group in terms of how the different personalities of group members, including the groupworkers, converge to create a certain *mood* that can be identified and in ways that are constantly changing.

Tuckman's five stages of group life

One of the most influential conceptualisations of a group progressing can be found in Tuckman's (1965) five stages of group life, which describe how some groups pass through these stages sequentially. The following is a brief account of the five stages: *forming, storming, norming, performing* and *mourning* (*ending* or *adjourning*).

Forming
The group is characterised by anxiety, with a dependence on the leader. The group is involved in attempting to discover its *code of conduct*, testing out what behaviours are acceptable and what the norms of the group will be, such as whether the group will be supportive, critical, serious, fun, helpful or otherwise. A group in this mode will approach the task with the feeling of *'what shall we do?'*

Storming
At this point, the group is characterised by a sense of conflict, with rebellion against the leader, polarisation of opinion, conflict between sub-groups and a resistance to being controlled. Emotional resistance to the task and a sense of the task being impossible may pervade. This stage often represents a *testing out* of the leadership which, if positive, may lead to a climate where the group can begin to take seriously its task and the implications involved. A group in this mode will often approach the task with the feeling of *'it can't be done'* or *'I won't do it.'*

Norming
At this stage, the group is characterised by a sense of group cohesion and certain norms for the group begin to emerge. Earlier feelings of resistance start to be overcome and conflicts patched up, with the group beginning to offer mutual support to members. A determination to achieve the task will be accompanied by an open exchange of views and sense of co-operation. A group in this mode will often approach the task with the feeling of *'we can do it'*.

Performing
At this stage, the group is characterised by a focus on the task that it was created to achieve. Roles within the group are functional and flexible, with interpersonal

problems having been patched up. Individuals feel safe to express differences of opinion and trust the group to find acceptable and appropriate compromises. There is a sense of energy and purpose within the group in relation to the task and, as a result, solutions to problems begin to emerge. In this mode, the feeling is often *'we are doing it!'*

Mourning (*ending* or *adjourning*)

This fifth stage was added by Tuckman in 1977 and is marked by a sense of mourning at the adjournment of the group. Individuals are about to leave the group and as a result, the discussion focuses either around past shared experiences or suggestions and attempts to hold the group together. There is a desire for the group not to end – leading to suggestions for the group to meet at a later date. In this mode, the feeling is often *'this can't end!'*

It is important to note that the different phases are not always easy to identify or clear-cut. Some groups do not go through these processes sequentially – instead, some jump backwards and forwards from one stage to another, and groups can spend different lengths of time in each phase. One of the main disadvantages of Tuckman's conceptualisation is that it can easily be used in a way that over-simplifies the different stages and, therefore, denies the complex dynamics that may be evident and the role of the groupworkers and individual members within that dynamic. For these reasons, it is best used as a guide – as a perspective that can be helpful when attempting to identify the major features that are evident in a group's progress and development at a particular point in time.

Bion's theory of group development

In a different conceptualisation, Bion (1961) asserted that every group has two aspects: a 'work group' and a 'basic assumptions' group. A 'work group' is focused on the task for which it was formed and as such, it is a group that is able to recognise and work on painful or difficult issues, such as conflict and fundamental differences among group members. A 'basic assumptions' group uses a variety of unconscious devices to avoid anxiety and, as a result, the group tends to avoid working on painful or difficult thoughts, feelings or experiences, such as feelings of conflict. Bion used the term 'basic assumptions' to mean those unconscious assumptions that are inevitably a part of group life and in this aspect of group functioning, Bion identified three types of 'basic assumptions': *dependency*, *pairing* and *fight/flight*.

The dependency basic assumption group

This group looks towards a leader for all things and consequently denies much of the knowledge and skill that is present in the group. People experience dependency in groups, not just in relation to others (e.g. leader) but also in relation to favoured or habitual practices (e.g. deliberating for long periods on how to choose and use ground rules). As a result, people become caught in self-limiting processes which inhibit change, learning, creativity and innovation.

The pairing basic assumption group
This group encourages two of the members of the group to communicate or make some form of contact on behalf of the whole group, with the other members staying out of it. It is possible that different 'pairings' are present within the group at the same time (e.g. a sexual partnership or protective relationship based on the dominance of one person over another). The notion of pairing also highlights the issues of intergroup relations – both inside and outside of a group. What is important in this context is who represents a particular aspect of the group, or particular cultural form, and who carries the relatedness of the group.

The fight/flight basic assumption group
This group uses strategies to take *flight* from what is difficult in the here-and-now. This can sometimes be understood to mean that participants physically take flight from the group, which may happen, but flight can take different forms such as anecdotal ramblings, arriving late or leaving early – in effect, any action that avoids dealing with what is happening and the group's task in the here-and-now. When *fight* is in operation, this may be characterised by differences, conflict, aggressiveness and hostility between one member and another, or between a group member and the leader. Groups are very powerfully affected and controlled by issues of competition and avoidance and the fear of attack or criticism.

Bion's theories effectively describe the defences that group members can adopt and how these interfere with the task and the possibility of becoming a 'working group'. In order to work with these defences, Bion stressed the importance of openness; paying attention to the emotional experiences present in the group (in the here-and-now); offering interpretations to illuminate the group processes and the 'basic assumptions' being played out and how these stances inhibit the group's attempt to accomplish its task. (For a more detailed account of the importance of defences in social work, see Trevithick, 2011).

Thinking about human behaviour in terms of unconscious defences can help to avoid labelling people or describing participants solely in terms of their behaviour. For example, Yalom and Leszcz's (2005) account of the *monopolist*, the *silent patient*, or the *help-rejecting complainer* (someone who constantly communicates 'yes but' to any suggestion) indicates a tendency to describe people in terms of their behaviour. Similarly, Northen and Kurland write of the *monopoliser*, the *isolate* and the *scapegoat* (2001: 242–246). In any group, people take up positions or communicate in certain ways because of the influence of the past, in response to what is happening in the present and also because the dynamic of the group invites or compels them to put themselves forward in a particular way. This means that the dynamic of the group can encourage the expression of certain types of behaviour. This may be evident when the dynamic produces a situation where a particular participant is compulsively silent or silenced or where someone talks incessantly, and fills the group with empty words. These examples indicate a complex collusion among other members of the group.

A different feature of the processes occurring in groups has been conceptualised in terms of *groupthink* (Janis, 1982), which describes the way that a group's judgements can deteriorate to the point where the need for agreement or compliance among group members is given priority over the motivation to try to obtain accurate knowledge to make appropriate decisions, thereby limiting the scope of the subject being explored. It can be evident when the position adopted by one influential individual, often the chairperson or designated leader, is accepted unquestioningly and in ways that eliminate or wipe out the possibility of exploring other ways to think about an issue.

Practical issues when setting up and running groups

How a group is structured, and the groupwork approach adopted should where possible be determined by the people for whom the group is intended. If this kind of negotiation is not possible, then the approach chosen should be the one that is considered to be the most appropriate in terms of meeting the needs of participants. Negotiating details of this kind – including with employers – can be a time-consuming activity, but the greater the preparation, the greater the likelihood that the group will be successful. Some groups adopt a specific theory base, such as groups that draw on behaviourism, humanism or psychodynamic theory, whilst others may draw heavily on a particular practice perspective, such as the concept of empowerment or mutual aid (Schwartz, 1961). A different type of group may be more action oriented, such as tenants' groups, community action groups, or those set up to campaign on a specific issue. A popular approach to emerge in the late 1960s and 1970s, and one that has continued to be influential, is feminist groupwork (Butler and Wintram, 1991; Cohen and Mullender, 2003).

These different approaches may be adopted to address a range of different personal and social problems, such as groups for people with mental health problems or for foster carers. Whatever the approach or leadership style adopted, groups may be organised in terms of:

- A *closed group*, that is, one that is made up of a fixed number of people, often for a stipulated time period. Therapeutic groups, or behaviour management groups that follow a set programme or manual, are often organised on this basis. The optimum membership is considered to be roughly 6–10 people.
- An *open group*, such as a drop-in group where there is no requirement for participants to attend every session. Nevertheless, the expectation is that the group will run irrespective of how many people turn up.

Most of the examples I have cited so far in relation to my own work – a boys' group, a girls' group, a women's group – were all closed groups but the depression groups that I ran included both closed and open groups. Both closed and open groups have advantages and disadvantages but I consider the flexibility that is a feature of drop-in groups to be particularly helpful when working with people who find it difficult to sign up to something on a regular basis. The fact that there is no attendance requirement can mean that people are more likely to attend a drop-in group because they have found it valuable or helpful in some way. In my experience, what people particularly value is the reciprocal nature of the help and support that the group can offer. Schwartz describes a *helping group* as follows:

> *The group is an enterprise in mutual aid, an alliance of individuals who need each other, in varying degrees, to work on certain common problems. The important fact is that this is a helping system in which clients need each other as well as the worker. This need to use each other, to create not one but many helping relationships, is a vital ingredient of the group process and constitutes a common need over and above the specific tasks for which the group was formed.*

(Schwartz, 1961: 226)

What is stressed in Schwartz's account is the importance of mutual aid and the inter-relationships that can be created in groups. This quotation also emphasises the different focus and purpose that groups can involve and also the fact that as human beings, we need each other in order to grow, to develop and to change our lives. As groupworkers, we can learn a great deal about ourselves, as well as other people, in this process.

Leadership

An influential categorisation describes group leadership in terms of:

- *democratic* leadership
- *authoritarian* leadership
- *laissez-faire* leadership

(Lewin *et al.*, 1939)

Some groupwork texts tend to promote one form of leadership over another – particularly democratic leadership – whereas it is important to consider all forms of group leadership as having the potential to meet specific needs. Also, in the life of a group it may be necessary to change leadership styles at that particular point in time. For example, I once ran a 'girls' group' with a number of colleagues. This group was based on a highly *democratic* style of leadership, with group members deciding what activities they wanted to be involved in. However, at different points in the group's life, a more *authoritarian* stance became essential when a serious fight broke out. The situation called for clear sanctions to be set in place in order to address the bullying and intimidating behaviour we encountered. *Laissez-faire* literally means 'leave well alone' and is a style of leadership that is more appropriate when group members are highly motivated and able to work independently. This style of leadership was rarely considered appropriate in the girls' group I have just described but highly appropriate for a parents' group that I once set up. A different way that leadership roles have been characterised is in terms of a *director, enabler* and *resource person* (Douglas, 1979). These titles essentially describe where the participants are located across a spectrum that ranges from leader-controlled to member-controlled, as illustrated in the following diagram:

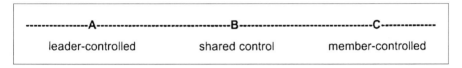

```
---------------A--------------------------------B--------------------------------C--------------
   leader-controlled              shared control              member-controlled
```

Within this picture, the organisation of the group may involve *sole leaders* or *co-leaders* or incorporate different leadership features. For example, in a parents' group that I once led, an 'expert' in the area of substance use and abuse was invited to run a session to provide information on the kind of behaviour that can be an indicator of whether a young person is taking illegal drugs. In my experience, *sole leadership* works well with people who are highly motivated and self-directing, such as an action group but in a group where strong emotions or unpredictable behaviour might be a feature, to have a sole leader is inadvisable because of the risks involved should someone become upset and need immediate one-to-one work. For example, for ten years I ran several groups a week for women suffering from depression where we had three group leaders. This was to ensure that if any woman, or any two women, became too upset to remain in the group and needed to step out, they could be accompanied by a groupworker. Meanwhile the group could continue to function (Trevithick, 1998).

A point to note is the extent to which group leaders can be the target of projections. The term projection describes the process by which a person's emotions, thoughts, fantasies, dispositions etc. are ascribed to someone else. Yalom and Leszcz describe the range of reactions that leaders can provoke:

> . . . *some members become helplessly dependent on the leaders, whom they imbue with unrealistic knowledge and power; others blindly defy the leaders, who are perceived as infantalising and controlling; others are wary of leaders, who they believe attempt to strip members of their individuality; some members try to split the co-therapists in an attempt to incite parental disagreements or rivalry . . . some compete bitterly with other members, hoping to accumulate units of attention and caring from the therapists; some are enveloped in envy when the leader's attention is focused on others; others expend energy in a search for allies among other*

members, in order to topple the therapists; still others neglect their own interests in a seemingly selfless effort to appease the leaders and other members.

(Yalom and Leszcz, 2005: 14)

Again, whilst these reactions are likely to be more intense in therapeutically-oriented groups, they can occur in all other types of groups where leadership is a feature.

Setting up a group

Before setting up a group it is important to consider the following points:

- Who the group is for.
- The aims and purposes it is designed to achieve.
- How to advertise the group and recruit and select group members.
- What resources are needed (staff numbers and commitment, rooms, crèche, equipment, supervision, training, transport, tea/coffee).
- Any community, agency or political issues that need to be considered.
- Selection process (if any) to be adopted for both the groupworkers and group participants.
- The structure of the group (its size, whether open or closed, duration in terms of how long it will run, at what time, for how long for each session, etc.).
- What specific practice approach will be adopted (if any).
- How any crises will be addressed.
- What follow-up work might be needed after the group.
- How it is planned to record group events and developments.
- How the effectiveness of the group will be evaluated.
- What follow-up work might be needed to evaluate the group's effectiveness over time.

A factor that is sometimes neglected is the opportunity for groupworkers to discuss the assumptions and practice philosophy that we bring to our work and how these assumptions inform our understanding of human beings and the situations we encounter (Konopka, 1983; Trevithick, 2012). As stated earlier, the greater the preparation, the greater the likelihood of success.

Interventions

In order to know how to intervene effectively, we need to have learned a number of *skills*. I describe a skill as five common characteristics: it is an action with a specific *goal*, that can be *learnt*, that involves *actions performed in sequence*, that can be organised in ways that involve *economy of effort* and that can be *evaluated* in terms of its effectiveness. Although these characteristics are described separately, they interweave and overlap in ways that, when effectively communicated in the form of an intervention, indicate skilled performance. Thus, if we define skills in terms of what we have learnt, then interventions describe how we put that learning into practice, that is, the actions we perform to influence events. Indeed, we do not know how well a skill has been learned until we attempt to put that skill into practice – in the form of an intervention.

The word *intervention* is used a great deal in social work, including groupwork, but is rarely defined. It comes from the Latin *inter* (between) and *venire* (to come) and means *coming between*. As such, interventions lie at the heart of everyday social interactions and reflect the desire to shape events and to influence others. In groupwork, all forms of communication could be considered to constitute an intervention, whether verbal or non verbal in character, and are expressed in order to have some impact on the dynamic of the group (Kennard *et al.*, 2000). One sign of a successful group is the extent to which all members feel able to communicate openly and freely. The role of the groupworker is slightly different because his or her task is to aid communication and to do so in a purposeful way. In this context, an intervention constitutes knowledge, skills and values in action and can be defined as:

> *The purposeful actions we undertake as professionals in a given situation, based on the knowledge and understanding we have acquired, the skills we have learned, and the values we adopt.*
>
> (Trevithick, 2012)

In general, interventions can be directed in four different ways, or in any combination. They may be directed toward:

- one or more group members
- the group as a whole (e.g. 'what does the group think?')
- parts of the whole group, e.g. pairs, threesomes, all younger/older group members, all parents
- the other group leaders

However, before intervening it is important for groupworkers to be clear whether it is appropriate and helpful to intervene at a particular point, whether the timing is right and what kind of impact is being sought. These considerations tend to be determined to a considerable extent by the purpose of the group. For example, if a group has been set up to explore emotions, then the interventions used are likely to be of a more emotional nature whereas in an action-oriented group, the interventions are likely to be focused in the more cerebral or problem solving and information sharing forms of communication. However, it is important to stress that even in action-based groups, an emotional content is always present and may need to be explored if a failure to do so inhibits the effectiveness and purpose of the group.

In effect, groupwork skills and interventions are similar to the generalist skills that are commonly used in social work. For example, almost all of the eighty generalist skills that I have identified elsewhere could be considered relevant to groupwork (Trevithick, 2012). Other authors conceptualise groupwork interventions slightly differently. For example, Northen and Kurland identify nine 'clusters of skills' that include: 'structuring, support, exploration, information-education, advice-giving, confrontation, clarification, forms of feedback and interpretation' (2001: 81) whereas in a chapter entitled 'Intervening in groups', Whitaker describes 25 possible interventions (2000: 233–236). Within the list of skills that different authors cite, interventions are often underpinned by the skills of observation, listening, speech and analysis and tend to be undertaken for the following reasons:

- To impart information.
- To create or re-establish a climate of safety.
- To maintain the structure or ground rules for the group.
- To open up new possibilities or avenues of explorations.
- To guide the direction of the group (e.g. through the use of self-disclosure).
- To interpret behaviour, the unconscious communication of the group or the dynamic of the group.
- To initiate a particular course of action (e.g. to remind members that the group is about to end).
- To model a way of dealing with a particular dilemma or situation (e.g. how to respond when a group member begins to cry or threatens to walk out).

The opportunity to learn how to intervene effectively calls for time to be set aside where certain skills and interventions can be rehearsed and practiced. This is best achieved where guidance is provided beforehand and honest feedback is available afterward. The capacity for critical thinking, self-reflection and self-criticism are also essential attributes that are often enhanced by the provision of quality supervision.

Record keeping and the evaluation of effectiveness

The record keeping, monitoring and evaluation systems to be adopted need to be worked out before the group has started. In this regard, it is important to be familiar with: agency recording and evaluation requirements; what purpose this information is designed to serve; and who will be allowed access to these records, such as senior staff, other professionals and supervisors. The Data Protection Act 1984 and Access to Personal Files Act 1987 give service users certain rights in relation to accessing their records. In order to rigorously evaluate the effectiveness of the groupwork and its outcomes, where possible it is important to collect baseline data. This data can be used to identify and indicate the frequency, intensity or severity of a particular problem at specific points in the life of the group, often at the beginning of the group and then at other designated times, such as the mid-point and end of the group. This information can then be compared and any changes identified. Of particular interest is the extent to which any changes or benefits can be attributed to the groupwork undertaken.

Conclusion

In a climate where we see a growing tendency to individualise and personalise whole areas of human experience, groupwork has an important role to play to combat the dangers that accompany social isolation, social exclusion and neglect by bringing people together. In this context, I consider groupwork to have much greater potential for empowerment and personal and social change than one-to-one work. I have argued in this chapter that to be effective in our work calls for a sound knowledge and skills base – which includes an understanding of how 'public issues' (Mills, 1959: 130) often underpin the 'personal troubles' that people encounter. In order to emphasise the importance of groupwork theory underpinning practice, I have outlined a number of subjects and given examples of the different ways that we can work with people in groups. Broadening our scope to include wider systemic and social perspectives is essential and so too is the need to bring people together. In the current context within which social work is located, the need to develop groupwork knowledge and skills in order to work effectively with people in groups could not be more urgent.

References

Belbin, R.M. (1993) *Team Roles at Work.* Oxford: Butterworth-Heinemann.

Bion, W.R. (1961) *Experiences in Groups, and Other Papers.* London: Tavistock.

Bowlby, J. (1979) *The Making and Breaking of Affectional Bonds.* London: Tavistock.

Butler, S. and Wintram, C. (1991) *Feminist Groupwork.* London: Sage.

Cohen, M. and Mullender, A. (Eds.) (2003) *Gender and Groupwork.* London: Routledge.

Dorling, D. (2010) *Injustice: Why Social Inequality Persists.* Bristol: Policy Press.

Douglas, T. (1976) *Groupwork in Practice.* London: Tavistock.

Douglas, T. (1979) *Group Processes in Social Work: A Theoretical Synthesis.* Chichester: Wiley.

Howe, D. (1996) Surface and Depth in Social-Work Practice. In Parton, N. (Ed.) *Social Theory, Social Change and Social Work.* London: Routledge.

Howe, D. (1998) Relationship-based Thinking and Practice in Social Work. *Journal of Social Work Practice*, 16(2): 45–56.

Janis, I.L. (1982) *Groupthink: Psychological Studies of Policy Decisions and Fiascoes.* 2nd edn. Boston: Houghton Mifflin.

Joseph Rowntree Foundation and New Policy Institute (2009) *Monitoring Poverty and Social Exclusion.* Available at: http://www.jrf.org.uk/publications/monitoring-poverty-2009 [accessed 1 June 2011].

Kennard, D., Roberts, J. and Winter, D.A. (2000) *A Work Book of Group-Analytic Interventions.* London: Jessica Kingsley.

Konopka, G. (1983) *Social Groupwork: A Helping Process.* 3rd edn. Engelwood Cliffs, NJ: Prentice-Hall.

Lewin, K., Lippit, R. and White, R.K. (1939) Patterns of Aggressive Behaviour in Experimentally Created Social Climates. *Journal of Social Psychology*, 10: 271–301.

Malekoff, A. (2009) Adolescents. In Gitterman, A., Salmon, A. and R. (Eds.) *Encyclopedia of Social Work with Groups.* Abingdon: Routledge.

Marmot Review (2010) *Fair Society, Healthy Lives: The Marmot Review.* Available at: http://www.marmot-review.org.uk [accessed 1 June 2011].

Mills, C.W. (1959) *The Sociological Imagination.* Oxford: Oxford University Press.

Northen, H. and Kurland, R. (2001) *Social Work with Groups.* 3rd edn. New York: Columbia University Press.

Schwartz, W. (1961) The Social Worker in the Group. *The Social Welfare Forum: Official Proceedings from the National Conference on Social Welfare.* New York: Columbia University Press.

Tosone, R. (2009) Psychodynamic model. In Gitterman, A., Salmon, A. and R. (Eds) *Encyclopedia of Social Work with Groups.* Abingdon: Routledge.

Trevithick, P. (1998) Psychotherapy and Working Class Women. In Seu, B. and Heenan, C. (Eds.) *Feminism and Psychotherapy: Reflections on Contemporary Theories and Practices.* London: Sage.

Trevithick, P. (2003) Effective Relationship-Based Practice: A Theoretical Exploration. *Journal of Social Work Practice*, 17(2): 173–186.

Trevithick, P. (2011) Understanding Defences and Defensive Behaviour in Social Work. *Journal of Social Work Practice*, 25(4): 389–412.

Trevithick, P. (2012) *Social Work Skills and Knowledge: A Practice Handbook.* 3rd edn. Maidenhead: Open University Press.

Tuckman, B. (1965). Developmental Sequence in Small Groups *Psychological Bulletin*, 63(6) 384–399.

Whitaker, D. (2000) *Using Groups to Help People*, 2nd edn. London: Routledge.

Wilkinson, R. and Pickett, K. (2009) *The Spirit Level: Why More Equal Societies Almost Always Do Better.* London: Allen Lane.

Winnicott, D.W. (1986) *Home Is Where We Start From.* Harmondsworth: Penguin.

Yalom, I. and Leszcz, M. (2005) *The Theory and Practice of Group Psychotherapy.* 5th edn. New York: Basic Books.

Part Three: The Future of Practice in an International Context

Chapter 15

Critical Social Work[1]

Mel Gray, Paul Stepney, and Stephen A. Webb

Social work sits in a small corner of a larger world stage which, given the current global financial crisis, appears to have reached a critical point in its development. How should social work orientate itself and what positive mandate can it take up in this context? It would be facile to write a chapter on critical social work without some reference to the global upheavals presently confronting us in a most dramatic way. In this chapter, we seek to make a distinctive case for Critical Social Work as an approach that confronts and seeks to change relations of domination and oppression in society.

Caught in a wave of pragmatic social engineering and fiscal regulation of major global economies, corporations, and banks, the lessons from recent social work theorising, especially those from a postmodern perspective, provide little by way of orientation or practical guidance. At best, such theorising serves as a warning of the danger of doing business with unregulated markets in social care and the need for a sound social and economic analysis to underpin the theory-to-practice debate. It is hard to imagine how the much-vaunted celebrations of diversity and empowering tactics of postmodern social work can have much to offer in such times of severe economic crisis.

In the UK, the savage public spending cuts introduced by the new coalition government of David Cameron, allied to the communitarian rhetoric associated with the 'Big Society' (Cameron, 2009) are ostensibly designed to reactivate moral responsibility, that is, to encourage citizens to take greater responsibility for their own welfare. The guiding principles here are mutual self-help, voluntarism, civic responsibility, interdependence, and diversity. However, what diversity shall be celebrated when they come to shut down your local community-based social services office and axe other public services? Thus for all the celebrations and condemnations of postmodern amnesia, the questions of social justice and radical transformation – and of their relevance for political practice – remain more than ever on the social work agenda (Webb, 2009).

---

[1] As will become clear in this chapter, Critical Social Work, when capitalised, denotes a perspective with its roots in critical theory (Gray and Webb, 2009).

According to Blond (2010: 1) there has been a widespread collapse of culture, values, and beliefs which, at the local level, translates into a host of problems including:

> . . . *increasing fear, lack of trust, increase in violent crime (especially gun and knife crime [our addition]), loneliness, depression, private and public debt, family break up, unresponsive public services, powerlessness, rise of racism, longer working hours . . . seemingly immovable poverty and the permanence of inequality.*

This litany of social problems is mirrored at the structural level in market economies by the epochal decline of industrial employment, decades of accumulated financial debt, financial capital severed from national industry, sweat-shop exploitation and human rights abuse, the relocation of poorest workers to slums on the very edge of social life, the real estate and housing bubble implosion, huge population increases in prison incarceration, cocktails of pharmaceutical drugs incessantly targeting the rising tide of mental illness, and the growth of banal media-saturated life routines. It is a calamitous diagnosis that makes for a burgeoning social justice agenda for the profession often on the receiving end of this tumultuous fallout.

According to many social commentators, we are now entering a new phase of a protracted long downturn in the fortunes of late capitalism. As Watkins (2010: 6) notes, 'Running into trillions of dollars in direct and indirect support, the bailouts of the financial institutions will weigh on domestic economies – above all in the US and UK – for years to come'. Dulcified by bouts of social work intervention for certain designated categories of 'service' users, postmodern globalisation can now be seen for what it is – a long process of decay subordinate to the management of highly differentiated populations (Clarke, 2001). We are witnessing a post-industrial stupor, undermining long-term employment prospects, democratic culture, and anti-capitalist resistance.

Adding to the costs of post-industrial change is, of course, the problem of global warming. Carbon emissions appear to be rising by the same amounts they were supposed to fall, because of the failed Kyoto Protocol and Copenhagen Climate Summit. There are no historical analogies from which to draw succour to deal with this urgent climate change problem. The current terrifying state of affairs around greenhouse gas emissions prompted Mike Davis to pen a bleak article *Who Will Build the Ark?* As a warmer world takes its grip, he explains how cities of poverty may well become the coffins of hope:

> *Since most of history's giant trees have already been cut down, a new Ark will have to be constructed out of the materials that a desperate humanity finds at hand in insurgent communities, pirate technologies, bootlegged media, rebel science, and forgotten utopias.*

Davis (2010: 30)

The net effect of global capitalism having run aground on the reefs of inequality and racial division, intensified by incapacitated governments sailing on the tide of reckless capital and rising debt, is the advent of new modes and possibilities for a resurgent radical politics – in our terms a 'Critical Social Work'. There is no lack of critique or radical sentiment today. We are witnessing an overload of anti-capitalist critiques on the horrors of neoliberalism. Žižek (2010: 86–87) maintains that the stagnancy of capital and the fear of crisis have led to a permanent state of economic emergency which 'brings with it the threat of far more savage austerity measures, cuts in benefits, diminishing health, education and social services and more precarious employment'.

With the erosion of UK social services under the new Cameron–Clegg coalition government, and more broadly, the collapse of properly functioning welfare states in advanced liberal societies (previously reformed under the banner of modernisation), radical social workers may be fast approaching a moment of truth from which they should take stock before propelling themselves forward: they wanted real change – now they have it. However, this exposes the ambiguity of human agency in a structurally shaped world, neatly captured by Marx (2008: 15) when he noted, 'men make their own history, but do so not under conditions of their own choosing'. As we shall see, a critical stance in social work promises to prefigure the general practice culture that an effective Left requires, defending the conditions for a broader and richer critical culture and a more engaged political practice.

Why Critical Social Work?

Critical Social Work is a generic term for a set of practices drawing upon critical theory to promote greater social and economic justice through transformational change. It may be viewed as a committed approach that locates individual experience within wider social structures and seeks to challenge oppression through progressive welfare policy and practice (Gray and Webb, 2009). Practitioners seek to mobilise a range of interests at the local level through collective action and the development of more preventative and rights-based services (Stepney, 2010).

Critical social work may be situated within a historical context as part of a 'radical tradition' of social change emerging during the 1970s (Ferguson and Woodward, 2009) leading to the growth of community work and local political action. It was informed by Marxist and feminist critiques of traditional welfare resulting in the publication of various critical texts (see, for example, Bailey and Brake, 1975). Here it was suggested the care function of welfare could also be seen as part of the state's control of the working class and the reproduction of relationships of domination and subordination ultimately serving the interests of capital (Mullaly, 2007). It is also associated with the growth of new global social movements (Castells, 1977) placing concerns about, for example, the emancipation of women, institutional racism, and discrimination in mental health on the mainstream political agenda.

The task of Critical Social Work is to elucidate alternatives to practices stemming from oppressive regimes and by-products of global capitalism, as expressed and felt at the local level. It seeks to promote *genuinely* radical change in the political and economic structure of neoliberal society in the name of social justice and equality. In the absence of an organised political movement, this is no easy task. It is made harder because certain sectors in mainstream social work appear to have accepted global capitalism and liberal democracy as 'the only game in town'. In order to avoid the two alternatives of liberal rationalism and cultural postmodernism, Critical Social Work urgently needs a *new politics* to respond to the social and economic conditions described above.

The critical social work tradition, while denoting a very general set of intellectual and practical representations, breaks with the order of conventional opinion in social work – public sector managerialism, a protectionist evidence-based social engineering, the necessity of inequalities, and the state instruments for protecting these. While Critical Social Work forms an intellectual pattern that is always actualised in a different context, there is a common set of principles uniting its agenda. 'Critical Social Work', in this sense, is a heuristic device implicitly used in political action or argument, even if the term itself does not appear. At a basic level, it means taking a stance on fundamental issues impacting upon service users and practitioners as well as the wider society. Critical Social Work thus reflects a 'zone of political engagement' for students, researchers, and practitioners. In social work, the zone of engagement represents a position people take up, either as a refusal, resistance, or in defiance of certain contemporary arrangements, whether these are along the lines of class, gender, race, age, sexual orientation or disability. It also indicates 'taking a stance' as a sign of commitment alongside those who are oppressed, exploited or treated unjustly. In some important respects, it signifies a disavowal with certain ways of thinking and practising in the service of the oppressor or the exploiter. It represents a feeling of dissent symptomatic of tension with dominant worldviews and a further commitment to a project of social transformation.

This resistance is expressed either against the body of social work itself or the institutional and structural arrangements of society beyond it. In extending the transformative agenda from the political sphere, Critical Social Work is unique in opposing the vulgar reductionism of effects in social work called for in the name of public sector managerialism, evidence-based practice, and risk-aversive technologies. Social work, perhaps inadvertently, scoops up some of the material logic of advanced capitalism and reproduces it in face-to-face dealings with service users, thereby helping to reinforce relationships of domination and exploitation. Critical Social Work embodies a theory of practice to expose both the designated and latent effects of this process. Thus we take Critical Social Work practice to be a perspective that sees itself as part of a progressive political project, a project which begins with a rejection of contemporary social arrangements and seeks to establish another more equitable and just state of affairs.

One of the distinctive and enduring claims made by Critical Social Work is that theory and practice, ideas and their application, should not be treated as separate entities. Critical Social Work shows how the paradoxes emerging from the traditional 'theory *and* practice' problem in social work evolve from the '*and*'. It identifies the way in which theory and practice are linked internally by their common participation in a structure in which the mode of activity is expressed. Hence they cannot be placed one after the other as cause and effect: rather, they are two moments of a circular process. In this sense, theory and approach, or theory and practice, are not merely different ways of looking at the world.

In developing Critical Social Work, no one preconceived method or set of skills for practice is assumed, so it is useful to think in terms of an approach. Choosing a method, or honing a set of skills, implies an approach. It is precisely by stressing the reflective and dialogical aspects of action that Critical Social Work overcomes the false distinction between theory *and* practice. By showing that social work comprises a *cycle of action-reflection-action* the critical arm bypasses the simplifying theory-practice distinction and leads to 'praxis-oriented research' as a way of overcoming the schism between 'knowing' and 'doing'. Knowledge increases critically reflective capabilities and directs attention to the possibilities of social transformation. From this perspective, theory illuminates lived experience to increase the intellectual, moral, and political capabilities of service users and social workers alike. Such praxis-oriented research also explicitly comprises activities to challenge dominance and its effects in terms of injustice and inequality.

Although Critical Social Work's fundamental emancipatory promise and its structural critique of social work have been influential, as a counterbalance to mainstream thinking, it seems fitting to re-examine its relevance in the dramatically changed social context of rising neoliberalism and its current impact on social work (Ferguson, 2008). Here, we can identify the movement's successes but also the disturbing convergence of some of its ideals with the demands of an emerging new form of capitalism – post-Fordist, 'disorganised', and transnational, where aspects of critical social work, such as empowerment, 'celebration of difference', and service-user involvement, have unwittingly supplied a key ingredient to neoliberalism and the modernisation of the welfare state, while welfare agencies have incorporated the rhetorical and emotive language of empowerment into their mission statements and policies (Stepney, 2006).

A distinctive politics of Critical Social Work inheres in a renewed commitment to a progressive agenda for the profession and a resurgent wave of thinking aimed at articulating a set of alternatives (Webb, 2010). Social work is not just about self-foundation based on knowledge, values, and skills formation, but also about self-assertion. Crucially, it is through this notion of self-assertion that social work can best be understood as an agent of change and a collective enterprise underpinned by progressive values. As *a set of professional practice and values still committed to justice, caring, and equality*, a number of core ethical concerns joined to a progressive political agenda make Critical Social Work unique. In order to properly understand what a 'politics' comprises, the next section examines the rich legacy of ideas inherited from the broader social science tradition of critical theory. It is here the roots of Critical Social Work are to be found.

Critical theory

Critical social work is informed by a number of theoretical traditions and this makes it a rather slippery approach to define. It follows that there are numerous versions drawing on such traditions as Marxism, feminism, postmodernism, critical realism, a strengths perspective and constructive approaches, thus reflecting a very diverse field (Stepney, 2010). All draw upon critical theory to develop practices that aim to be progressive by linking the wider structural context of problems with outcomes through the conduit of human experience (Kazi, 2003). The term is something of a misnomer as there is no single overarching critical theory but rather a diverse range of critical theories sharing certain pivotal assumptions. Mostly, critical theory is associated with the work of the German Institute for Social Research that subsequently became known as the Frankfurt School. Among its key thinkers were Horkheimer, Adorno, Marcuse, and Habermas. Collectively, critical theories are:

1. Aimed at producing *enlightenment* in the agents who hold them, that is, at enabling them to determine what their true interests are.
2. Inherently *emancipatory*, that is, they free agents from a kind of coercion which is, at least, partly self-imposed, from self-frustration of conscious human action.
3. Different epistemologically in essential ways from natural science theories: theories in natural science are objectifying while critical theories are *reflective* (Geuss, 1981).

Against this backdrop, Habermas (1972) draws a distinction between different forms of knowledge based on our particular interest in that knowledge. Where our aim is to understand facts about the world, our interest is in *empirical-analytical* knowledge that can be subjected to verification or falsification. Where our interest is in understanding the world and the meaning of phenomena, we are drawn to *historical-hermeneutical* knowledge which requires the interpretation of events in particular contexts and time. Where our interest is to find the true motives behind our interpretations and understanding of facts and events, we need a form of knowledge Habermas calls *emancipatory* knowledge. This is associated with a type of freedom ensuing from discovering the truth and this knowledge can only be reached through critical reflection (see Lovat and Gray, 2008, for a particular social work application of these ideas).

There appears to be a synergy between Habermasian theory and the diverse forms of knowledge upon which social workers draw. However, to some extent, social workers have taken critical reflection out of this broader context of understanding, influenced by psychologist Schön's (1983) notion of the reflective practitioner. For Habermas, critical reflection is a particular form of reasoning with its roots in Kantian ethics and philosophy. All reasoning is a logical process, but what elevates it to a form of critical thinking is the process of reasoning in context with the understanding ideas that are shaped by societal processes which privilege some forms of knowledge over others. Here notions of power and ideology become central. Thus critical theory, as expounded by Habermas and other members of the Frankfurt School, 'is a reflective theory which gives agents a kind of knowledge inherently productive of enlightenment and emancipation' (Geuss, 1981: 2). It comes at a time where analytical philosophy and a faith in neo-positivism have come to assume prominence in, for example, the push for evidence-based practice (Gray, Plath, and Webb, 2009; Stepney, 2010; Webb, 2001). However, critical theorists note the limitations of positivism for explaining causal processes, or how society functions, how institutions are shaped by and, in turn, shape ideas.

Importantly, critical theorists acknowledged the inevitability of change but sought to understand the laws and processes governing change. How did social change come about and what could be learnt from these processes to inform future change? Could enlightened agents contribute to change in a proactive manner if they understood the processes not only shaping their ideas but also the dynamics of social change? Their starting point for such understanding was the idea of 'ideology as worldview'. Critical theorists perceived logic in the way people's ideologies or worldviews were shaped. Essentially they were a collection of ideas, values, beliefs, and attitudes with some measure of coherence arising in particular social, historical, and cultural contexts (Geuss, 1981). Hence critical theorists saw human beings, not as atomistic individuals, but as social beings shaped by society, culture, and history.

Critical theory has come to be associated mostly with its *critique* of society as it is; with highlighting prevailing ideologies shaping false consciousness or deluded self-beliefs; and with associating these with issues of power or, specifically, dominant and subordinate political interests. Critical theory critiqued the way in which the dominant order shaped people's beliefs and sought to change them. It highlighted the way in which these dominant beliefs promoted the interests of powerful groups while workers or lower social strata groups bore the brunt of unequal, unjust, exploitative, and oppressive social conditions. In other words, those with the most power would ensure social institutions would promote laws and structures to maintain their privileged position in society, and therefore the job of the underdog was to undermine these dominant interests.

There is a resonance here for the social work profession in the notion that *critical ideas* can change the world. There was a time when social work had a clear political project (see Bailey and Brake, 1975; Pearson, 1975) where it perceived its role of changing oppressive and unjust social conditions as achievable. But to some extent, this has been lost and the time is right to devise a new politics for Critical Social Work. Social work's revolutionary zeal and idealism has been diminished by the oppressive conditions created by risk-averse, punitive neoliberal welfare regimes – permeated by what Furedi calls a 'culture of fear'. The task of Critical Social Work is to uncover the exact ways in which these contemporary conditions are moulding and shaping the profession and making it lose touch with its political fervour and commitment. The link here is the way in which neoliberalism shapes the cultural environment in which social workers work and their clients live (Ferguson and Woodward, 2009). Neoliberalism makes these environments highly regulated through regimes of new public management concerned with promoting the values of efficiency over and above quality, justice, and care. In pursuing the mantra of 'what works' and evidence-based practice, it creates structures that severely curtail professional autonomy and thereby reshape practice (Gray *et al.*, 2009; Webb, 2001).

Similar processes influence the life chances of clients or service users; for example, the strict conditions attached to the receipt of benefits allows little room for manoeuvre and forces recipients to conform to their participation requirements. At the same time, social workers become agents of enforcement imposing these restrictions on clients. A Critical Social Work perspective would warn the profession of the danger of aligning itself with Cameron's call for a reactivation of moral responsibility to promote civic obligation, self-help, and voluntary association in the community (Cameron, 2009). The 'Big Society' debate may be regarded as a convenient panacea to the problems of a deeply divided and unequal society at a time of drastic cutbacks in welfare spending (explored in more detail by Paul Stepney in Chapter 1). Several notions offer a theoretical prism through which to critique this state of affairs, but central to our concern for developing a Critical Social Work is developing a critique of the notion of *governmentality* as an axis around which modern forms of power, knowledge, and ideology cohere.

Governmentality

Governmentality is essentially concerned with the machinations of power, the production of circuits of power at the level of the everyday, and how these are shaping new forms of welfare governance. As Fairbanks (2012) notes:

*Foucault described governmentality as follows: (i) The ensemble formed by the institutions, analyses, procedures, calculations that allow the exercise of a very specific and complex form of power that has as its target **population**; as its principle form of knowledge **political economy**; as its essential technical means **security** (read welfare); (ii) the tendency which over time has led steadily towards the pre-eminence over all other forms (sovereignty and discipline) of this type of power which may be termed government – resulting in the formation of a whole series of governmental apparatuses and a whole complex of knowledges operating in the social; and (iii) the process of governmentalisation . . . the tactics of government that make possible the continual definition and redefinition of what is within the competence of the state and what is not. The state, as such, can only be understood in its survival and its limits on the basis of the general tactics of governmentality.*

(in Gray, Midgley and Webb, 2012: 63)

Developmentally, new forms of power arise in the wake of attacks on the welfare state from the left and right of politics resulting in what sociologists have referred to as the shrinking realm of the social (Connell, 2000) through targeted, conditional income transfers (Castles and Mitchell, 1991) and an increasing embrace of economic solutions for social problems. This has led to a *fiscalisation of discourses* about public services, creating a 'cult of efficiency' that has been central to the modernisation of the welfare state (Clarke, 2008). Market mechanisms relating to the supply and demand of services have been deployed to increase competition and improve outcomes, but within parameters of cost containment, efficiency, and effectiveness (Stepney, 2010).

The modernising of welfare is clearly a global phenomenon but, as yet, little has been done to connect the idea of neoliberalisation (Harvey, 2005) with the path-dependent development processes of different welfare-state regimes (Esping-Andersen, 1990). All one can say at present is that, in Europe, there is evidence of some convergence in policy outcomes, but under conditions of neoliberalism 'welfare states are now on a shared trajectory of more limited social rights' (Timonen, 1999: 255).

More specifically, neoliberalism, new public management, and techniques and rationalities of advanced liberal government have reconfigured social policies and programmes in a radical departure from 'old' welfare state planning in which the government played a major role in providing for the well-being of citizens. Within the modernised or reconfigured welfare state, sometimes regarded as 'the death of the social' (Rose, 1996), or 'a post-welfarist social regime' (Dean, 2010/1999) the citizen has become a consumer or user with 'choice' within a field of constructed quasi-markets in services and expertise. Services have been rationalised, restructured, marketised, and privatised in massive welfare modernisation programmes in developed Western contexts. Alongside the attempt to facilitate consumer choice, there is also a return to disciplinary, coercive, and paternalist modes of welfare governance. The double facilitative-disciplinary logic underlying neoliberal reform is seen as the core feature in the transformation of welfare governance, which Soss, Fording, and Schram (2011) have labelled 'neoliberal paternalism'.

On the one hand, social work interventions are now increasingly organised through quasi-markets, policies of *contracting* out of and *fees* for services (user-pay models), increased *competition* between service providers, and the streamlining of services to produce greater *efficiencies* measured in terms of cost-benefit ratios. Within this marketised scenario, the welfare recipient has been reconfigured as a consumer or service user with choice – one who can 'choose' to participate in the state-sponsored welfare-to-work programmes and, at least, show a desire to participate or become economically active by reaping the rewards of the state's 'activation' programmes. This represents the neoliberal aspect of welfare governance. However, on the other hand, participating in these programmes has become a condition of maintaining benefits. Failure to do so now means an exit from welfare. Non-participants are breached. The state or nongovernmental organisations running the programme thus assume the welfare recipient to be someone who needs to be disciplined or corrected so she or he might learn to exercise 'choice' wisely. This is the paternal side of welfare reform. The dual policy involves an intensification of *governmentality* (the use of expertise working through individual capacities and freedom) together with the exercise of state *sovereignty* (coercive measures underwritten by law).

One problem with this new form of welfare governance is the presentation of itself in a powerful cocktail of economic, social, and moral language: economic participation, consumer choice, active welfare, mutual obligation, and social inclusion are just some of the terms used to describe this new welfare settlement. Essentially, the system disciplines those capable of exercising choice as citizen consumers and those who, for whatever reason, are incapable of making responsible choices and must be guided, obligated, or even coerced into so doing. A key category here is the unemployable. As noted by Terranova (2003), 'governments do not like the completely unemployable. The potentialities of work must be kept alive, the unemployed must undergo continuous training in order both to be monitored and kept alive as some kind of postindustrial reserve force'. So at the 'hard' end of the social inclusion agenda is a trampoline policy concerned with *how to move people off welfare and bounce them into work –* how to make them *productive* members of society or *economic participants.* Taking into account the varieties of work in which individuals are engaged, including the *value of social care*, these sharp distinctions become less obvious as new mixtures of welfare support, economic participation, and social care mark alternatives to the 'neoliberal workfare state' (Jessop, 1999: 358). Against a backdrop of radical change in the way clients are regulated, administered, and controlled, the governmentality agenda is having enduring effects on how social workers intervene, and whether they can act in a politically attuned way.

Practice Focus One: A study of rationalising practices in psychiatric outpatient clinics in central Finland

The introduction of a new managerial audit system in community mental health teams in central Finland can be located within the trajectory of governmentality, since it has been found to reshape practice by reinforcing certain modes of working and discouraging others. Practitioners were required to reduce time for therapeutic work and family support in favour of meeting managerial targets, leading to short-term interventions compromising their ability to meet client need. In this way, the governmentality agenda reduced professional autonomy and intensified aspirations for efficiency and effectiveness over quality.

(Saario and Stepney, 2009)

Please pause and reflect on this practice focus. Can you identify specific ways in which new forms of governance and managerial audit have produced diverse and contradictory effects on practice? Undertake a brief contextual analysis of one of these events. What steps can the practitioner take to prevent practice being reshaped in this way?

Agamben traces the net effects of micro-governmentality regimes on the social and defines our contemporary 'biopolitical society' as one inhered by constant but fluid forms of social control. Whether western society is governed by political parties of the right or left:

> . . . these terms simply name the two poles – the one that aims at desubjectivation, without any scruples, and the one that wants to cover it with the hypocritical mask of the good citizen of democracy – of the same machine of government.
>
> (Agamben, 2007: 46–47)

The task of Critical Social Work is clearly urgent in the face of this all-encompassing governmentality agenda. Governmentality designates a constellation of flows of power in which the State apparatus no longer generates subjects (as citizens or clients) but increasingly merely administers and regulates individuals' bare lives and basic needs.

A distinctive agenda for Critical Social Work

The idea of a distinctive agenda is suggestive of a break with some form or function of critical social work as it has previously been articulated. Indeed, we would suggest it takes the form of a re-examination of its concepts and procedures, its recent history, and the ways they have become intertwined with the logic of social emancipation. In particular, it searches for a new 'militant figure', serving as a theoretical provocation to disturb the tranquil waters of 'individualising' interventions resting on a foundation of evidence-based practice, task-centredness, risk assessment, and resource management. It adheres to transformative possibilities around a politics of equality and justice for social work freed from the dominion of the market (Ferguson and Woodward, 2009). To reconfigure the social landscape of what can be thought and done is to alter the field of the possible by cracking open the static and striated blocks of hierarchical regimes. Indeed, this means placing Critical Social Work as the *leitmotif* and centrepiece for a positive theory of political and social organisation in an otherwise normative, generic social work. As we shall see, demarcating this enclosure for Critical Social Work against its mellifluous counterpart is an important part of building a stable group identity for progressive social workers on the Left 'what might be supported and mobilised as a "New Social Work Left"' (Gray and Webb, forthcoming).

Certain strands in critical social work reflect a narrow grasp of social theory and lack any close analysis of the impact of late-capitalist conditions on social work, or alternatively fail to demonstrate how social work feeds into, challenges, or sustains these conditions. While certain postmodernist treatments have attempted to advance a critical social work discourse, they are often reactive, rethinking and relabeling old theory with one or two new 'ideas', hence Freirian critical community practice that is critical but non transformational (Butcher *et al.*, 2007) and, to some extent, the 'new structural social work' (Mullaly, 2007). Such strands tend to extol a utopian vision without recognising the extraordinary resilience of neoliberalism and advanced capitalism. They may idealise service users, fail to see them as complex human agents, and over-emphasise external forces of oppression in the process denying the real human suffering arising from complex internal and external sources. Overlooked is the possibility 'critical' practice might spring from other sources, like practitioners themselves, trade unions, indigenous groups, and social movements already in existence. Most importantly, the organising concepts have tended to be overdetermined by fashionable literary and linguistic concepts with little bearing on social work.

To make this distinction, Gray and Webb (2009) differentiated between Critical Social Work (capitalised) as having a narrow meaning with links to critical theory as outlined above and critical social work (lower case) as having a broad meaning denoting all other uses. Many texts with reference in their title to 'critical social work' or 'critical practice' fall into the second category and draw on common components to which some key thinkers have contributed. For example, critical postmodernism draws on Foucault's theorising of power and emphasises critical reflection but its roots are in social constructionism rather than critical theory (Fook, 2002). The 'best practice' agenda, strengths perspective, and empowerment approach are other examples. All reflect an ambivalence which can be read either as endorsing a critical social work approach or one evoking neoliberal affinities based on individualist accounts of change and notions of individual responsibility and choice in a market economy of social care provision as set out above (Gray, 2011).

Gray and Webb (2009) and Stepney (2010) view 'Critical Social Work' as emerging from various intellectual movements, including Marxism, feminism, race theory, critical realism, and postcolonial criticism which identified dimensions of economic and political domination in modern societies. It embodies a specific set of values. It constitutes a political project seeking to explain and transform various circumstances in which social workers and service users find themselves, while connecting these to a structural analysis of those aspects of society leading to oppression, injustice, and exploitation. It essentially involves an examination of *the relations of domination which meaning serves to sustain in social work and the wider society.* To analyse ideology in relation to social work, one should analyse the socio-historical conditions in which ideological forms are produced and received, conditions which include the relations of domination these forms serve to sustain. It creatively constructs meaning animated by a *critical concern* shared with the emancipatory project. It offers a practical means of moving from the social world as it is to the world as we would wish it to be.

Thus the Critical Social Worker inevitably analyses the coercive workings and organisation of power, especially as manifested in hierarchical relations of

---

Practice Focus Two: Transfer of care of older people in the UK

There has been a highly charged debate around the issue of so called 'bed-blocking' concerning the hospital discharge of older people, with legislation in the UK introduced in 2003 allowing municipal authorities to be fined for delayed discharges. The research evidence is contested and has been interpreted in different ways, in particular between those who cite data about the problem of delayed discharge and an emerging crisis in the care homes market (Glasby and Henwood, 2007) and those who have produced empirical evidence on changing admission and death rates in nursing homes to support a more critical position (Ford and Stepney, 2003). It can be shown that, while delays in discharge do occur and can have negative effects on older people, premature discharge constitutes a more common problem hitherto given insufficient recognition by policy makers. When older people are prematurely discharged back into the community, without adequate domiciliary services and support, the result is increased risk of harm which may quickly lead to breakdown, readmission to hospital, or worse (Ford and Stepney 2003). A Critical Social Work practitioner would seek to incorporate notions of fairness and justice, alongside effectiveness criteria, into their work to counteract the jeopardised citizenship of older people.

Please consider how the current 'crisis in care' of older people has impacted on your own practice. Carry out a micro-level analysis of the way ideology and power combined to structure events in your work with one service user.

domination and exploitation. Social workers actually know a great deal about power and its machinations, but have hitherto been timid in building on what they know. They have learnt a great deal from the likes of Foucault, Gramsci, Habermas, and Bourdieu, but have been distracted from analysing the central apparatus of exercising power as structural forms, and often remiss in understanding the distinctiveness of the modern state in its relation to social work (Badioa, 2008). Certainly, the analysis of governmentality as everyday flows of power, or circuits of power, has been tremendously suggestive for critical social work, but it overlooks the complex relations between state institutions and social work. For instance, the deep regulation of social and personal life through law and instrumental rationality can be deeply disadvantageous to particular groups even in a democratic society.

Critical Social Work would benefit from focusing on the tense relationship between civil society and the state, between the ideologies, apparatuses, agencies, and processes associated with political organisation based on the state. Identifying causal mechanisms and getting at structure through the contextual analysis of events is what Critical Social Work does best. These events are arenas of social and political practice in which actors – service users and social workers – are seen as manipulating 'norms', which are neither consistent nor fully coherent, as they pursue their ambitions and personal interests within the late capitalist schema.

An examination of the way in which ideology and power are intimately coupled as part of an ongoing sequence of 'social events' offers a method for Critical Social Work to study structure through micro-level analysis. A Critical Social Worker confronting a sequence of events will ask how far they reflect contingent clashes of local context connected to wider issues and to what extent they manifest deep social and political cleavages. This not only helps explain regularities and regulation of state institutions but also the strategising of actors interacting with one another. The focus is on both 'social action' as governmentality and of the underlying social structure and normative rule of social order. Modern society can usefully be conceptualised as so many ways of distributing, maintaining, and challenging power, with ideology as one of its central mechanisms. Social work is intimately caught up in the machinery of power and the articulation of dominant ideology. It is composed of a specific set of *social practices* that either help constitute or rebuff the essential mechanism of modern power. In its use of critical tools deployed via the analysis of ideology and power, Critical Social Work decisively confronts those practices which reinforce or maintain relations of domination and exploitation.

Conclusion

In this chapter we have put forward a distinctive agenda for Critical Social Work drawing on critical theory as part of a political project committed to achieving greater social and economic justice. The current global financial crisis, and the inequalities and divisions deriving from it, provide a backdrop to the debate and signal the urgency for social work to rediscover its change-agent role. Such an approach framed from critical perspectives can drive practice agendas and has the capacity to leaven the instrumentality of effectiveness measures with strategies of emancipation. The end result is a Critical Social Work (what Gray and Webb (forthcoming) refer to as the 'New Social Work Left') with the ability to confront relations of power, domination, and oppression in society so social workers might be better placed to transform them.

References

Agamben, G. (2007) *What is an Apparatus? and Other Essays.* Stanford: Stanford University Press.

Badioa, A. (2008) The Communist Hypothesis. *New Left Review*, 37, 29–42.

Bailey, R. and Brake, M. (Eds.) (1975) *Radical Social Work.* London: Edward Arnold.

Blond, P. (2010) *Red Tory: How Left and Right Have Broken Britain and How We Can Fix it.* London: Faber and Faber.

Butcher, H., Banks, S., Henderson, P. and Robertson, J. (2007) *Critical Community Practice.* Bristol: Policy Press.

Cameron, D. (2009) The Big Society. Hugo Young Memorial Lecture, London, 29 November.

Castells, M. (1977) *The Urban Question.* London: Edward Arnold.

Castles, F.G. and Mitchell, D. (1991) *Three Worlds of Welfare Capitalism or Four.* ANU, Graduate Program in Public Policy.

Clarke, J. (2001) Globalisation and Welfare States: Some Unsettling Thoughts. In Sykes, R., Palier, B. and Prior, P. (Eds.) *Globalisation and European Welfare States.* Basingstoke: Palgrave. 19–37.

Clarke, J. (2008) Performance Paradoxes: The Politics of Evaluation in Public Services. In Davis, H. and Martin, S. (Eds.) *Public Services Inspection in the UK.* London: Jessica Kingsley. 120–134.

Connell, R. (2000) Sociology and World Market Society. *Contemporary Sociology*, 29(2) 291–296.

Davis, M. (2010) Who Will Build the Ark? *New Left Review*, 61(1), 29–46.

Dean, M. (2007) Governing the Unemployed Self in an Active Society. In Vij, R. (Ed.) *Globalization and Welfare.* Basingstoke: Palgrave.

Dean, M. (2010/1999) *Governmentality: Power and Rule in Modern Society*, London: Sage.

Esping-Andersen, G. (1990) *Three Worlds of Welfare Capitalism.* Princeton: Princeton University Press.

Fairbanks, R. (2012) Welfare Governance. In Gray, M., Midgley, J. and Webb, S.A. (Eds.) *Sage Handbook of Social Work.* London: Sage.

Ferguson, I. (2008) *Reclaiming Social Work: Challenging Neo-Liberalism and Promoting Social Justice.* London: Sage.

Ferguson, I. and Woodward, R. (2009) *Radical Social Work in Practice: Making a Difference.* Bristol: The Policy Press.

Fook, J. (2002) *Social Work: Critical Theory and Practice.* London: Sage.

Ford, D. and Stepney, P. (2003) Hospital Discharge and The Citizenship Rights of Older People: Will The UK Become a Test-bed for Eastern Europe? *European Journal of Social Work*, 6: 3, 257–72.

Geuss, R. (1981) *The Idea of Critical Theory: Habermas and the Frankfurt School.* New York: Cambridge University Press.

Glasby, J. and Henwood, M. (2007) Part of the Problem or Part of The Solution? The Role of Care Homes in Tackling Delayed Hospital Discharge. *British Journal of Social Work*, 37: 299–312.

Gray, M. (2011) Back to Basics: A Critique of The Strengths Perspective in Social Work. *Families in Society: Journal of Contemporary Social Services*, 92: 1, 5–11.

Gray, M. and Webb, S.A. (2009) Critical Social Work. In Gray, M. and Webb, S.A. (Eds.) *Social Work Theories and Methods.* London: Sage.

Gray, M. and Webb, S.A. (forthcoming) *The New Politics of Critical Social Work.* Basingstoke: Palgrave.

Gray, M., Plath, D. and Webb, S.A. (2009) *Evidence-based Social Work: A Critical Stance.* London: Routledge.

Habermas, J. (1972) *Knowledge and Human Interests.* London: Heinemann.

Harvey, D. (2005) *A Brief History of Neoliberalism.* New York: Oxford University Press.

Jessop, B. (1999) The Changing Governance of Welfare: Recent Trends in its Primary Functions, Scale, and Modes of Coordination. *Social Policy & Administration*, 33(4) 348–359.

Kazi, M. (2003) *Realist Evaluation in Practice.* London: Sage.

Lovat, T. and Gray, M. (2008) Towards a Proportionist Social Work Ethic: A Habermasian Perspective. *British Journal of Social Work*, 38: 1100–14.

Marx, K. (2008) *The 18th Brumaire of Louis Boneparte* (reprint from original published in 1852), Rockville MD: Wildside Press.

Mullaly, B. (2007) *The New Structural Social Work.* 3rd edn. Don Mills, Ontario: Oxford University Press.

Pearson, G. (1975) *The Deviant Imagination.* Basingstoke: Macmillan.

Rose, N. (1996) Governing 'Advanced' Liberal Democracies. In Barry, A. Osborne, T. and Rose, N. (Eds.) *Foucault and Political Reason.* London: UCL Press.

Saario, S. and Stepney, P. (2009) Managerial Audit and Mental Health: A Study of Rationalising Practices in Finnish Psychiatric Clinics. *European Journal of Social Work*, 12: 1, 41–56.

Schön, D. (1983) *The Reflective Practitioner: How Professionals Think in Action.* New York: Basic Books.

Soss, J., Fording, R.C. and Schram, S.F. (2011) *Disciplining the Poor: Neoliberal Paternalism and The Persistent Power of Race.* Chicago: University of Chicago Press.

Stepney, P. (2006) Mission Impossible? Critical Practice in Social Work. *British Journal of Social Work*, 36: 8, 1289–1307.

Stepney, P. (2010) Social Welfare at The Crossroads: Evidence-Based Practice or Critical Practice? *The International Journal of Interdisciplinary Social Sciences*, 5(5) 105–120.

Terranova, T. (2003) *Free Labor: Producing Culture For The Digital Economy*. Electronic book review. Retrieved 10 December 2010 http://www.electronicbookreview.com/thread/technocapitalism/voluntary

Timonen, V. (1999) A threat to Social Security? The Impact of EU Membership on The Finnish Welfare State. *Journal of European Social Policy*, 9: 3, 253–261.

Watkins, S. (2010) *Shifting Sands. Editorial.* New Left Review, 61: 1, 12.

Webb, S.A. (2001) Some Considerations on The Validity of Evidence-Based Practice in Social Work. *British Journal of Social Work*, 31: 1, 57–79.

Webb, S.A. (2009) Against Difference and Diversity in Social Work: The Case of Human Rights. *International Journal of Social Welfare*, 18: 2, 307–16.

Webb, S.A. (2010) (Re)Assembling the Left: The Politics of Redistribution and Recognition in Social Work. *British Journal of Social Work*, 40: 8, 2364–79.

Žižek, S. (2010) A Permanent State of Emergency. *New Left Review*, 64. Retrieved on 22-02-11 from http://www.newleftreview.org/?view=2853

Chapter 16

Research Minded Practice in Social Work

Martyn Jones

Introduction

Let's assume it would be reasonable to expect that social workers, involved in the lives of other people, should know what they are doing. That seems self-evident. We expect our doctors to know what they are doing when we go to see them. Why would it be different? But what does it mean to say we expect social workers to know what they are doing. Just what is it we expect them to know, and how would we know if they knew it? Not so easy. We might feel reassured if we checked up on their qualifications. At least we'd know they had some relevant education and training. Or, from word of mouth, we might hear they were good at their job. That helps. But, who is to say the education and training is adequate, or the grapevine is working properly? Why should I trust those social workers to have anything to do with my life?

There is a lot the social worker has to do to gain the trust of others, and sometimes of course that's never going to be possible – or, arguably, appropriate. And there is a lot the social workers are going to have to know if they are to do their job well. Added to which, social work is the kind of job where you can never know it all – indeed, it's the kind of job where you should never think you can know it all. Social work occupies an unusual place. It remains unsure of itself and its claims to expertise – happily perhaps for its recipients. Because, of course, the sort of expertise social workers need isn't quite the same as the expertise sought in doctors, or accountants, or engineers.

In discussing research minded practice for social work, we have to recognise we are approaching some tricky territory. It is the case, if only by anecdote, that most students of social work do not greet with glee the prospect of studying research and for many practitioners research remains something done and talked about elsewhere (Gibbs and Stirling, 2010). What is it about research that has rendered it somewhat counter-cultural in the world of social work practice? There are many answers to that question, but amongst them is the possibility of mutual misunderstanding and scepticism – social work research of social work practice, and vice versa.

A chapter on research minded practice appears in this book presumably because of an assumption that research matters not just to social work per se but to the practice of social work. That is a big assumption. But it is one that increasing numbers of academics, researchers, managers, policy makers and practitioners – not to mention clients, service users and community members – are keen to promote (Evans and Hardy, 2010). In short, contemporary social work is required not only to engage with the question of research but to create closer connections between practice and research (Corby, 2006). In this chapter, we will be examining various facets of this trend and suggesting that research minded practice can not only assist social workers in knowing what they are doing but also contribute to improved ways of doing it – to the ultimate benefit of the people in whose lives they are involved. However, getting there is going to mean significant reciprocal learning, considerable capacity building, and not a little supportive infrastructure.

On the matter of misunderstanding

What does research need to learn about social work practice? Let's start at the beginning. Social work claims to look both ways, towards the person and towards their environment. This dual focus is often said to be what gives social work an inkling of distinctiveness – understanding and acting at the interface between the personal and the social (Chenoweth and McAuliffe, 2008). There is no reason why this dual focus approach would apply solely to the client or their community. It can reflect back upon the social worker and their environment as well. The somewhat timeless saying that recommends 'start where the client is' does hold an important clue: 'start where the social worker is'. Lesson one for research: consider the social worker in relation to their practice environment.

This may sound simple. However, major misunderstandings will arise in the search for research minded practice unless there is an appreciation of the way practice is both shaped by and shaping the contexts in which it occurs (Adams, Dominelli and Payne, 2009). And, naturally, the contexts are varied and complex. To accomplish their practice, social workers have to mediate a mix of imperatives from organisation, policy, law, ethics, their profession and their own personal histories. Lesson two: research can only ever be one amongst a number of influences upon practice. That is not to say research cannot or should not be a significant – sometimes, *the* significant – influence. But it is to recognise from the outset that, to find its place, there will need to be an awareness of other influences in the mix.

It has also been part of the social work tradition that social workers would be out to 'make a difference' and a difference for the better. Social work is unavoidably a moral activity. It has no choice but to walk through the moral maze conjured up by the question, what do we mean by 'better'? Respect for persons, social justice, human rights – these are common means of navigating the maze but the ethical path is rarely self-evident (Hugman, 2005). Added to which, there can be no room for complacency when social work's heritage includes too many examples of claiming to be acting for the better when this has been far from the case. Lesson three: if research wishes to connect more closely with practice, be prepared to traverse a value-rich land together.

And if social work does aim to introduce a difference, whether that's overtly towards more socially just arrangements or the difference that comes simply from being alongside someone in distress, then it has to be self-questioning about the power and authority vested within it. It's hard to conceive of any form of social work that is devoid of power (Smith, 2008). Yet, this is not necessarily a familiar place for research. So much of the research tradition has been directed towards the pursuit of knowledge with a view of power at one remove – as if we can nullify the power invested in research by gaining informed consent from participants or leaving it to decision-makers to determine whether or not reported recommendations are to be implemented (D'Cruz and Jones, 2004). This positioning of research may itself be appropriate but, if research and practice are to be meaningfully joined, then perhaps there's a fourth lesson for research: be ready to re-think the ways in which research itself may be infused with power and authority.

Lastly for now, lesson five for research: social work is controversial, under-resourced, over-stretched, emotionally and intellectually exhausting but immensely fulfilling, inspiring and passionate. This is not going to be a dull partnership.

Okay, let's come at this from the other end. What does social work need to appreciate about research if we are to move towards research minded practice? It may be a surprise to some social workers that research comes in many guises. There is plenty of room to stereotype research dismissively, as the persistent image of the white coated, laboratory technician suggests. But if we think of research as searching anew for fresh understandings, insights, and even explanations, of what we take for granted, then a world of possibilities opens up. Being open-minded and methodical in the ways we go about this still leaves a lot of room to move. Certainly there are traditions and principles in the accustomed ways of practising research that need to be understood – but the diversity that is research needs to be appreciated in much the same way as it does for social work (Alston and Bowles, 2003). Lesson one for social work: give research a chance; it takes time to get to know.

In recognising that research can be a stranger to social work, it is also the case that some meeting points can quickly be found. Social workers have to use careful thinking and information gathering processes in going about their work. They have to make sense of the information they generate from the people and situations they encounter, and be aware of the many ways this can be interpreted and acted upon. At a very general level, research and social work both go about making knowledge. But this is what is at the heart of research. So, one can find in research a familiarity with the debates and challenges bound up in the pursuit of knowledge (McLaughlin, 2007). And, over time, research has evolved particular approaches to going about this, ranging from the painstakingly methodical to the vibrantly creative. Lesson two for social work: if you want to sharpen your critical thinking, information processing and knowledge making skills, research has a lot to offer.

In moving towards research minded practice, it is important also to appreciate that there are not only many ways in which researchers go about making knowledge, there are also many different commitments in research to the relationship between knowledge and action (for example, Patton, 2008; Reason and Bradbury, 2008). And whilst social work does involve knowledge making, it is at heart an action-oriented activity. Closer connections between research and social work practice can arise as we recognise their shared interest in putting knowledge into action. This may be helped by the realisation that, perhaps surprisingly for some, much attention is paid within research to the question of its practical effect. Of course, there are disparate views about this (Hammersley, 1995). Nevertheless, lesson three for social work: research is ready to get its hands dirty and does indeed have a life outside of the ivory towers.

Thinking of practical effect, there is a related aspect of research that it is worth social work pondering. And, perversely, it has to do with those ivory towers – they do bestow on the mystique of research a particular status in western society. It remains the case that research, especially when carried out according to long established customs, enjoys certain respectability, and consequently is harder (though of course not impossible) to dismiss (Banks, 2009). In the cut and thrust of practice and policy development, and the promotion of pressing social issues, research can be a powerful ally. Lesson four for social work: making friends with research can open important doors.

To embrace research, social work requires an element of humility. Research, good research, affords critical new insights into all the areas within which social work moves. Much of research is driven by a passion to discover and understand – and a wish for that knowledge to translate into a more just and compassionate response (Pease, 2010). Research, like social work, has to struggle with the ethics and politics of its practice. But social work is not alone in striving to make a difference for the better. Lesson five: research can enhance our understandings and our capacities in working together for the greater good.

The term 'research minded practice' is a useful starting point for suggesting the kind of relationship that might emerge from a stronger, mutual understanding between research and social work (Hardwick and Worsley, 2011). It is proposing a certain mind-set based on different assumptions, where research is no longer counter-cultural but embedded and enriching. Whilst it begins with a readiness to learn about the other, finding an accommodation between research and social work practice is never going to be straightforward. The idea that practitioners might want to hold research in mind offers a softer approach when compared with the somewhat strident view that practice should be based on – or even, to a lesser extent, informed by – evidence generated through research (for contrasting approaches, see Sheldon and Chilvers, 2000; Shaw, 2005; Trinder, 2000; Webb, 2001). This may seem a subtle, perhaps semantic difference, but it is an important one. The aspiration is more modest but, in that, potentially more achievable. And looking at how the two can learn from one another may enable a more open exploration of the potential benefits to both.

Mutual learning

When we talk about research minded practice, we are talking about three main ideas: firstly, that research generates knowledge relevant to and useful in practice; secondly, that the processes of research can be aligned with the processes of social work; and thirdly, that practitioners can themselves be researchers.

Starting with the first idea, we can quickly appreciate that there are several strands to relevant knowledge that comes out of research. Research generates knowledge about the people, situations and issues with which social work is engaged, and about the way social work is carried out. This knowledge can be both descriptive (telling us how it is) and explanatory (telling us why it is) (Babbie, 2010). For example, research might tell us about the rates and experiences of homelessness. It might show how those rates correlate with changes in the rental market, the occurrence of violence in the household, how those experiences are shaped according to barriers encountered through disability or ethnicity and what social workers experience in their practice with people who are homeless. Research also generates evaluative knowledge, which can be used to review the appropriateness and effectiveness of social work practice (Shaw and Lishman, 1999). For example, research might indicate whether or not intensive case management helps people transition into more secure housing arrangements. These kinds of research knowledge – descriptive, explanatory and evaluative – are produced in very many ways. And behind each of these ways of generating knowledge (methodologies) there are more abstract philosophies about how the world can, or should, be known (epistemologies).

It is customary to understand this transmission of knowledge across research and social work practice as primarily one way. That is to say, that social work practice can learn from what research has found out about, for instance, homelessness, or child abuse, or depression, or poverty, or caring, or communication, or advocacy. And similarly, that social work can learn from what research has to show about the impact of different forms of practice. For this transmission to occur, those engaged in practice would need to be able to 'read' research. They would need to have sufficient access to and literacy in research materials, the time to spend on this, and the ability to filter the material both in terms of its trustworthiness and its applicability (Orme and Shemmings, 2010). Clearly, this is a big expectation – and, in addition, there is the matter of translating that knowledge into practice, with the implication that in so doing practice will become transformed for the better. It all requires more than simply professional develop-ment and a positive attitude on behalf of the individual, as we shall be discussing later. As big as this is, however, it is only one half of the story. It is the half that sees research as being done 'over there', making the challenge one of transporting what's useful and relevant from over there into a different place, the place of practice.

The generation and use of research knowledge is not just a one-way street. When it comes to the generation of knowledge, research can learn much from social work. To begin with, social work is well positioned to point to what it is that warrants being researched in the first place. By virtue of the work they do, social workers are confronting complex social and personal issues on a daily basis. They gain a very special insight into the nature of these issues, and the challenges they present to practice, often before they emerge into public consciousness. They also have opportunity to facilitate the voicing of these issues by service users and community members, who of course themselves have legitimacy in helping define and moderate research agendas (Evans and Jones, 2004). Research minded practice, then, involves not only a readiness to learn from research formed and conducted by others – it involves actively contributing to the questions that give direction to research.

Given the contested and sensitive nature of the areas in which social work occurs, those seeking to research such matters would do well to learn from the experience of practitioners who are familiar with them and in particular their ethical and political dimensions. Practitioners can assist research by facilitating access to relevant people and organisations. But rather than be perceived just as friendly gatekeepers, meaningful and ongoing consultation from an early stage can help highlight what may need to be considered if the research is to be conducted in an appropriately sensitive and ethical way. This may include practitioners facilitating the participation of service users or community members as the research is being designed, for example, or pointing to organisational politics that will require careful negotiation if the research is to proceed. Similarly, when planning how the research findings are to be disseminated effectively, practi-tioners will have considerable, pertinent wisdom on the networks, languages and communication pathways that are likely to have greatest impact.

A research minded practitioner can be positioned as both a recipient of research knowledge and a contributor to the ways in which research is formulated, designed, implemented and disseminated. These represent a signifi-cant relationship between research and social work practice. Yet, they are just the beginning. To forge a deeper relationship, we have to explore further how research knowledge translates into the actual practice of social work (Ruckdes-chel and Chambon, 2010). This requires looking at the next two main ideas: the alignment of processes in research and social work practice; and practitioners as researchers.

In seeking points of convergence between research and social work practice, we can look not only to the knowledge that is generated but also to the processes of knowledge generation and utilisation. At one level, this is about recognising that research and social work practice both aspire to such common cognitive processes as diligent inquiry, open-mindedness, critical thinking, ethical reasoning, reflection and creativity (Gray, Plath and Webb, 2009). Arguably, bringing these qualities to knowledge-making fosters good research and good social work practice, and the professional capacities they imply are part of a shared developmental project. Those who identify primarily as researchers can attest to the length of time it may take to develop these qualities, and social workers may well say the same thing. And this is likely to be the case because what lies behind cognitive qualities of this kind is a highly developed ability to go beyond prescriptive rules of practice, whether these are rules of conducting research or rules of doing social work (Fook, Ryan and Hawkins, 2000). Both activities require the ability to make new rules – to engage in the process of knowledge-making as well as knowledge-application – according to the novelty of the situation or issues as they arise (Dreyfus and Dreyfus, 1986).

It is almost thirty years ago since Schon (1983) first explored so prominently the connection between knowledge and action in professional activity. His commentary on the limitations of a technical, rational view of professional practice spurred on what has since been described as a practice movement (Watson, 2002). Across a range of professions, a collection of ideas steadily gained momentum making space for tacit knowledge, reflective practice, communities of practice, and constructivist approaches more generally, in our appreciation of the intricacies of practice achievements (Benner, 1984; Fook, 1996; Gould and Taylor, 1996; Parton and O'Byrne, 2000; Taylor and White, 2000; Wenger, 1998). These socio-cultural models have been in tune with a sense that professional practice occurs in a complex, uncertain and unpredictable environment, requiring innovative responses and the capacity to design new ways of tackling emergent issues. They focus to a greater or lesser extent on the power inherent in accustomed ways of thinking, acting and being, ways that work to sustain structured inequalities and dominant interests (Thompson, 2010).

What does this mean for the joining of research and social work practice? As we seek convergence through shared processes of knowledge-making, it means that we construe the relationship between research and social work practice in a fundamentally different manner. This differently formed relationship emanates from the assumption that expertise in knowledge-making doesn't reside with those who happen to be called researchers. Instead, this expertise is viewed as, to use the popularised but evocative term, distributed. In some respects, the desired relationship is reminiscent of Freire's pedagogy (Kincheloe, 2007). The social worker isn't to be approached as an empty vessel ready to be filled up with research knowledge. Rather, a dialogue is sought as interested parties explore jointly the salient issues from their respective, and respected, positions. New perspectives and practices are generated in the contexts within which the dialogue progresses – and as such are intimately bound to the specifics of the time and place in which they occur.

Whilst controversial, the distinction between Mode 1 and Mode 2 knowledge production, drawn by Gibbons and colleagues (1994) some ten years after Schon's seminal work, attempted to capture this kind of research partnering. Mode 2 takes place outside of traditional sites of knowledge production (universities) and within the 'contexts of application', in places where the knowledge-making is entwined with the challenges of invention. It involves close interaction between a diversity of partners, coming together on the basis of their complementary areas of expertise, and working collectively on practical issues to generate successful innovations. From this vantage point, the traditional Mode 1 criteria that mark an activity as research (being done by designated researchers, from an academic knowledge base, reviewed by research peers, resulting in published research findings, and so on) may be missing but the socially engaged knowledge production processes that are involved constitute a valued form of research in its own right (Nowotny *et al.*, 2001).

This casts a particular light on research minded practice. By broadening out what can be understood as doing research, it is no less challenging to social work practice than expecting greater mindfulness of research knowledge. It holds an invitation to practitioners to engage purposefully in processes that generate new and innovative ways of working, fitting to their unique situation and responsive to emerging issues (Gray, 2008). This implies the scope to loosen their hold on familiar practices, traverse borders to form surprising networks, and find the confidence to experiment with new ideas. Recognising the expertise of service users and community members, and their part in such knowledge-making processes, will itself have a most profound effect on the transformation of professional practice. And if there is any substance to the claim that the pace of social change will not be diminishing anytime soon, then this dimension of research minded practice is going to be very important indeed.

We have anticipated in part the third of the three main ideas of research-minded practice, the consideration of practitioners as researchers. It will hopefully be evident by now that research minded practice does not stop at practitioners accessing and using research knowledge generated by others (researchers) important though that is. If research is to be incorporated into social work practice, practitioners do need to reach out and find the relevance of research knowledge for their work. As we have seen, this requires some lessons to be learned and barriers to be broken down. Where it does appear, research is hardly the most loved subject on the professionally qualifying curriculum. A stronger association, however, rests on greater identification by practitioners of themselves as researchers.

The present institutional form of research militates against this. There is, for example, a rite of passage, undertaking and completing a doctorate of philosophy (PhD) which signifies research status. And we should not be under any illusion; doing high-end research requires a long and seemingly arduous journey. Those who get there have had to demonstrate special capacities in research, and no doubt the social work profession needs people with PhDs. In some ways, then, it could be taken as nonsense and even dangerous to suggest that practitioners who have not travelled this path might also construe themselves as researchers. Yet, there is a contrary view that would question whether research should be understood in such narrow terms and as the province of an elite group.

By identifying themselves as researchers, practitioners do not need to be making any grandiose or misguided claims. Conceiving themselves in this way, they are more likely to participate in and initiate research-oriented activities as part of their core responsibilities. They may not be employed as researchers, but they can act as researchers in their day to day work – to the benefit of their practice, their employing organisation and the client communities it serves (Powell and Ramos, 2010). As discussed above, practitioners can promote areas for research and actively support valued research projects being undertaken by paid researchers. With some training and mentorship, they can conduct small scale research projects themselves, including evaluative projects on their own or others' practice. They can systematically and critically examine their own professional knowledge and its underpinning values and assumptions, and break out of routinised responses and patterns of interaction. They can form alliances with research bodies and in collaboration seek to influence policy makers on shared social goals. They can offer their research capacities and connections as a resource to service users and community members, facilitating the engagement of marginalised populations in research related activities. They can become involved in trans-disciplinary and trans-sector teams developing new approaches to emergent issues. They may even decide on a career turn, and cross the road to become an official researcher themselves.

Building research minded practice cultures: gaining some traction

Having sketched a portrait of research minded practice, we need to ask ourselves the question: what are its chances? At the outset, it was suggested that there were some lessons to be learned within the cultures and habits of research and social work practice if they were to achieve a closer union. But they also need to be prepared for the organisational and policy environment of social work and human services. Otherwise, the chances are not great.

So we have to ask ourselves a follow up question: to what extent are the benefits of research minded practice sought by contemporary human service organisations and policy making processes? On the surface, the answers may seem encouraging. There is a championing of evidence-based policy and practice, promoted to modernise the social work profession and improve the effectiveness of public services. Furthermore, organisations are invited to be dynamic, innovative and perpetually learning in order to secure their performance and ongoing relevance (Senge *et al.*, 1999). Against this backdrop, one might think that the scene is set for research minded practice to flourish given the contribution it could make to such objectives. What could possibly get in the way?

Contemporary human service organisations are replete with mechanisms for ensuring accountability and managing outcomes (Jordan, 2010; McDonald, 2006; Webb, 2006). Evidence-based practice fits these requirements neatly – and rather too neatly for some. McDonald points to the limitations of evidence-based practice as a professional response to the neoliberal contexts of service delivery (McDonald, 2003). Her critique offers some warnings for research minded practice. If we allow research agendas to be driven by managerial priorities for organisational accountability and fiscal efficiency, and the outcomes of research to be reduced to simplistic formulations of best practice, we will have limited severely the potential of research to invigorate our professional contribution.

Social workers within human service organisations occupy a contradictory space. The regulation of their professional behaviours through administrative processes designed to optimise organisational performance stands in tension with an organisation's reliance on their embodied expertise and ethical appreci-ation when it comes to delivering human services in all its complexity (Gould and Baldwin, 2004). Compliance and risk aversion at the expense of judgement and risk tolerance will prove costly (see *The Munro Review of Child Protection*, 2011, for a related discussion). Practitioners serious about research minded practice will need to be very clear and very vocal on the point that this represents both a threat and an opportunity for those organisations operating within a neoliberal policy environment. It will take committed and courageous organisational and policy leadership to provide the necessary backing. And to gain the backing will require a professional presence that recognises the multiple and conflicting imperatives facing that leadership (Stepney and Rostila, 2011).

To go down the path of research minded practice does require the acquisition of a certain mind-set on behalf of the individual social work practitioner. This can be nurtured through professional education and socialisation, and their contribu-tion can be significant. However, the sustainability and lasting impact of research minded practice will be realised only through a concerted and systematic approach at a range of organisational and policy levels in support of such a move (Orme and Powell, 2008; Orme, Ruckdeschel and Briar-Lawson, 2010). These might include, for example: developing research literacy within the workforce;

facilitating access to research knowledge through user-friendly materials and databases; incorporating reflective research capability within supervisory relationships; fostering practice innovation research networks; establishing collaborative research partnerships between field agencies and universities; implementing policies on knowledge exchange capacity; defining career pathways for advanced practitioner-researchers; acknowledging and rewarding special contributions to research minded practice; and so on. Of course, all such initiatives imply a funding commitment as well, at a time when human service organisations remain resource poor and service programs stretched.

The problem is that research minded practice cannot usefully be thought about as an add-on – as something that practitioners can do when they find a spare moment. Neither can it be thought about as simply an alternative, a 'smarter' way of doing more with less. It is about building a different workforce and professional capability and creating the infrastructure to support it. This will require an investment, stemming from a strategic and policy commitment. Despite the seemingly relentless trend to govern professional practice through ever tighter and intrusive administrative systems, there are signs that contradictions do surface and that openings can be found to progress research oriented practice initiatives.

Within the Australian context, a large non-government human services organisation is seeking to build its research culture from the ground up. With a history of a strong partnership with a local university, there are existing collaborations on nationally funded research projects and on student-led research activity. The organisation has now committed money to enhancing practice-based research, engaging practitioners in proposing topics for investigation, and developing a professional development program in research literacy. Another non-government human service organisation is engaging their front-line managers and supervisors in work with a local university on developing a practice evaluation tool that is designed particularly to generate data on well-being outcomes in contrast to the plethora of output measures required by the tendered service provision contracts. The tool is to be integrated into everyday practice, and practitioners involved in the organisational learning processes that ensue. A recent study of policy research in Australian non-government human services organisations (Goodwin and Phillips, 2011) has highlighted the growing role of these organisations in knowledge generation and their incipient potential to work for social justice in policy development, strengthened in part through the legitimacy that comes with their proximity to service users and clients.

These are but a few pointers to the traction that can be gained when looking to a broader approach for embedding research minded practice into professional and organisational worlds. Encouragingly, there is increasing activity in this area, though the challenges should not be underestimated. Research minded practice is symbolic of a new kind of professionalism – one which can be confronting for professionals themselves but also to the role they play within human services organisations. Conducted with due ethical awareness, however, the ultimate beneficiaries can be the service users and community members in whose lives those professionals and organisations are involved.

Conclusion

Rapid changes in the use of communication technologies, widespread migration and displacement of peoples, increasing occurrence of natural disasters together with concerns for food and water security, widening disparities in the share of national and international wealth, all such shifting contextual trends – and countless and unforeseeable more – continue to create and reinforce emergent or endemic social issues that find their way into the everyday lives of marginalised and disadvantaged populations. If social work is to play a meaningful part in engaging with those populations, then it will require all the professional resources at its disposal. This includes knowledge generated through research and the creative capacities of knowledge making, which can foster practice that is research minded towards the goals of well-being and social justice.

Social work practice remains one of the most challenging occupations in contemporary society. It is driven by social values to face complex and often distressing situations whilst finding its place in the realities of its operating organisational and policy environment – an intensely intellectual, moral and practical activity. To remain nimble and relevant, social work practice will need to draw on multiple knowledges and have the ethical fluency to negotiate defensible and strategic possibilities for action. Research minded practice is a catalyst for this kind of professionalism. The incentive goes beyond achieving greater cohesion between research and practice, as valuable as that might be for the enrichment they can bring to one another. Within a social work tradition of privileging process as much as task, it is perhaps the process of pursuing research minded practice that matters most. For in striving towards practice that is ethically research minded, social work can preserve and advance a professionalism that is other-serving, open to influence and critique, and determined to find the best possible ways of walking alongside those who, for a challenging period in their lives, find themselves in the company of a social worker.

Acknowledgements

I would like to take the opportunity to acknowledge those who have played an important part in my own adventure with social work research – those many service users, practitioners, managers and fellow academics with whom I have had the pleasure to work. Particular mention to Professors Bill Jordan and Jan Fook for their formative mentorship; colleagues previously associated with Exeter University, including the editors Deirdre and Paul; Dr Heather D'Cruz for the ongoing, stimulating conversations; and current colleagues at RMIT University, Professor Catherine McDonald and Drs John Whyte, Sharon Andrews and Lisa Harris. Their influence has been significant; responsibility for what I have done with it is mine.

References

Adams, R., Dominelli, L. and Payne, M. (Eds.) (2009) *Practising Social Work in a Complex World.* (2nd edn.) Basingstoke: Palgrave Macmillan.

Alston, M. and Bowles, W. (2003) *Research for Social Workers: An Introduction to Methods.* (2nd edn.) Crows Nest: Allen & Unwin.

Babbie, E.R. (2010) *The Practice of Social Research.* (12th edn.) Belmont, CA: Wadsworth Cengage Learning.

Banks, G. (2009) *Challenges of Evidence-Based Policy Making.* Canberra: Australian Government Productivity Commission.

Benner, P. (1984) *From Novice to Expert: Excellence and Power in Clinical Nursing Excellence.* Menlo-Park, CA: Addison-Wesley.

Chenoweth, L. and McAuliffe, D. (2008) *The Road to Social Work and Human Services Practice.* (2nd edn.) Melbourne: Cengage Learning.

Corby, B. (2006) *Applying Research in Social Work Practice.* Maidenhead: Open University Press.

D'Cruz, H. and Jones, M. (2004) *Social Work Research: Ethical and Political Contexts.* London: Sage.

Dreyfus, H. and Dreyfus, S. (1986) *Mind Over Machine: The Power of Human Intuition and Expertise in The Era of The Computer.* New York: The Free Press.

Evans, C. and Jones, R. (2004) Engagement and Empowerment, Research and Relevance: Comments on User-Controlled Research. *Research Policy and Planning,* 22(2) 5–14.

Evans, T. and Hardy, M. with Shaw, I. (2010) *Evidence and Knowledge For Practice.* Cambridge: Polity.

Fook, J, Ryan, M. and Hawkins, L. (2000) *Professional Expertise: Practice, Theory, and Education For Working in Uncertainty.* London: Whiting & Birch.

Fook, J. (Ed.) (1996) *The Reflective Researcher: Social Theories of Practice Research.* Sydney: Allen & Unwin.

Gibbons, M., Limoges, C., Nowotny, H., Schwartzman, S., Scott, P. and Trow, M. (1994) *The New Production of Knowledge: The Dynamics of Science and Research in Contemporary Society.* London: Sage.

Gibbs, A. and Stirling, B. (2010) Reflections on Designing and Teaching a Social Work Research Course For Distance and on-Campus Students. *Social Work Education,* 29(4) 441–449.

Goodwin, S. and Phillips, R. (2011) *Researching the Researchers: Policy Research in Non-Government Organisations in The Human Services Sector – Research Report 2011.* Sydney: University of Sydney.

Gould, N. and Baldwin, M. (Eds.) (2004) *Social Work, Critical Reflection and The Learning Organisation*. Aldershot: Ashgate.

Gould, N. and Taylor, I. (Eds.) (1996) *Reflective Learning For Social Work*. Aldershot: Arena.

Gray, M. (2008) Knowledge Production in Social Work: The 'Gold Standard' of Mode 2? *Transcending Global-Local Divides*, 34th Biannual Congress of the International Association of Schools of Social Work (IASSW) Durban, South Africa, 20–24th July.

Gray, M., Plath, D. and Webb, S. (2009) *Evidence-based Social Work: A Critical Stance*. London: Routledge.

Hammersley, M. (1995) *The Politics of Social Research*. London: Sage.

Hardwick, L. and Worsley, A. (2011) *Doing Social Work Research*. London: Sage.

Hugman, R. (2005) *New Approaches in Ethics For The Caring Professions*. Basingstoke: Palgrave Macmillan.

Jordan, B. (2010) *Why the Third Way Failed: Economics, Morality and The Origins of the 'Big Society'*. Bristol: Policy Press.

Kincheloe, J.L. (2007) Critical Pedagogy in The Twenty-First Century: Evolution For Survival. In McClaren, P. and Kincheloe, J.L. (Eds.) *Critical Pedagogy: Where Are We Now?* New York: Peter Lang Publishing.

McDonald, C. (2003) Forward Via The Past? Evidence-Based Practice as Strategy in Social Work. *The Drawing Board: An Australian review of public affairs*, 3(3) 123–142.

McDonald, C. (2006) *Challenging Social Work: The Institutional Context of Practice*. London: Palgrave Macmillan.

McLaughlin, H. (2007) *Understanding Social Work Research*. London: Sage.

Munro, E. (2011) *The Munro Review of Child Protection: Final Report – A Child Centred System*. England: Department for Education, Cm 8062.

Nowotny, H., Scott, P. and Gibbons, M. (2001) *Re-thinking Science: Knowledge and The Public in an Age of Uncertainty*. Cambridge: Polity.

Orme, J. and Powell, J. (2008) Building Research Capacity in Social Work: Process and Issues. *British Journal of Social Work*, 38(5) 988–1008.

Orme, J. and Shemmings, D. (2010) *Developing Research Based Social Work Practice*. Basingstoke: Palgrave Macmillan.

Orme, J., Ruckdeschel, R. and Briar-Lawson, K. (2010) Challenges and Directions in Social Work Research and Social Work Practice. In Shaw, I., Briar-Lawson, K., Orme, J. and Ruckdeschel, R. (Eds.) *The Sage Handbook of Social Work Research*. London: Sage.

Parton, N. and O'Byrne, P. (2000) *Constructive Social Work*. London: Macmillan.

Patton, M.Q. (2008) *Utilisation-Focused Evaluation.* (4th edn) London: Sage.

Pease, B. (2010) Challenging the Dominant Paradigm: Social Work Research, Social Justice and Social Change. In Shaw, I., Briar-Lawson, K., Orme, J. and Ruckdeschel, R. (Eds.) *The Sage handbook of Social Work Research*. London: Sage.

Powell, J. and Ramos, B. (2010) The Practice of Social Work Research. In Shaw, I., Briar-Lawson, K., Orme, J. and Ruckdeschel, R. (Eds.) *The Sage Handbook of Social Work Research*. London: Sage.

Reason, P. and Bradbury, H. (Eds.) (2008) *Handbook of Action Research: Participative Inquiry and Practice.* (2nd edn.) London: Sage.

Ruckdeschel, R. and Chambon, A. (2010) The Uses of Social Work Research. In Shaw, I., Briar-Lawson, K., Orme, J. and Ruckdeschel, R. (Eds.) *The Sage Handbook of Social Work Research.* London: Sage.

Schon, D.A. (1983) *The Reflective Practitioner: How Professionals Think in Action.* New York: Basic Books.

Senge, P., Kleiner, A., Roberts, C., Ross, R., Roth, G. and Smith, B. (1999) *The Dance of Change: The Challenges of Sustaining Momentum in Learning Organisations.* New York: Doubleday.

Shaw, I. (2005) Evidencing Social Work. In Sommerfield, P. (Ed.) *Evidence-based Social Work: Towards a New Professionalism?* Bern: Peter Lang.

Shaw, I. and Lishman, J. (Eds.) (1999) *Evaluation and Social Work Practice.* London: Sage.

Sheldon, B. and Chilvers, R. (2000) *Evidence-based Social Care: A Study of Prospects and Problems.* Lyme Regis: Russell House.

Smith, R. (2008) *Social Work and Power.* Basingstoke: Palgrave Macmillan.

Stepney, P. and Rostila, I. (2011) Towards an Integrated Model of Practice Evaluation Balancing Accountability, Critical Knowledge and Developmental Perspectives. *Health Sociology Review*, 20(2) 133–146.

Taylor, C. and White, S. (2000) *Practising Reflexivity in Health and Welfare: Making Knowledge.* Buckingham: Open University Press.

Thompson, N. (2010) *Theorising Social Work Practice.* Basingstoke: Palgrave Macmillan.

Trinder, L. (2000) A Critical Appraisal of Evidence-Based Practice. In Trinder, L. and Reynolds, S. (Eds.) *Evidence-based Practice: A Critical Appraisal.* Oxford: Blackwell.

Watson, V. (2002) Do We Learn From Planning Practice? The Contribution of The Practice Movement to Planning Theory. *Journal of Planning Education and Research*, 22(2) 178–187.

Webb, S. (2001) Some Considerations on The Validity of Evidence Based Practice in Social Work. *British Journal of Social Work*, 31: 1, 57–79.

Webb, S. (2006) *Social Work in a Risk Society: Social and Political Perspectives.* London: Palgrave Macmillan.

Wenger, E. (1998) *Communities of Practice: Learning, Meaning and Identity.* Cambridge: Cambridge University Press.

Chapter 17

The Big Society and Social Work: A New Direction for Practice?

Bill Jordan

The Conservative Party emerged from the General Election of May, 2010, with the largest representation in the House of Commons. It had campaigned – to the bafflement of many commentators – on a programme framed by the concept of the 'Big Society', as an alternative to New Labour's 'Big State.' This did not play particularly well with voters; yet David Cameron made it clear from the outset of his term as Prime Minster that it would be the touchstone of his reforms of the country's institutions.

Since then, critics have portrayed the Big Society as no more than a cloak for a Thatcherite privatisation of the public sector. But I shall argue that it was a response to New Labour's centralised, rationalist, economically-informed, managerial blueprint for social relations and collective life, addressing specific weaknesses in the Third Way model in ways which are relevant for social work practice. Above all, in its emphasis on civil society, on well-being and on relationships, it offers to supply a very different basis for organisation and policy in social care and children's services from the regime imposed by New Labour.

It is understandable that resistance to the coalition government's programme should focus on cuts to public services, and the opportunities offered to the voluntary and commercial sectors for taking over aspects of state provision. I shall argue that the priority given to reducing the fiscal deficit is indeed in tension with the Big Society agenda, but that does not imply that the latter is no more than a smokescreen for privatisation. Instead, I shall suggest that these are two sides of a strategy that addresses problems shared by most European countries and the USA – that the parts of their economies not directly linked with global markets have experienced huge challenges since the crash of 2008–9, and require a new basis for survival in an integrated world economy increasingly dominated by such rising powers as China, India, Brazil, Indonesia and Russia.

The Third Way approach, which was derived from the theory of information, incentives and contracts (Bolton and Dewatripont, 2005; Laffont and Martimort, 2002) took its cues from the World Bank's model of global development (Stiglitz, 2001, 2002; Stiglitz and Greenwald, 2003). According to this perspective, countries like the UK could modernise and rationalise their whole infrastructures to make every organisation efficient and responsive to the signals emanating from world markets. To achieve this, the financial sector should be given a leading role, with the banks as key institutions, because they were the best-informed agents in the economy. The public sector was therefore redesigned on business lines, so that its organisations mimicked the workings of firms, both in their management structures, and in the way staff were induced to adopt practices in line with the requirements of cost-effective principles (Jordan, 2010). The whole of society could thus be mobilised towards prosperity according to a single rationale, led by its 'world class' financial intermediaries, the City of London.

Try as it might to evade its complicity in the catastrophic collapse of the banking sector, New Labour was hopelessly discredited by the consequences of the crash. But it was also undone by other features of its model. The very nature of the systems it installed, requiring compliance with impersonal electronic management tools, checklists and tick-boxes, was designed to dispense with involvement, enthusiasm and commitment, as well as judgement and experience. Both staff and service users found that the new services, even though they were generously funded, could be mechanistic and soulless. Above all, they rested on individual assessments, and addressed individual behaviour, often cutting across family, kinship, neighbourhood and community bonds, and ignoring (or even combating) traditions, cultures and loyalties.

In his pre-election speeches and articles, David Cameron (2009; 2010) seized on all these features of New Labour's programme. He insisted that power had been centralised and passed to officials; the Big Society would redistribute it to the people and their communities. He wanted to strengthen civil society and associational bonds. He also emphasised that well-being (overall satisfaction with quality of life) was more important than economic growth and material possessions, and that relationships of all kinds were the most important elements in well-being.

Accordingly, his model of the public services, including social work, was far more decentralised, and allowed staff and service users, as well as local politicians and associations, more influence. Asked in January 2011 about what the Big Society implied for the organisation of social provision, the minister responsible for its implementation, Francis Maude, replied that there was no one model – the outcomes would be 'uneven and lumpy' with each district deciding on its own patterns (BBC Radio 4, 2011a).

At the same time, other signals suggest that practice will be allowed to use professional expertise, critique and judgement as more important elements; the *Munro Review of Child Protection* (2011) indicates this direction, and has government backing. But another influential principle will be the involvement of local activists, and accountability to local communities. This is derived as much from the development of alternatives to the Third Way model (Participle, 2011) as from government policy. This chapter will attempt to draw together these themes at a time of transition in the policy framework for social work.

Tough Love: Third Way social policy

To understand the direction in which this programme of change is being steered by the coalition government, we need to grasp the overall rationale of the Third Way regime which it replaced. The Blair–Brown leadership of New Labour aimed to regenerate the UK's economy and society, using public sector modernisation to repair the damage done in the Thatcher–Major years. On its analysis, the shortcomings of the governments of the 1980s and early 1990s could be traced to their neglect of large parts of the country's public infrastructure, and hence the population: Margaret Thatcher's embrace of global market forces had not gone far enough. In a relentless stream of legislation, initiatives and guidance, New Labour set about the redesign of the collective landscape, with the aim of changing citizens' orientations towards the state and each other, and indeed their very identities as participants in the national project.

New Labour's grandiose vision for 'national renewal' was set out in a series of speeches and articles by Tony Blair, and in policy documents issued soon after its 1997 election victory. It was expressed in terms of abstract values such as 'equality', 'inclusion', 'opportunity', 'responsibility' and 'community'.

> We are putting our values into practice; we are the only political force capable of liberating the potential of our people. Knowing what we have to do and knowing how to do it.

> (Blair, 1999)

The goal, expressed in initiatives such as Sure Start, was to equip all citizens for participation in a competitive, economic and political environment. The Social Investment State (Giddens, 1998) would allow all children to grow up able to contribute to and benefit from this framework, under a contract between the state and each individual member, 'on terms which are fair and clear' (Blair, 1998: v). The positive parts of this programme were expressed through the incentives to work in the national minimum wage and the support to working families through tax credits, as well as the counselling and training supplied in the New Deals for benefits claimants. With these entitlements went duties to be 'independent', to support one's family from earnings if possible, to save for retirement and to avoid being a burden on taxpayers (DSS, 1998: 80).

The ethos of 'tough love' with which this informed the public services (Jordan, B. with Jordan, C., 2000; Jordan, 2001) meant that social workers were required to deal with those who failed to live up to the standards of this new contract, and who failed to take the opportunities offered. Already before New Labour came to power, local authority social work was moving towards a style of practice which was legalistic, formal, procedural and arm's length, concerned with assessing and managing risk and dangerousness (Kemshall and Pritchard, 1996; Parton *et al.*, 1997). Practice was mainly involved in allocating services and exercising surveillance through systems of rationing and control that made little use of interpersonal skills. In its White Paper *Modernising Social Services* (DoH, 1998) New Labour consolidated these trends, regulating them through a series of new supervisory and monitoring bodies, setting new standards and targets against which to measure performance, establishing agencies to enforce these, and remodelling services to promote 'independence' and 'choice'. Those measures were followed up by very detailed objectives and performance indicators, with long lists of definitions and quality standards, expressed in arcane language and acronyms, worthy of the pen of Jeremy Bentham (e.g. Social Services Inspectorate, 1999).

The openly-stated aim behind these reforms was a cultural transformation, in which both staff and service users would be changed – once the 'old, passive' mould of the post-war welfare state was broken – into active, choosing consumers, within organisations explicitly modelled on banks and supermarkets (DSS, 1998: 26). In reality, as evidence of disorder, alienation and deviance accumulated; and as scandals such as the deaths of Baby Peter in Haringey, Fiona Pilkington and her daughter in Leicestershire, and David Askew in Manchester, pointed to the shortcomings in the various agency partnerships which had been established; the stubborn residue of problems in deprived districts, and the limitations of the new systems and initiatives, became apparent. As early as 2006, the Conservatives began to develop a theme, 'Broken Britain', which focused on the failure of the Third Way vision for inclusion, and the persistence of marriage breakdown, lone parenthood, poverty, truancy, delinquency, drug and alcohol abuse among those without a stake in the new order (Centre for Social Justice, 2006).

New Labour could probably have shrugged off this attack if the property boom had been sustained and bank credit had continued to fuel consumer spending. But the financial crash undermined the foundations of its programme, by revealing that the very basis in economic rationality on which it was supposed to rest was fatally flawed (Tett, 2009). If the bankers on whose shoulders this grandiose edifice rested could themselves invest billions in fantasy bubbles, what hope was there for the mass of credit-card borrowers and mortgage-holders?

But by the same token, 'tough love' had not transformed social services users into independent consumers, or conflict-ridden families into self-responsible citizens. Instead, the micro-management methods and electronic systems which had taken over these services, and to which staff's time and energies had been increasingly devoted, were now the objects of critical scrutiny. Modernisation had failed to reach the parts of society most in need of it. The extent to which New Labour had fallen short of its aims was symbolised, in the May 2010 election campaign, by Gordon Brown's televised encounter with Gillian Dalley in Rochdale, soon after which a national audience heard him describe the pensioner and former social services worker as a 'bigoted woman'.

The Third Way project had turned against its core supporters and supposed principal beneficiaries.

A new direction?

The revival of localism, particularity and community signalled by the Big Society turn might equally well be seen as an acceptance of uneven economic development. Just as the European Union project, which had aimed to include the notoriously spendthrift, fiscally unsound and administratively suspect Mediterranean countries in a prosperity generated by the prudent Germans, began to unravel with the crash, so the defeat of New Labour demonstrated that no single coherent, state-led rationale could draw the whole UK population into advantageous participation in global capitalism.

New Labour had tried to integrate the economy and society by appointing the banks as custodians of the former, and expecting state officials to steer people towards them for their needs – a process which has been described as the 'financialisation of citizenship' (Inman, 2010). The coalition government aimed to re-orientate citizens towards each other, to get them to co-operate in what David Cameron often called 'collective action' (Cameron, 2010). This had several ironies, since collective action by trades unions, local authorities and other interest groups was exactly what Margaret Thatcher had sought to suppress; and the first manifestations of this new phenomenon took the form of protests, notably by students against increases in university fees and cuts in education maintenance allowances.

The concealed assumption behind this new direction was that, in the wake of the crash, many parts of the economy and specific districts (perhaps whole regions) should strive to emulate Spain's Basque country (Ramesh, 2011) or Italian communes, which thrived on traditional methods of producing local specialities, and on cultures which valued ways of life outside the global flow. Although this strategy could not be acknowledged as creating backwaters, it effectively accepted that local niches, based on co-operatives, associations, mutuals, social enterprises and promoting the particularities of place and history, represented the best hope of achieving success and harmony in such environments.

In this, Cameron, Maude, Letwin and other ministers from the Conservative Party drew on the work of Phillip Blond (2009a; 2009b; 2009c; 2010) whose inspiration in turn came from the Tory writers Cobbett, Carlyle, Ruskin and Disraeli, and from dissident Liberals Belloc and Chesterton. Blond was radical in wanting redistribution of property in favour of communities, co-operatives, local trust funds and social enterprises: he saw the failure of Thatcherism as lying in the consolidation of a monopoly state, and advocated the dispersal of resources and authority to workers and community groups in a process of rapid decentralisation.

These ideas are not confined to the Conservatives. They clearly draw on some of the 'community politics' pioneered by the Liberal Democrats, but they are also now being taken up by advisers to Ed Miliband, who see the Third Way as having been an elitist Fabian project, which turned its back on working-class solidarities and traditions. 'Blue Labour' theorists such as Maurice (now Lord) Glasman and Marc Stears (BBC Radio 4, 2011b, *The Guardian*, 2011) acknowledge their affinities with the 'Red Tory' Blond, and seek a 'Good Society' with some of the features of the Big Society approach.

Another common theme in post-Third Way thinking is the effort to address 'well-being' rather than increased consumption, as part of a move away from materialistic individualism. Among political leaders, David Cameron was the first to recognise that the message from research on this topic (Kahneman *et al.*, 1999; Helliwell, 2003; Layard, 2005) was that, in addition to good health and work satisfaction, relationships of all kinds were the key components in overall quality of life, and that this had important implications for government. The UK came 22nd out of 25 EU countries, above only Lithuania, Latvia and Slovakia, on this measure (Innocenti, 2007) while another study put it *last* among 21 affluent OECD countries for children's and young people's well-being (Bradshaw *et al.*, 2006).

Here the implications for social work are obvious, since the relationships at stake for well-being are both close and intimate bonds (partnerships and parenthood), those of kinship, and also those formed through participation in community groups and associations (activists are happier than those who follow lives of private consumption). The quality of all these relationships outweigh the final third of income in people's pockets and purses, and Cameron has been quick to emphasise the need for a long-term programme to improve the quality of all these elements in social relations.

> We will feel it in the strength of our relationships – the civility and courtesy we show each other . . . This is not the work of one parliamentary term or even two . . . It will take more than a generation.
>
> (Cameron, 2009)

These priorities have been endorsed by a series of independent research reports of direct significance for social work practice. The Joseph Rowntree Trust's study of *Contemporary Social Evils* conducted a survey of public attitudes to these, and discovered that 'individualism and greed' were considered to have contributed to 'a more fragmented, more stratified society' (Unwin, 2009: 4).

Similarly, The Children Society's *Good Childhood Report* found that there was a single main factor contributing to unhappiness in childhood and adolescence:

> One common theme . . . links all these problems: excessive individualism . . . By excessive individualism we mean the belief that the prime duty of the individual is to make the most of their own life, rather than to contribute to the good of others . . .

The pursuit of personal success relative to others cannot create a happy society,
since one person's success necessarily involves another's failure.

(Layard and Dunn, 2009: 5–6)

So the coalition government's emphasis on strengthening family life and civil society, on co-operation and collective action, on participation and group membership, all fit well with a growing critique among social commentators on trends in UK society under the New Labour regime. I have argued that, smuggled in with this new attention to relationships of affection, loyalty, solidarity and belonging is a kind of economic dualism; the basis for these new features of civil society is expected to be an acceptance of modest localism and niche production of specialist (not to say homespun) commodities and services. All this is of direct relevance for the future of social work practice in the new regime.

Implications for practice

In the Conservative Party's election manifesto, there were no radical plans to overhaul social care or children's services to parallel those for re-organising the NHS or encouraging academies and free schools. More modestly, the example of a social care team becoming a co-operative to supply local services was given (Conservative Party, 2010: 27) as an illustration of the new approach to devolution in the public services.

But another part of the proposed shift towards the Big Society is the idea that professionals will take more responsibility for decisions, and that this greater exercise of their judgement will be at the expense of the controlling influence of the central state (Conservative Party, 2010: 37). This idea found its first clear illustration in the Interim Report of the *Munro Review of Child Protection*, strongly endorsed by the government, which argued for a strengthening of 'professional reasoning' to judge how best to work with parents, through 'critical reflection' in supervision (Munro Report, Executive Summary, para. 15: 11–12).

> *The current managerial style puts too much emphasis on the bureaucratic aspect of*
> *the work. Radical reform is needed to give due weight to the importance of the*
> *cognitive and emotional requirements of the work, the need for continuing profes-*
> *sional development, and for access to research in order to help workers perform to*
> *a high level. The scale of rules and procedures may help to achieve a minimum*
> *standard of practice, but inhibits the development of professional expertise and*
> *alienates the workforce, thus contributing to serious problems of recruitment and*
> *retention.*

(*ibid*, para. 14: 11)

This round condemnation of the whole New Labour approach to the provision of professional child protection services fits well with the decentralising and relationship-focused aspects of the Big Society programme. In a few sentences, Munro addresses a whole range of discontents among social work staff and academic critics of the Third Way approach – the mechanistic view of human problems, the technocratic methods of supervision, management and quality control, the electronic basis for recording and reviewing, the lack of adequate reflection on emotional and social factors, and the whole culture and morale of agencies. The Review demands a new environment for the improvement of practice in this field, and its critique of the New Labour 'modernised' version is largely compatible with the coalition government's programme.

Another pointer to the future for practice comes from an organisation, Participle Ltd, which has no theoretical or political links with the Conservative programme, yet has come up with principles for the development of social care which are highly compatible with the Big Society. The Southwark Circle (one of several such projects) is sponsored by that borough's council, and consists of a network of volunteers and paid staff whose members exchange all kinds of services, and are involved in many group activities. The designers of the scheme spent time living with some older people and consulting with many others, to make sure it fitted their requirements. The aim is to maximise the active involvement of local people in potential and actual need.

The project received an initial investment of £800,000, but it is reckoned to be on target to save the council £24 million over five years; it was self-supporting within three years (Bunting, 2010). On their website, the Southwark Circle (Participle, 2011) describes itself as a membership organisation that provides on-demand help with practical tasks, through local, reliable neighbourhood helpers, a social network for teaching, learning and sharing. It describes its history as derived from the idea that 'people can be each others' solution.' Tokens for an hour's help cost £12, so it is not a cheap option; but Participle claims that the scheme represents the future of social care and the public services generally.

> *We believe there needs to be a new settlement between individuals, communities and government – new ways for people to get involved in determining their lives in a meaningful way.*
>
> (Participle, 2011)

The new approach would make professional staff accountable to such membership organisations, and this has been put into practice in a project in Swindon for multi-problem families. The latter recruit the professionals who will help them and set the terms and goals on which they engage with them. They insist that the scheme is based on love, trust, respect and non-judgementalism, and claim that this approach is saving the public services considerable sums of money (Bunting, 2011).

Conclusions

I have argued that some of the ideas behind the Big Society programme represent overdue shifts in the basis for social work in UK local and national government agencies, and in the voluntary sector (which had become increasingly reliant on government contracts under New Labour). The Third Way attempt to rationalise the whole social order through the adoption of an economic model of relationships had led to a form of practice which was mechanistic, driven by external, official objectives, and framed by a narrow focus on individual behaviour. Not just the organisation of social work, but practice itself, had become infected by these characteristics, and in these respects the new direction is to be welcomed.

However, I have also argued that the Big Society signals an unacknowledged dualism in public policy. While the Chancellor of the Exchequer sets about an attempt to rehabilitate the City of London as a global financial hub, and to reverse the decline of the UK manufacturing sector in world markets, the Prime Minister and a close group of his political supporters, including Francis Maude and Oliver Letwin, with the backing of several brighter MPs such as Jesse Norman (2010), are pushing through a programme to revive those parts of the economy and society most damaged by the failures of the Third Way project.

The new direction accepts that a different logic must apply to many of the businesses and social enterprises which make up the economies of the larger part of the country – a rationale of localism, niche production and a collective life with closer horizons than the global perspective unsuccessfully sought by New Labour. It looks at the run-down high streets of many provincial towns, the shabby backstreets and neglected infrastructure and the deprivation of some social housing districts, and seeks to mobilise their populations to act together to restore a sense of communal pride and purpose. This would be reflected as much in prospering local banks, building societies, shops and services as in schools, clinics and care centres.

Some critics have seen all this as middle-class nostalgia for a lost world of rural contentment, an attempt to recreate the social relations of the Archers' Ambridge (Raban, 2010). Others, as we have noted, claim that it conceals the true intentions behind government cuts and privatisations (Kettle, 2010). But I have argued that the Third Way programme was unsustainable, not least in social work and the other public services, and that some new direction was required across a broad range of policy issues.

Yet the Big Society begs a number of questions about a new collective landscape. As yet, there are few clues about the relationships between the two economies and societies it will construct – the parts linked with global markets, and those focused on local communities. Here the radical Phillip Blond insists that the world of monopoly finance and business must be required to resource the transfer of power and self-sufficiency to the periphery, through major redistributions of wealth, and the establishment of new institutions to fund community development. There is as yet no evidence of a similar radicalism in coalition government thinking. Instead, cuts to local authority funding, disproportionally applied to cities with higher levels of deprivation, suggest the imposition of new austerity on those already at a disadvantage.

The obvious weakness of the Big Society perspective is that the communities it seeks to mobilise are not starting from the same resource base. Some are much wealthier than others, in terms of the skills and experience of their members, and in terms of their private and public infrastructures. Collective action could widen the gulf between them, and increase the differentials in well-being between their residents. Nothing in the Big Society programme suggests that the coalition has a clear plan to avoid this outcome.

This applies also to issues for the most vulnerable individuals in society. While the ideas put forward by Participle and other groups are positive, they ultimately require a National Care Service to supply the funds for those who need care. Before the election of 2010, the Conservatives dropped out of a last-minute attempt by New Labour's Andy Burnham to reach a political consensus over such a scheme; the Conservatives declared in favour of private insurance, an approach rejected across the northern countries of the EU, and which – from French experience – can be expected to cover no more than 20 per cent of the population.

Finally, the future relationship of social work to the new community development thrust is unclear. The Conservative Manifesto foresaw new 'independent community organisers', to be trained to promote collective action in civil society throughout the country, as well as a national citizenship service for 16–18 year-olds (Conservative Party, 2010: 38). The Third Way project separated social work from community development, and neglected the latter. It would be consistent with the Big Society approach to reconnect these parts of social work's historical legacy, linking practice with the drive towards a more collective view of its methods and tasks.

References

BBC Radio 4 (2011a) Interview with Francis Maude. *PM*, 12 January.

BBC Radio 4 (2011b) Blue Labour, *Analysis*, 21 March.

Blair, T. (1998) Preface to DSS (1998) *A New Contract for Welfare*. Cm 3805, London: Stationery Office.

Blair, T. (1999) Speech to Labour Party Conference, September.

Blond, P. (2009a) The New Conservatism Can Create a Capitalism that Works for the Poor. *The Guardian*, 3 July, p 33.

Blond, P. (2009b) Without a Concept of Virtue, our Politics and our Banks are Doomed. *The Independent*, 1 June.

Blond, P. (2009c) Rise of the Red Tories. *Prospect Magazine*, 28 February, issue 155.

Blond, P. (2010) *Red Tory: How Left and Right have Broken Britain, and How We can Fix It.* London: Faber and Faber.

Bolton, P. and Dewatripont, M. (2005) *Contract Theory.* Cambridge, MA: MIT Press.

Bradshaw, J., Hoelscher, P. and Richardson, D. (2006) Children and Young People's Well-being in the EU 25. *Journal of Social Indicators Research*, 80, 133–177.

Bunting, M. (2010) A New Model of Welfare would Work with the Grain of our Relationships. *The Guardian*, 28 June, p. 25.

Bunting, M. (2011) Up Close and Personal. *The Guardian* (Society) 9 February, p. 1.

Cameron, D. (2009) The Big Society. *Hugo Young Memorial Lecture*, London, 10 November.

Cameron, D. (2010) Labour are Now the Reactionaries, We are the Radicals – As this Promise Shows. *The Guardian*, 9 April.

Centre for Social Justice (2006) *Broken Britain.* (6 Volumes) London: Centre for Social Justice.

Conservative Party (2010) *Invitation to Join the Government of Britain.* London: The Conservative Party.

DoH (1998) *Modernising Social Services: Promoting Independence, Providing Protection, Raising Standards.* Cm 4169, London: Stationery Office.

DSS (1998) *A New Contract for Welfare.* Cm 103805, London: Stationery Office.

Giddens, A. (1998) *The Third Way: The Renewal of Social Democracy.* Cambridge: Polity.

Guardian (2011) Blue Labour: A Vision of the Future, or in Thrall to the Past? 22 April, p. 21.

Helliwell, J.F. (2003) How's Life? Combining Individual and National Variables to Explain Subjective Well-being. *Economic Modelling*, 20: 331–360.

Inman, P. (2010) Avarice: the True Villain behind the Global Slump. *The Guardian*, 12 April, p. 30.

Innocenti Report, Card 7 (2007) *Child Poverty in Perspective: An Overview of Child Well-being in Rich Countries.* Florence: UNICEF.

Jordan, B. (2001) Tough Love: Social Work, Social Exclusion and the Third Way. *British Journal of Social Work*, 31: 527–540.

Jordan, B. (2010) *Why the Third Way Failed: Economics, Morality and the Origins of the Big Society.* Bristol: Policy Press.

Jordan, B. with Jordan, C. (2000) *Social Work and the Third Way: Tough Love as Social Policy.* London: Sage.

Kahneman, D., Diener, E. and Schwartz, N. (eds.) (1999) *Well-being: The Foundations of Hedonic Psychology.* New York, NY: Russell Sage Foundation.

Kemshall, H. and Pritchard, C. (Eds.) (1996) *Good Practice in Risk Assessment and Risk Management.* London: Jessica Kingsley.

Kettle, M. (2010) The Big Society is Bound to End up as Something Meaner. *The Guardian*, 2 April.

Laffont, J.J. and Martimort, D. (2002) *The Theory of Incentives: The Principal-Agent Model.* Princeton, NJ: Princeton University Press.

Layard, R. (2005) *Happiness: Lessons from a New Science.* London: Allen Lane.

Layard, R. and Dunn, J. (2009) *A Good Childhood: Searching for Values in a Competitive Age.* London: Children's Society/Penguin.

Munro Review of Child Protection (2011) *Interim Report: The Child's Journey.* London: Department of Health.

Norman, J. (2010) *The Big Society: The Anatomy of the New Politics.* Buckingham: Buckingham University Press.

Participle Ltd (2011) *Our Mission: The Public Realm: Re-imagined, Redelivered.* http://www.participle.net/about/our_mission/

Parton, N., Thorpe, D. and Wattam, C. (1997) *Child Protection, Risk and the Social Order.* London: Macmillan.

Raban, J. (2010) Parson Blond's Foggy Sermon. *The Guardian*, Review Section, 24 April: 18–19.

Ramesh, R. (2011) Co-ops and Txokos: Why the Big Society Thrives in Basque Country. *The Guardian* (Spain: Society) 30 March,

Social Services Inspectorate (1999) *Children's Services Planning: Planning to Deliver Change.* London: Social Services Inspectorate, Department of Health.

Stiglitz, J.E. (2001) An Agenda for Development for the Twenty-First Century. In Giddens, A. (Ed.) *The Global Third Way Debate*, Cambridge: Polity, 340–357.

Stiglitz, J.E. (2002) *Globalisation and its Discontents.* London: Allen Lane.

Stiglitz, J.E. and Greenwald, B. (2003) *Towards a New Paradigm in Monetary Economics.* Cambridge: Cambridge University Press.

Tett, G. (2009) *Fool's Gold: How Unrestrained Greed Corrupted a Dream, Shattered Global Markets and Unleashed a Catastrophe.* London: Little, Brown.

Unwin, J. (2009) Introduction. In Utting, D. (Ed.) *Contemporary Social Evils.* Bristol: Joseph Rowntree Foundation/Policy Press, 1–4.

Index

Social work and mental health
The value of everything
By Peter Gilbert with Peter Bates, Sarah Carr, Michael Clark, Nick Gould and Greg Slay

This new edition of *The Value of Everything: Social Work and its Importance in the Field of Mental Health* (RHP, 2003) promotes integration and multi-disciplinary work, and sets social work as one of the most vital components in a truly whole-person and whole-systems approach to mental health. It 'draws strongly on an eclectic range of sources and interweaves writing from across several disciplines.' BJSW.

978-1-905541-60-7

Social work assessment and intervention
Second edition
By Steven Walker and Chris Beckett

Acclaimed in its first edition, now extensively revised, restructured and updated, this comprehensive guide to empowering practice for social workers and the people with whom they work 'addresses overarching issues such as rationing of services and thresholds of need which are particularly pertinent in the "Big Society" of today. There is much that is useful in this book.' Rostrum. Using case illustrations, evidence based guidance, and practical activities combined with extensive references, this valuable learning resource will help students, practitioners, managers, trainers and policy-makers to synthesise social work knowledge and theory to provide holistic support and effective services.

978-1-905541-68-3

Crisis intervention
By Neil Thompson

This clear and concise introduction to theory and methods is an extensively revised and updated version of *Crisis Intervention Revisited* (Pepar, 1991). It clears up misunderstandings and oversimplifications that have at times caused the immense value of crisis theory to have been lost; and takes fuller account of the sociological dimension of crisis, such as issues of discrimination on the grounds of gender, race/ethnicity, and age.

978-1-905541-67-6

Power and empowerment
By Neil Thompson

'A useful gateway to the complexity of power and empowerment . . . as succinct an introduction as one could wish for . . . It is a book which speaks a strong commitment to social justice and which also provides a welcome antidote to the tendency to polarise "powerful" and "powerless" – Neil Thompson provides an altogether more subtle and compelling analysis . . . I can see experienced practitioners and practice teachers enjoying it. This is a book that goes well beyond the rhetoric.' Professor Mark Doel, Sheffield Hallam University.

978-1-903855-99-7

Engagement in practice
Theory and practice for successful engagement
By Gillian Squirrell

For anyone working with communities, this book explores: various forms and meanings of engagement and participation; opportunities for engagement; the skills and attitudes needed for undertaking engagement ethically and effectively; different types of engagement practice for different circumstances, purposes, intended outputs and stakeholder groups; preparing stakeholders for what is involved; reducing the risks of exclusion; possible pitfalls in some types of engagement activities; evaluating engagement work.

978-1-905541-75-1

Supervision: praxis and purpose
Developing a critical model of practice for those working with children and young people post Munro
By Brian Belton, Justin Hill, Tina Salter and John Peaper

Not the sort of book that asks readers to agree with all of it; rather, by considering supervision in various settings, including social work, youth work and coaching, it aims to challenge readers to 'reconsider different perspectives that have informed supervision practice over the years.' As the LCSB manager – an RSW – notes in his PSW review, it 'endorses Munro's stance on supervision, namely that it needs a practice framework premised on evidence to be truly effective . . . (and) in its methodology of carefully unpicking strands of theory, provides a useful commentary on theories in a way that goes beyond the subject matter of supervision . . . I certainly found this inspiring.'

978-1-905541-78-2

Managing uncertainty and change in social work and social care
By Ken Johnson and Isabel Williams

'Aims to assist social care staff to understand the factors that lead to change and uncertainty, to reflect on their personal and professional reactions and experiences, and to develop skills and approaches to tackle change in a positive and constructive manner.' Health & Social Care in the Community.

978-1-905541-07-2

Social control and the use of power in social work with children and families
Edited by Toyin Okitikpi

Ten contributors: examine the extent of social work powers in working with children and families; consider whether social workers are not only aware of their powers but also know how they utilise them when working with 'at risk' cases; discuss how the 'rule of optimism' could be redefined and still safeguard vulnerable children and young people; examine the ethics of exercising power; look at critical reflection and power in social work.

978-1-905541-71-3

Evidence-based social work
A guide for the perplexed
By Tony Newman, Alice Moseley, Stephanie Tierney and Annemarie Ellis

'Written in an easy-to-read style this book makes the inaccessible, accessible. How do you find the evidence, what matters and what doesn't? With the many research findings how do you sort the wheat from the chaff? How do you make sense of the statistics. The answers are all in this excellent book. I strongly recommend it.' Ann Buchanan, Univ of Oxford.

'Written in plain English . . . illustrates how evidence-based social work can be put into practice, and how it improves outcomes for those with whom we work.' Professional Social Work.

978-1-903855-55-3

Religion and spirituality
By Bernard Moss

'Intended to help staff engage with people's religion and spirituality, if appropriate . . . It guides the reader through ways of celebrating diversity, fostering resilience and challenging discrimination.' Care & Health.

'Indispensable for holistic service provision . . . displays an impressive degree of cultural sensitivity toward people of faith . . . represents an important contribution to the mainstreaming of spirituality in social work practice.' Journal of Social Work.

978-1-903855-57-7

Social work and well-being
By Bill Jordan

'The current emphasis, by traditionally unsentimental or hardnosed economists, on the importance of people's well-being sits nicely with social work's "old" emphasis on relationships and feelings. Jordan rebuts the view that the latter are fuzzy concepts lacking in intellectual rigour, instead arguing that they are vital and necessary if social workers are to move themselves and their clients beyond concerns with material consumption and instrumental outcomes.' Community Care.

'An intelligent and sensitive analysis of some vitally important issues.' Neil Thompson.

978-1-905541-13-3

Barefoot Helper
Mindfulness and creativity in social work and the helping professions
By Mark Hamer

'Might help you to do your job better, stay sane and be happy.' Addiction Today.

'A refreshing discourse on regaining the soul of social work by becoming more authentic people ourselves . . . who knows, it could be the start of social work ridding itself of its corporate dullness and becoming the exciting, creative profession that seduced many of us in the first place.' Wellbeing.

'I endorse it wholeheartedly.' The Guardian's barefoot doctor.

978-1-905541-03-4